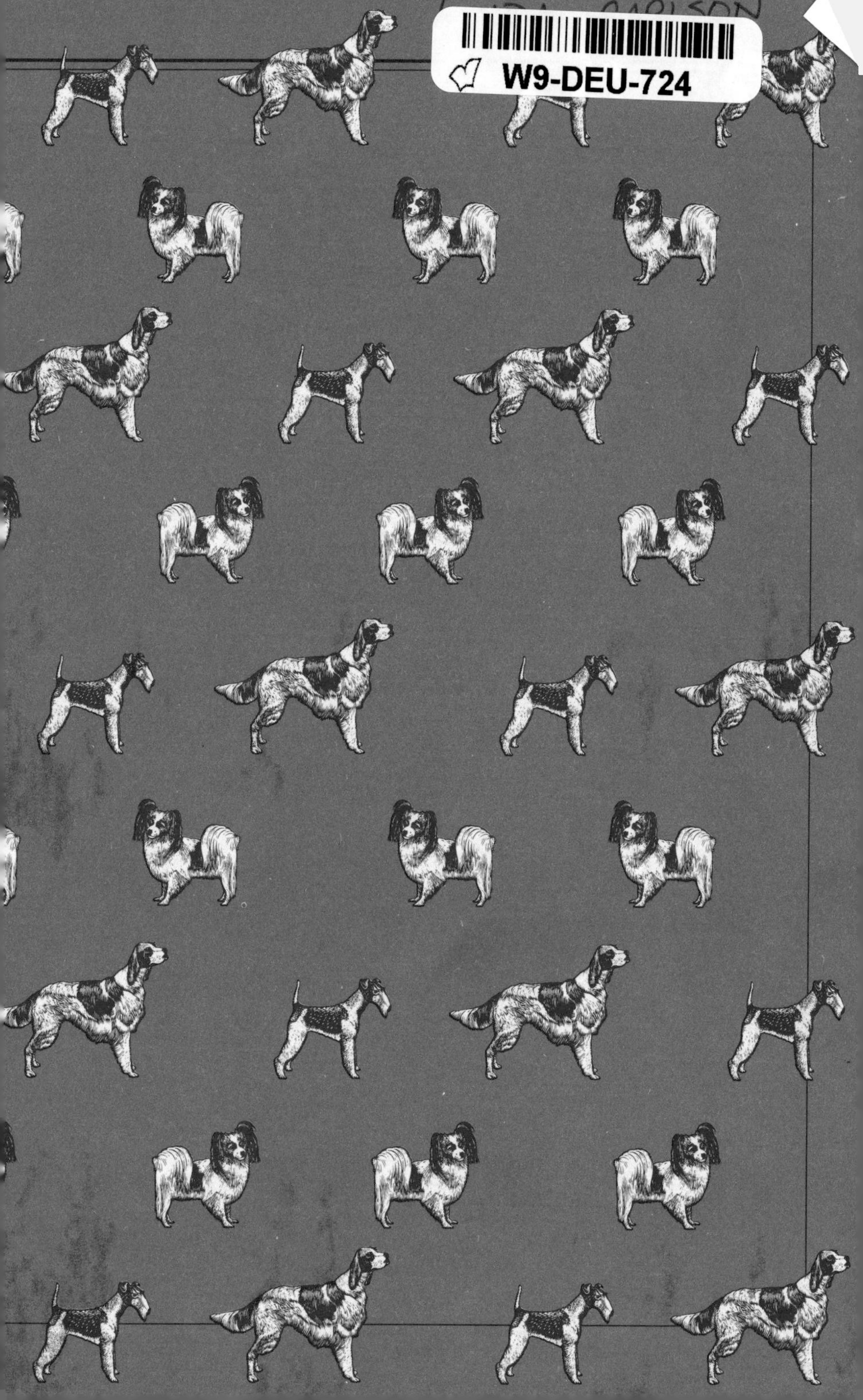

EYEWITNESS HANDBOOKS

DOGS

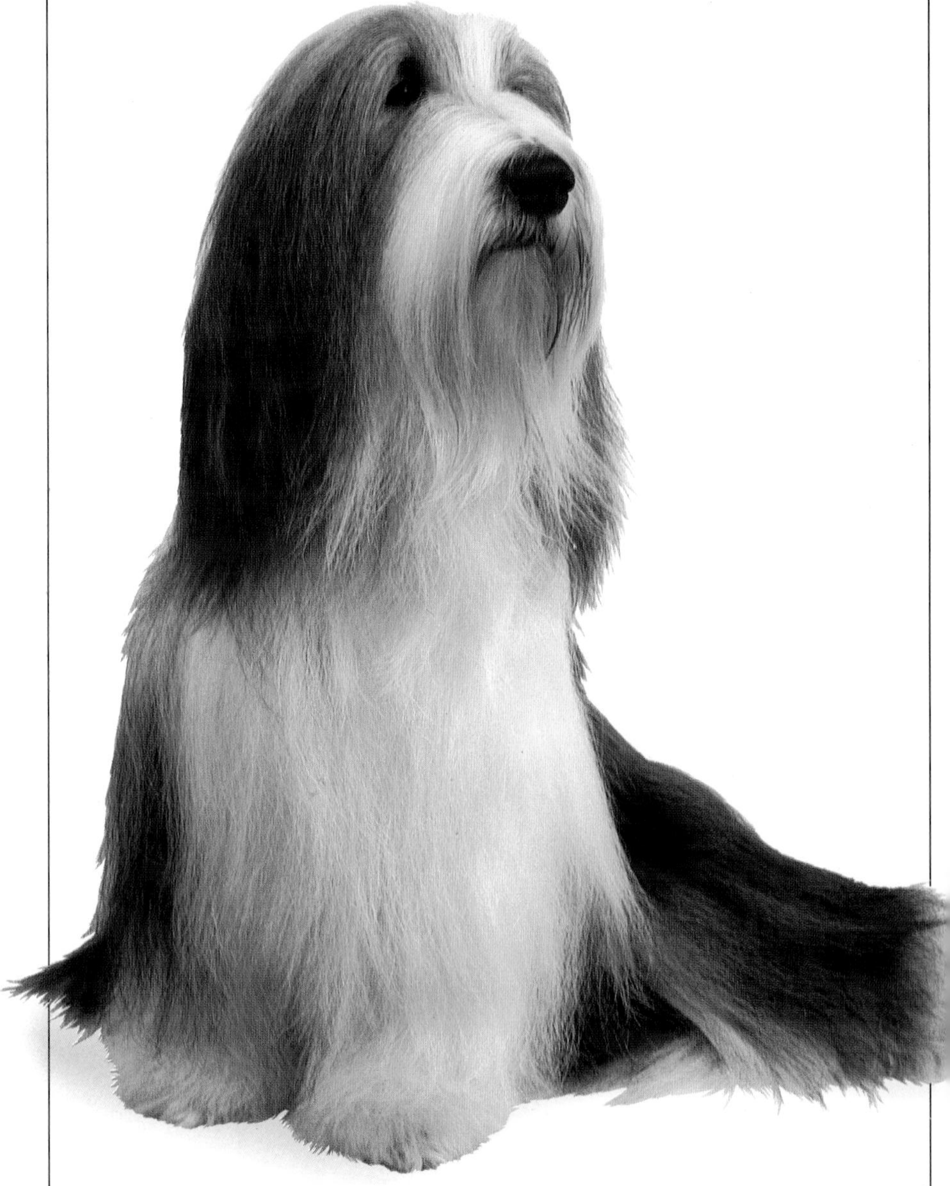

EYEWITNESS HANDBOOKS

DOGS

DAVID ALDERTON

Photography by
TRACY MORGAN

Stoddart

A Dorling Kindersley Book

Editor Damien Moore
Art Editors Vicki James, Shaun Mc Nally
Series Editor Jonathan Metcalf
Series Art Editor Spencer Holbrook
Production Controller Caroline Webber

First published in Canada in 1993 by
Stoddart Publishing Co. Ltd,
34 Lesmill Road, Don Mills, Canada, M3B 2T6

First published in Great Britain in 1993
by Dorling Kindersley Limited,
9 Henrietta Street, London WC2E 8PS

Canadian Cataloguing in Publication Data:

Alderton, David, 1956-
Dogs
(Eyewitness Handbooks)
ISBN 0-7737-2611-X

1. Dogs - Pictorial works. 2. Dogs - Identification.
I. Title. II. Series.
SF430.A64 1993 636.7'1'022 C92-095001-9

Computer page make-up by Damien Moore
Text film output by The Right Type, Great Britain

Reproduced by Colourscan, Singapore
Printed and bound by Kyodo Printing Co., Singapore

CONTENTS

AUTHOR'S INTRODUCTION

Despite the variety of shapes and sizes of today's domestic dog breeds, all are directly related to the wolf. The process of domestication began over 12,000 years ago, probably in disparate regions in the northern hemisphere, at a time when wolves had a far wider distribution than they do today. The early semi-wild dogs were probably kept as guard dogs and for herding and guarding stock, rather than as companions.

ARCHAEOLOGICAL evidence has now revealed that marked distinctions in the sizes of domestic dogs had already become apparent over 9,000 years ago, even in dogs living in the same region. This trend seems to have gathered momentum, with the characteristic build of many of today's breeds being established by Roman times. By this stage in their history, dogs were being kept largely for the same purposes as they are today: hunting; working with livestock; guarding property; and acting as companions. Highly selective breeding and natural adaptation to various climatic conditions led to the emergence of countless new forms of dog through the Middle Ages. By the 1800s, many of the highly intelligent and specialized gundog breeds known today had evolved.

OFF TO THE HUNT
This medieval hunting scene depicts a distinctly greyhound-type breed in pursuit of its quarry. Leaner, sleeker dogs were better adapted for speed.

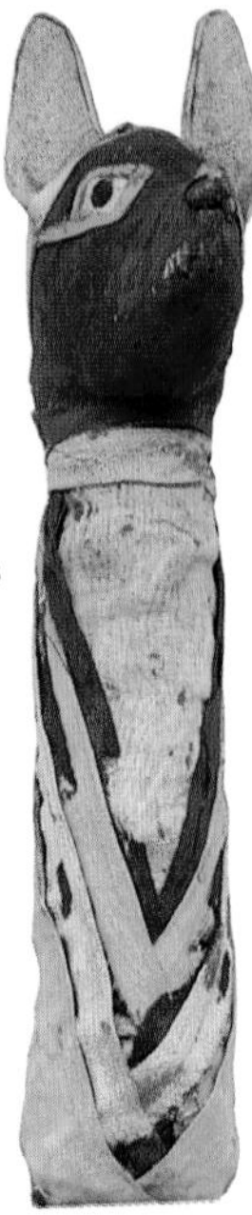

ANCIENT GODS
Dating from about 200 BC, this mummified dog was prepared by the Egyptians to resemble the jackal god, Anubis.

BREED STANDARDS

In the past, many dogs may have been similar in general appearance to the way they are today, but they were not then classified in specific breeds. The most significant change in this respect occurred very recently in canine history.

As dog shows became fashionable in the late 19th century, the need arose for specific criteria against which individual dogs could be compared and judged. Enthusiasts in Great Britain grouped together in 1873 to form what became known as the Kennel Club. This led directly to the establishment of stud books and set standards for certain dog breeds. It also set basic rules for shows. Similar organizations followed in other

EARLY FOXHOUND
Many hounds have been developed to pursue a particular quarry; foxhounds are bred to have the pace, stamina, and tenacity needed for fox hunting.

countries: the American Kennel Club was formed in 1884, and its Canadian counterpart in 1888.

BREED RECOGNITION

Nowadays, certain breeds, such as the German Shepherd Dog, have become popular throughout the world. Others, however, such as the American coonhounds, remain far more localized, perhaps even restricted to one specific region of a single country. The main purpose of this book is to serve as a guide to identifying these breeds, whether worldwide or local. Official recognition of breeds, however, depends largely on the individual countries and organizations. Breed standards often differ slightly between countries, as do the regulations concerning ear cropping and tail docking.

Wherever possible, and with the cooperation of top breeders in countries throughout the world, this book includes illustrations of top class examples of the dogs as representatives of their breeds.

CHARLES CRUFT
The founder of the famous Crufts dog show started his career as a dog food salesman.

EARLY SHOW
Great Danes come under scrutiny at the 1933 Crufts dog show (below).

AGILITY EVENTS

At an agility event, both purebred and mongrel dogs are judged on their competence in negotiating obstacles and obeying verbal commands.

SHOWING

Not all opportunities to show a dog are dependent on the animal's adherence to breed standards. Nor are they as demanding, on dogs or owners, as championship shows such as Crufts or Westminster. Open shows follow the same format as the championship shows, but they are considerably smaller: the best-of-breed winners compete for the best-in-show award. For dogs and owners new to showing, these can prove to be excellent venues at which to learn what is expected by judges.

Field trials (to put gundogs through their paces) and sheepdog trials are specialized events. At sheepdog trials, a dog herds a flock over a preset course into an enclosure. Points are given for speed and concentration, and penalties are incurred for barking and nipping when dogs grow impatient. The teamwork between man and dog displayed at these events is perhaps the most striking example of the progress that has been made since man and wolf first embarked on their curious alliance over 12,000 years ago.

TOP DOG

The winner's cup or ribbon is not only a reward for a good performance on the day – it is the culmination of months of dedicated hard work.

How This Book Works

FOLLOWING the Introduction and the Identification Key, the main breed section of the book is divided into six dog groups: companion dogs, gundogs, herding dogs, hounds, terriers, and working dogs. The breeds are ordered according to country of origin, ranging worldwide from the USA to Australia. The annotated example below shows how a typical entry is organized.

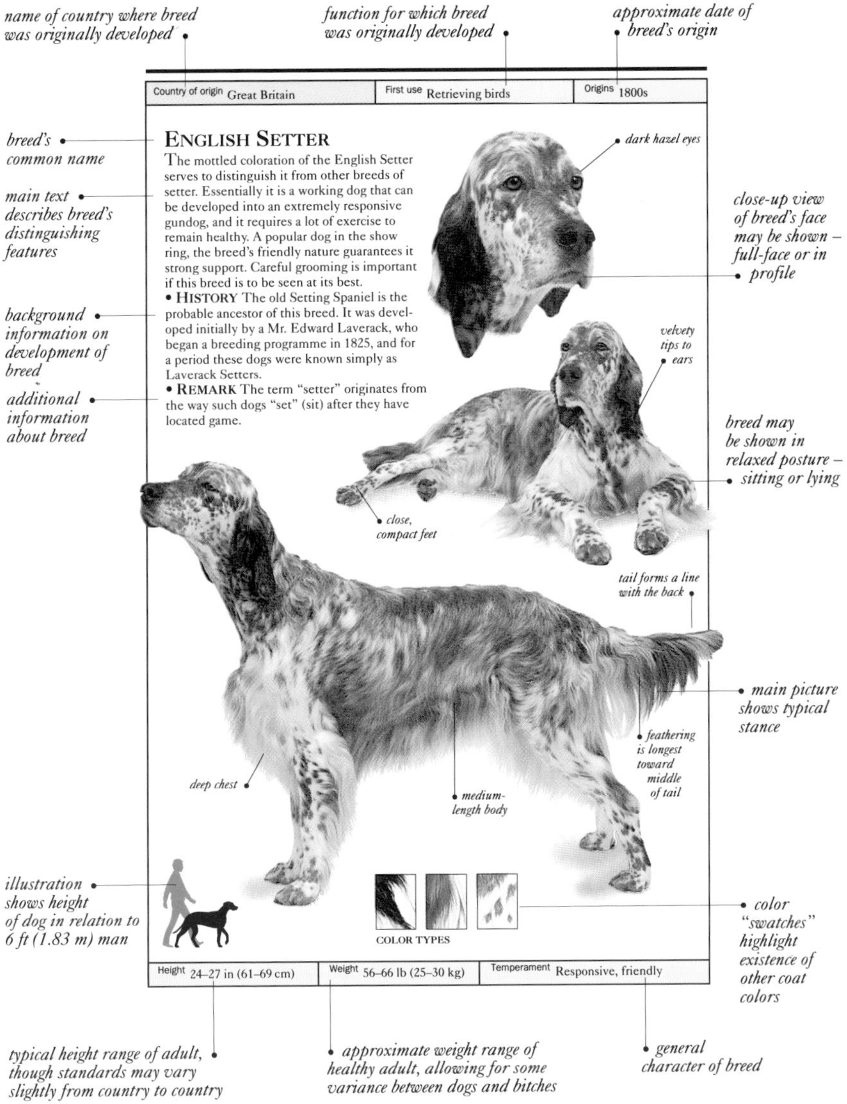

Country of origin Great Britain	First use Retrieving birds	Origins 1800s

ENGLISH SETTER

The mottled coloration of the English Setter serves to distinguish it from other breeds of setter. Essentially it is a working dog that can be developed into an extremely responsive gundog, and it requires a lot of exercise to remain healthy. A popular dog in the show ring, the breed's friendly nature guarantees it strong support. Careful grooming is important if this breed is to be seen at its best.

• **HISTORY** The old Setting Spaniel is the probable ancestor of this breed. It was developed initially by a Mr. Edward Laverack, who began a breeding programme in 1825, and for a period these dogs were known simply as Laverack Setters.

• **REMARK** The term "setter" originates from the way such dogs "set" (sit) after they have located game.

COLOR TYPES

Height 24–27 in (61–69 cm)	Weight 56–66 lb (25–30 kg)	Temperament Responsive, friendly

dark hazel eyes
velvety tips to ears
close, compact feet
tail forms a line with the back
feathering is longest toward middle of tail
deep chest
medium-length body
name of country where breed was originally developed
function for which breed was originally developed
approximate date of breed's origin
breed's common name
main text describes breed's distinguishing features
background information on development of breed
additional information about breed
close-up view of breed's face may be shown – full-face or in profile
breed may be shown in relaxed posture – sitting or lying
main picture shows typical stance
illustration shows height of dog in relation to 6 ft (1.83 m) man
color "swatches" highlight existence of other coat colors
typical height range of adult, though standards may vary slightly from country to country
approximate weight range of healthy adult, allowing for some variance between dogs and bitches
general character of breed

THE DOG FAMILY

THE EARLIEST MEMBERS of the Canidae family, which includes all living dogs, jackals, and foxes, can be traced back some 30 million years. Today there are 13 genera and 37 recognized species of these carnivores spread all over the world, although the distribution of some, such as the Gray Wolf (*Canis lupus*), has contracted greatly in recent times. Other species, such as the Red Fox (*Vulpes vulpes*), have adapted to urban living and their range is now much wider. All modern domestic dogs (*Canis familiaris*) are descended from the Gray Wolf and still retain much of the wolf's instincts. Wolves have the same social instinct that

OTHER GENERA

SPECIES
African Wild Dog *(Lycaon pictus)*
Arctic Fox *(Alopex lagopus)*
Bat-eared Fox *(Otocyon megalotis)*
Dhole *(Cuon alpinus)*
Maned Wolf *(Chrysocyon brachyurus)*
Raccoon Dog *(Nyctereutes procyonoides)*
Bush Dog *(Speothos venaticus)*
Small-eared Dog *(Atelocynus microtis)*
Crab-eating Fox *(Cerdocyon thous)*

GENUS *CANIS*

SPECIES
Gray Wolf *(C. lupus)*
Red Wolf *(C. rufus)*
Coyote *(C. latrans)*
Golden Jackal *(C. aureus)*
Simien Jackal *(C. simensis)*
Silver-backed Jackal *(C. mesomelas)*
Side-striped Jackal *(C. adustus)*
Dingo *(C. dingo)*
Domestic Dog *(C. familiaris)*

AFRICAN WILD DOG
A hunter of the African plains, the African Wild Dog lives in family groups. Its numbers have fallen dramatically in recent years, and the species is now considered endangered.

DOMESTIC DOG
There are now more than 300 different breeds of domestic dog, but they are not recognized by zoologists as separate species. All are grouped under the heading of *Canis familiaris.*

GRAY WOLF
Known to have evolved about 300,000 years ago, the highly social Gray Wolf is the largest wild dog. It is a fearless hunter but wary of humans, by whom it has been persecuted for centuries.

dogs display in their loyalty towards their masters; they have the territorial instinct exploited in guard dogs; and they have the hunting instinct refined in gundogs, hounds, and terriers. The Gray Wolf even has the herding instinct – one of the pack specializes in isolating a victim from its herd by using similar skills to a sheepdog.

DINGO

For many years dingoes were thought to be wild dogs. They are now known to be feral – that is, domestic dogs that have reverted to living wild.

CANIDAE

GENUS *VULPES*

SPECIES

Red Fox *(V. vulpes)*
Gray Fox *(V. cinereoargenteus)*
Island Gray Fox *(V. littoralis)*
Swift Fox *(V. velox)*
Fennec Fox *(V. zerda)*
Indian Fox *(V. bengalensis)*
Blanford's Fox *(V. cana)*
Cape Fox *(V. chama)*
Corsac Fox *(V. corsac)*
Tibetan Sand Fox *(V. ferrilata)*
Pale Fox *(V. pallida)*
Kit Fox *(V. macrotis)*
Rüppell's Fox *(V. rueppelli)*

GENUS *DUSICYON*

SPECIES

Chilla *(D. griseus)*
Colpeo Fox *(D. culpaeus)*
Small-eared Fox *(D. microtis)*
Pampas Fox *(D. gymnocercus)*
Sechura Fox *(D. sechurae)*
Hoary Fox *(D. vetulus)*

RED FOX
This highly adaptable canid has adjusted well to urban living, emerging at night from its den to feed on garbage. Apart from the domestic dog, it is the most widely distributed member of the family.

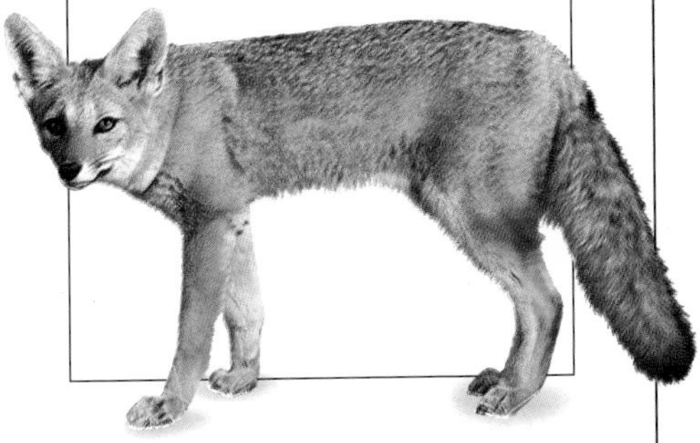

CHILLA
As with wild dogs in other parts of the world, the Chilla, or South American Fox, has been hunted for its fur, and this has had an adverse effect on some populations. In comparison with other canids little is known about South American foxes.

DOMESTIC DOG GROUPS

DOMESTIC DOGS may be classified in many different ways, but the fundamental means of separating breeds is on the basis of their function. Although many breeds are now kept as pets, irrespective of their origins, most were first used to carry out specific tasks, such as herding, hunting, and guarding. Their temperament, physique, and behavior have developed accordingly. For the purposes of this book, six major categorizations have been employed.

GUNDOGS (SPORTING GROUP)
This sporting group is bred to work closely with people, and gundogs are characterized by their responsive natures, and high intelligence. The gundog category includes spaniels, setters, retrievers, poodles, and pointers. Many gundogs have multiple uses: they can track the game, indicate the target for the hunter, and retrieve the game if it is shot.

COMPANION DOGS
(TOY GROUP/ NON-SPORTING GROUP)
This group consists of dogs generally characterized by their small size and gentle nature. The idea of keeping dogs as pets was popularized by the royal courts.

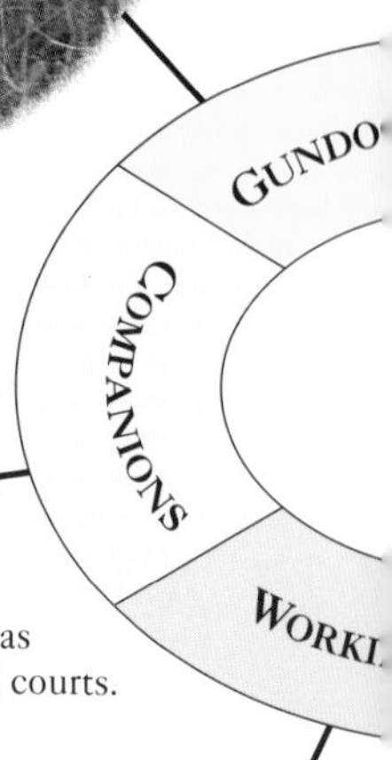
GUNDO
COMPANIONS
WORKI

WORKING DOGS (WORKING GROUP)
Around the world, the working group of dogs has been trained for a wide variety of specific tasks, including pulling sleds across snow and ice. In many countries they are employed to guard property and livestock; in others they are little more than livestock themselves, and have been traditionally used to provide food and fur.

HERDING DOGS (HERDING GROUP)

This herding group is an ancient category, since dogs have been employed to control the movements of livestock for centuries. They are most commonly used to herd sheep and cattle, but have also been trained to control deer, and even chickens. A good sheepdog possesses an "eye," with which it fixes the sheep, persuading them to move with minimal disturbance. The development of herding dogs has tended to be localized, which is reflected in the diversity of such breeds today. They are active, intelligent dogs with some of the more distinctive coats.

HOUNDS (HOUND GROUP)

The hound group is probably the most ancient category, bred to pursue game. It includes the fastest members of the dog family: the elegant sight hounds, such as the Greyhound, that run fast after game. But other hounds, such as the Bloodhound, have been bred for stamina, and these, mostly short-coated, breeds trail their quarry by scent rather than sight.

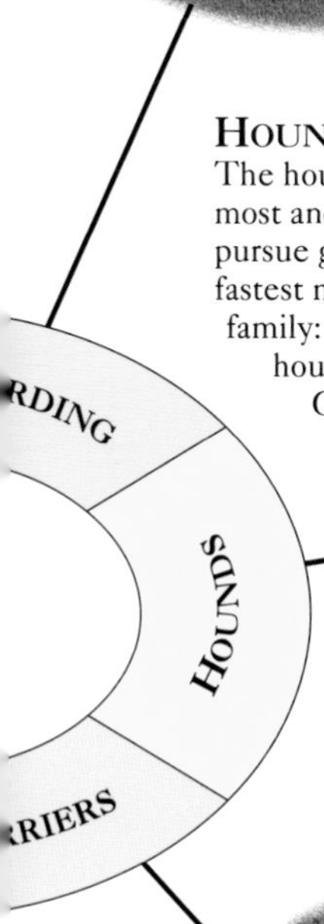
RDING
HOUNDS
RRIERS

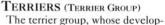

TERRIERS (TERRIER GROUP)

The terrier group, whose development has been centered in Great Britain during the last 100 years, are small but tenacious. Bold and fearless by nature, they are also highly inquisitive. They make first-class rodent-killers, and their small size allows them to "go to earth" in pursuit of quarry, such as foxes, driving them out to be chased by hounds. They make personable companions and enjoy exploring their surroundings.

WHAT IS A DOG?

ALL DOGS are primarily carnivorous, with teeth especially adapted for eating meat and gnawing bones. Because they were originally hunters, dogs are equipped with acute senses for detecting prey, and have very powerful muscles, allowing them to run at a great pace, with bursts of speed when necessary. All canids walk on their toes (rather than on the soles of their feet like bears), which allows them greater agility – often an important factor when tackling prey much larger than themselves. Dogs also evolved the ability to work together in a pack, thus overcoming the problem of hunting larger animals.

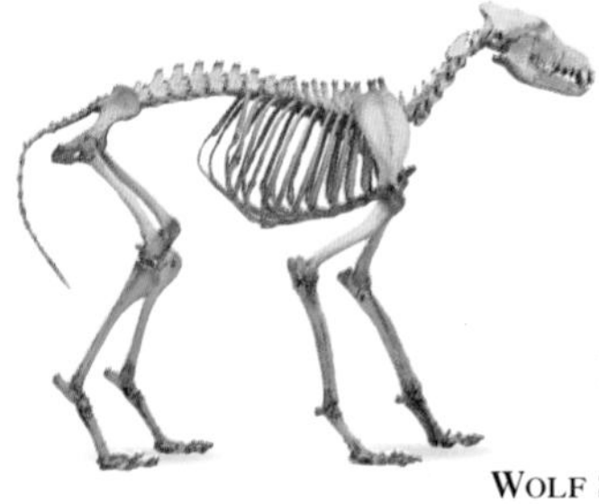

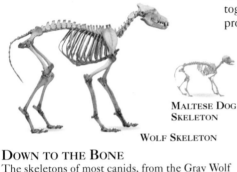

MALTESE DOG SKELETON

WOLF SKELETON

DOWN TO THE BONE

The skeletons of most canids, from the Gray Wolf to the smallest lapdog, are strikingly similar in shape, but natural evolution and man's selective breeding have resulted in some distinctive differences, primarily in the length of limbs and the skull shape. Usually, limb bones are long in relation to the height of the animal.

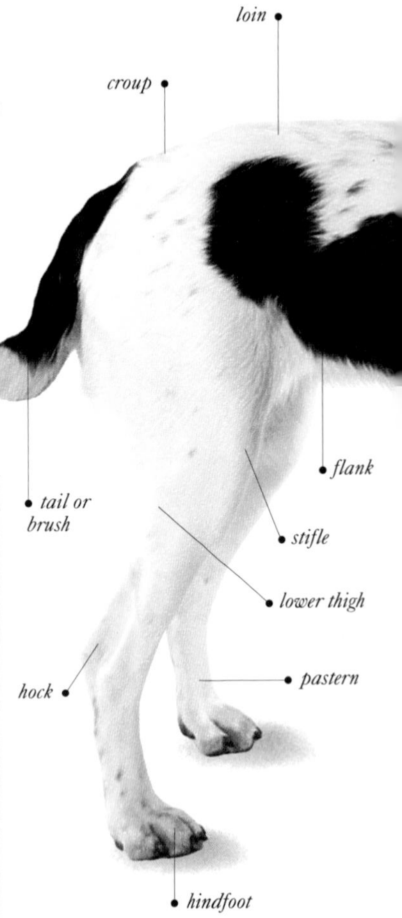
loin
croup
flank
tail or brush
stifle
lower thigh
pastern
hock
hindfoot

CROPPING AND DOCKING

Cropping ears to make them erect is a common practice in many countries, but illegal in the UK. In breeds where it is traditional, tail docking is usually carried out soon after birth. It seems to cause little pain, but has become controversial. For each breed there is a standard docking length, but the difference between docked breeds is variable.

cropped ears

docked tail

Skull Shape

The difference between the tiny, rounded (brachycephalic) skull of the selectively bred Japanese Chin, and the elongate (dolichocephalic) skull of its ancestor, the Gray Wolf, illustrates the extent of man's influence on the development of the domestic dog.

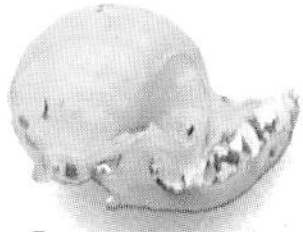

Japanese Chin Skull

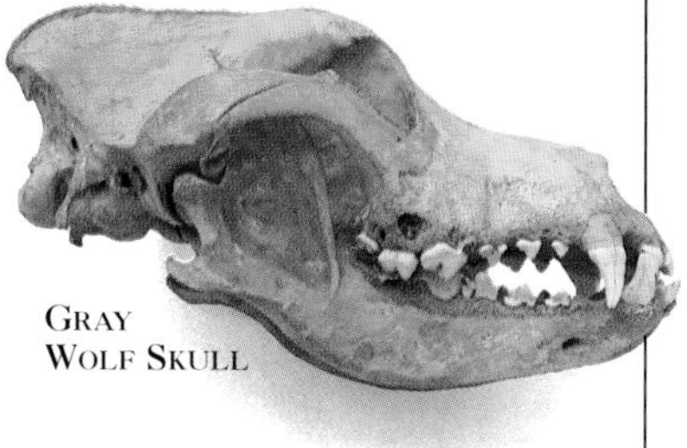

Gray Wolf Skull

crest
occiput
nape
stop
withers
muzzle
chest
shoulder
elbow
forearm
stopper pad
wrist
dew claw
forefoot

Size

Some hounds occur in standard and short-legged, or "basset," forms. Many short-legged forms were originally developed to take part in hunts conducted on foot rather than on horseback.

Short-legged Form

Standard Form

Dew Claws

The dew claw (equivalent of a thumb) is the innermost digit on each foot. It is of no use to most domestic dogs, and is commonly removed at a very early age. However, the Puffin Dog has double dew claws, which assist its mobility in rough terrain.

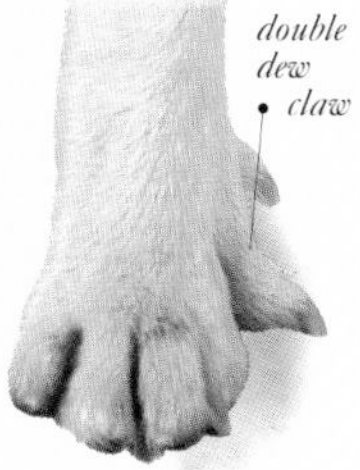
double dew claw

Coat Types

A dog's coat is made up of two basic types of hair: the longer, outer, guard hairs, which are fairly coarse in texture; and the softer secondary hairs that make up the undercoat, and through which the guard hairs protrude. Variations on this basic pattern do occur, however, and not all breeds have both types of hair. A dog's coat is an important feature in its development: dogs bred in cold climates are likely to have dense coats; hunting dogs tend to have short, sleek coats; and terriers are often bred with wiry coats for protection against the elements.

Care Considerations

The type of coat is an important consideration when choosing a dog. As a guide, those with short, smooth coats, such as Dalmatians, are easiest to care for, needing little more than a polish with a hound glove and an occasional bath. In contrast, dogs with wiry coats, such as Schnauzers, must be regularly combed. For show purposes, their coat must be stripped and plucked about once every three months; pets can be clipped about every two months and excess hair trimmed from around the eyes and ears. Breeds with longer coats, such as the Rough Collie, need daily grooming to prevent the coat from becoming matted. Many breeds will benefit from a bath every three months or so, both to keep their coat clean and to reduce their doggy odor. Excessive bathing, however, is not recommended.

Desert Dweller

Its short coat allows this young Dingo to tolerate the Australian desert sun.

Long-haired Coat

Wire-haired Coat

Smooth Coat

COLOR TYPES

While some breeds occur in just a single color form, in other cases a much wider range of combinations exists. The color panels accompanying the breed entries in this book serve to give a general indication of some alternative color types for each particular breed. The panels themselves are not exact color replicas, but reflect major color groupings, as set out below. In the case of patterned varieties, precise distribution of the colors may be laid down in the breed standard. Not all colors in a particular breed may be recognized for exhibition purposes.

LIVER
Includes reddish brown, sable, and cinnamon shades.

BLACK BRINDLE
Includes "pepper and salt," a gray/black combination.

CREAM
Includes white, and light shades such as ivory, blond, and lemon.

RED/TAN
Includes red, red-fawn, tawny, rich chestnut, orange roan, chestnut roan.

BLUE
Includes merle (blue-gray), and speckled blue (with black).

DARK BROWN
Includes mahogany and blackish brown.

BLACK AND TAN
Clearly defined colors which result in good contrast.

GOLD
Includes russet gold, fawn, apricot, wheaten, and tawny.

CHESTNUT RED AND WHITE
Includes combinations of white with orange, fawn, red, chestnut.

BLUE MOTTLED WITH TAN
Includes blue and brindle, and bluish black and tan.

BLACK AND WHITE
Includes black or brindle markings with white.

BLACK, TAN, AND WHITE
Otherwise known as tricolor.

GRAY
Includes all shades from silvery to blue-black gray, and gray or black brindle.

LIVER AND TAN
A combination of two reddish shades.

LIVER AND WHITE
A coloration often associated with gundog breeds.

TAN AND WHITE
A color combination seen in many breeds of hound.

BLACK
Some breeds are pure black, but may become gray around the muzzle with age.

GOLD AND WHITE
Includes white with lemon, gold, or orange spots.

RED BRINDLE
Includes orange or mahogany brindle.

FUR COLORS
A black and a yellow Labrador. There is also a liver-colored variety.

SENSES AND INSTINCTS

SINCE THE PROCESS of domestication began, selective breeding over 4,000 generations or more has changed the physical appearance of some dogs dramatically. But even the tiny Chihuahua (see p.41) displays many behavioral characteristics of its ancestor, the wolf. Like the wolf, the domestic dog communicates by means of calls and body language, with its ears and tail being especially expressive. The dog retains the same strong social instincts as the wolf.

SENSITIVE EARS

HEARING

Dogs generally have a very acute sense of hearing and are able to hear sounds that are too high-pitched for human ears. This greater hearing range assists dogs in tracking down their quarry and in communicating with each other. Recently, dogs have been used to help deaf people, some being trained to indicate such sounds as a ringing telephone.

SENDING A MESSAGE

COMMUNICATION

Wolves keep in touch with each other by howling, a means of communication well developed in northern spitz breeds, which work in groups. Pack hounds tracking a scent may also bay, which is useful to the hunter when the dog is not visible.

ON THE SCENT

KEEN EYESIGHT

SIGHT

The position of the eyes, toward the sides of the head, gives dogs a wider field of vision than human beings, making them more aware of their environment. Dogs also have better vision at dusk because the cells in the retina, where the image is focused, respond well to low light. However, color vision is limited.

SMELL

The keen sense of smell common to all dogs is most fully developed in breeds such as the Bloodhound, which uses it to track quarry. Dogs rely on the nose, as well as Jacobson's Organ in the mouth, to detect scent particles.

Scent Marking

Dog urine contains highly individual chemical scent markers, or pheromones. A male will convey the boundaries of his territory to other dogs by using urine as a marker. After puberty, male dogs spray urine by lifting their leg, rather than squatting like a bitch, in order to hit a target such as a tree or a post. They may also scratch the ground, leaving a scent from the sweat glands between their toes. There is a distinct difference in scent marking between the sexes, and male dogs urinate perhaps three times more frequently than bitches.

Identifying a Stranger

Ready to Fight

Aggression

Male dogs meeting in antagonistic situations carry out a well-defined series of gestures, indicating submission (below), or threatening aggression without actually attacking their opponent. The dog stands upright, tail erect, raising its hackles (the hairs along its back). The neck extends forward and the mouth opens into a snarl.

Offering No Defence

Submission

If a dog wants to submit, it will probably crouch down with its tail between its legs and its ears down. In some cases it may run off, with the dominant dog in pursuit. Alternatively, it may roll over on to its back, like a puppy, and may urinate a little if it has no easy means of retreat. A submissive dog is not likely to be attacked.

Companionship

Despite their need to establish a "pecking order," dogs are social by nature and generally get along well together. Dogs bred as companions tend to be less noisy than hounds, since barking is not considered a desirable trait where dogs are living in close proximity to people. A companion dog will wag its tail and open its mouth slightly in greeting when a member of the family returns home.

Faithful Friend

PUPPIES

MOST PEOPLE prefer to own a dog from puppyhood, so that they can train it themselves. A puppy will settle more rapidly into unfamiliar surroundings than older individuals, and is less likely to display the behavioral problems sometimes encountered in adult dogs. Even so, some disruption and damage in the home is likely to follow a puppy's acquisition. Carpets, for example, may be soiled or chewed, and puppies may bark or yelp a great deal when first left on their own. This calls for tolerance on the part of owners. Sensible training and adequate attention to the puppy's needs should reduce such problems to a minimum. Dogs are creatures of routine, and will soon learn to respond as required.

GOLDEN RETRIEVER AND PUPS

THE BREEDING PERIOD

Domestic bitches (female dogs) usually have two periods of "heat" each year, while wild bitches come into season only once during this time. Both wild and domestic dogs have a gestation period of about two months before the litter is born. The off-spring, known as pups or cubs, are helpless at birth, and are suckled and cleaned by their mother until they start to be weaned on to solid food at about four to six weeks old.

HEALTHY PUPS

Young dogs tend to play vigorously and then sleep for long periods. This is not a sign of ill health. Similarly, in a new home, a pup will be less active than an adult dog. Key health indicators to look for are a good appetite and firm stool with no trace of blood. The skin is normally loose, but watch for a potbellied appearance, which could indicate worms. Deworming is a vital process for the pup's continued good health. Your vet will be able to advise you on essential vaccinations.

PLAYFUL PATTERDALES

The Developing Pup

The coat of a pup may be less profuse than its mother's (as in the example of the Old English Sheepdog, shown right), but the distribution of markings is unlikely to change as the pup matures.

By the time it is six months old, the pup should be housetrained. It should also be walking readily on a leash and can soon be allowed to exercise freely. Choose a quiet spot away from roads, and away from distractions such as other dogs or farm animals. If the dog runs off, do not chase it, because it is likely to see this as a game. Instead, stand still and call it back. It should return after its enthusiasm for its newfound freedom wears off.

Old English Sheepdog and Pup

Shar Pei Pup

Cocker Spaniel Pup

Relative Sizes

All young puppies, no matter what their breed, are of a relatively similar size at birth. Only later do the larger breeds, like the Shar Pei (far left) start to grow at a faster rate than the smaller breeds, like the Cocker Spaniel (near left). Avoid exercising young dogs too strenuously, especially the larger breeds, because this puts stresses on their frame. It is better just to give them daily walks, with the opportunity to run free if they wish.

Toward Adulthood

Changes become apparent as pups grow older. In certain breeds, such as the German Shepherd Dog, the ears will start to become erect. In a few cases this does not happen, but generally the ears should have started to lift by the time the puppy is approaching six months old. In breeds in which pups are noticeably paler at birth than the adult dogs (as in the case of the Australian Cattle Dog, shown right), coat coloration is also likely to have darkened by six months. Other characteristics, such as eye color, may also be more adult-like by this age.

Australian Cattle Dog and Pup

Choosing a Dog

When choosing a dog, the potential owner is influenced by a number of factors, such as health, appearance, and character, but the size of the adult dog is generally the chief concern. However, size can often be deceptive, as some large dogs, such as the Greyhound, can be much less active in the home than smaller breeds. Unfortunately, the more dogs are kept as companions the more their origins become obscured, though the instincts that first shaped their development often remain largely intact. Too many people choose a dog on the basis of its appearance alone without giving adequate consideration to the breed's ancestry, which is a factor that affects both its character and behavior.

Papillon

Small is Beautiful

Toy dogs such as the Papillon have a built-in advantage over larger breeds – their appetite is smaller, and so they are less expensive to feed. They are quite easy to train and tend to be keen to please their owners. They thrive on affection and are usually good with children. However, it does not always follow that small dogs need less space; many small dogs, especially terriers, are very active and like nothing better than to run loose in open country.

Beagle

Hounds

Some smaller hounds, such as the Beagle, have much to recommend them as pets, often having short, easy-care coats and lively, active natures. All scent hounds can be difficult to train, however, and will be reluctant to return to their owners if they pick up a scent. Pack dogs by nature, they can be greedy eaters.

Spaniels

Gundogs were developed to have a close rapport with their owners, and breeds such as the English Springer Spaniel make admirable house companions, provided they have plenty of opportunity to exercise and plenty of time devoted to their needs. Grooming is a must, and particular attention should be paid to the heavy, pendulous ears, or they may become a source of problems in later life. Infections in the ears are common in spaniel breeds. One simple precaution is to invest in a very deep food bowl. The ears should then hang down outside the bowl, where they are less likely to become soiled by food.

English Springer Spaniel

POINTS TO CHECK

backbone not prominent
coat free from lice or fleas
clear ears
eyes clear and free from discharge
clean anal area
pup should walk and run freely
potbelly may indicate worms
check for presence of dew claws

CHOOSING A PUP

Having decided on the breed, you may be able to obtain a puppy locally. Breeders can be traced through the dog magazines or via the national kennel club. The cost of pups varies depending on their pedigree and the relative rarity of the breed. Pups are generally fully weaned and ready for their new home at about nine weeks old. Arrange for a veterinary check-up as soon as possible to ensure that the pup is in good health. However, not everybody wants, or can afford to buy, a pedigree dog and, in terms of companionship, mongrels (dogs of mixed breed) can be delightful pets. But remember that it may be hard to determine the ultimate size of a mongrel.

DOBERMANN

GUARD DOGS

Breeds suitable for guard work, such as the Dobermann, have recently undergone a surge in popularity. Many guard dogs, however, retain strong working instincts and are dominant by nature. Consequently, they require firm training from a very early age if they are not to become a liability as they grow older.

GREAT DANE

THE BIGGER THE BETTER

The size of dogs such as the Great Dane can be off-putting. But size is no reliable indicator of a dog's temperament, for this is a gentle, largely placid breed. There are certainly drawbacks in keeping an animal of this size: feeding costs are considerable, and they need plenty of living space.

Pet Care

A VARIETY OF EQUIPMENT is needed for grooming, feeding, and exercising a dog. It is important, however, to choose the right equipment for your particular choice of breed, as requirements differ somewhat. Choosing the right equipment for the right stage in your dog's life will save you unnecessary trouble and expense. It may be better to defer the purchase of a bed, for instance, until the teething phase has passed, at around nine months of age. A cardboard box will do until then. Otherwise, your expensive purchase may be damaged beyond repair.

Grooming and Coat Care

Regular grooming is vital from an early age, not only to keep the dog's coat in good condition, but also to accustom it to the procedure, which the dog will then readily accept throughout its life. Some breeds require more coat care than others, depending on the quality of the hair, the length of the coat, and the lifestyle of the dog. Regular grooming sessions are a perfect opportunity for you to check for any health problems your dog may be experiencing, such as rashes, hair loss, sores or wounds, or any lumps or swellings that may need attention from a veterinarian. If you intend to show your dog, these sessions will also accustom the animal to being handled.

double-headed brush for finishing off
wire comb for untangling
flea comb

Combs and Brushes

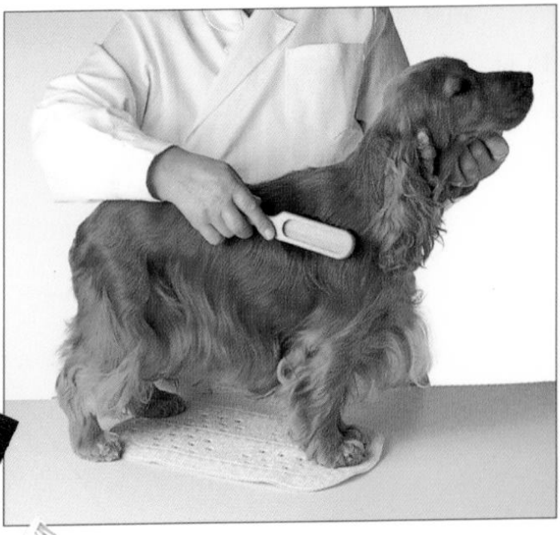

Brushing

Regular brushing to remove tangles and snags is the first step to keeping your dog's coat in good condition. You will have better access to all of the coat if you can persuade the dog to remain standing throughout this process.

Sleeping Quarters

Encouraging a dog to use its own sleeping quarters from an early age will deter it from sleeping on your bed or using the sofa and chairs as a substitute.

Dog Beds

When you decide that the purchase of a bed is in order, make sure that it is fully washable, for this is the site where fleas typically deposit their eggs. By cleaning the bed on a regular basis, you may be able to spare yourself an explosive epidemic of these troublesome parasites. If you are buying a bed for a young dog, make sure that it is sufficiently large to accommodate the dog comfortably once it is fully grown.

LIGHTWEIGHT NYLON LEASH

COLLAR AND TAG

PULL TOY

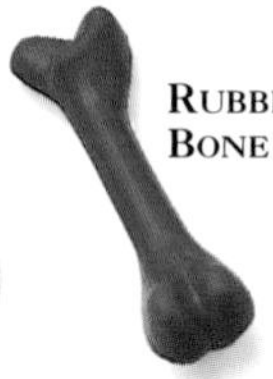

RUBBER BONE

COLLARS, LEASHES, AND TOYS

Pups from six to seven weeks old should be introduced to wearing a collar. Proper training of all dogs must include learning to walk calmly on a collar and leash with their owner. A leather collar can be unbuckled and made longer as your dog grows. Adjust it so that it fits loosely, but is not so slack that the dog can pull its head free of it. In case your dog wanders, be sure to attach a tag to the collar stating your address and telephone number.

Dogs, even when fully grown, enjoy play, and your pet store should have a wide range of suitable toys. Play sessions are not only fun for the dog, they also represent good exercise. Pull toys and rubber bones help to keep the dog's teeth in good condition, but avoid small items that pups may swallow.

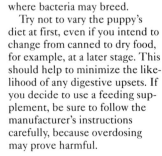

CERAMIC BOWL

STAINLESS-STEEL BOWL

NUTRITIONAL CARE

Food and water bowls should be made from a material that can be properly cleaned. Replace ceramic bowls once they are chipped or cracked, for such defects are sites where bacteria may breed.

Try not to vary the puppy's diet at first, even if you intend to change from canned to dry food, for example, at a later stage. This should help to minimize the likelihood of any digestive upsets. If you decide to use a feeding supplement, be sure to follow the manufacturer's instructions carefully, because overdosing may prove harmful.

HEALTH CARE

TEETH CARE

You can now buy specially made toothpaste and brushes for your dog. These will help to ensure healthy teeth and gums throughout its life.

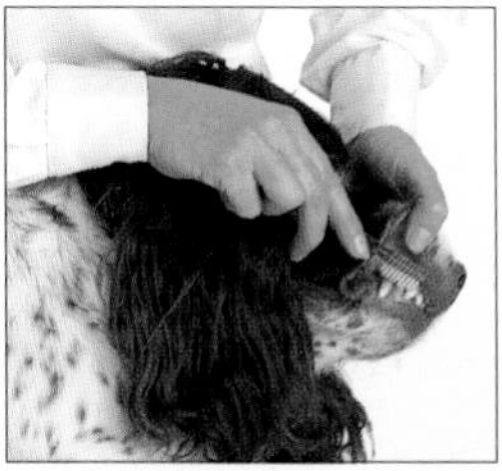

GIVING MEDICINE

If your dog is cooperative you should be able to administer medicine orally using a spoon. If not, use a dropper. Give it slowly or the dog is likely to spit it out.

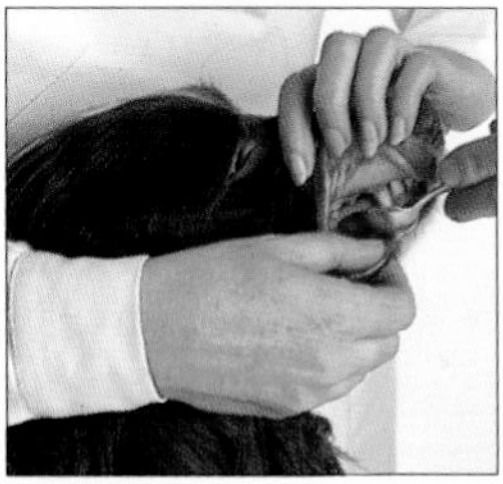

EAR CLEANING

Remove dead hair with your fingers, use a dropper to put oily cleanser into the ear canal, massage the base of the ear to spread it, then clear oil or wax at the surface with cotton wool. Never poke into the ear canal.

SHOWING YOUR DOG

MANY OWNERS of purebred dogs are great show enthusiasts and travel considerable distances in the hope of success in the show ring. For the vast majority of participants, however, there are no financial rewards for all their hard work. This is one arena where the amateur still reigns supreme, with people taking part simply because they enjoy the opportunity to show their dogs, meet other people who have similar interests, and share in the excitement as the final winners are chosen. For information on shows, consult the specialist dog press.

BATH TIME

For the show dog, a bath is the first stage of preparation for the ring. Place the bath in a draft-free spot, and use warm water and shampoo formulated for dogs. Hold the dog's head up so that water runs away from its eyes and nose. Thoroughly rinse out the shampoo, towel dry, and, for long-haired breeds, use a hairdryer before brushing.

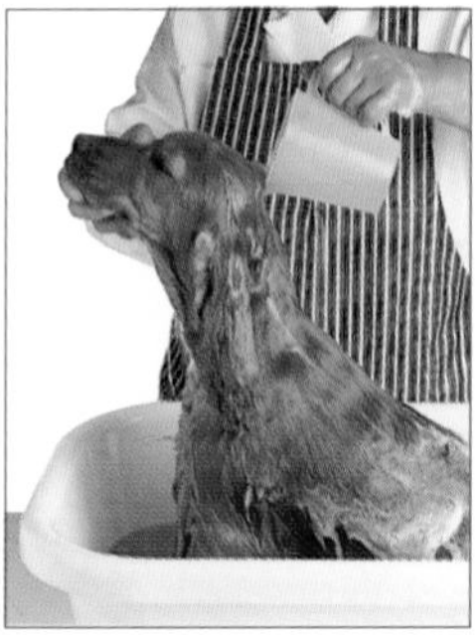

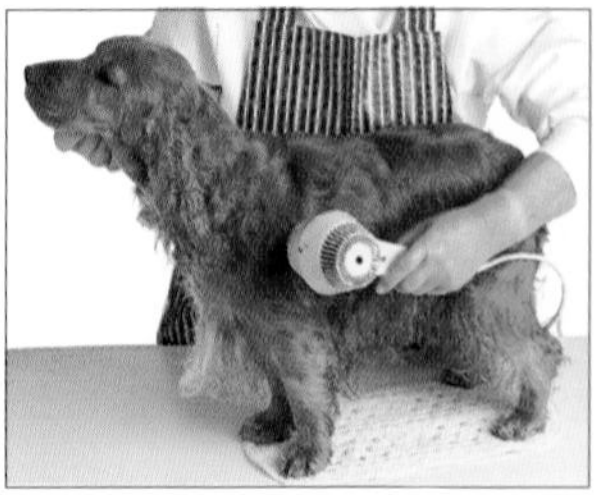

HAIRDRYER
Use a low-heat setting only.

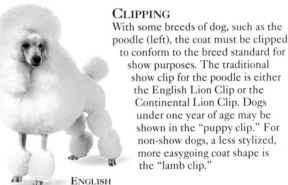

CLIPPING

With some breeds of dog, such as the poodle (left), the coat must be clipped to conform to the breed standard for show purposes. The traditional show clip for the poodle is either the English Lion Clip or the Continental Lion Clip. Dogs under one year of age may be shown in the "puppy clip." For non-show dogs, a less stylized, more easygoing coat shape is the "lamb clip."

CONTINENTAL LION CLIP

ENGLISH LION CLIP

KEEPING CLEAN

With a long-haired dog, you may have to go to considerable lengths to keep it clean and tangle-free after it has been bathed in the run-up to its appearance in front of the judges. Here (right), a Yorkshire Terrier has been bathed and had its hair tied up until show time. Its marvelous, flowing, full-length coat is then revealed, with just a single bow remaining.

HAIR SAFELY TIED UP AFTER BATHING

COMBED AND READY

PET'S SUPPLIES

The Big Day

The show ring is the culmination of much hard work by the owners. A good show dog is trained to display itself to best advantage in front of the judge. A calm disposition is essential, for the dog must tolerate close examination and handling by a stranger, and it must ignore the unsettling presence of the other dogs. In turn, a judge needs a thorough knowledge of the official breed standards in order to assess the dog's appearance, stance, presence, movement, and temperament.

A Dog Show in Progress
A class of Afghan Hounds and their handlers wait anxiously for the verdict of the judge.

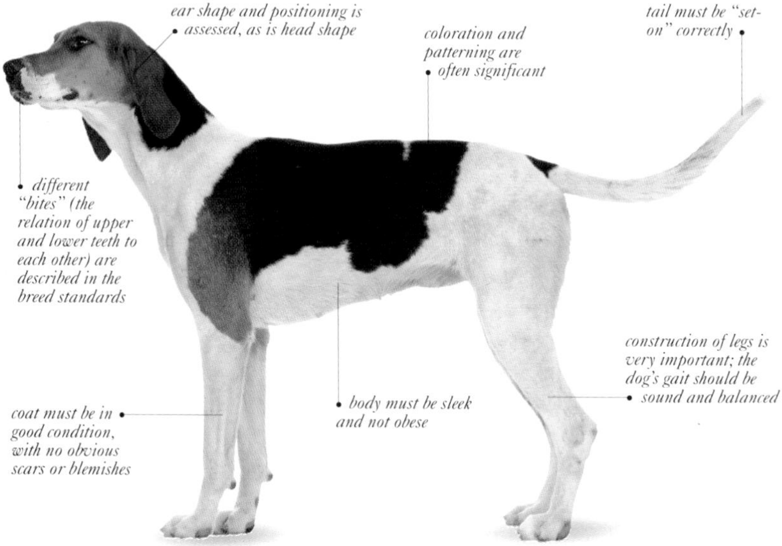
ear shape and positioning is assessed, as is head shape
coloration and patterning are often significant
tail must be "set-on" correctly
different "bites" (the relation of upper and lower teeth to each other) are described in the breed standards
construction of legs is very important; the dog's gait should be sound and balanced
body must be sleek and not obese
coat must be in good condition, with no obvious scars or blemishes

Breed Standards

The breed standard in every country where a breed is recognized usually specifies such things as the height and weight of the dog; the proportions of the body with reference to specific body parts; coloration; and the appearance and texture of the coat, ears, tail, eyes, and feet. Typical faults that count against a dog are also listed at the end of the standard.

Dog Identification Key

THE SYSTEM OF IDENTIFICATION used here assumes no prior knowledge of dog character or function, but offers instead a method of recognition based on noting key physical characteristics, as defined below and opposite. On the following pages (pp.30–37), all the breeds in the book are separated into groups, first by size (small, medium, or large), then by head shape (round, long, or square), ear type (long, erect, or short), and finally by coat type (short, long, or wiry). At the end of this trail appears a typical dog of that type (e.g., small, round-headed, long-eared, and short-coated), together with the page numbers on which all breeds with similar features appear. In a few cases, a breed may appear in more than one group.

Size

This is the most evident feature that separates breeds. Three categories are used – small, medium, and large – and they refer to the highest point of the shoulder (the withers). This is also the measure for show purposes, and is the figure given in the actual breed entries.

Head Shape

This is obviously a less precise feature than height, but, again, the breeds have been divided into three broad categories: round-headed, long-headed, and square-headed. Round-headed breeds tend to be short-nosed; long-headed breeds have long noses, which may taper; square-headed breeds often have relatively short, muscular jaws.

LARGE
MEDIUM
SMALL

SIZE VARIANTS
The sizes shown are: large, over 24 in (61 cm); medium, 18–24 in (46–61 cm); and small, under 18 in (46 cm).

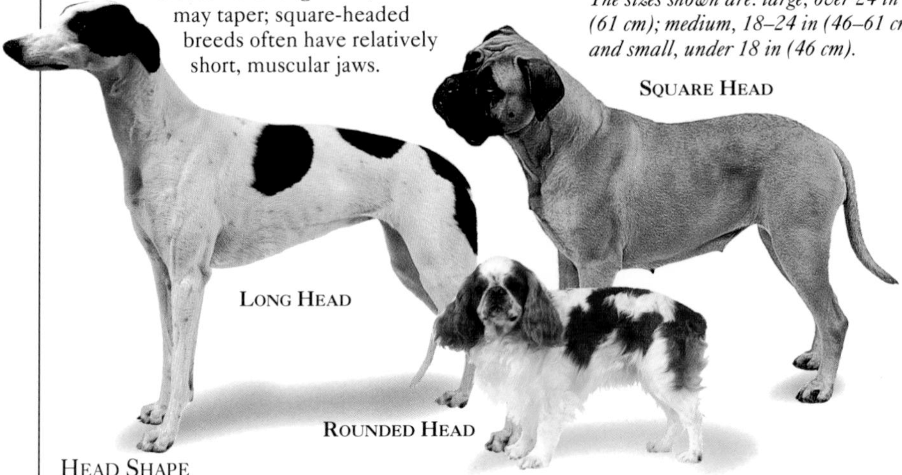
SQUARE HEAD
LONG HEAD
ROUNDED HEAD

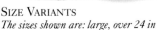

HEAD SHAPE
This can give an indication of the dog's ancestry. Sight hounds, like the Greyhound, typically have a long muzzle. Breeds originally bred for fighting tend to have a short, squarish muzzle.

LONG EARS
SHORT EARS
ERECT EARS

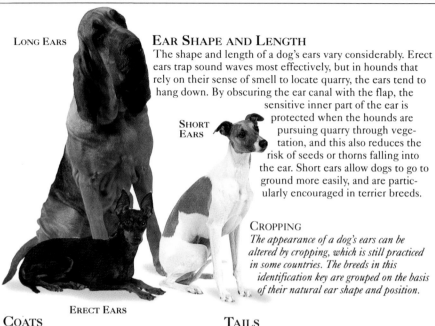

EAR SHAPE AND LENGTH

The shape and length of a dog's ears vary considerably. Erect ears trap sound waves most effectively, but in hounds that rely on their sense of smell to locate quarry, the ears tend to hang down. By obscuring the ear canal with the flap, the sensitive inner part of the ear is protected when the hounds are pursuing quarry through vegetation, and this also reduces the risk of seeds or thorns falling into the ear. Short ears allow dogs to go to ground more easily, and are particularly encouraged in terrier breeds.

CROPPING
The appearance of a dog's ears can be altered by cropping, which is still practiced in some countries. The breeds in this identification key are grouped on the basis of their natural ear shape and position.

COATS

Another significant feature that can help to identify a dog is its coat type. Coats can be divided into short- or long-haired, on the basis of their length, while the third category, wire-haired, is distinguished by texture. Some breeds, such as the Dachshunds, have been developed in all three coat types, while others may occur in both short- and long-haired forms, although one type often tends to predominate today.

SHORT HAIR
Creates a smooth, sleek appearance, with the hair tight against the skin.

LONG HAIR
Usually combines with a dense undercoat to give weatherproofing.

WIRE HAIR
A harsh and dense type often found on breeds working in undergrowth.

TAILS

Tails show considerable variation in length and shape, but recognition of the various types is not essential for breed identification. Tails can be altered artificially by docking.

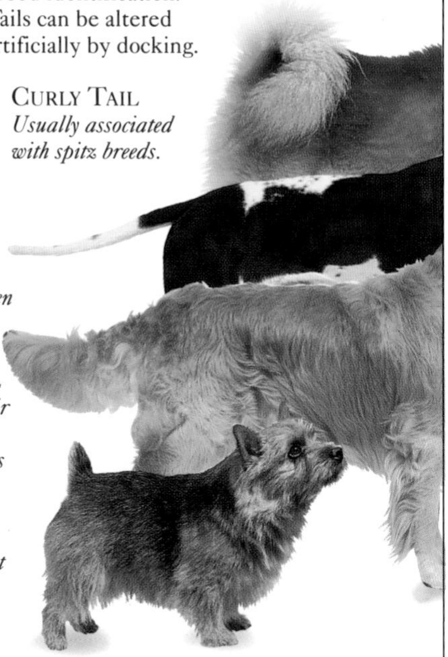

CURLY TAIL
Usually associated with spitz breeds.

LONG TAIL
Used as a means of communication; enables a dog to be seen in undergrowth.

FEATHERED TAIL
Formed by longer hair on lower tail surface. Associated with setters and other gundogs.

DOCKED TAIL
Mainly carried out on terriers, this procedure creates a short, erect tail.

Breeds Grouped by Key Characteristics

Small Dogs

This group includes all breeds under 18 inches (46 cm) in height. Once you have established that the dog belongs to this category, you should identify the head shape (see p.28), followed by the ear and coat type. You will then be able to locate a breed of that physical type in one of the bands below or on pages 32 to 33,

Round-headed

Long-eared

Short-haired

Beagle *146(b)*

Long-haired

Tibetan Terrier *55(b)*

OTHERS *38, 40(b), 43(b), 46(b), 49, 51(t), 52, 53(b), 55(t), 56(t & b), 57(b), 58, 59(b), 60, 63*

Wire-haired

Dandie Dinmont Terrier *213(t)*

Long-headed

Long-eared

Short-haired

Basset Hound *146(t)*

Italian Greyhound *50*

OTHERS *40(t), 43(t), 47(b), 48, 50, 59(t), 146(b), 155(t), 158–59, 173(t & b), 175, 186(b), 187, 209(b)*

Long-haired

Cesky Terrier *230(b)*

Erect-eared

Short-haired

Miniature Bull Terrier *212(t)*

English Toy Terrier *210(t)*

OTHERS *42, 54, 107(b), 111(t), 111(b), 132(t), 197, 206, 210(b), 246(t), 249(b), 291(t), 295(b)*

Long-haired

German Spitz: Mittel *44(b)*

OTHERS *39(t), 44(t), 45(t & b), 51(b), 57(t), 132(b), 221(t), 225* where there will also be page references for all similar breeds featured in the book.

"Small" dogs include the so-called toy breeds, and many terriers. Their size makes them popular as companions today, although some were quite localized in former years. Some terriers share a common ancestry, and may resemble each other, while true companion dogs show a much wider variation in appearance.

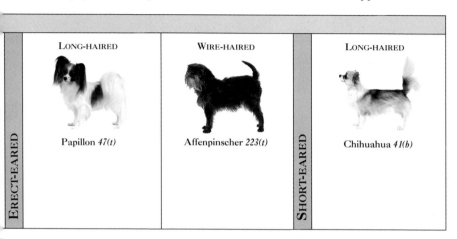

ERECT-EARED

LONG-HAIRED

Papillon *47(t)*

WIRE-HAIRED

Affenpinscher *223(t)*

SHORT-EARED

LONG-HAIRED

Chihuahua *41(b)*

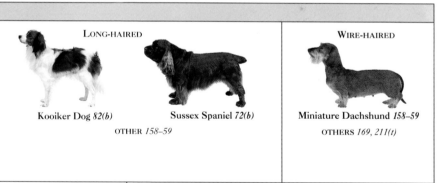

LONG-HAIRED

Kooiker Dog *82(b)*

Sussex Spaniel *72(b)*

OTHER *158–59*

WIRE-HAIRED

Miniature Dachshund *158–59*

OTHERS *169, 211(t)*

LONG-HAIRED

Shetland Sheepdog *109(b)*

WIRE-HAIRED

Australian Terrier *220(b)*

Podengo Portugueso Pequeno *197*

OTHERS *211(b), 217(t), 225*

SMALL, LONG-HEADED DOGS *continued*

SHORT-EARED

SHORT-HAIRED

Parson Jack Russell Terrier *215(t)*

Japanese Terrier *292(t)*

Smooth Fox Terrier *216(t)*

OTHERS *218(t), 221(b), 222, 223(b), 228(b)*

SQUARE-HEADED

ERECT-EARED

SHORT-HAIRED

Boston Terrier *208(b)*

OTHER *263(t)*

LONG-HAIRED

Skye Terrier *217(b)*

OTHER *219*

WIRE-HAIRED

Cairn Terrier *213(b)*

OTHER *218(b)*

MEDIUM-SIZED DOGS

THIS GROUP INCLUDES all dog breeds between 18 and 24 inches (41–61 cm) in height. Once you have established that the dog actually belongs to this category, you should identify the head shape (see p.28), followed by the ear shape and length, and the coat type. You will then be able to locate a breed of that physical

ROUND-HEADED

LONG-EARED

SHORT-HAIRED

Labrador *69*

OTHER *136*

LONG-HAIRED

Polish Lowland Sheepdog *123(t)*

OTHERS *66(b), 67(t), 95, 106, 123(b), 136, 266*

WIRE-HAIRED

Wire Fox Terrier *215(b)*

Lakeland Terrier *214(t)*

Welsh Terrier *216(b)*

OTHERS *214(b), 215(t), 221(b), 224, 228(t)*

SHORT-EARED

SHORT-HAIRED

Pug *53*

OTHERS *39(b), 212(b)*

WIRE-HAIRED

Sealyham Terrier *220(t)*

OTHER *229*

type below or on pages 34 to 37, where there will also be page references for all similar breeds featured in the book.

Many common breeds are medium sized, including various gundogs, sheepdogs, and hounds, though others remain localized, even within their country of origin. Nevertheless, rare-breed shows are gradually introducing many of them to a wider audience.

ERECT-EARED

LONG-HAIRED

Chow Chow *288*

SHORT-EARED

LONG-HAIRED

Briard *116–117*

MEDIUM-SIZED, LONG-HEADED DOGS *continued*

LONG-EARED

SHORT-HAIRED

Weimaraner *76–77*

OTHERS *61, 62, 67(b), 70–71, 72(t), 74, 79, 82(t), 87, 88–89, 90, 91, 92(t), 93, 98, 101, 102, 103, 104, 120–21, 138, 139(t & b), 140, 141, 142–43, 144, 145, 147, 151(b), 152, 153, 154(t & b), 155(b), 156, 157, 160(t & b), 161, 164, 165, 166–67, 168, 170–71, 174, 178, 180, 182, 183, 184–85, 188, 189(t), 190, 191, 195, 199, 201, 205, 230(t & b), 272, 274, 279, 280(t), 284(t)*

LONG-HAIRE

Afghan Hound *20*

OTHERS *64, 65, 66(t*
68, 73, 75, 76–77, 80–
83(t & b), 84, 86, 94

ERECT-EARED

SHORT-HAIRED

Pharoah Hound *193*

Sarloos Wolfhound *125*

OTHERS *109(t), 112, 113, 115, 119, 129, 192(b), 194, 198, 204, 233(b), 234–35, 239(t), 245(t & b), 246(b), 247(t & b), 248, 249(t), 281, 284(b), 285(t & b), 286, 287, 290, 292(b)*

LONG-HAIRE

Keeshond *46(t)*

OTHERS *108, 114(t & b), 124, 126, 128*

SHORT-EARED

SHORT-HAIRED

Sloughi *203*

Chinook *233(t)*

OTHERS *107(t), 150, 151(t), 186(t), 196*

Irish Red and White Setter *85*

OTHERS *96, 103, 105, 110, 134(t & b), 135, 137, 149, 275, 280(t), 267, 270–71, 295*

WIRE-HAIRED

Spinone *100*

Briquet Griffon Vendéen *177(t)*

OTHERS *78, 97(t & b), 99, 122, 165, 176, 177(b), 179, 180, 181, 189(b), 192(t)*

Berger de Picard *118*

OTHERS *239(b), 243, 262, 268*

WIRE-HAIRED

Laekenois *127*

Podengo Portugueso: Medio *198*

OTHERS *194, 226*

LONG-HAIRED

Soft-coated Wheaten Terrier *227*

Border Collie *107(t)*

WIRE-HAIRED

Airedale Terrier *209(t)*

MEDIUM-SIZED, SQUARE-HEADED DOGS *continued*

LONG-EARED

SHORT-HAIRED

Dogue de Bordeaux *263(b)*

OTHERS *238, 242, 260, 273, 280(b), 293*

LONG-HAIRED

Bouvier des Flandres *130–31*

OTHERS *133(b), 273*

LARGE DOGS

THIS GROUP INCLUDES all breeds over 24 inches (61 cm) in height. Once you have established that the dog belongs to this category, you should identify the head shape (see p.28), followed by the ear and coat type. You will then be able to

LONG-HEADED

LONG-EARED

SHORT-HAIRED

Great Dane *252–53*

OTHERS *243, 283, 291(b)*

LONG-HAIRED

Pyrenean Mastiff *278*

OTHERS *200, 258–59, 261, 264–65, 282*

SQUARE-HEADED

LONG-EARED

SHORT-HAIRED

Neopolitan Mastiff *276–77*

Mastiff *236–37*

ERECT-EARED

LONG-HAIRED

Pumi *133(b)*

SHORT-EARED

SHORT-HAIRED

Boxer *255(t)*

OTHERS *207, 208(t), 231, 232, 289, 294*

locate a breed of that physical type in one of the bands below, where there will also be page references for all similar breeds featured in the book.

As might be expected, these breeds are relatively few in number, though some can trace their ancestry back to the oldest forms of the domestic dog.

WIRE-HAIRED

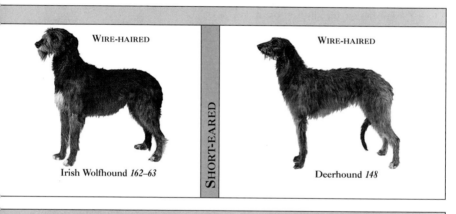

Irish Wolfhound *162–63*

SHORT-EARED

WIRE-HAIRED

Deerhound *148*

SHORT-EARED

LONG-HAIRED

Landseer *256–57*

Newfoundland *240–41*

COMPANION DOGS

BRED ESSENTIALLY AS PETS, and not as working dogs, companion dogs appear in a wide variety of shapes and sizes. They are often simply scaled-down versions of much larger dogs, but some, such as the Chihuahua (see p.41), were created specifically as companions, with no hint of a working ancestry. Others, like the Bulldog (see p.39) and the Basenji (see p.59), were developed from former working stock. Companion dogs are typically loyal and affectionate by nature, but concerns have been expressed regarding the constitution of some members of this group. A hindlimb weakness centered on the knees (called luxating patellas) is one type of problem found in some companion breeds. However, by careful selection of adult breeding stock, breeders are continually seeking to eliminate such weaknesses.

Country of origin	First use	Origins
USA	Companion	1972

KYI LEO

One of the newest breeds to enter the dog world, the Kyi Leo is a small, solidly built animal with a profuse covering of long hair and an alert, friendly face. Usual coat coloration is black and white, but other colors are also commonly seen.

• **HISTORY** The ancestry of this newcomer is in no doubt at all: it is the result of crossings between the Lhasa Apso and the Maltese. Originating in California, the Kyi Leo is specifically designed for life as a companion dog and does not regard the lack of a garden or yard as a particular hardship.

• **REMARK** The Kyi Leo is an "easy-care" dog. Its long coat does require frequent brushing to remain in good condition, but no clipping is necessary.

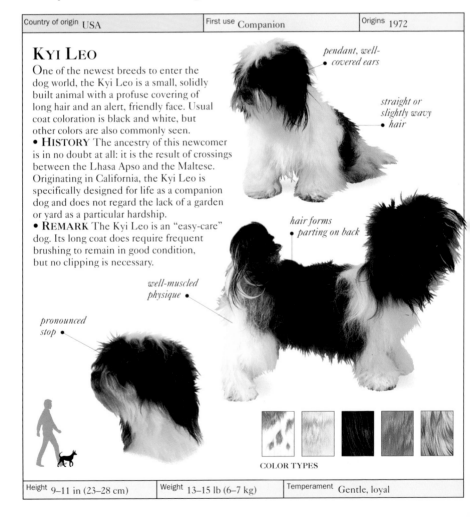

pendant, well-covered ears
straight or slightly wavy hair

hair forms parting on back
well-muscled physique

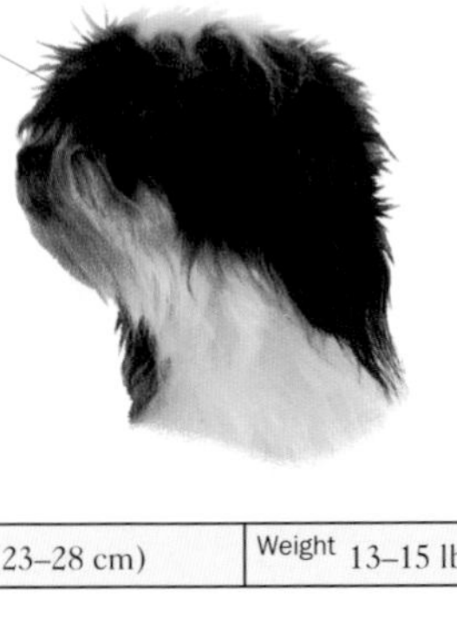
pronounced stop

COLOR TYPES

Height	Weight	Temperament
9–11 in (23–28 cm)	13–15 lb (6–7 kg)	Gentle, loyal

Country of origin USA	First use Companion	Origins 1900s

Toy American Eskimo

The face, coat, and lush tail of this dog identify it as a spitz-type breed. The pointed muzzle and erect ears are foxlike, its coat is long and thick, and its tail is well-plumed and carried in a curl over the back. Although a small dog, it is nevertheless sturdy, well-muscled, and powerful with a broad back. Solid white is the preferred coat color, although it can sometimes be found with cream- or fawn-colored markings.

• **History** Descended from the German Spitz, American breeders favored the white form and concentrated their efforts into developing this single color type.

• **Remark** Apart from size, all three American Eskimo dogs are judged against the same standard.

erect, triangular ears
plumed tail, set high and carried over the back
short, sturdy legs

Height 11–12 in (28–31 cm)	Weight 6–10 lb (3–5 kg)	Temperament Affectionate, obedient

Country of origin Great Britain	First use Baiting bulls	Origins 1800s

Bulldog

With a musculature almost out of proportion to its size, the Bulldog is a low-set, but powerful, mastiff-type dog. Its head is enormous, the circumference of which may equal its height. Its eyes are set low. White often predominates in the coat in the case of pieds; other colours include fawn and brindle.

• **History** Until the banning of bull-baiting in England in 1835, this breed was very popular. Since then it has been made considerably gentler by selective breeding.

• **Remark** Birth by cesarean section is not uncommon, as the large head size of the pups may block the birth canal.

• **Other Names** English Bulldog.

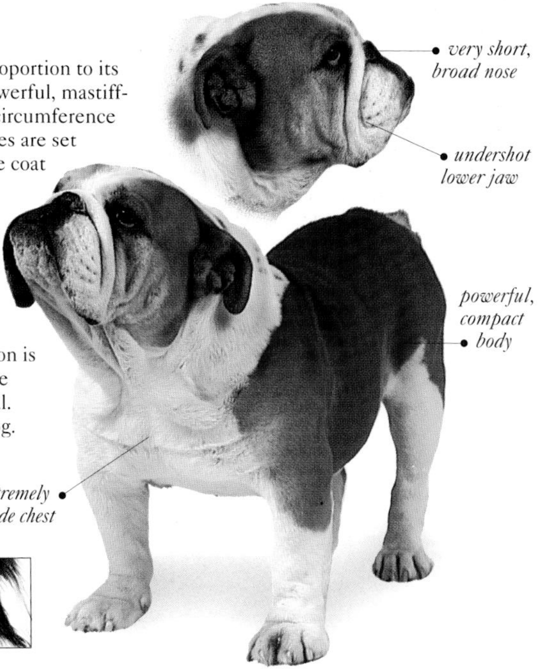
very short, broad nose
undershot lower jaw
powerful, compact body
extremely wide chest

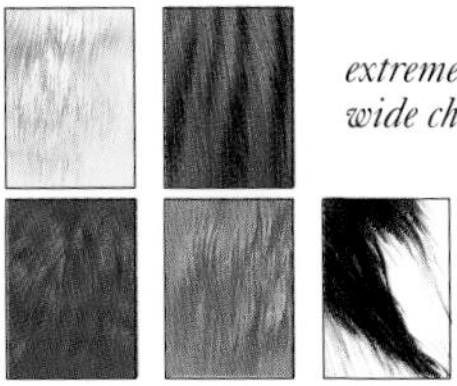
COLOR TYPES

Height 12–14 in (31–36 cm)	Weight 50–55 lb (23–25 kg)	Temperament Affectionate, docile

Country of origin Great Britain	First use Companion	Origins 1920s

CAVALIER KING CHARLES

A modern recreation of the old type of King Charles Spaniel (below), the Cavalier can be distinguished by its longer nose and heavier build. Both breeds have identical coloration. The chestnut and white of each breed is described as the Blenheim, after the palace of the Duke of Marlborough in England, where spaniels of this color were first developed.

• **HISTORY** Toy spaniels were a common sight around the palaces of Europe during the 17th century and were often portrayed in paintings of the period. Cavaliers were first registered by the British Kennel Club as a separate breed in 1945.

• **REMARK** The prefix "Cavalier" was chosen to distinguish it from the King Charles Spaniel.

long, well-feathered ears
relatively flat, undomed skull
long, silky coat with no curls

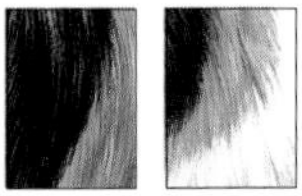
COLOR TYPES

Height 12–13 in (31–33 cm)	Weight 10–18 lb (5–8 kg)	Temperament Friendly, obedient

Country of origin Great Britain	First use Companion	Origins 1600s

KING CHARLES SPANIEL

Squarely built with a distinctive domed skull, this breed's affectionate nature has made it a popular pet for centuries. The large, dark eyes are particularly appealing.

• **HISTORY** This breed was greatly favored by King Charles II of England (1630–85). He regularly exercised his dogs in St. James's Park, London.

• **REMARK** The breed today is larger than its ancestors.

• **OTHER NAMES** English Toy Spaniel.

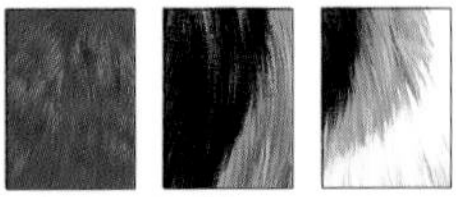
COLOR TYPES

domed skull
short back
short nose, with wide, turned-up muzzle
deep, broad chest

Height 10–11 in (25–27 cm)	Weight 8–14 lb (4–6 kg)	Temperament Obedient, affectionate

Country of origin Mexico	First use Companion	Origins 1800s

Chihuahua

Differing coat lengths separate the two varieties of this tiny, plucky dog. The smooth-coated form has a short, glossy coat, while the long-haired form has a significantly longer, slightly wavy coat. The long-haired form is the result of crossings of Smooth-coated Chihuahuas with Yorkshire Terriers (see p.219) and Papillons (see p.47). Selective breeding has since taken place to ensure that in all other respects the two forms are indistinguishable. Common colors are fawn, chestnut, steel-blue, and silver, often seen in combinations.

• **History** The name "Chihuahua" derives from the Mexican state of that name, where this dog may have originated. It was first seen in the USA toward the end of the 19th century, before being taken to Europe. Most of today's bloodlines are descended from the original 50 dogs taken to the USA.

• **Remark** The Chihuahua can be sensitive to cold. It also shivers when excited or nervous.

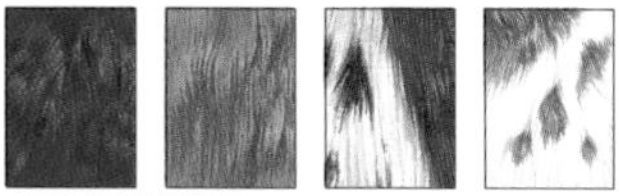

COLOR TYPES

relatively muscular hindquarters
short, soft, glossy coat

SMOOTH-COATED CHIHUAHUA

short, pointed muzzle

ruff on neck
muscular, well-feathered legs

LONG-HAIRED CHIHUAHUA

coat may be slightly wavy but never curled
long tail resembles a plume
dainty feet

Height 6–9 in (15–23 cm)	Weight 2–6 lb (1–3 kg)	Temperament Bold, playful

Country of origin Mexico	First use Companion	Origins 1500s

MEXICAN HAIRLESS

Three forms of this breed are now recognized: the Standard (shown here), the Miniature, and the smaller Toy version. There is also a so-called "Powder-puff" version of each size, which does have a coat of hair but cannot be exhibited. The Mexican Hairless has a noble stance, not unlike that of a sight hound, and the build of a terrier.

• **HISTORY** Utilized as bed-warmers, pets, and, less comfortingly, as ritual sacrifices, this dog was widely kept in ancient Aztec settlements.

• **REMARK** A breeding program initiated by the Mexican Kennel Club in the 1950s saved this dog from certain extinction. They are, however, still quite scarce, even today.

• **OTHER NAMES** Tepeizeuintli, Xoloitzcuintli.

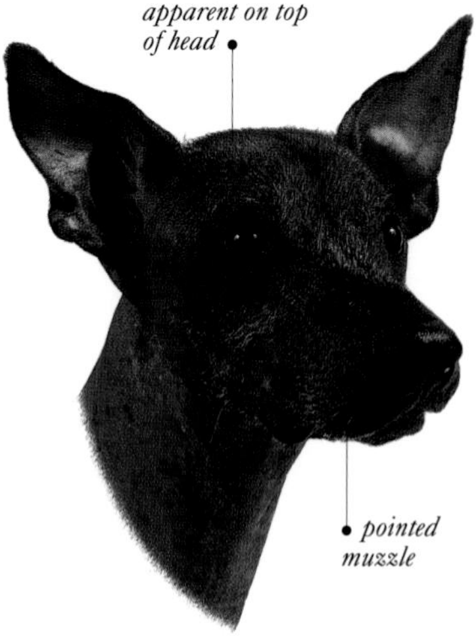
traces of hair apparent on top of head
pointed muzzle

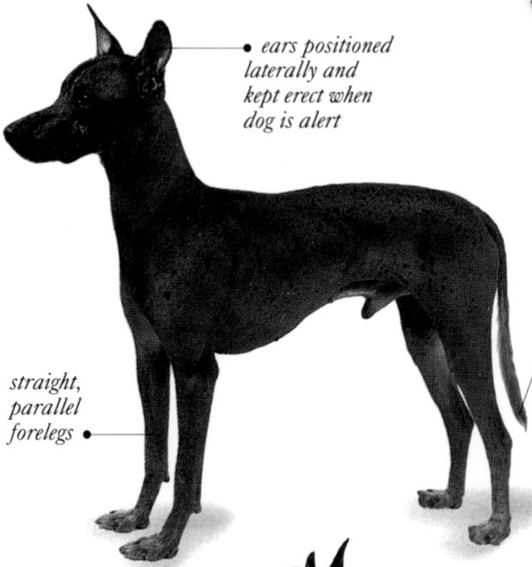
ears positioned laterally and kept erect when dog is alert
straight, parallel forelegs
tip of tail shows traces of hair

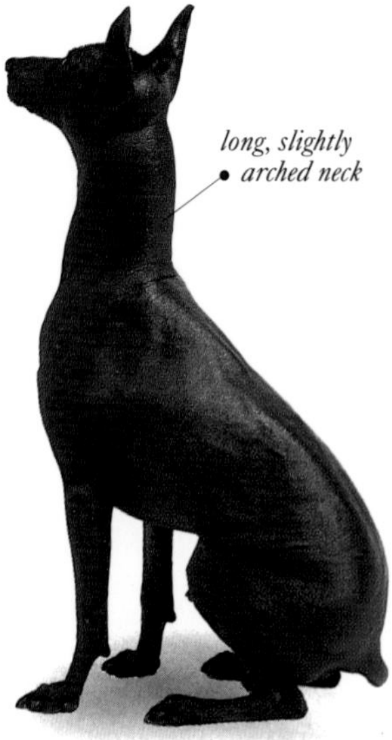
long, slightly arched neck

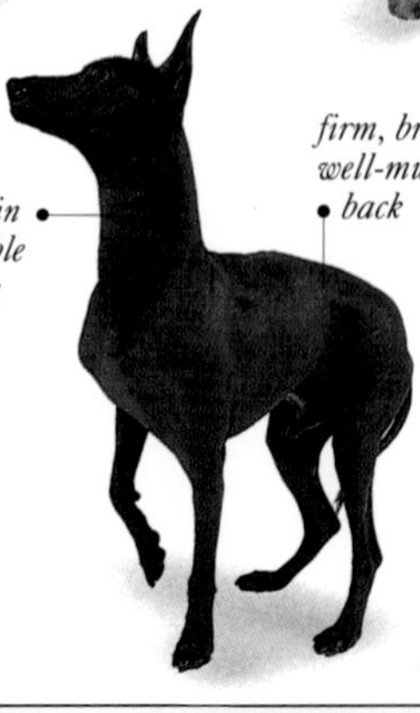
exposed skin is susceptible to sunburn
firm, broad, well-muscled back

COLOR TYPES

Height 11–12 in (28–31 cm)	Weight 9–18 lb (4–8 kg)	Temperament Lively, alert

Country of origin	First use	Origins
Peru	Warming beds	1200s

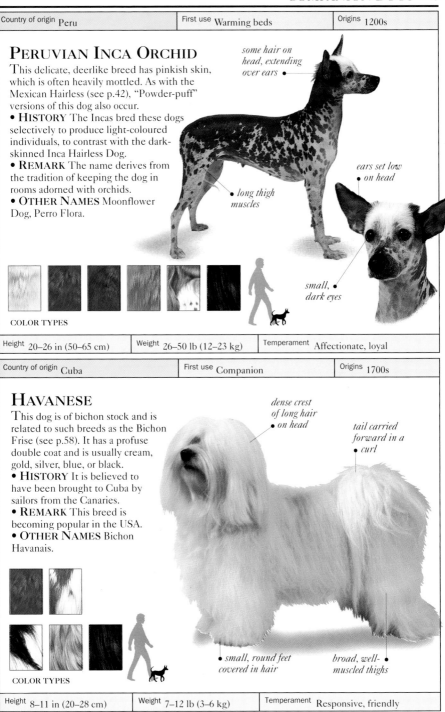

PERUVIAN INCA ORCHID

This delicate, deerlike breed has pinkish skin, which is often heavily mottled. As with the Mexican Hairless (see p.42), "Powder-puff" versions of this dog also occur.

- **HISTORY** The Incas bred these dogs selectively to produce light-coloured individuals, to contrast with the dark-skinned Inca Hairless Dog.
- **REMARK** The name derives from the tradition of keeping the dog in rooms adorned with orchids.
- **OTHER NAMES** Moonflower Dog, Perro Flora.

some hair on head, extending over ears
long thigh muscles

ears set low on head
small, dark eyes

COLOR TYPES

Height	Weight	Temperament
20–26 in (50–65 cm)	26–50 lb (12–23 kg)	Affectionate, loyal

Country of origin	First use	Origins
Cuba	Companion	1700s

HAVANESE

This dog is of bichon stock and is related to such breeds as the Bichon Frise (see p.58). It has a profuse double coat and is usually cream, gold, silver, blue, or black.

- **HISTORY** It is believed to have been brought to Cuba by sailors from the Canaries.
- **REMARK** This breed is becoming popular in the USA.
- **OTHER NAMES** Bichon Havanais.

dense crest of long hair on head
tail carried forward in a curl
small, round feet covered in hair
broad, well-muscled thighs

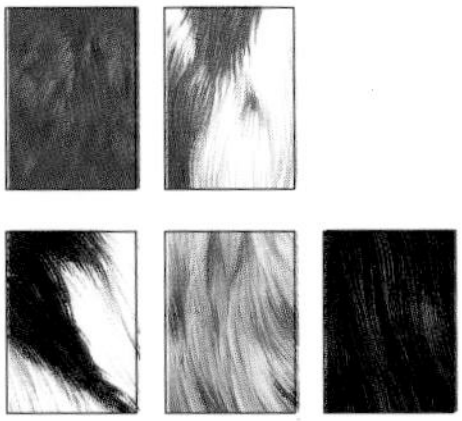

COLOR TYPES

Height	Weight	Temperament
8–11 in (20–28 cm)	7–12 lb (3–6 kg)	Responsive, friendly

Country of origin Germany	First use Companion	Origins 1800s

GIANT GERMAN SPITZ

The face of this breed is a little foxlike. The outercoat is long and harsh, while the undercoat is dense and soft. The Giant German Spitz, as its name suggests, is the second largest of this German group of spitz dogs, and is bred in solid colors only.

• **HISTORY** The ancestors of these dogs were probably brought to Holland and Germany by the Vikings.

• **REMARK** Certain colors became associated with particular regions, such as the black with Wurttemberg.

• **OTHER NAMES** Deutscher Gross Spitz.

tail curls up and lies over back
erect, triangular ears
round, catlike feet

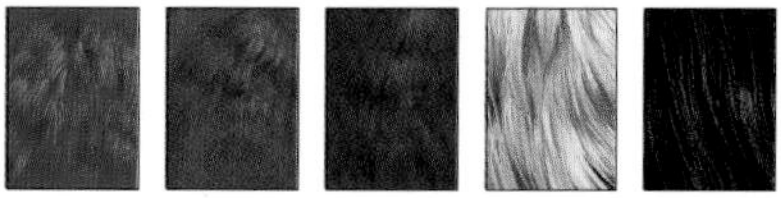

COLOR TYPES

Height 16 in (41 cm)	Weight 40 lb (18 kg)	Temperament Lively, playful

Country of origin Germany	First use Working on farms	Origins 1800s

GERMAN SPITZ: MITTEL

The mittel, or standard, form of the German Spitz is the third largest of the five varieties. Like the Giant (above), it is usually bred in solid colors. In British show rings all varieties and markings are acceptable.

• **HISTORY** The watchful demeanor of these dogs initially led to their being highly valued on farms, but they also make rewarding companions.

• **REMARK** Like the other German Spitz, the Mittel has a harsh, long outercoat and a soft, woolly undercoat.

• **OTHER NAMES** Deutscher Mittel Spitz.

luxuriant tail

oval eyes
compact, firm condition

COLOR TYPES

Height 11½–14 in (29–36 cm)	Weight 25 lb (11 kg)	Temperament Lively, playful

Country of origin Germany	First use Lapdog	Origins 1800s

GERMAN SPITZ: KLEIN

The German Spitz breeds are compact and squarely built, and can be distinguished essentially on the basis of size. The Spitz is protected from harsh weather by its thick coat, which varies greatly in color, and has a dense undercoat.

• **HISTORY** The German Spitz is descended from much larger sled-pulling spitz breeds.

• **REMARK** Since 1985, this breed has undergone a revival outside Germany.

• **OTHER NAMES** Deutsche Spitz.

tail curls over back
small, triangular ears
no color restriction
short, sturdy legs

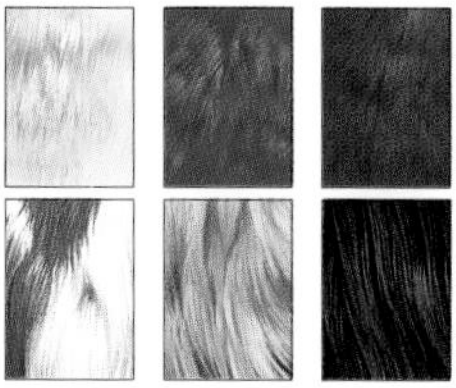

COLOR TYPES

Height 9–11 in (23–28 cm)	Weight 18–22 lb (8–10 kg)	Temperament Lively, playful

Country of origin Germany	First use General companion	Origins 1800s

POMERANIAN

The smallest member of the German Spitz group, the Pomeranian is characterized by an upright tail that tilts forward over its body. This breed is a devoted and affectionate companion. The coat takes three years to reach full maturity. The solid colors include white, red orange, gray, and black.

• **HISTORY** This breed is thought to have developed in northern Germany from larger spitz dogs.

• **REMARK** Despite its diminutive size it makes a good watchdog.

erect, foxlike ears

harsh, long hair on tail

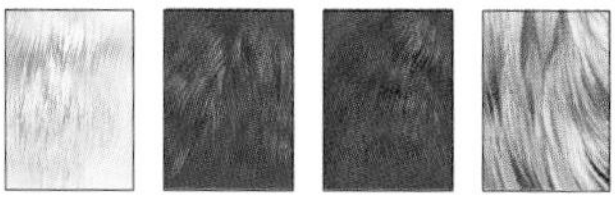

COLOR TYPES

Height 8–11 in (20–28 cm)	Weight 4–5½ lb (2–3 kg)	Temperament Friendly, active

Country of origin Netherlands	First use Barge companion	Origins 1500s

KEESHOND

This lively breed is distinguished by its wolf gray coat. Its coloration tends to be lighter on the head, creating the impression of dark "spectacles" around the eyes.

• **HISTORY** It is named after the Dutchman de Gyselaer, whose nickname was Kees.

• **REMARK** A fine watchdog, the Keeshond provides good security as well as company.

• **OTHER NAMES** Wolf Spitz, Chien Loup.

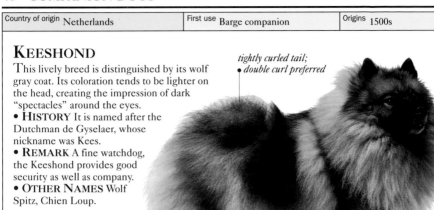

tightly curled tail;
double curl preferred
no feathering
below hocks

dense ruff

Height 17–19 in (43–48 cm)	Weight 55–66 lb (25–30 kg)	Temperament Independent, affectionate

Country of origin Belgium	First use Companion	Origins 1600s

CONTINENTAL TOY SPANIEL: PHALENE

Closely related to the Papillon (see p.47), the Phalene can be readily distinguished from the Papillon by its ears, which hang down on the sides of its head.

• **HISTORY** The breed was popular in Italy during the Renaissance, and was well known in European royal circles.

• **REMARK** In the USA, the Phalene is not distinguished from the Papillon, which is accepted in both ear forms.

• **OTHER NAMES** Épagneul Nain, Continental Phalene.

white blaze
on face
high-set
bushy tail
harelike feet

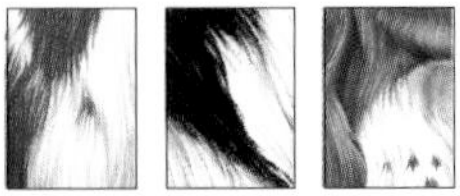

COLOR TYPES

Height 8–11 in (20–28 cm)	Weight 9–10 lb (4.1–4.5 kg)	Temperament Friendly, alert

Country of origin France	First use Companion	Origins 1600s

Papillon

This dainty little dog is closely related to the Phalene (see p.46); in the USA the Phalene is considered a drop-eared version of the Papillon, but the same breed. The name *Papillon*, the French for "butterfly," refers to the shape of the Papillon's erect ears.

• **HISTORY** This breed often featured in paintings by the Flemish artist Van Dyke.

• **REMARK** Daily grooming is essential.

• **OTHER NAMES** Épagneul Nain.

symmetrical head markings and blaze
slightly round skull
fine, harelike feet with long hair between toes

very large, well-fringed ears

Height 8–11 in (20–28 cm)	Weight 9–10 lb (4–4.5 kg)	Temperament Friendly, alert

Country of origin France	First use Companion	Origins 1400s

Toy Poodle

Identical in all respects to its larger relatives except in height, this is the smallest of the three varieties of poodle. Pictured here is the lion trim, preferred for showing.

• **HISTORY** Miniaturization of the Standard Poodle gave rise to this breed. They were portrayed by the German artist Dürer in 1500.

• **REMARK** In the USA Toy Poodles are those 10 in (25 cm) or less in height. The coat needs clipping every six to eight weeks.

• **OTHER NAMES** Caniche.

tail carried at an angle to body
long, fine head
deep, relatively wide chest
dense, very profuse coat
well-sprung ribs

small, oval feet

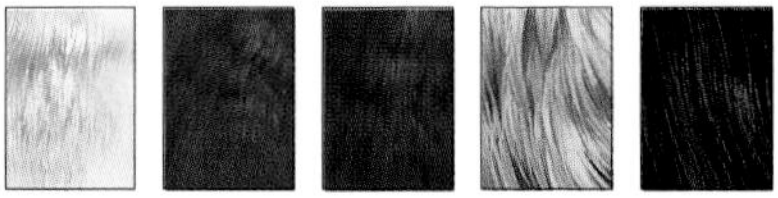

COLOR TYPES

Height 10–11 in (25–28 cm)	Weight 15 lb (7 kg)	Temperament Loyal, sociable

Country of origin France	First use Water dog	Origins 1600s

MINIATURE POODLE

Well-proportioned and squarely built, the Miniature Poodle lies between the larger Standard (see p.254) and the tiny Toy (see p.47) in size. This intelligent breed has a sporty disposition, and is easy to train.

- **HISTORY** Poodles probably derive from the Pudel, an old German water dog.
- **REMARK** From the late 1940s to the 1960s, the Miniature Poodle was the most popular dog breed in the world.
- **OTHER NAMES** Barbone, Caniche.

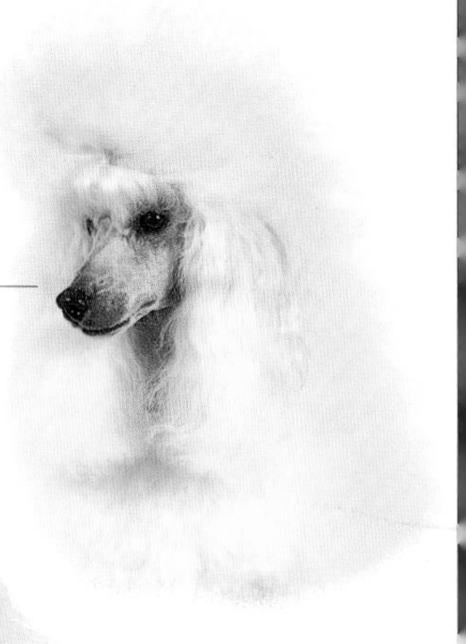
long, wide ears

strong neck

thick, harsh-textured coat
straight forelegs
muscular hind legs

long, straight muzzle
small, oval feet

COLOR TYPES

Height 11–15 in (28–38 cm)	Weight 26–30 lb (12–14 kg)	Temperament Intelligent, lively

Country of origin France	First use Companion	Origins 1500s

LÖWCHEN

With its long, silky coat trimmed in the traditional "lion clip," this dog is easily distinguished from other members of the bichon group. The tail is clipped along part of its length, leaving just a plume of hair, completing this attractive, lively breed's distinctive parody of the "king of the beasts."

• **HISTORY** This breed found favor with the European aristocracy at an early stage in its development. It is featured in a painting by Goya of the Duchess of Alba in the late 1700s. However, its popularity declined to the extent that by 1960 it was considered to be the world's rarest dog breed.

• **REMARK** This intelligent, good-natured breed has recently undergone a welcome growth in popularity, particularly in the USA.

• **OTHER NAMES** Little Lion Dog.

short head with dark nose
long, silky "mane"

large, dark, round eyes
tail curls forward over back
well-muscled hindquarters
long, pendant, well-fringed ears

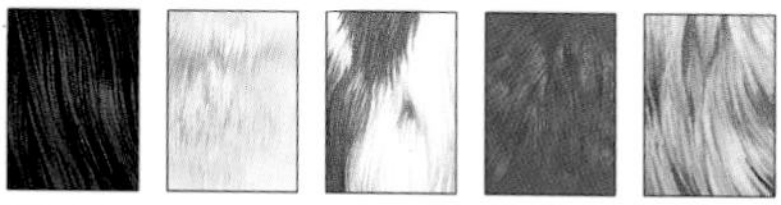

COLOR TYPES

Height 10–13 in (25–33 cm)	Weight 8–18 lb (4–8 kg)	Temperament Active, affectionate

Country of origin Italy	First use Lady's companion	Origins 500 BC

ITALIAN GREYHOUND

A miniature form of the Greyhound, this breed is far less fragile than it looks. It has a gait similar to the larger dog's, and the same rapid acceleration, facilitated by long, muscular hindquarters. The long, graceful neck heightens its refined air.

• **HISTORY** This breed has survived since the time of the Pharaohs. More recently, however, it has suffered from the introduction of English Toy Terrier blood (see p.210).

• **REMARK** Similar dogs have been found, mummified, in Egyptian tombs.

• **OTHER NAMES** Piccolo Levrieri Italiani.

ears well back on head
flat and narrow skull

ITALIAN GREYHOUND PUPPIES

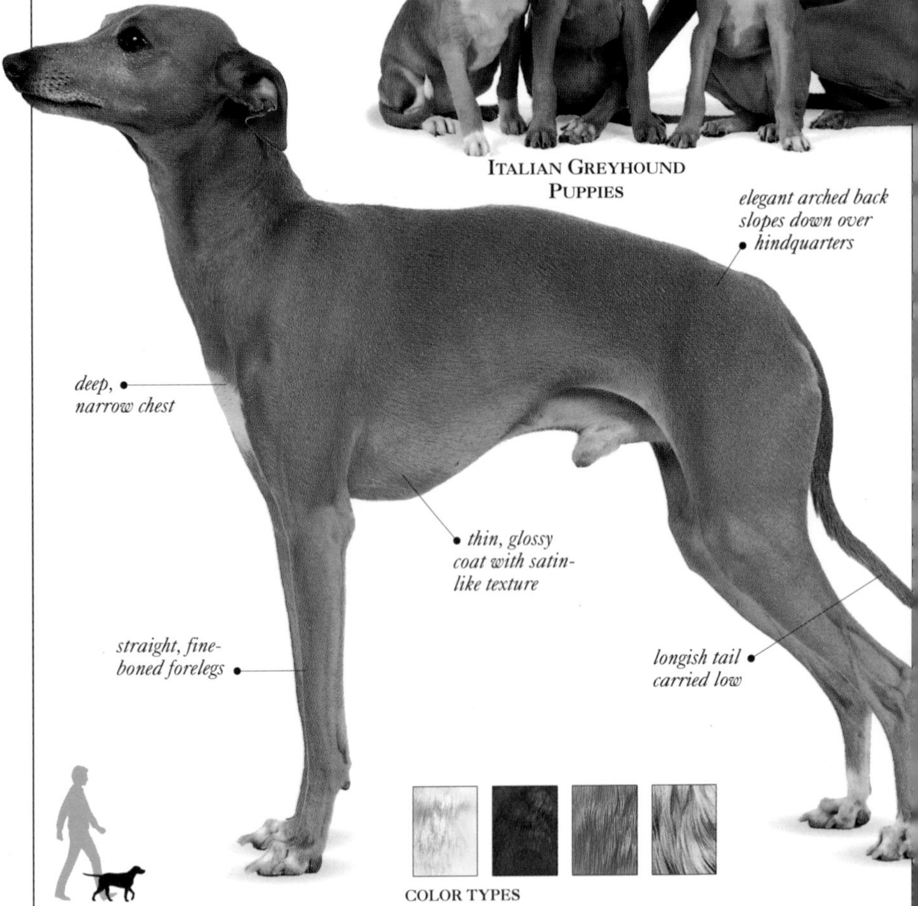
elegant arched back slopes down over hindquarters
deep, narrow chest
thin, glossy coat with satin-like texture
straight, fine-boned forelegs
longish tail carried low

COLOR TYPES

Height 13–15 in (33–38 cm)	Weight 8 lb (3.6 kg)	Temperament Quiet, affectionate

Country of origin	First use	Origins
Italy	General companion	1200s

BOLOGNESE

Descended from bichon stock, thus having the characteristic white, cottony coat associated with this group, the Bolognese may in fact have blond markings, although these are not considered desirable. This is a square-built and solid dog for its size.

- **HISTORY** The breed's ancestry dates back to the bichons that first appeared in southern Italy in the 13th century. It became a popular court dog but is now relatively scarce.
- **REMARK** The Bolognese has always been a companion dog and bonds very closely with people.
- **OTHER NAMES** Bichon Bolognese.

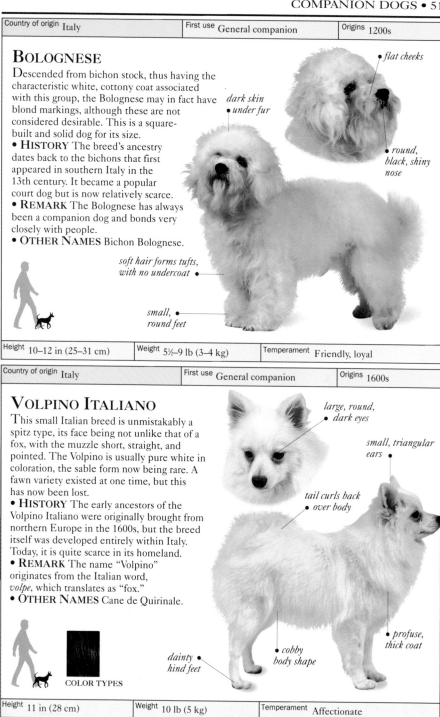

flat cheeks
dark skin under fur
round, black, shiny nose
soft hair forms tufts, with no undercoat
small, round feet

Height	Weight	Temperament
10–12 in (25–31 cm)	5½–9 lb (3–4 kg)	Friendly, loyal

Country of origin	First use	Origins
Italy	General companion	1600s

VOLPINO ITALIANO

This small Italian breed is unmistakably a spitz type, its face being not unlike that of a fox, with the muzzle short, straight, and pointed. The Volpino is usually pure white in coloration, the sable form now being rare. A fawn variety existed at one time, but this has now been lost.

- **HISTORY** The early ancestors of the Volpino Italiano were originally brought from northern Europe in the 1600s, but the breed itself was developed entirely within Italy. Today, it is quite scarce in its homeland.
- **REMARK** The name "Volpino" originates from the Italian word, *volpe*, which translates as "fox."
- **OTHER NAMES** Cane de Quirinale.

large, round, dark eyes
small, triangular ears
tail curls back over body
profuse, thick coat
cobby body shape
dainty hind feet

COLOR TYPES

Height	Weight	Temperament
11 in (28 cm)	10 lb (5 kg)	Affectionate

Country of origin China	First use Companion	Origins 100s

PEKINGESE

The Pekingese is a short-legged breed of dog with a characteristic rolling gait. It has a relatively compact, flattened face fringed with longer hair, which gives the impression of the dog having a mane. This breed makes a bold and alert watchdog for the home.

• **HISTORY** It was first seen in the West after the British overran Beijing in 1860. Prior to this, the Pekingese had been the jealously guarded, exclusive possession of the Chinese emperor.

• **REMARK** Pekingese used to be known as "sleeve dogs," because they could be carried in the long, flowing sleeves of Chinese courtiers.

• **OTHER NAMES** Peking Palasthund.

large, round, dark eyes

very evident stop to nose
well-feathered tail is set high and curled over to one side
long, silky coat

broad nose with large nostrils
large head with broad skull
skull is flat between ears
heart-shaped ears set level with skull

COLOR TYPES

Height 6–9 in (15–23 cm)	Weight 7–12 lb (3–6 kg)	Temperament Independent, lively

Country of origin China	First use Companion	Origins 1500s

PUG

Squarely and solidly built, the Pug is a compact, yet very well-proportioned little breed with an unmistakable, flat, wrinkled face. It has a very distinctive, endearing expression.

• **HISTORY** Originally developed in the Orient about 400 years ago, the breed arrived in Europe via Holland, where it gained immense popularity. It was later perfected in Britain.

• **REMARK** This intelligent, long-lived dog may have been larger in the earliest days of its development.

• **OTHER NAMES** Carlin, Mops.

tightly curled tail
strong, muscular legs

square, compact body
fine, smooth, soft coat

COLOR TYPES

Height 10–11 in (25–28 cm)	Weight 14–18 lb (6–8 kg)	Temperament Loyal, affectionate

Country of origin China	First use Chinese court dog	Origins 1600s

SHIH TZU

Often confused with the Tibetan Lhasa Apso (see p.56), the Chinese Shih Tzu has a denser, slightly wavy coat and a face that has been described as similar to a chrysanthemum. This impression is given by the tendency of the hair on the bridge of the dog's nose to grow upward. Generally, this facial hair is tied up on the top of its head.

• **HISTORY** The Shih Tzu was developed in Beijing, China, by crossing miniature Chinese breeds with Tibetan breeds.

• **REMARK** For many years this breed was a great favorite of the Emperors of China.

• **OTHER NAMES** Chrysanthemum Dog.

long facial hair

well-spaced eyes
tail held high and heavily plumed
long, dense outercoat with good undercoat

COLOR TYPES

Height 10½ in (27 cm)	Weight 10–16 lb (5–7 kg)	Temperament Gentle, loyal

Country of origin China	First use Companion	Origins 100 BC

Chinese Crested Dog

This nimble little dog comes in two varieties. One form, the Hairless, only has hair as a crest on its head and toes, and a plume on its tail. The Powder Puff variety is covered with long, soft hair. Both are found in a mixture of colors.

• **History** Known for centuries in China, this dog first came to prominence in the Han dynasty, but was not exhibited in the West until the Westminster Show in New York in 1885. It was not until 1975 that a specialist breed club was established in the USA.

• **Remark** The texture of the skin of the Hairless should be smooth and fine-grained. This dog is vulnerable to sunburn.

Powder Puff

ears are normally erect

long, slightly rounded skull
deep, broad chest
Powder Puff has undercoat and a soft veil of long hair

skin may be plain or spotted, and may lighten in summer
no hair above first joint of leg

long, tapering, fairly straight tail

ears sometimes droop under weight of hair
hare-like feet

Hairless

hairless body

Height 9–13 in (23–33 cm)	Weight 5–12 lb (2–5.5 kg)	Temperament Affectionate, lively

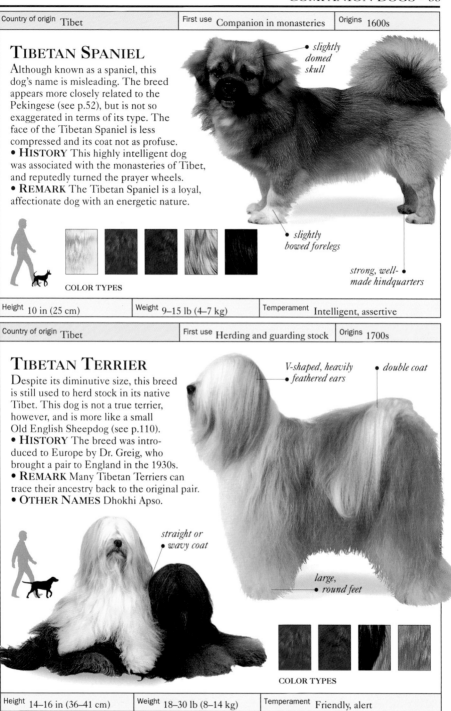

Country of origin Tibet	First use Companion in monasteries	Origins 1600s

TIBETAN SPANIEL

Although known as a spaniel, this dog's name is misleading. The breed appears more closely related to the Pekingese (see p.52), but is not so exaggerated in terms of its type. The face of the Tibetan Spaniel is less compressed and its coat not as profuse.

• **HISTORY** This highly intelligent dog was associated with the monasteries of Tibet, and reputedly turned the prayer wheels.

• **REMARK** The Tibetan Spaniel is a loyal, affectionate dog with an energetic nature.

slightly domed skull
slightly bowed forelegs
strong, well-made hindquarters

COLOR TYPES

Height 10 in (25 cm)	Weight 9–15 lb (4–7 kg)	Temperament Intelligent, assertive

Country of origin Tibet	First use Herding and guarding stock	Origins 1700s

TIBETAN TERRIER

Despite its diminutive size, this breed is still used to herd stock in its native Tibet. This dog is not a true terrier, however, and is more like a small Old English Sheepdog (see p.110).

• **HISTORY** The breed was introduced to Europe by Dr. Greig, who brought a pair to England in the 1930s.

• **REMARK** Many Tibetan Terriers can trace their ancestry back to the original pair.

• **OTHER NAMES** Dhokhi Apso.

V-shaped, heavily feathered ears
double coat
large, round feet

straight or wavy coat

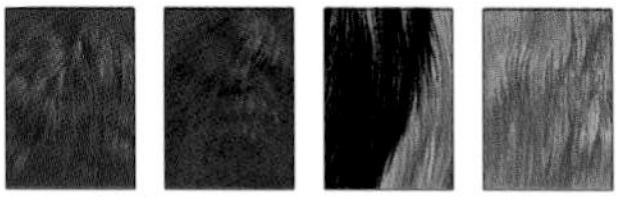

COLOR TYPES

Height 14–16 in (36–41 cm)	Weight 18–30 lb (8–14 kg)	Temperament Friendly, alert

Country of origin	First use	Origins
Tibet	Companion in monasteries	600s

LHASA APSO

long parting
from back of head
feathered ears

Although small in stature, the Lhasa Apso is a hardy dog with a fine sense of hearing. It makes an excellent watchdog. While the name "Lhasa" probably refers to the capital of Tibet, "apso" may mean "goatlike" – referring to the long, coarse coat, which is its most distinctive feature. Hair falls well over its eyes, and it has a prominent beard and mustache.

• **HISTORY** This is the first of the Tibetan breeds to have been recognized by the AKC, in 1935. The present of a Lhasa Apso was a traditional gift of the Dalai Lama.

• **REMARK** The Lhasa Apso's long, cascading coat needs plenty of grooming.

straight forelegs

COLOR TYPES

Height	Weight	Temperament
10–11 in (25–28 cm)	13–15 lb (6–7 kg)	Gentle, loyal

Country of origin	First use	Origins
Japan	Companion to aristocracy	700s

JAPANESE CHIN

long hair
on ears

There is a distinct similarity between this breed and the Pekingese (see p.52), but the Japanese Chin is both taller and of a lighter build. The coat of a puppy is relatively short compared with that of an adult dog.

• **HISTORY** Queen Victoria, an enthusiastic dog lover, had two Japanese Chins.

• **REMARK** Early examples of the breed were apparently quite delicate and tended to be even smaller than those seen today.

• **OTHER NAMES** Japanese Spaniel, Chin.

large, dark eyes
slender feet

COLOR TYPES

Height	Weight	Temperament
9 in (23 cm)	4–7 lb (2–3 kg)	Intelligent, alert

Country of origin	First use	Origins
Japan	Companion	1800s

Japanese Spitz

This delightful spitz breed has a striking, long coat, which must always be pure white in color. This feature distinguishes it from the miniature form of the American Eskimo (see p.39), which is otherwise extremely similar.

• **HISTORY** The Japanese Spitz is thought to bear no direct relationship to the American Eskimo; rather, it is believed to have been developed from the native Siberian Samoyed (see p.287).

• **REMARK** The Japanese Spitz is rapidly increasing in popularity in Europe.

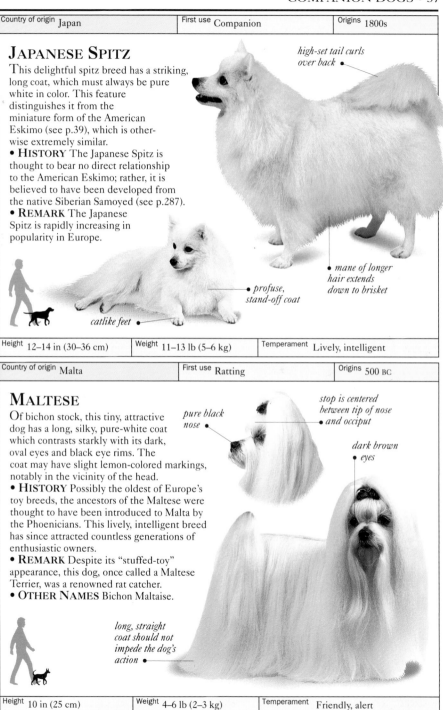

high-set tail curls over back
mane of longer hair extends down to brisket
profuse, stand-off coat
catlike feet

Height	Weight	Temperament
12–14 in (30–36 cm)	11–13 lb (5–6 kg)	Lively, intelligent

Country of origin	First use	Origins
Malta	Ratting	500 BC

Maltese

Of bichon stock, this tiny, attractive dog has a long, silky, pure-white coat which contrasts starkly with its dark, oval eyes and black eye rims. The coat may have slight lemon-colored markings, notably in the vicinity of the head.

• **HISTORY** Possibly the oldest of Europe's toy breeds, the ancestors of the Maltese were thought to have been introduced to Malta by the Phoenicians. This lively, intelligent breed has since attracted countless generations of enthusiastic owners.

• **REMARK** Despite its "stuffed-toy" appearance, this dog, once called a Maltese Terrier, was a renowned rat catcher.

• **OTHER NAMES** Bichon Maltaise.

pure black nose
stop is centered between tip of nose and occiput
dark brown eyes
long, straight coat should not impede the dog's action

Height	Weight	Temperament
10 in (25 cm)	4–6 lb (2–3 kg)	Friendly, alert

Country of origin Spain	First use Companion to royalty	Origins 1400s

BICHON FRISE

This bichon is distinguished by its double coat, which gives it a fluffy appearance. The coat is fine and silky, consisting of soft, corkscrew curls. These are trimmed back over the eyes to emphasize the rounded appearance of the face.

• **HISTORY** Originally, the Bichon Frise was popular in the royal courts of Europe. By the 1800s, however, the breed had lost favour and was more likely to be seen in circuses or accompanying organ grinders.

• **REMARK** Its long association with people makes the Bichon Frise a responsive pet.

• **OTHER NAMES** Tenerife Dog.

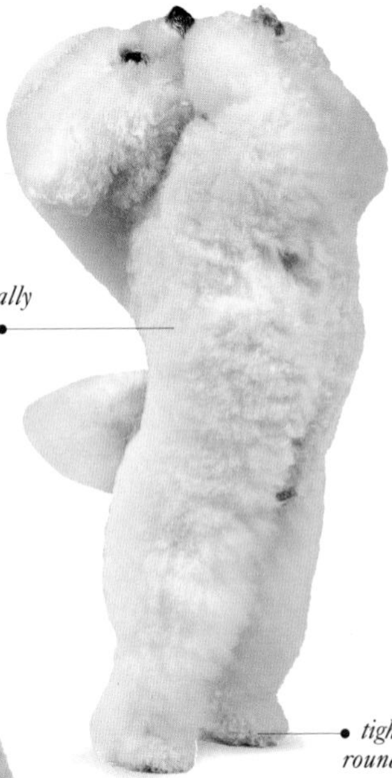
naturally agile
tight, round feet

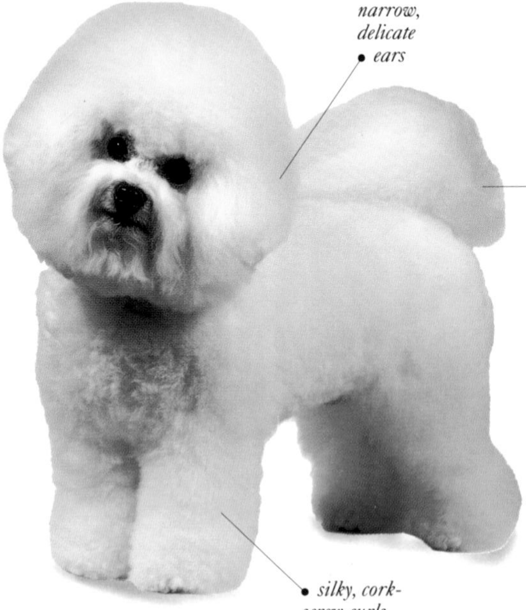
narrow, delicate ears
tail curls over back
silky, cork-screw curls

strong, straight forelegs

Height 9–12 in (23–31 cm)	Weight 7–12 lb (3–6 kg)	Temperament Friendly, active

Country of origin Zaire	First use Hunting dog	Origins 1500s

BASENJI

The most distinctive feature of the alert, finely built Basenji becomes apparent only when it is disturbed – instead of barking like other dogs, it has unique yodeling and chortling calls.

• **HISTORY** The Basenji was developed as a hunting dog in the Congo and it may be related to similar dogs portrayed on ancient Egyptian artifacts. The breed caused a sensation when it was first shown at Crufts, in England, in 1937. The owner called them "basenji," which is an African word for "bush thing."

• **REMARK** Green vegetables are favored by these dogs and should form part of their regular diet. Bitches come into heat only once a year instead of twice.

• **OTHER NAMES** Congo Dog.

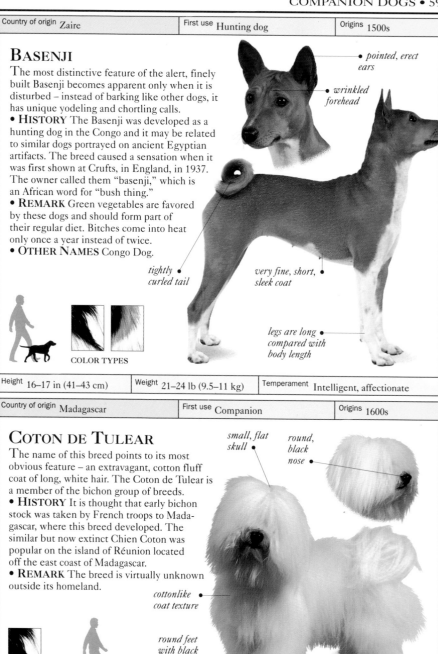

pointed, erect ears
wrinkled forehead
tightly curled tail
very fine, short, sleek coat
legs are long compared with body length

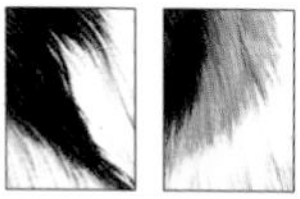

COLOR TYPES

Height 16–17 in (41–43 cm)	Weight 21–24 lb (9.5–11 kg)	Temperament Intelligent, affectionate

Country of origin Madagascar	First use Companion	Origins 1600s

COTON DE TULEAR

The name of this breed points to its most obvious feature – an extravagant, cotton fluff coat of long, white hair. The Coton de Tulear is a member of the bichon group of breeds.

• **HISTORY** It is thought that early bichon stock was taken by French troops to Madagascar, where this breed developed. The similar but now extinct Chien Coton was popular on the island of Réunion located off the east coast of Madagascar.

• **REMARK** The breed is virtually unknown outside its homeland.

small, flat skull
round, black nose
cottonlike coat texture
round feet with black nails

COLOR TYPES

Height 10–12 in (25–30 cm)	Weight 12–15 lb (5.5–7 kg)	Temperament Lively, loyal

GUNDOGS

ORIGINALLY a sporting companion, the lively, loyal nature of the gundog has won it a place in the home as a family pet. Setters, spaniels, pointers, and retrievers are all classified as gundogs, and are characterized by their very responsive and friendly dispositions. However, they do require a great deal of exercise. Their longish, water-resistant coats protect them in all weather, a feature bred into them in their sporting days. A number of gundog breeds have a localized distribution, while others, such as the Spinone (see p.100), are now well known in show rings around the world. Field trials are held regularly to test and maintain their working abilities.

Country of origin	First use	Origins
USA	Hunting small game	1800s

AMERICAN COCKER SPANIEL

Smaller than its English counterpart (see p.63), and with a much longer coat, the American Cocker Spaniel was developed in the USA in the last century. A black American Cocker must be jet black, with no trace of brown or liver shadings. To be classified as black and tan, tan markings must comprise no less than 10 percent of the coat. The color "tan" can vary from shades of cream to dark red.

- **HISTORY** This dog was bred from English Cocker Spaniels taken to the USA. It was first recognized as a separate breed in 1946.
- **REMARK** This keen and industrious breed specialized in retrieving quails.
- **OTHER NAMES** Cocker Spaniel.

clearly defined stop
lobular ears
muscular, well-boned hindquarters
profuse covering of wavy or flat silky hair

rounded head shape
rounded, firm feet with thick pads

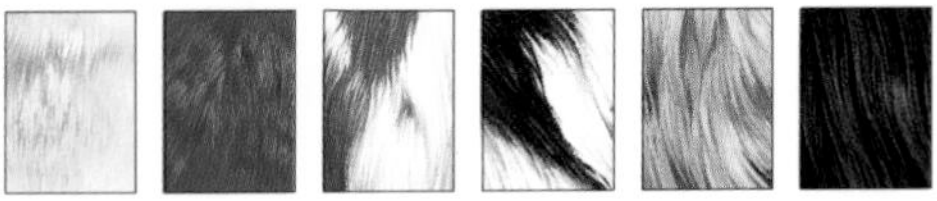

COLOR TYPES

Height	Weight	Temperament
14–15 in (36–38 cm)	24–28 lb (11–13 kg)	Active, friendly

Country of origin USA	First use Retrieving water fowl	Origins 1800s

Chesapeake Bay Retriever

The broad skull, wedge-shaped forehead, and powerful jaws of this breed make it ideal as a retriever. Its very dense coat serves to protect it from the cold waters of the Chesapeake Bay region of the USA, where it was first developed. The oily texture of the hair gives this retriever a distinctive smell.

• **History** The breed evolved from two pups rescued from a ship that ran aground off the coast of Maryland, in 1807. The two dogs were trained to retrieve duck, a skill that was refined through crossings with Flat, and Curly-coated Retrievers and Otter Hounds.

• **Remark** The webbed toes of this breed assist in swimming.

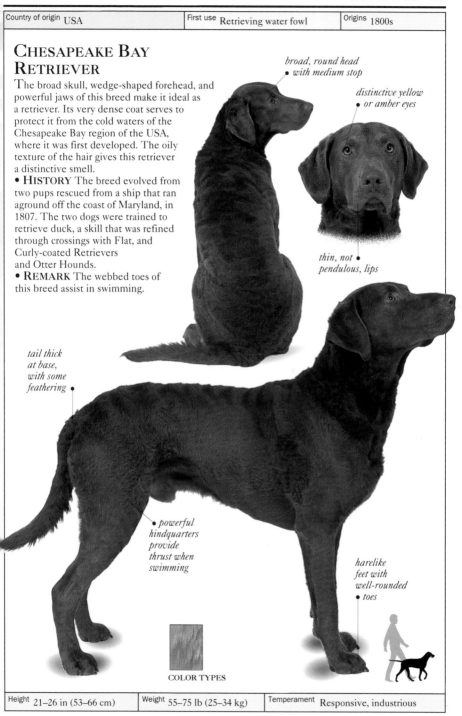

broad, round head with medium stop

distinctive yellow or amber eyes
thin, not pendulous, lips

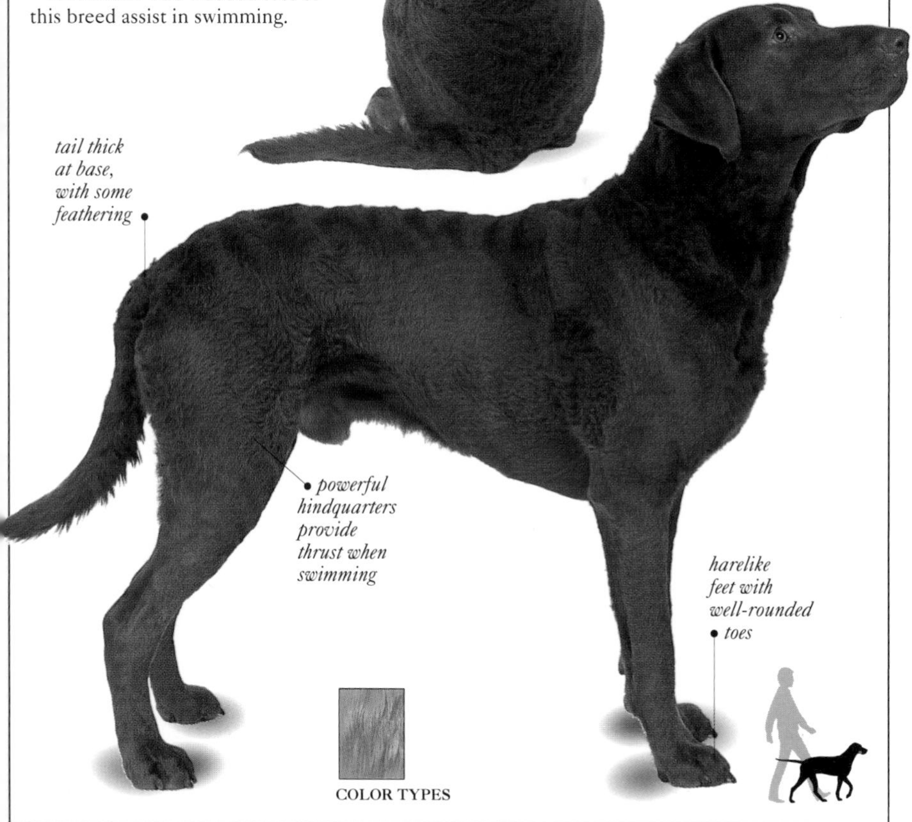
tail thick at base, with some feathering
powerful hindquarters provide thrust when swimming
harelike feet with well-rounded toes

COLOR TYPES

Height 21–26 in (53–66 cm)	Weight 55–75 lb (25–34 kg)	Temperament Responsive, industrious

Country of origin	First use	Origins
Great Britain	Tracking and retrieving game	1800s

CLUMBER SPANIEL

This large, bulky spaniel is not as speedy in the field as some of its more streamlined relatives, but it is vigorous and works well, especially in areas of heavy cover. The Clumber has a large wide head, a pronounced stop, and deep-set eyes. Its attractive, pure-white, silky coat is heavily feathered on the neck and chest. Lemon- or orange-colored markings are permissible.

• **HISTORY** The Duke of Newcastle was instrumental in developing this breed in Britain at the family home in Clumber Park. He may have obtained the ancestral stock from France. Later, Prince Albert, as well as his son, who became King Edward VII, both favored this spaniel, as did King George V.

• **REMARK** Despite royal patronage, this spaniel has never been generally popular.

massive, square skull with heavy brow and deep stop
lemon markings on ears preferred
long ears, shaped like vine leaves

plain white body preferred

well-feathered tail
thick, powerful neck
short, well-boned legs
exceedingly powerful hindquarters

Height	Weight	Temperament
19–20 in (48–51 cm)	65–80 lb (29–36 kg)	Dedicated, responsive

Country of origin Great Britain	First use Retrieving game	Origins 1800s

Cocker Spaniel

This breed of gundog has a broad nose for scenting, a generous square muzzle, a pronounced stop, and a precise yet delicate bite, ideal for retrieving game. Its long coat is silky in texture but not curly. In solid-colored dogs, white markings are permissible only on the chest.

- **History** The Cocker Spaniel was originally developed in Wales and southwestern parts of England to flush woodcock, a popular game bird.
- **Remark** Its long ears hang close to the ground and often harbor ticks and burrs, which can lead to disease and injury.
- **Other Names** English Cocker Spaniel.

long, silky hair on ears

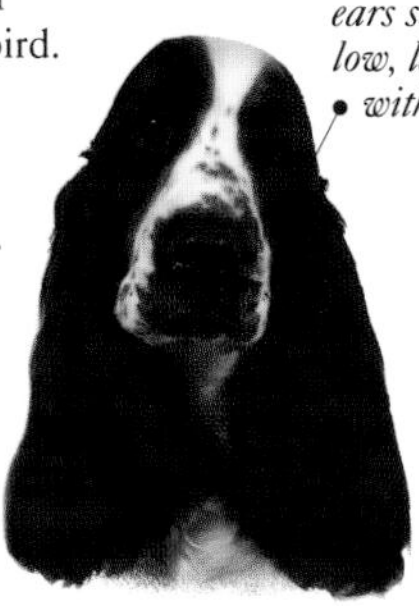
ears set low, level with eyes

strong, compact body
flat, silky coat with feathering

tail set low and may be moderately docked
medium-length, muscular neck merging into sloping shoulders
stifles well bent
straight, well-boned legs
thickly padded feet

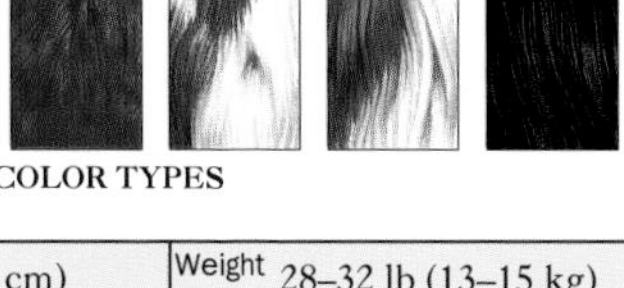
COLOR TYPES

Height 15–16 in (38–41 cm)	Weight 28–32 lb (13–15 kg)	Temperament Responsive, affectionate

Country of origin	First use	Origins
Great Britain	Retrieving water fowl	1800s

CURLY-COATED RETRIEVER

This robust, agile breed of retriever has a tidy general appearance. Its body is covered with a tightly curled, black- or liver-colored coat, which does not need trimming. By contrast, its facial hair is distinctively smooth.

• **HISTORY** The precise ancestry of the Curly-coated Retriever is unclear, but Water Spaniels are probably responsible for its distinctive coat. Early Labradors may also have contributed to its development, along with poodles.

• **REMARK** The Curly-coated Retriever is one of the oldest breeds of retriever and is still a popular choice in Australia and New Zealand for quail and water fowl hunting. They enter water without hesitation, and their water-resistant coat dries quickly.

long head

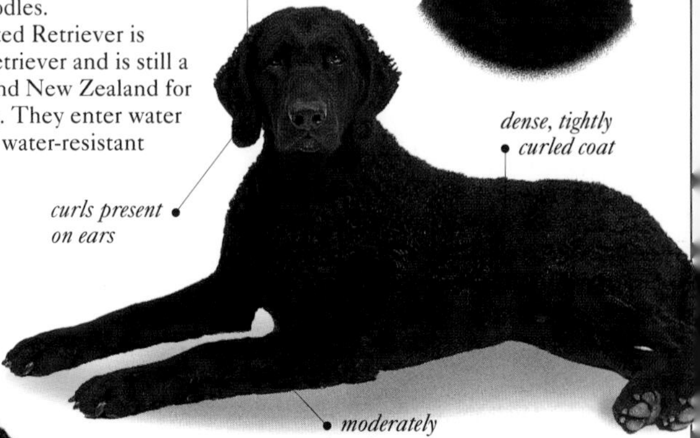
small ears lying close to head
dense, tightly curled coat
curls present on ears
moderately long legs

deep shoulders and muscular body
tail tapers toward point
straight forelegs
strong hind-quarters and low hocks
round, compact feet

COLOR TYPES

Height	Weight	Temperament
25–27 in (64–69 cm)	70–80 lb (32–36 kg)	Responsive, friendly

Country of origin Great Britain	First use Retrieving birds	Origins 1800s

English Setter

The mottled coloration of the English Setter serves to distinguish it from other breeds of setter. Essentially it is a working dog that can be developed into an extremely responsive gundog, and it requires a lot of exercise to remain healthy. A popular dog in the show ring, the breed's friendly nature guarantees it strong support. Careful grooming is important if this breed is to be seen at its best.

• **History** The old Setting Spaniel is the probable ancestor of this breed. It was developed initially by a Mr. Edward Laverack, who began a breeding program in 1825, and for a period these dogs were known simply as Laverack Setters.

• **Remark** The term "setter" originates from the way such dogs "set" (sit) after they have located game.

dark hazel eyes

velvety tips to ears
close, compact feet

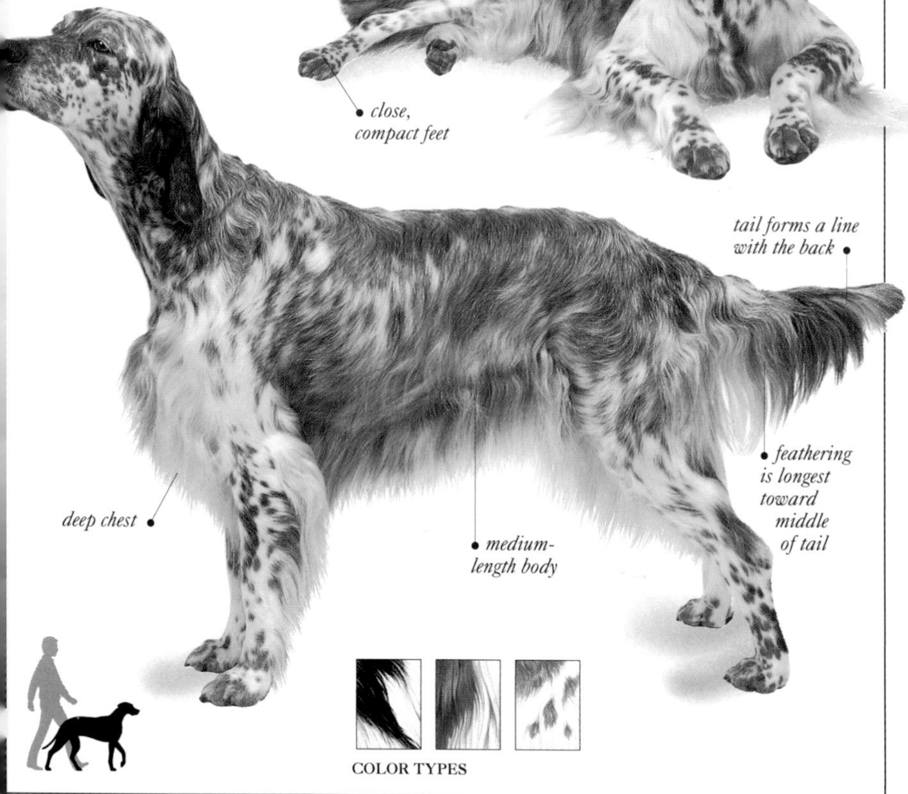
tail forms a line with the back
feathering is longest toward middle of tail
deep chest
medium-length body

COLOR TYPES

Height 24–27 in (61–69 cm)	Weight 56–66 lb (25–30 kg)	Temperament Responsive, friendly

Country of origin	First use	Origins
Great Britain	Retrieving birds	1600s

Gordon Setter

The black-and-tan coloration of the Gordon is distinctive among setters. It is an adept sporting dog, being skilled at locating game, and is also an impressive sight in the show ring. Puppies are slow to mature, however, and appear rather uncoordinated.

• **History** The Gordon Setter was developed by the 4th Duke of Richmond and Gordon, at his ancestral seat in Banffshire, Scotland, from various breeds including bloodhounds and collies.

• **Remark** It is the only setter developed in Scotland.

clearly defined stop
silky, glossy coat
forelegs are well feathered

long muzzle

Height	Weight	Temperament
24½–26 in (62–66 cm)	56–65 lb (25–30 kg)	Obedient, loyal

Country of origin	First use	Origins
Great Britain	Flushing out game	1800s

English Springer Spaniel

As well as being the ancestor of most other contemporary spaniels, the English Springer is also one of the tallest. A division between working and show strains has arisen, the former being shorter and stockier.

• **History** This gundog was originally used to "spring" (flush) game from the ground.

• **Remark** The Springer makes a good family pet if it receives sufficient exercise.

strong jaws
weather-resistant coat

lobe-shaped ears

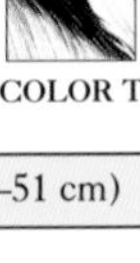

COLOR TYPES

Height	Weight	Temperament
19–20 in (48–51 cm)	49–53 lb (22–24 kg)	Willing, active

Country of origin Great Britain	First use Retrieving birds	Origins 1800s

FIELD SPANIEL

The Field Spaniel has a long body in relation to its height, and a silky, flat coat. The breed was originally divided into two categories, the lighter of which became the Cocker Spaniel (see p.63).

• **HISTORY** After the Field Spaniel was separated from the Cocker in 1892, crossings with Sussex Spaniels (see p.72) led to a temporary deterioration in type and soundness, which threatened the breed's existence.

• **REMARK** Although popular as a gundog, the breed has not done well in the show ring.

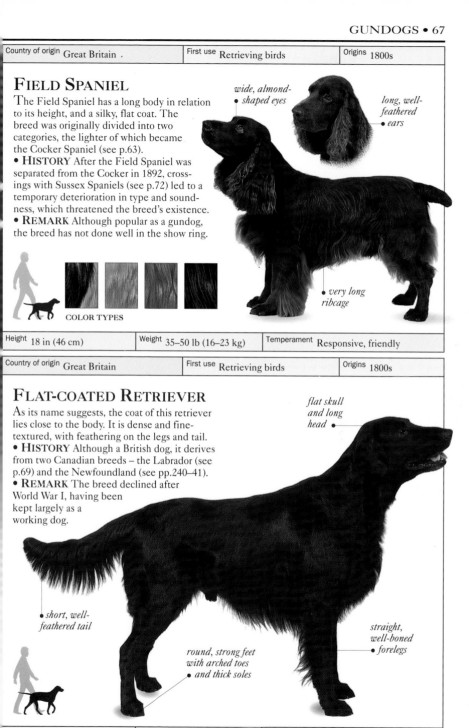

wide, almond-shaped eyes
long, well-feathered ears
very long ribcage

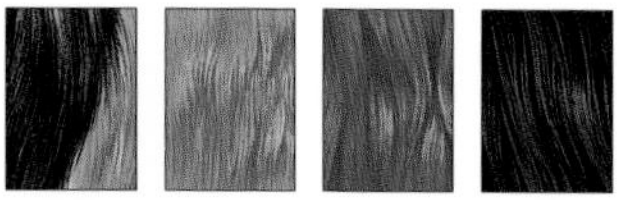

COLOR TYPES

Height 18 in (46 cm)	Weight 35–50 lb (16–23 kg)	Temperament Responsive, friendly

Country of origin Great Britain	First use Retrieving birds	Origins 1800s

FLAT-COATED RETRIEVER

As its name suggests, the coat of this retriever lies close to the body. It is dense and fine-textured, with feathering on the legs and tail.

• **HISTORY** Although a British dog, it derives from two Canadian breeds – the Labrador (see p.69) and the Newfoundland (see pp.240–41).

• **REMARK** The breed declined after World War I, having been kept largely as a working dog.

flat skull and long head
short, well-feathered tail
round, strong feet with arched toes and thick soles
straight, well-boned forelegs

Height 22–23 in (56–58 cm)	Weight 60–70 lb (27–32 kg)	Temperament Attentive, friendly

Country of origin Great Britain	First use Retrieving birds	Origins 1800s

Golden Retriever

The coloration of this retriever has helped to make it one of the most popular of all breeds. The coat can vary from shades of cream to gold, but must not be red. The Golden Retriever is a responsive dog to train, and provided it receives plenty of exercise, it makes an excellent family companion.

• **History** Although it has been suggested that this retriever evolved from Russian circus dogs, it is more likely it was bred from crossings that started with a yellow Flat-coated Retriever (see p.67) and a Tweed Water Spaniel, with Irish Setter, Labrador, and Bloodhound introduced later.

• **Remark** Until 1920 it was known as the Golden Flat-coat.

• **Other Names** Yellow Retriever or Russian Retriever.

broad skull and powerful muzzle

ears level with eyes

well-spaced, brown eyes
black nose preferred

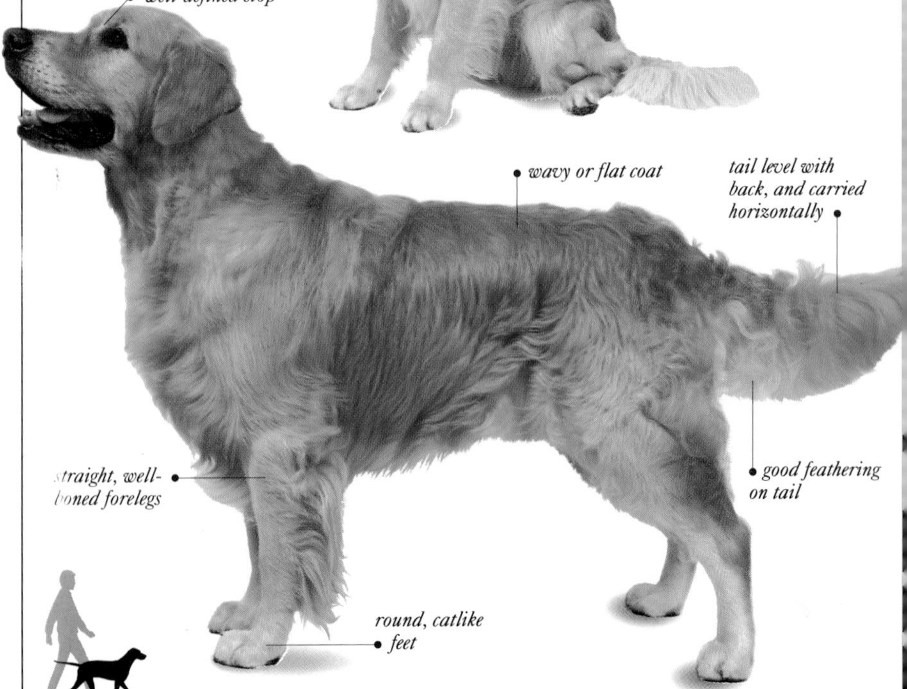
well-defined stop
wavy or flat coat
tail level with back, and carried horizontally
straight, well-boned forelegs
good feathering on tail
round, catlike feet

Height 20–24 in (51–61 cm)	Weight 60–80 lb (27–36 kg)	Temperament Responsive, alert

Country of origin	First use	Origins
Canada	Helping fishermen	1800s

Labrador Retriever

The tail is the most distinctive feature of this intelligent, short-coated retriever. It has a thick base, tapering along its length, with no signs of feathering. A short coupled, solid dog, it has a broad skull, wide nose, and powerful neck.

• **HISTORY** The Labrador Retriever came from Newfoundland, where it used to help haul the fishermen's nets ashore. Today, apart from being a gundog, Labradors often act as guide dogs, have been trained to detect drugs and explosives, and are popular as companions.

• **REMARK** Unless regularly exercised, Labradors tend towards obesity.

wide skull and slightly pronounced brow
smooth, black, chocolate, or yellow double coat

long shoulders
otter-like, medium-length tail

well-developed hindquarters
wide, powerful, chest with barrel-shaped ribcage
well-arched toes and thick pads

COLOR TYPES

Height	Weight	Temperament
21½–22½ in (54–57 cm)	55–75 lb (25–34 kg)	Responsive, friendly

Country of origin	First use	Origins
Great Britain	Tracking hares	1600s

POINTER

This breed has an agile and athletic build. The muzzle has a distinctively concave profile and is often raised high as the dog tests the air. The Pointer is prized for its exceptional sense of smell. It displays considerable pace on the field, covering enormous distances. This elegant dog retains strong working instincts and requires a great deal of exercise if it is to be kept as a pet.

• **HISTORY** The Pointer has been a hunting dog since the 17th century. Originally it was trained to detect hares, which were then run down, or "coursed," by Greyhounds.

• **REMARK** In the presence of game, this dog freezes in a characteristic "pointing" stance to indicate the quarry's direction.

• **OTHER NAMES** English Pointer.

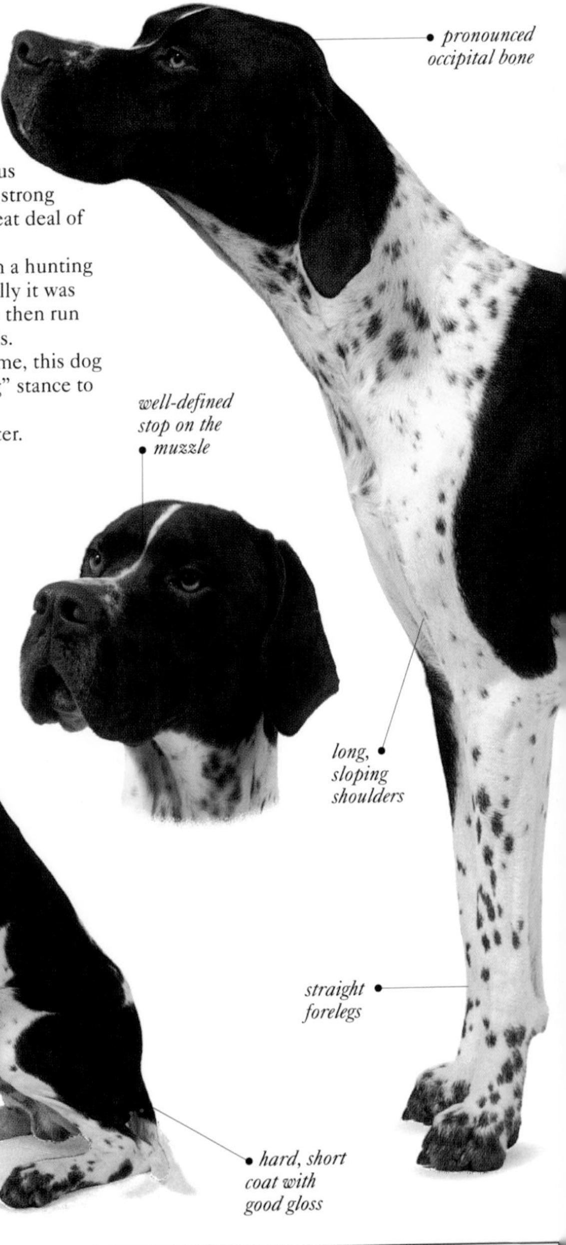
pronounced occipital bone
long, sloping shoulders
straight forelegs
well-defined stop on the muzzle

wide chest
hard, short coat with good gloss

Height	Weight	Temperament
24–27 in (61–69 cm)	44–66 lb (20–30 kg)	Responsive, lively

long, sloping neck
medium-length ears, lying close to head
hite areas lways evident
feet well-cushioned

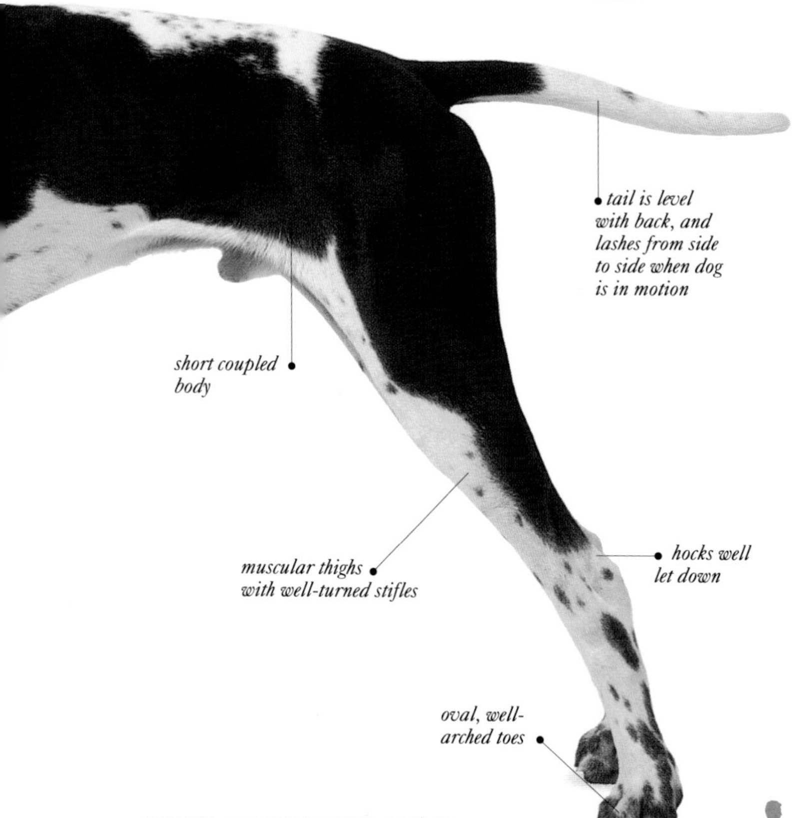
tail is level with back, and lashes from side to side when dog is in motion
short coupled body
muscular thighs with well-turned stifles
hocks well let down
oval, well-arched toes

COLOR TYPES

Country of origin	First use	Origins
Great Britain	Springing hidden game	1500s

WELSH SPRINGER SPANIEL

Although possibly sharing common origins with the English Springer (see p.66), the Welsh Springer Spaniel is generally smaller, has a finer head, and always has rich, dark red markings on a white coat.

HISTORY A clue to the possible age of this breed comes from a 16th-century manuscript that refers to what could be an early ancestor of the Welsh Springer Spaniel.

• **REMARK** The description "springer" refers to the breed's ability to "spring" hidden game.

slightly domed skull
long, muscular neck
silky, dense coat, never wavy or wiry
thick pads on round feet

square, medium-length muzzle

Height	Weight	Temperament
18–19 in (46–48 cm)	35–45 lb (16–20 kg)	Attentive, friendly

Country of origin	First use	Origins
Great Britain	Scenting game	1700s

SUSSEX SPANIEL

The Sussex is a lower, longer, slower dog than other spaniels. Its abundant, flat coat is rich golden liver in color, the hairs becoming golden at their tips.

• **HISTORY** This is one of the oldest spaniel breeds, first recognized in 1855.

• **REMARK** Unusually for spaniels, the Sussex will "give tongue" (bay) when on the scent of game, in the fashion of hounds.

broad skull and wrinkled brows

long body
short, strong legs

Height	Weight	Temperament
15–16 in (38–41 cm)	40–50 lb (18–23 kg)	Friendly, determined

Country of origin	First use	Origins
Canada	Retrieving ducks	1800s

Nova Scotia Duck Tolling Retriever

This muscular, medium- to heavy-boned retriever has a dense, water-repellent coat. The feathering is paler than the ground color, which can be various shades of red, often with white markings.

- **HISTORY** This dog was developed in Canada in the late 19th century to perform a unique role in hunting. It is used to toll (lure) curious ducks within range of the concealed hunters' guns by creating a disturbance at the edge of the water.
- **REMARK** Foxes occasionally lure their prey toward them in this cunning fashion.

wedge-shaped head
brown nose

deep chest
light feathering

slight waves on back
water-repellent coat
muscular body
well-muscled legs

COLOR TYPES

Height	Weight	Temperament
17–21 in (43–53 cm)	37–51 lb (17–23 kg)	Responsive, active

Country of origin Denmark	First use Scenting and pointing game	Origins 1700s

Old Danish Pointer

By the standards of most pointers, this dog is not tall, but it is nevertheless a robust animal, well balanced, with muscular thighs, a heavy head, and a long and powerful neck with dewlap. Its short coat is brown and white in color, some ticking being permitted.

• **HISTORY** The origins of the Old Danish Pointer are uncertain, but it may have resulted from crossings between Spanish Pointers, brought to Denmark by Gypsies, and local bloodhound breeds. The breed is little known outside its Danish homeland.

• **REMARK** Its excellent scenting abilities makes it ideal for tracking wounded animals.

• **OTHER NAMES** Gammel Dansk Honsehund.

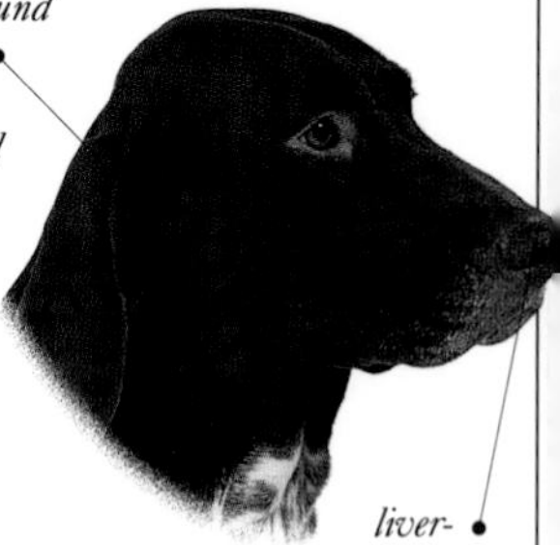
long, pendant ears, round at tips
liver-colored nose

broad forehead
some ticking evident in coat

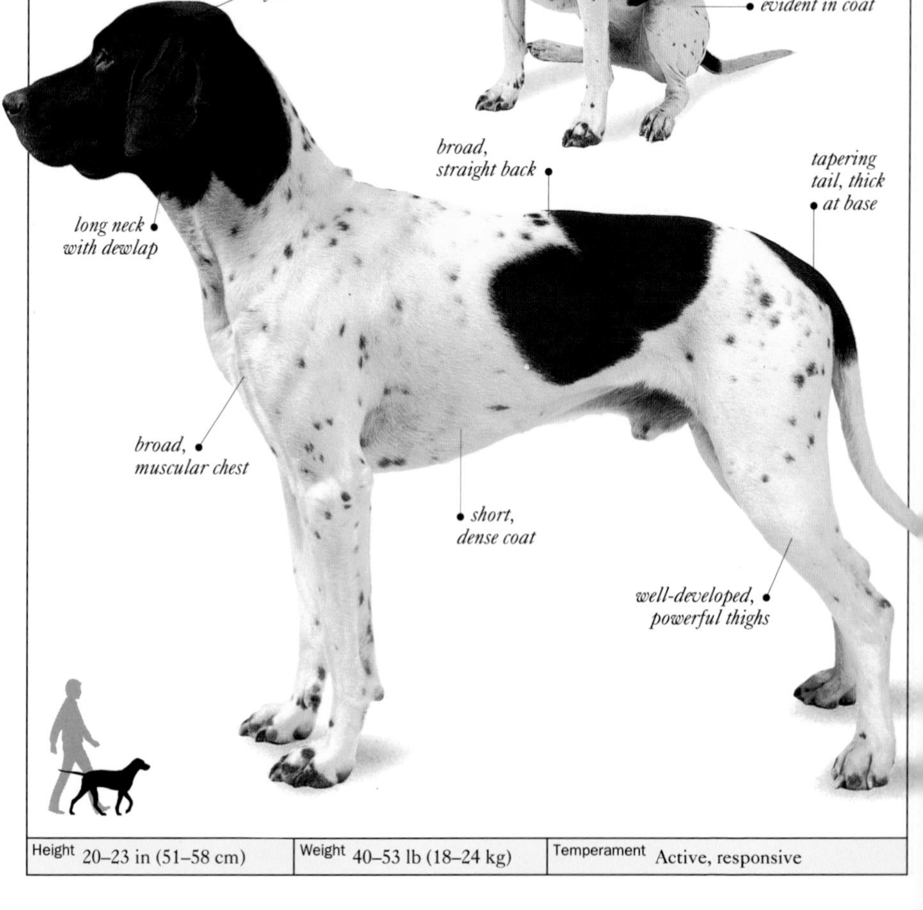
hazel-colored eyes
long neck with dewlap
broad, straight back
tapering tail, thick at base
broad, muscular chest
short, dense coat
well-developed, powerful thighs

Height 20–23 in (51–58 cm)	Weight 40–53 lb (18–24 kg)	Temperament Active, responsive

Country of origin Germany	First use Hunting quail	Origins 1900s

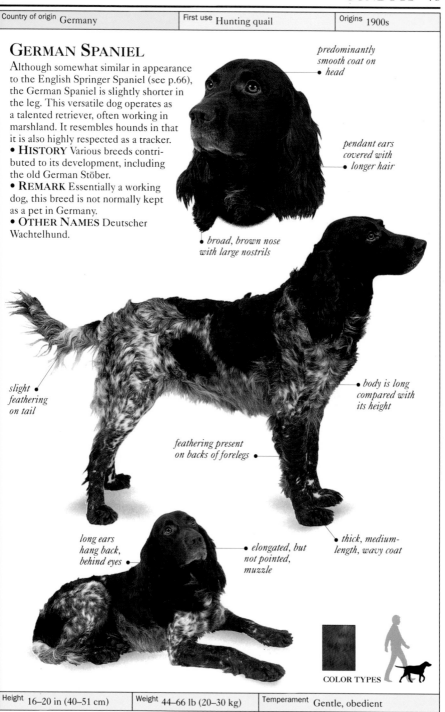

GERMAN SPANIEL

Although somewhat similar in appearance to the English Springer Spaniel (see p.66), the German Spaniel is slightly shorter in the leg. This versatile dog operates as a talented retriever, often working in marshland. It resembles hounds in that it is also highly respected as a tracker.

- **HISTORY** Various breeds contributed to its development, including the old German Stöber.
- **REMARK** Essentially a working dog, this breed is not normally kept as a pet in Germany.
- **OTHER NAMES** Deutscher Wachtelhund.

predominantly smooth coat on head
pendant ears covered with longer hair
broad, brown nose with large nostrils

slight feathering on tail
body is long compared with its height
feathering present on backs of forelegs
thick, medium-length, wavy coat

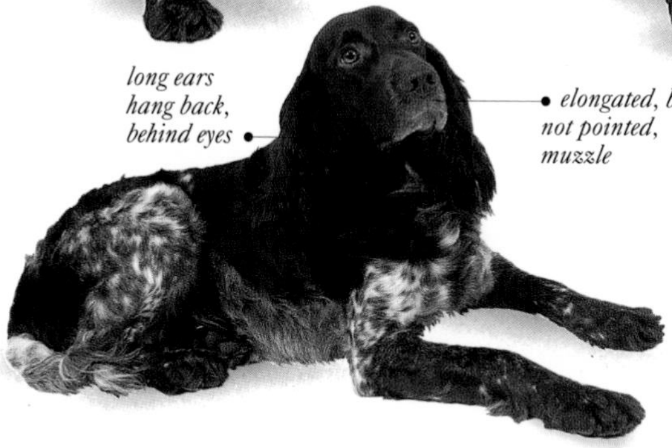
long ears hang back, behind eyes
elongated, but not pointed, muzzle

COLOR TYPES

Height 16–20 in (40–51 cm)	Weight 44–66 lb (20–30 kg)	Temperament Gentle, obedient

Country of origin Germany	First use Tracking large game	Origins 1600s

WEIMARANER

A sleek, uniformly gray coat color and fine, aristocratic features are the hallmarks of this medium-size hunting dog. It has a strong muzzle and only a moderate stop. The Weimaraner, originally known as the Weimar Pointer, comes from a long tradition of German hunting dogs, many of which have found favor in other countries all over the world. This indefatigable breed has long, muscular limbs, a good sense of smell, and an obedient and friendly character – all the attributes of a good, all-around hunting dog. It is one of only seven breeds of hunt, point, and retrieve dogs. Long-haired and short-haired forms of the Weimaraner are found, although the long-haired form is not officially recognized in the USA. The coat color is slightly lighter on the head and on the ears.

• **HISTORY** There is no confirmed history of the development of this dog. One theory suggests that the Weimaraner is the result of an albino mutation that appeared in some of the ancient German pointers. It may have descended from the German Braken, or from crossings between a regular pointer and an unnamed yellow pointer, overseen by Grand Duke Karl August of Weimar.

• **REMARK** The exact origins of this dog are unknown. However, the breed can be positively dated to the 1600s when it appeared in an early painting by the Flemish artist Van Dyck.

• **OTHER NAMES** Weimaraner Vorstehhund.

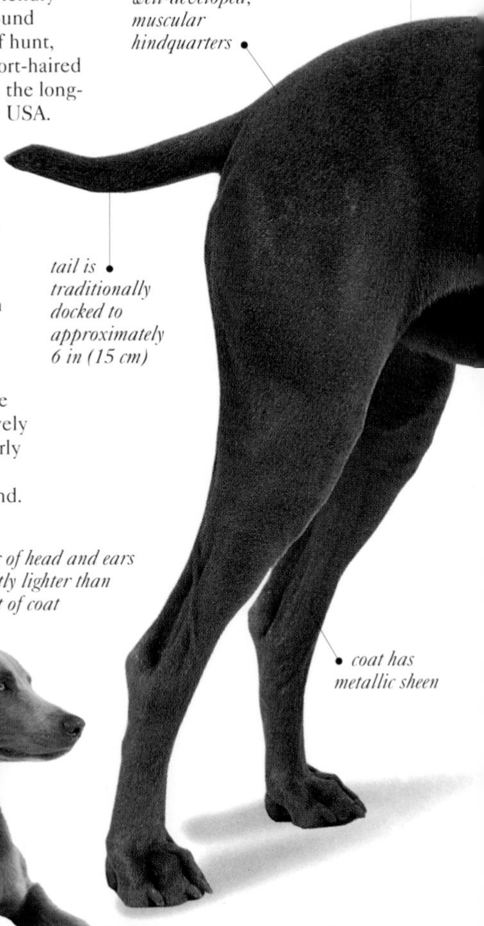
level back
well-developed, muscular hindquarters
tail is traditionally docked to approximately 6 in (15 cm)
coat has metallic sheen

color of head and ears slightly lighter than rest of coat
coat length 1–2 in (3–6 cm)
fringing evident

LONG-HAIRED WEIMARANER

Height 22–27 in (56–69 cm)	Weight 70–86 lb (32–39 kg)	Temperament Responsive, alert

long, lobular ears with round tips
short, smooth, and sleek coat
long muzzle
moderately long, clean-lined neck
amber-colored or blue-gray eyes
well-developed neck and deep shoulders
firm, compact feet and well-arched toes

SHORT-HAIRED WEIMARANER

Country of origin Germany	First use Retrieving birds	Origins 1800s

German Wire-haired Pointer

The harsh, wiry coat and the longer hair above the eyes and on the jaws distinguish this sturdy breed from the other forms of German pointer. The distinctive texture of the coat helps to prevent twigs and other debris from becoming entangled when the dog is working.

• **History** First recognized in Germany in 1870, the breed has developed into its present condition through the infusion of German Shepherd and griffon blood.

• **Remark** Highly valued as a gundog, it is able to fulfil a variety of tasks.

• **Other Names** Deutscher Drahthaariger Vorstehhund.

medium-length head
pronounced beard

harsh, flat outercoat
tail often kept nearly horizontal
powerful muzzle
straight forelegs
deep chest
well-arched toes with sturdy nails

COLOR TYPES

Height 22–26 in (56–66 cm)	Weight 45–75 lb (20–34 kg)	Temperament Active, responsive

Country of origin Germany	First use Pointing	Origins 1800s

SMALL MÜNSTERLÄNDER

This sturdy breed can be distinguished from its larger relative not only by its size, but also by its coloration, which is invariably liver and white. It is otherwise of similar type, a powerful, muscular dog very well-suited to working in the field for long periods of time.

• **HISTORY** The breed's origins can be traced back to Westphalia in Germany. It was developed from crossings involving French spaniels and dogs similar to the Dutch Partridge Dog (see p.82). It was used as a bird dog, and valued especially for its pointing skills. It reached its greatest prominence in the early 1900s.

• **REMARK** This good-natured dog is now becoming more popular outside Germany.

• **OTHER NAMES** Kleiner Münsterländer Vorstehhund, Heidewachtel, Spion.

predominantly liver-colored head
sleek coat with signs of feathering

variable amount of ticking
skin is tight over body

well-feathered tail
straight forelegs
strong, setter-like body
considerable feathering at back of hind legs
tight feet, with thick pads

Height 19–22 in (48–56 cm)	Weight 33 lb (15 kg)	Temperament Responsive, friendly

Country of origin	First use	Origins
Germany	Tracking and retrieving game	1800s

LARGE MÜNSTERLÄNDER

The Large Münsterländer can be instantly distinguished from its smaller relative (see p.79) by its distinctive coloration, which is a striking combination of black and white, rather than liver and white. The larger breed should also have ticking or roaning in the white.

• **HISTORY** Originally, the German Long-haired Pointer Club accepted only liver-and-white dogs for registration, and so black-and-white pups were often simply given away. It was from these that the Large Münsterländer evolved.

• **REMARK** The first breed club for this dog was formed in 1919.

• **OTHER NAMES** Grosser Münsterländer Vorstehhund.

strong, muscular neck
straight forelegs
strong black nails

broad, slightly round head
wide chest with good depth

Height	Weight	Temperament
23–24 in (59–61 cm)	55–65 lb (25–29 kg)	Responsive, friendly

dark brown, medium-size eyes
broad, round-tipped ears, lying flat on the sides
solid back, sloping slightly downward
well-formed black nose
tail is in line with back, tapering to the tip
taut abdomen
dense hair between toes

Country of origin Netherlands	First use Hunting game	Origins 1600s

DUTCH PARTRIDGE DOG

The coat of this medium-size, strongly built breed appears long, mainly because of fringes present on the ears. These extend down the neck, and are also seen on the legs and tail. When walking, the tail is held horizontally, and is slightly curled at the tip. It is held down when the dog is at rest.

• **HISTORY** This breed originated in the Drentse district of the Netherlands; it probably stems from the same ancestral stock as today's spaniels and setters. It frequently hunts pheasants and rabbits, as well as partridges.

• **REMARK** The Dutch Partridge Dog tends to rotate its tail in a circle when it has located game.

• **OTHER NAMES** Drentse Partijshond.

fringes on ears

coarse, straight coat
strong, sturdy legs with thick pads on feet

COLOR TYPES

Height 22–25 in (56–64 cm)	Weight 50 lb (23 kg)	Temperament Responsive, loyal

Country of origin Netherlands	First use Hunting small game	Origins 1700s

KOOIKER DOG

This lightly built, well-proportioned dog has well-feathered ears, a slightly wavy, moderate-length coat, and pronounced fringing to the legs, chest, and tail. In general appearance it is not unlike a small setter with a long, bushy tail.

• **HISTORY** This breed is well-known in the Netherlands and is reputed to have foiled an assassination attempt on Prince William II of Orange (1626–1650) by barking and waking him just in time.

• **REMARK** The bushy tail of the Kooiker is used to lure wild ducks so that they can be banded and then released.

• **OTHER NAMES** Kooikerhondje.

ears set high on head
conspicuous black nose
medium-length, wavy coat
well-feathered forelegs

white blaze on face
well-feathered ears with black tips

Height 14–16 in (35–41 cm)	Weight 20–24 lb (9–11 kg)	Temperament Industrious, intelligent

Country of origin	First use	Origins
Netherlands	Catching moles	1600s

STABYHOUN

This spaniel-like breed has a slightly elongated but well-balanced body, a wide head, and a muzzle tapering toward the nose. Its coat is long, sleek, and well feathered and is seen in dappled colors of black, brown, orange, and blue.

• **HISTORY** The breed originated in Friesland, in the Netherlands. Crossings between the Drentse Patrijshond, a larger Dutch gundog, and spaniels probably occurred.

• **REMARK** This popular gundog is able to locate, point, and retrieve game. It adapts well to family life.

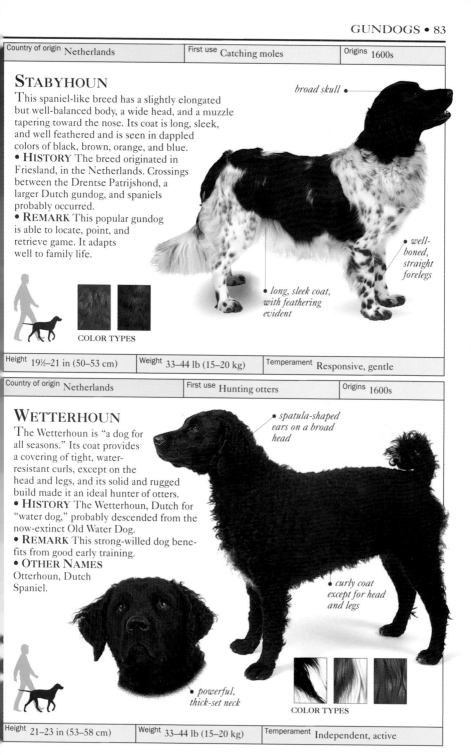

broad skull
well-boned, straight forelegs
long, sleek coat, with feathering evident

COLOR TYPES

Height	Weight	Temperament
19½–21 in (50–53 cm)	33–44 lb (15–20 kg)	Responsive, gentle

Country of origin	First use	Origins
Netherlands	Hunting otters	1600s

WETTERHOUN

The Wetterhoun is "a dog for all seasons." Its coat provides a covering of tight, water-resistant curls, except on the head and legs, and its solid and rugged build made it an ideal hunter of otters.

• **HISTORY** The Wetterhoun, Dutch for "water dog," probably descended from the now-extinct Old Water Dog.

• **REMARK** This strong-willed dog benefits from good early training.

• **OTHER NAMES** Otterhoun, Dutch Spaniel.

spatula-shaped ears on a broad head
curly coat except for head and legs

powerful, thick-set neck

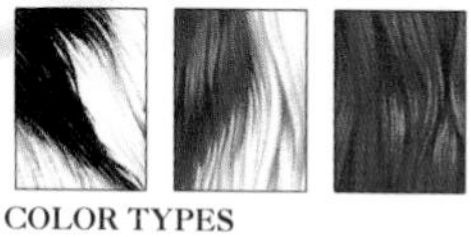
COLOR TYPES

Height	Weight	Temperament
21–23 in (53–58 cm)	33–44 lb (15–20 kg)	Independent, active

Country of origin	First use	Origins
Ireland	Retrieving water fowl	1800s

IRISH WATER SPANIEL

Standing taller than any other breed of spaniel, and with a unique coloration showing a purplish hue described as puce liver, this breed has a powerful presence. The coat is comprised of tight ringlets and is naturally oily and water-repellent. The first 4 in (10 cm) of tail has curly hair, while the rest to the tip is either bare skin or covered with straight hair.

• **HISTORY** The Irish Water Spaniel may have been developed from the Portuguese Water Dog or a poodle, crossed with native Irish spaniels. The breed's founder, Justin McCarthy, kept the breed's origins a closely guarded secret and refused to reveal details of its precise ancestry.

• **REMARK** This spaniel is a powerful swimmer and is large enough to retrieve game the size of geese from deep water.

large nose, the color of dark liver
long, oval ears

head set well above body
tight ringlets of hair cover body

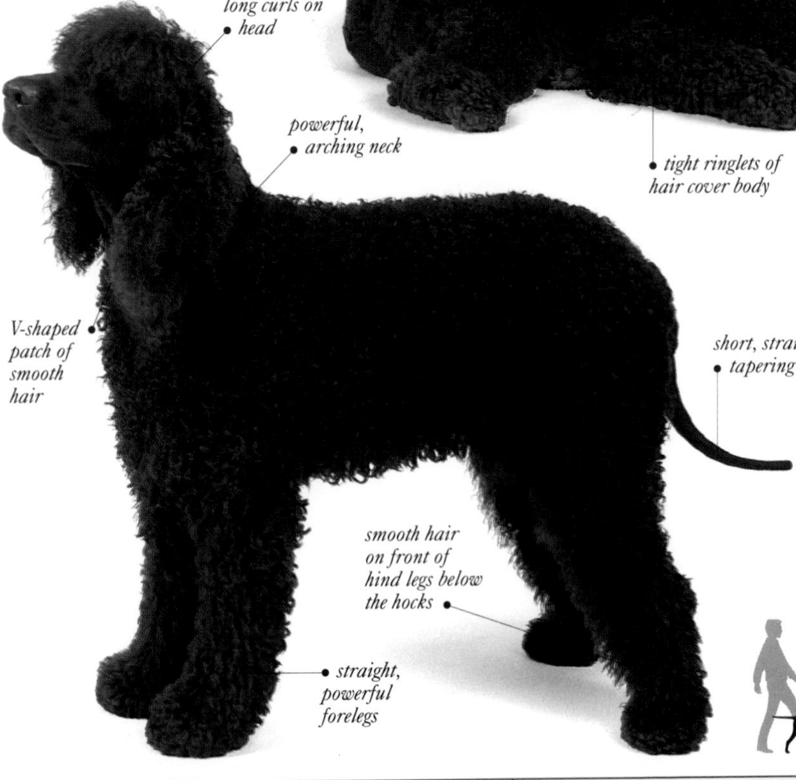
long curls on head
powerful, arching neck
V-shaped patch of smooth hair
short, straight, tapering tail
smooth hair on front of hind legs below the hocks
straight, powerful forelegs

Height	Weight	Temperament
20–23 in (51–58 cm)	45–65 lb (20–29 kg)	Responsive, playful

Country of origin Ireland	First use Retrieving game	Origins 1700s

IRISH RED AND WHITE SETTER

Well-proportioned and athletic, the Irish Red and White Setter is a powerful, good-natured dog. Similar to the Irish Setter (see p.86), it is more heavily built with a broader head and a more prominent occipital peak. The finely textured, feathered coat has a pure white ground color with solid red patches. Some mottling or flecking is common. Roaning, however, is frowned upon in show circles. Setters are renowned for their highly developed sense of smell and ability to excel at any kind of hunting in any type of terrain or weather conditions.

• **HISTORY** Originally called the Particolor Setter, this hardy breed derives from the same rootstock as the graceful Irish Setter. Although the Irish Red and White Setter is an excellent working dog in the field, it came very close to extinction before undergoing a revival in recent years.

• **REMARK** The Irish Red and White Setter makes an affectionate family pet, but requires a great deal of exercise and rigorous training.

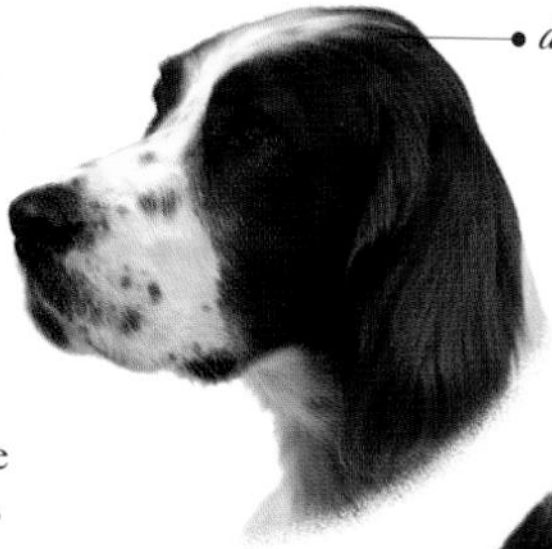
domed skull

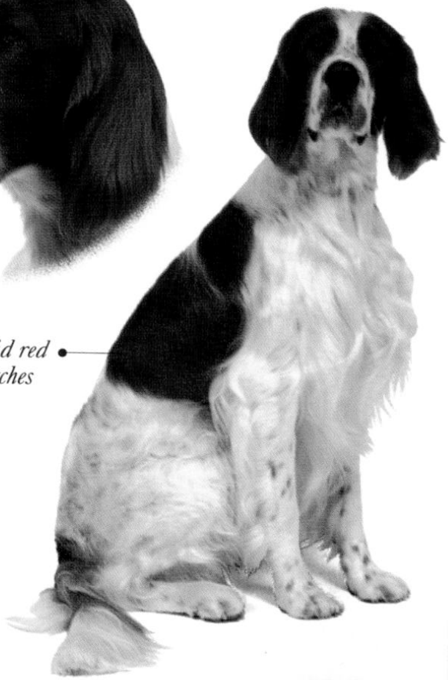
solid red patches

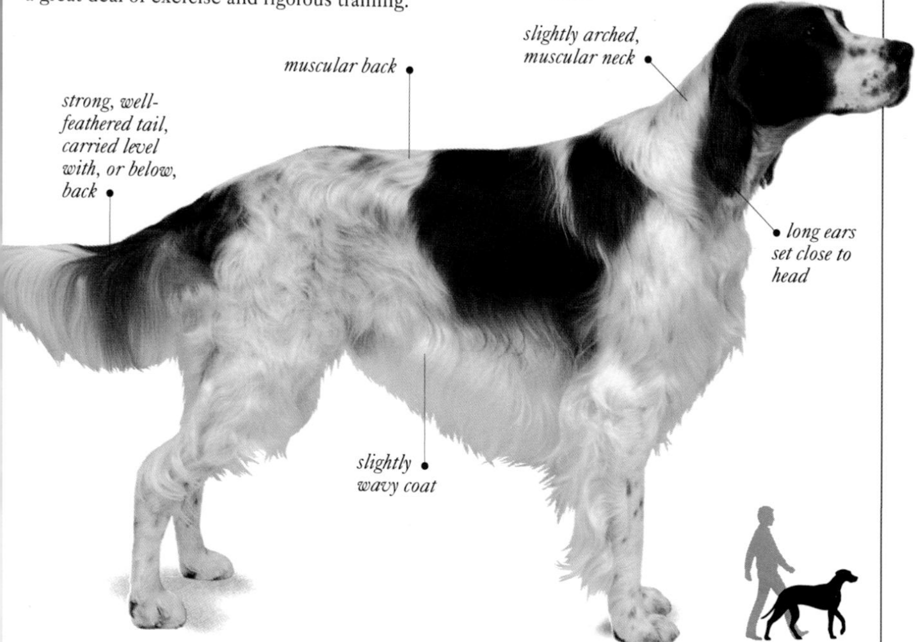
slightly arched, muscular neck
muscular back
strong, well-feathered tail, carried level with, or below, back
long ears set close to head
slightly wavy coat

Height 23–27 in (58–69 cm)	Weight 60–70 lb (27–32 kg)	Temperament Active, affectionate

Country of origin	First use	Origins
Ireland	Retrieving game	1700s

IRISH SETTER

In spite of its formal name, the Irish Setter is often better known simply as the Red Setter, due to its distinctive coloration. Built on racier lines than its red and white cousin, it is a lively, active dog, always ready for fun. It is popular as a pet but must have plenty of exercise. To ensure obedience it requires more training than other similar breeds. Ultimately, provided it is well trained, the Irish Setter should become a superb working companion.

• **HISTORY** The breed evolved in Ireland, where Irish Water Spaniels, Gordon Setters, and Springer Spaniels are all believed to have played a part in its development.

• **REMARK** A small amount of white on the chest is quite common, and will not lead to disqualification from a show ring.

• **OTHER NAMES** Red Setter.

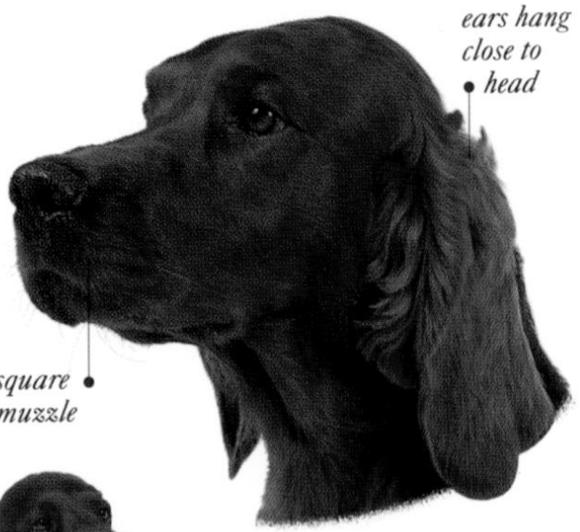
ears hang close to head
square muzzle

rich, chestnut coat

long, muscular neck
feathered, low-set tail
straight, sinewy forelegs
deep, narrow chest
long, fine feathering on back of legs

Height	Weight	Temperament
25–27 in (64–69 cm)	60–70 lb (27–32 kg)	Active, affectionate

Country of origin France	First use Hunting small game	Origins 1700s

Braque St. Germain

This pointer has a predominantly white coat broken by orange areas of variable size. Although slightly leggier than the English Pointer (see pp.70–71), the elegant Braque St. Germain is a dog of fine proportions.

- **History** The breed's ancestry dates back to two English Pointers given to King Charles X of France. When one died, the other was mated with a Braque Francais. The offspring laid the foundations of this breed.
- **Remark** This dog is not favored for retrieving from water, because its coat does not provide sufficient insulation when wet.
- **Other Names** St. Germain Pointer.

distinctive golden yellow eyes
long muzzle

well-defined orange patches

pinkish colored nose
ears set at eye level

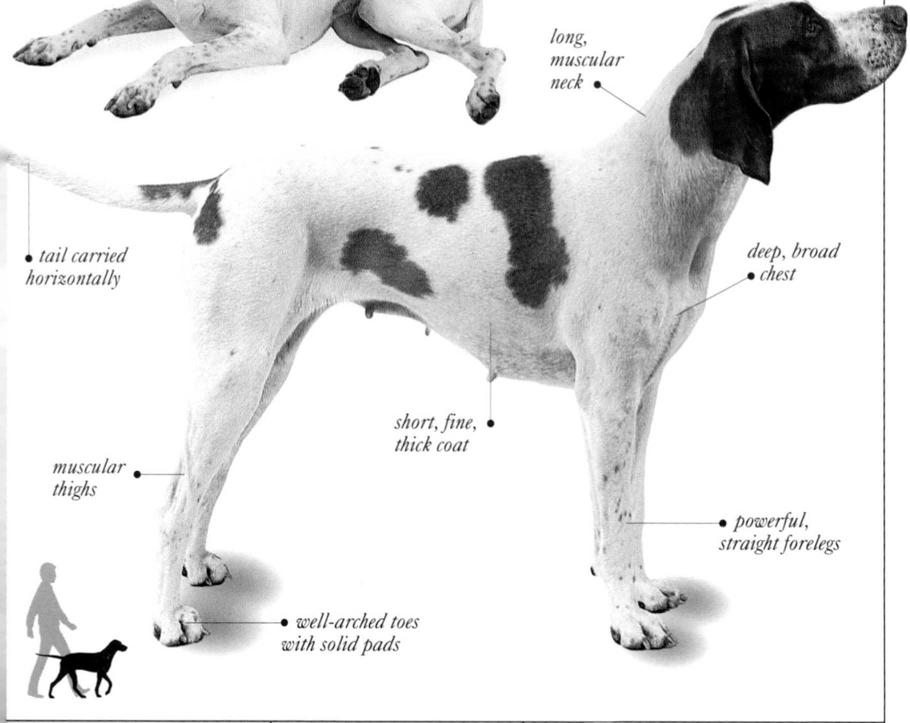
long, muscular neck
tail carried horizontally
deep, broad chest
short, fine, thick coat
muscular thighs
powerful, straight forelegs
well-arched toes with solid pads

Height 20–24 in (51–61 cm)	Weight 40–57 lb (18–26 kg)	Temperament Obedient, loyal

Country of origin France	First use Scenting and pointing game	Origins 1600s

LARGE FRENCH POINTER

One of France's oldest breeds, the Large French Pointer is an imposing dog, with a strong, well-muscled physique. The breed, which originated in the Pyrenean region of France, is a slightly taller dog than the better-known English Pointer (see pp.70–71), but in general physique they are very similar. A smaller version of the breed, from Gascony, has a more refined appearance.

• **HISTORY** It is popularly believed that the Large French Pointer is descended from the old, extinct Southern Hound, and that it is also closely related to the Italian and Spanish Pointers (see pp.101 and 102). There is certainly a houndlike aura attaching to this breed, which lends credence to this belief.

• **REMARK** During the latter part of the 19th century, the breed declined in popularity and was in danger of dying out. However, recent efforts among enthusiasts have resulted in a considerable boost in the numbers of these pointers. Although still not common, its future does now seem assured, as a new generation of hunters learns to appreciate its working skills.

• **OTHER NAMES** Braque Francais de Grande Taille.

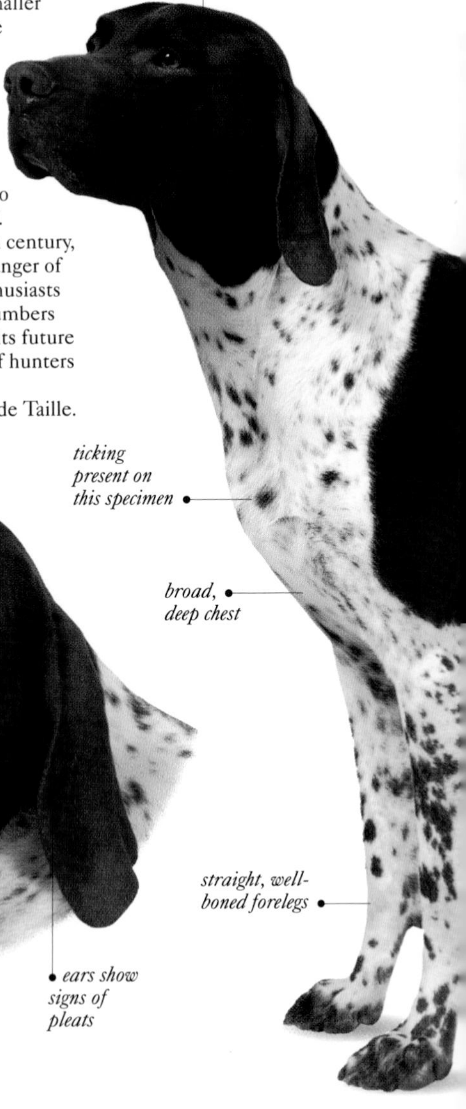
head often held upward to detect scents when working in open surroundings
ticking present on this specimen
broad, deep chest
straight, well-boned forelegs

convex head has broad, rectangular muzzle
fine hair covering on head and ears
ears show signs of pleats

Height 22–27 in (56–68 cm)	Weight 45–71 lb (20–32 kg)	Temperament Well-balanced, steady

short, dense,
thick coat
chestnut
or dark
yellow eyes
broad, chestnut-
colored nose

tail traditionally
docked
well-muscled
hindquarters
sound rump and
strong hind legs
oval,
well-cushioned
feet

Country of origin France	First use Pointing and retrieving game	Origins 1800s

AUVERGNE POINTER

The Auvergne Pointer is a large and relatively heavy gundog, with distinctive coloration and markings. It is an important breed characteristic that the ears and the area around the eyes are black. Elsewhere on the body, blue roaning, resulting from overlapping black and white hairs, is desirable. This patterning is known as "charbonnée," or "charcoaled," although some Auvergnes show clearly defined black markings on a white background.

• **HISTORY** It is thought that Gascony Hounds (see pp.170–71) contributed to the breed's ancestry, although any residual traces of tan markings now merit disqualification in the show ring.

• **REMARK** This pointer is still kept essentially for sporting purposes.

• **OTHER NAMES** Braque d'Auvergne.

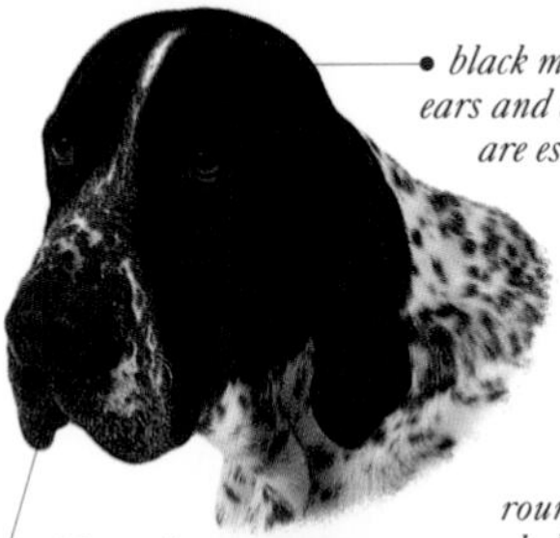
black markings on ears and around eyes are essential
wide, moist nostrils

round, domed skull with well-defined stop
long, straight forelegs

good sheen to coat
large, deep chest
very powerful hindquarters
large feet supported on well-cushioned pads

Height 22–24 in (56–61 cm)	Weight 49–62 lb (22–28 kg)	Temperament Responsive, lively

Country of origin France	First use Hunting game	Origins 1500s

BRAQUE DU BOURBONNAIS

The coat of the Braque du Bourbonnais is basically white with very evident roaning and as few clear patches of coloration as possible. This moderately large pointer is born with either no tail or a very rudimentary stump.

• **HISTORY** As its name implies, the Braque du Bourbonnais originated in the French province of Bourbon, and a dog very similar to today's breed can be found in paintings dating back to the 16th century. The breed flourished in France during the 1800s but then declined from about World War I. Enthusiasts have, however, now pooled their breeding stock to ensure its continued success as a fine French pointing dog.

• **REMARK** This versatile breed is equally at home in scrubland or marshes and is happy hunting all manner of game.

• **OTHER NAMES** Bourbonnais Pointer.

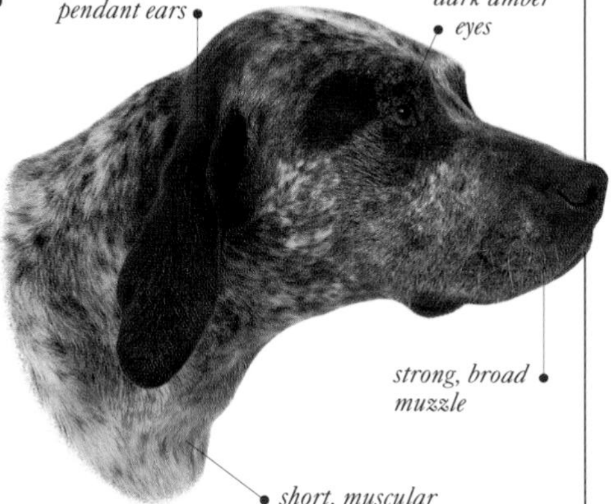
slightly curled, pendant ears
dark amber eyes
strong, broad muzzle
short, muscular neck and slight dewlap

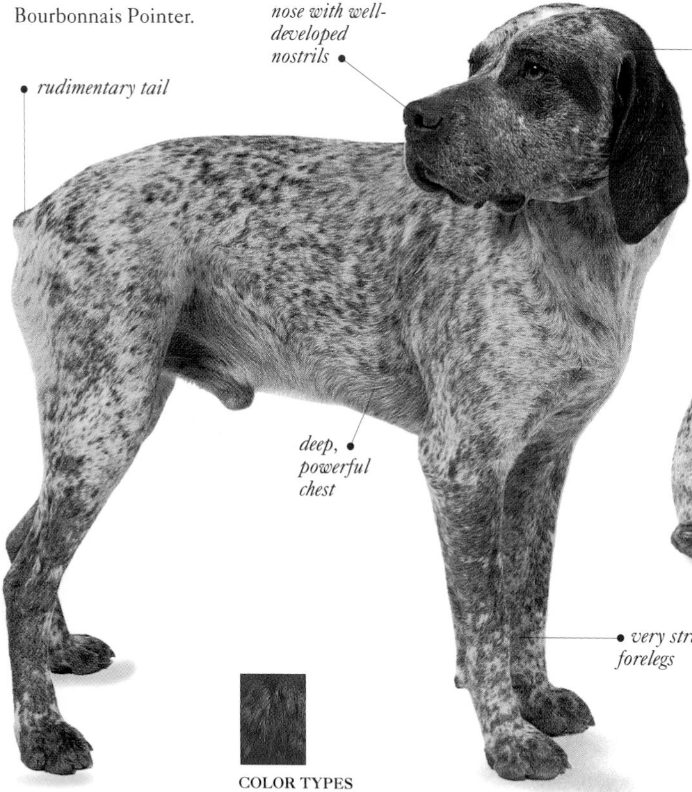
liver-colored nose with well-developed nostrils
pear-shaped head
rudimentary tail
deep, powerful chest
very straight forelegs

COLOR TYPES

Height 22 in (56 cm)	Weight 40–57 lb (18–26 kg)	Temperament Intelligent, affectionate

Country of origin France	First use Flushing and retrieving game	Origins 1600s

ÉPAGNEUL FRANCAIS

Being relatively tall and powerfully built, the Épagneul Francais, one of the oldest breeds of French spaniel, shows a distinct relationship to the setters. Its head is square, with a short neck which joins a muscular body of fine proportions. The coat is short and flat, with some feathering.

• **HISTORY** The ancestry of this breed is not known. Competition from other gundogs once brought it close to extinction, but it is now firmly re-established.

• **REMARK** The breed is not well known outside its native France.

• **OTHER NAMES** French Spaniel.

long, flat, feathered ears
feathered underparts
strong-boned legs
long, feathered tail
flat, straight coat with liver markings

Height 21–24 in (53–61 cm)	Weight 44–55 lb (20–25 kg)	Temperament Intelligent, responsive

Country of origin France	First use Retrieving water fowl	Origins 1700s

ÉPAGNEUL PICARD

This is another of the older French breeds of spaniel that displays an obvious relationship to the setters. The Picard can be distinguished by its characteristic tricolor appearance, with tan, liver, and white areas apparent in its coat.

• **HISTORY** Closely related to the Épagneul Francais (above), the Picard's ancestry is equally uncertain.

• **REMARK** This spaniel is highly prized as a water fowl retriever in the marshlands of Picardy, France.

• **OTHER NAMES** Picardy Spaniel.

broad, round skull
finer, longer hair on ears
flat, straight coat
ticking clearly evident in coat
large feet for body size
feathering apparent at back of legs

Height 22–24 in (56–61 cm)	Weight 44 lb (20 kg)	Temperament Intelligent, friendly

Country of origin France	First use Retrieving game	Origins 1700s

Brittany

Frequently described as a spaniel, the rather square-built Brittany appears to have more in common with the setters, certainly in terms of height and behavior. It is not a particularly gainly dog, the legs appearing somewhat out of proportion with the body. The tail is naturally short in length, but it is customarily docked to a maximum length of 4 in (10 cm).

• **HISTORY** An old breed, it underwent a revival in its native France in the early 1900s. It has since become popular in the USA.

• **REMARK** A good all-arounder in the field, the Brittany can hunt, point, and retrieve.

• **OTHER NAMES** Épagneul Breton.

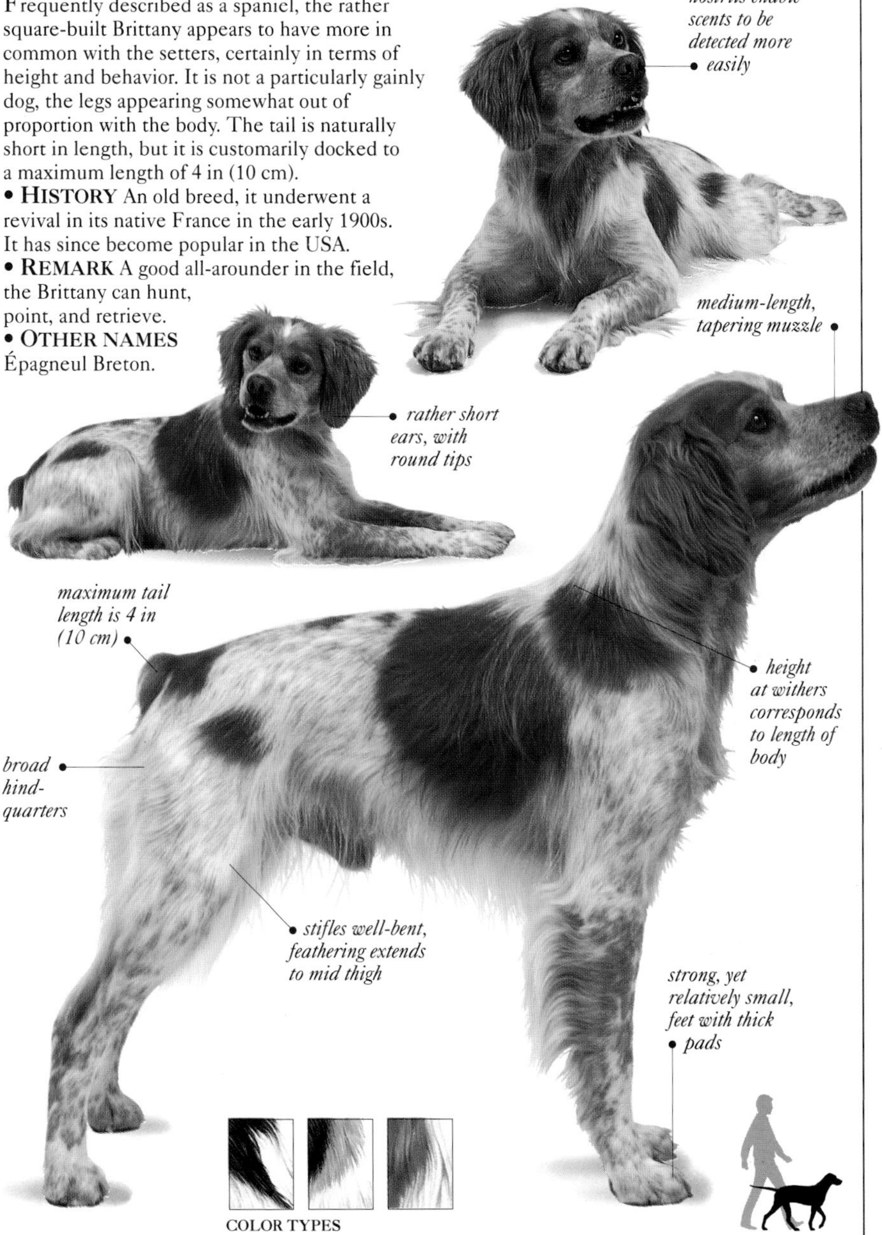
wide-open nostrils enable scents to be detected more easily
rather short ears, with round tips
medium-length, tapering muzzle
maximum tail length is 4 in (10 cm)
height at withers corresponds to length of body
broad hind-quarters
stifles well-bent, feathering extends to mid thigh
strong, yet relatively small, feet with thick pads
COLOR TYPES

Height 18–20½ in (46–52 cm)	Weight 28–33 lb (13–15 kg)	Temperament Loyal, obedient

Country of origin France	First use Flushing and retrieving game	Origins 1600s

ÉPAGNEUL PONT-AUDEMER

The presence of a curly topknot gives this spaniel a distinctive appearance. The rest of the liver, or liver-and-white, coat is long and curly, covering a medium-size, well-built dog.

• **HISTORY** Crosses involving the Irish Water Spaniel, or similar ancestral stock, gave rise to this breed. Old French spaniels probably also contributed to the bloodline. The breed was developed in the area of Pont-Audemer in Normandy. After World War II, the breed declined drastically, and Irish Water Spaniels were used to increase numbers.

• **REMARK** The Épagneul Pont-Audemer remains scarce today, but a society has been established to safeguard its future.

• **OTHER NAMES** Pont-Audemer Spaniel.

short hair on face
long, pendant, well-feathered ears
ticking may be apparent in white areas of coat

weather-resistant, wavy coat
tail traditionally docked to a third of full length
well-proportioned body

COLOR TYPES

Height 20–23 in (51–58 cm)	Weight 40–53 lb (18–24 kg)	Temperament Responsive, docile

Country of origin France	First use Retrieving water fowl	Origins 1600s

BARBET

The coat of the Barbet is thick and woolly, protecting the dog from freezing water conditions. It is shiny and may be curly or wavy, with a rather becoming tasseled appearance. The Barbet has played a central role in the development of many of today's water dogs.

• **HISTORY** Although the precise ancestry of the Barbet is unknown, it is an old breed, and is thought to be the forerunner of such breeds as poodles, Irish Water Spaniels, and Otterhounds. It is also thought to resemble the now-extinct English Water Dog.

• **REMARK** As well as retrieving water fowl, the Barbet would also return the fallen arrows of hunters who had missed their target.

• **OTHER NAMES** Griffon d'Arret à Poil Laineux.

long, pendant ears lying close to the head
large, prominent nostrils

good covering of long, water-resistant hair

solid, muscular body
undocked tail with slight upward curve
powerful, well-boned legs
large, round feet with webbing between toes

COLOR TYPES

Height 18–22 in (46–56 cm)	Weight 33–55 lb (15–25 kg)	Temperament Intelligent, obedient

Country of origin France	First use Hunting snipe	Origins 1800s

Épagneul Bleu de Picardie

The distinctive blue roan coloration of this breed helps to distinguish it from the Épagneul Picard (see p.92), another form of the same dog but with flecks and patches of liver and tan in its coat. In terms of its size, general proportions, and head shape, the breed conforms more to today's definition of a setter than a spaniel, and it looks a little like engravings of early Gordon Setters (see p.66).

• **History** This form of the Picard was developed in Picardy, France, and is descended from crossings of the blue belton (blue mixed with white) English Setter with the Picard itself. The result is a taller, lighter-boned dog with a better nose than that of the old type of French spaniel.

• **Remark** The Épagneul Bleu de Picardie is an extremely hardworking gundog that develops a very close bond with its master.

• **Other Names** Blue Picardy Spaniel.

hair longer and finer on ears
flat, relatively long, straight coat
good covering of hair on feet

dark brown, expressive eyes
ram-shaped muzzle with prominent nose

hair longer on tail than on body
deep chest
strong, well-boned legs
large feet

Height 22–24 in (56–61 cm)	Weight 44 lb (20 kg)	Temperament Intelligent, friendly

Country of origin France	First use Hunting and retrieving game	Origins 1800s

WIRE-HAIRED POINTING GRIFFON

The hard, coarse coat of this dog gives it rather an unkempt appearance. In reality it requires little grooming, aside from periodic brushing. Facially, this breed is characterized by bushy eyebrows and a heavy beard of long, thick hair.

• **HISTORY** The breed was developed by Dutchman Eduard Karel Korthals, possibly by crossing griffons with French Pointers.

• **REMARK** As well as pointing and retrieving, the versatile Wire-haired Pointing Griffon will also hunt rodents and pursue foxes.

• **OTHER NAMES** Korthals Griffon.

long, large head
powerful, straight forelegs
short legs compared with body
muscular hindquarters

COLOR TYPES

Height 22–24 in (56–61 cm)	Weight 50–60 lb (23–27 kg)	Temperament Independent, intelligent

Country of origin Czechoslovakia	First use Pointing game	Origins 1800s

CZESKY FOUSEK

The rough-textured coat of this breed varies in length from 1–3 in (2.5–7.5 cm), and is longest over the back and sides of the body. This is offset against a soft, thick undercoat.

• **HISTORY** Originated in Czechoslovakia, this dog was popular up until about 1914, but it was only the infusion of German Short-haired Pointer blood in the 1930s that saved it from extinction.

• **REMARK** The Fousek needs to be worked hard and does not take readily to domesticity.

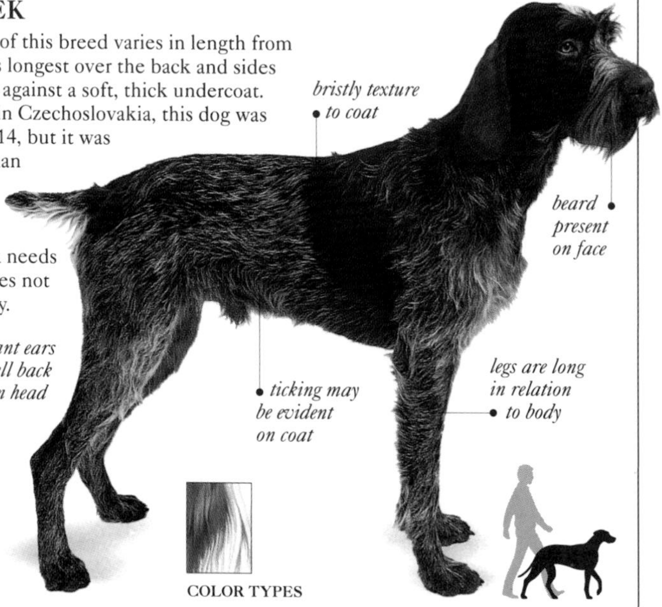
bristly texture to coat
beard present on face
ticking may be evident on coat
legs are long in relation to body

pendant ears set well back on head

COLOR TYPES

Height 24–26 in (61–66 cm)	Weight 60–75 lb (27–34 kg)	Temperament Intelligent, responsive

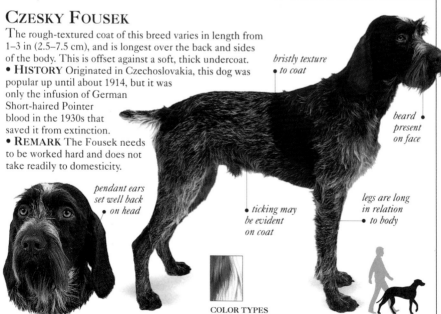

Country of origin	First use	Origins
Hungary	Hunting and retrieving game	1000s

HUNGARIAN VIZSLA

This medium-size, athletic gundog gives an immediate impression of being lean, lively, and muscular. Its coat is particularly striking, being smooth, shiny, sleek, and golden russet in color. White patches are undesirable.

• **HISTORY** It is thought that the ancestors of the Vizsla accompanied the Magyars in their invasion of Hungary. Its bloodline probably includes the ancient Transylvanian Hound and the Turkish Yellow Dog, with more recent additions of pointer blood.

• **REMARK** The Vizsla is adept at hunting, pointing, and retrieving in any terrain, including marshes.

• **OTHER NAMES**
Magyar Vizsla.

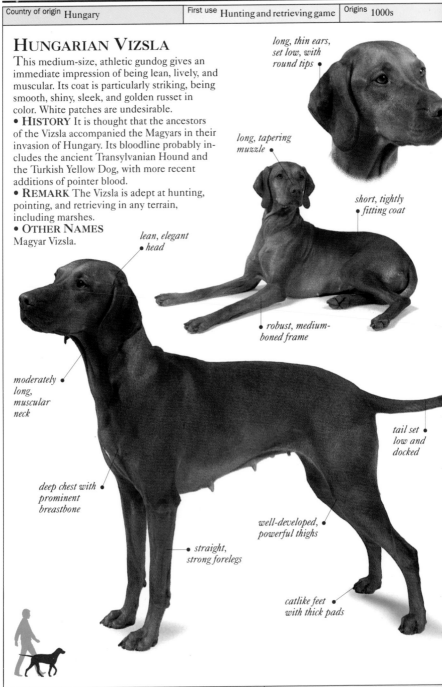

long, thin ears, set low, with round tips

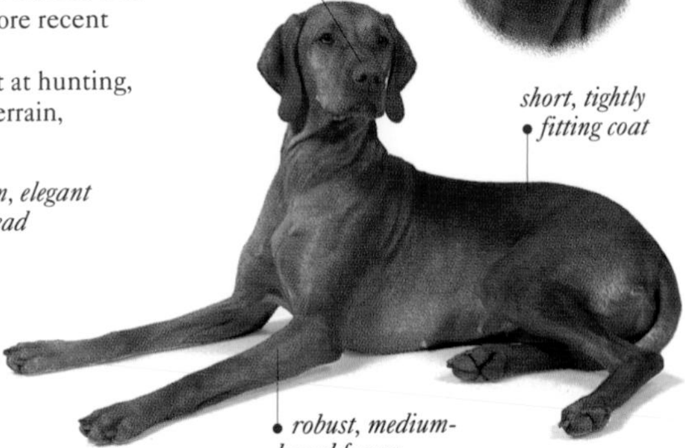
long, tapering muzzle
short, tightly fitting coat
robust, medium-boned frame

lean, elegant head
moderately long, muscular neck
tail set low and docked
deep chest with prominent breastbone
well-developed, powerful thighs
straight, strong forelegs
catlike feet with thick pads

Height	Weight	Temperament
22½–25 in (57–64 cm)	48½–66 lb (22–30 kg)	Gentle, responsive

Country of origin Hungary	First use Gundog	Origins 1930s

WIRE-HAIRED VIZSLA

The wire-haired form of the Vizsla is much rarer than its smooth-coated counterpart. It is a relative newcomer to the gundog scene and has yet to receive widespread recognition as a separate breed. In its Hungarian homeland, it is favored for working in water because it is less vulnerable to the cold.

• **HISTORY** Crossbreedings between the German Wire-haired Pointer and Vizslas, which took place during the 1930s, gave rise to this breed.

• **REMARK** The Hungarian word *vizsla* translates as "responsive," or "alert."

• **OTHER NAMES**
Drótszörü Magyar Vizsla.

noble head with tapering muzzle

beard and eyebrows evident
nails slightly darker than coat

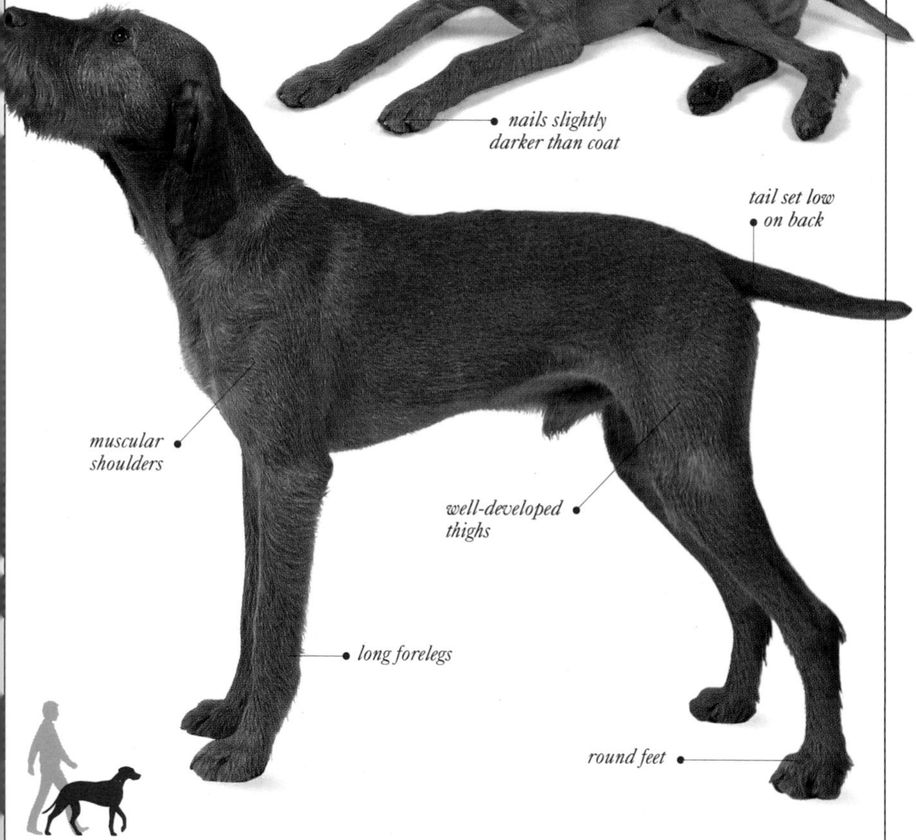
tail set low on back
muscular shoulders
well-developed thighs
long forelegs
round feet

Height 22–24 in (56–61 cm)	Weight 48–66 lb (22–30 kg)	Temperament Responsive, intelligent

Country of origin Italy	First use Retrieving game	Origins 1200s

SPINONE

The Spinone is one of the most talented of all the hunting dogs. Long appreciated in its homeland, it is becoming more popular elsewhere in Europe and in the USA, where it is recognized in the AKC's miscellaneous class. Its tracking abilities are particularly keen, and its "soft" mouth retrieves game unspoiled.

• **HISTORY** The ancestry of this dog dates back many centuries, and probably originated from griffon stock.

• **REMARK** A 15th-century fresco at the Ducal Palace in Mantua, Italy, depicts an early representation of the breed.

• **OTHER NAMES** Spinone Italiano, Italian Spinone.

friendly expression

large eyes, varying from yellow to ocher

sturdy back
docked tail not carried above the horizontal
long ears lie close to the head
hair slightly wiry to the touch
thick coat lies close to the body, with dense undercoat

COLOR TYPES

Height 24–26 in (61–66 cm)	Weight 71–82 lb (32–37 kg)	Temperament Responsive, loyal

Country of origin Italy	First use Gundog	Origins 1700s

Bracco Italiano

This agile, square-framed dog is one of the oldest surviving gundog breeds, and shows very clear signs of its origins from ancient hound stock. The muzzle is unusual, being square almost to the point of convex when viewed in profile. Its coat, which is short and dense, has a finer quality on the head, neck, and lower body. The body of the Bracco Italiano resembles other pointer breeds in overall appearance.

• **History** This was a popular dog during the Renaissance, and was often given as a gift from Italy to countries such as France and Spain. The Bracco Italiano declined in popularity by the 1800s, although it has recently undergone a revival in its homeland.

• **Remark** It has changed little over the centuries and tends to be a little stubborn.

• **Other Names** Italian Pointer.

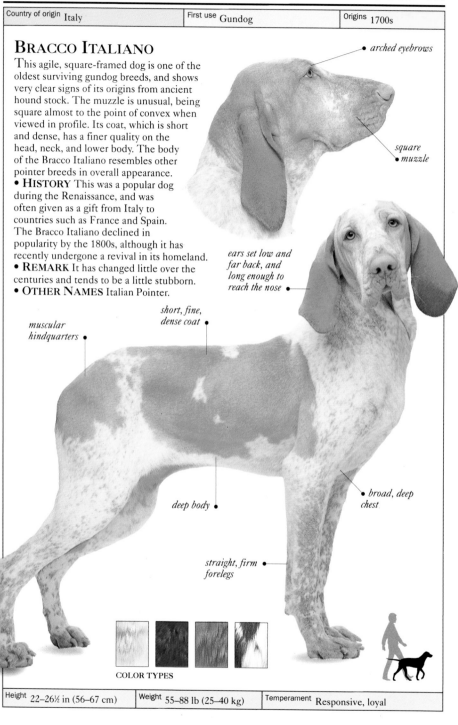

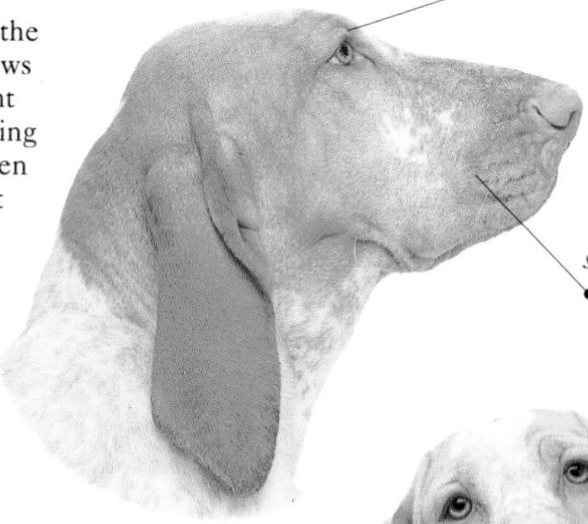
arched eyebrows
square muzzle

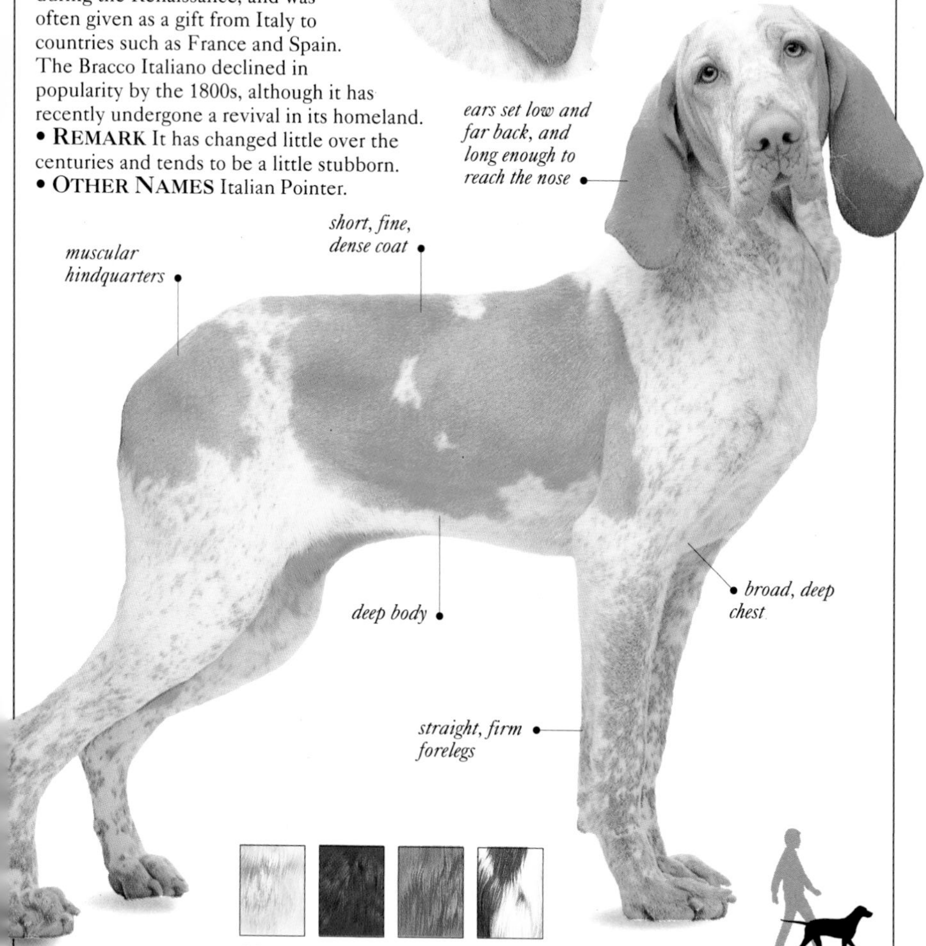
ears set low and far back, and long enough to reach the nose
short, fine, dense coat
muscular hindquarters
deep body
broad, deep chest
straight, firm forelegs

COLOR TYPES

Height 22–26½ in (56–67 cm)	Weight 55–88 lb (25–40 kg)	Temperament Responsive, loyal

Country of origin	First use	Origins
Spain	Hunting deer	1600s

PERDIGUERO DE BURGOS

This breed of pointer has a massive head in relation to a rather slender, well-muscled body. Its coat is short and finely textured, being exclusively liver and white in coloration, often with prominent ticking.

- **HISTORY** The ancestry of this dog is not certain, but it undoubtedly belongs to an old breed, possibly related to the ancient Sabueso Hound.
- **REMARK** The earlier form of this dog hunted deer; the quarry of today's breed is more likely to be partridge.
- **OTHER NAMES** Spanish Pointer.

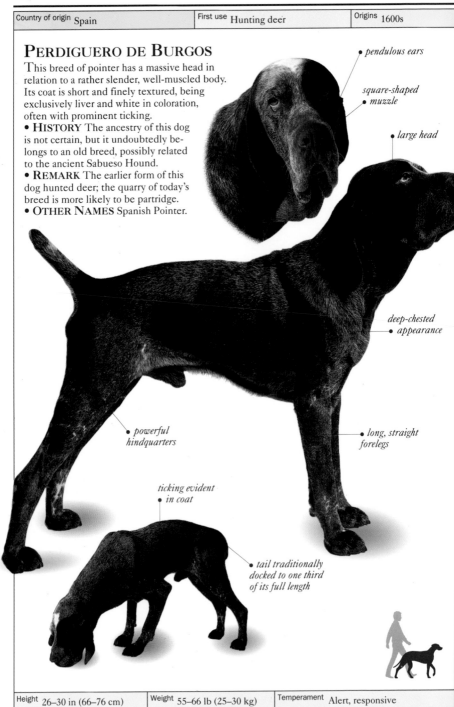

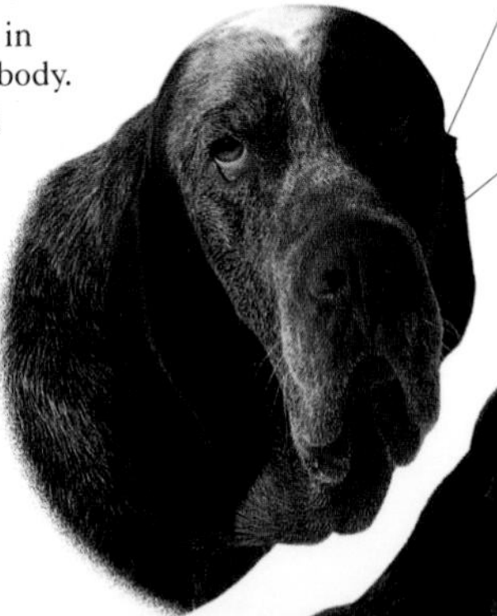
pendulous ears
square-shaped muzzle

large head
deep-chested appearance
powerful hindquarters
long, straight forelegs

ticking evident in coat
tail traditionally docked to one third of its full length

Height	Weight	Temperament
26–30 in (66–76 cm)	55–66 lb (25–30 kg)	Alert, responsive

Country of origin Portugal	First use Retrieving from the sea	Origins 1500s

PORTUGUESE WATER DOG

There are two coat types associated with this breed, neither of which has an undercoat. In the first form, the hair is longish and wavy, with loose curls. In the second, the coat is shorter and thicker, and with more compact curls.

• **HISTORY** This breed is centuries old and was a valued fisherman's dog in the Algarve region of Portugal, capable of retrieving objects lost overboard and carrying messages between boats.

• **REMARK** Numbers of this breed fell to just 50 in 1960, although it is now widespread in Europe.

• **OTHER NAMES** Cão de Agua.

long, wavy hair

characteristic plume on tail
short, straight, muscular neck
profuse coat
angulated hindquarters
deep chest
powerful forelegs

COLOR TYPES

Height 16–22 in (41–56 cm)	Weight 35–55 lb (16–25 kg)	Temperament Obedient, friendly

Country of origin	First use	Origins
Portugal	Hunting and retrieving game	1200s

PERDIGUERO PORTUGUESO

This is a medium-size breed of pointer, which is still kept for working purposes in its homeland. The long-haired form is now relatively scarce, with the smooth-coated type predominating. It has a broad head and a distinctive stop to the nose.

• **HISTORY** So effective are the hunting abilities of this ancient breed that game suffered a dramatic decline. An ownership ban, from which only royalty was exempt, was imposed in the late 16th century.

• **REMARK** The name "Perdiguero" comes from the Portuguese word for partridge, the breed's chief quarry.

• **OTHER NAMES** Portuguese Pointer.

large, preferably dark eyes
broad, black nostrils

ears have round tips
smooth, short coat

triangular ears
tail traditionally docked
round, straight, powerful neck
short, broad body
well-arched toes

COLOR TYPES

Height	Weight	Temperament
20½–22 in (52–56 cm)	35–60 lb (16–27 kg)	Active, obedient

HERDING DOGS

ORIGINALLY, HERDING DOGS tended to be large and powerful, capable of protecting livestock from predators such as wolves and bears. As such threats declined, smaller, more agile breeds were adopted to take a more active role in controlling the movements of the herds. With various exceptions, such as the German Shepherd Dog (see p.119), European herding breeds are less likely to be seen in the show ring, or in the home as family pets, but are still used for herding purposes. However, this is changing. Some breeds, such as the Tervuren (see p.128) are losing their popularity as herders, but finding new roles as companions and show dogs.

Country of origin USA	First use Herding sheep	Origins 1800s

AUSTRALIAN SHEPHERD

This attractive, long-haired breed has a bobtail and a striking, and remarkably varied, coat coloration: every dog has a unique pattern of markings. Eye coloration, too, is highly variable.

• **HISTORY** Despite its name, this breed was developed mainly in the USA. It is descended from collie stock, possibly crossed with other herding breeds. Its original ancestry can be traced back to the Basque region of France and Spain.

• **REMARK** This breed is highly prized wherever obedience is of vital importance, such as in search and rescue work.

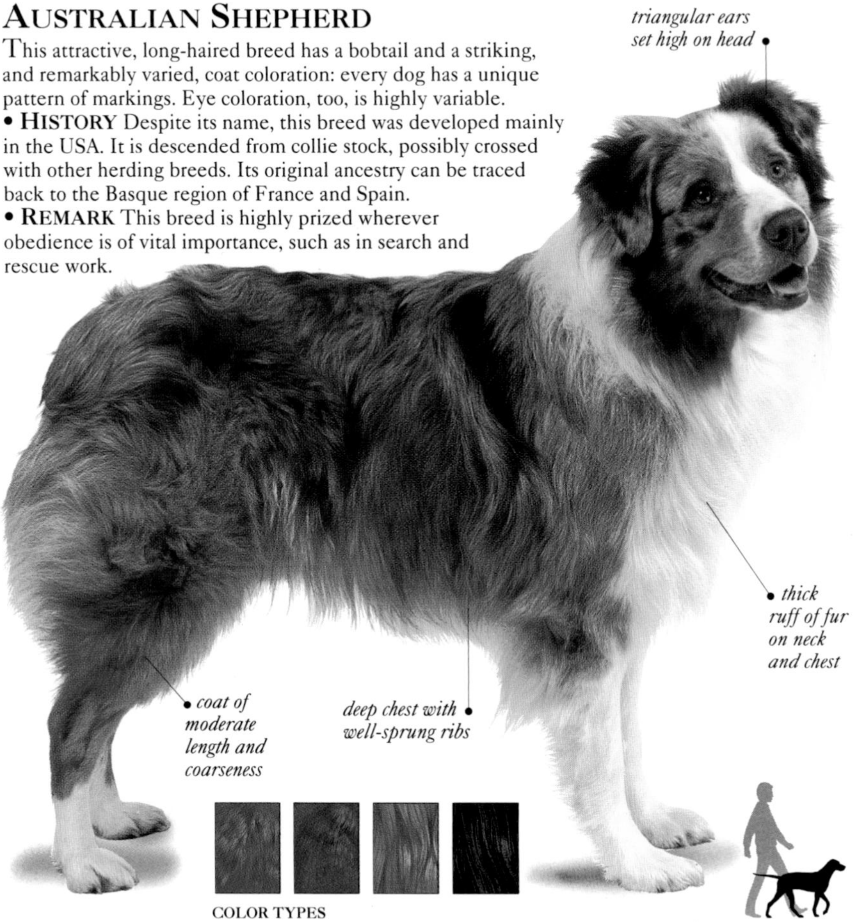
triangular ears set high on head
thick ruff of fur on neck and chest
coat of moderate length and coarseness
deep chest with well-sprung ribs
COLOR TYPES

Height 18–23 in (46–58.5 cm)	Weight 35–70 lb (16–32 kg)	Temperament Active, intelligent

Country of origin Great Britain	First use Herding sheep	Origins 1500s

Bearded Collie

Not dissimilar to the Old English Sheepdog in appearance (see p.110), the Bearded Collie is much lighter and more slender in shape. It has a medium-length, tousled coat covering an agile and athletic strong-limbed body.

• **History** The Bearded Collie is thought to have descended from Polish Lowland Sheepdogs brought to Scotland centuries ago by visiting sailors. Although an attentive and industrious worker, it seems to be adapting very well to its increasing popularity as a family pet and companion.

• **Remark** Hardy and well protected, it is quite content to sleep outdoors.

• **Other Names** Beardie.

flat, broad skull

ears largely covered with hair
straight, level back
tail set low on back
strong, well-boned forelegs
legs covered with shaggy hair

medium-size ears
oval-shaped feet with hair between toes
medium-length, harsh coat

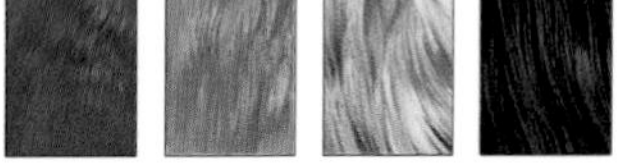

COLOR TYPES

Height 20–22 in (51–56 cm)	Weight 40–60 lb (18–27 kg)	Temperament Friendly, active

Country of origin	First use	Origins
Great Britain	Herding sheep	1700s

BORDER COLLIE

This graceful breed can be recognized by its distinctive black and white coloration, although a variety of colors are permissible. Its coat may be moderately long or smooth.

• **HISTORY** A standard was not approved by the Kennel Club of Britain until 1976, but this dog had long been valued by farmers in the border region between Scotland and England as an excellent sheep herder.

• **REMARK** The Border Collie has an effortless gait, lifting its feet just a short distance off the ground.

fairly broad skull
tapering muzzle
well-developed nostrils
white coloration should never predominate
broad, muscular hindquarters slope down to tail

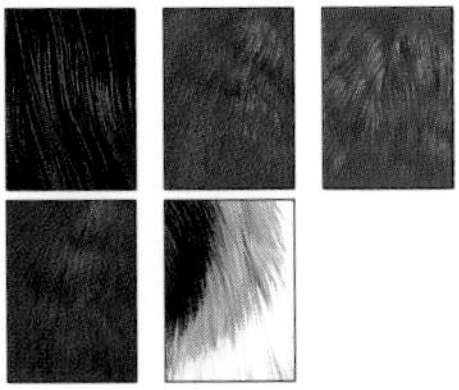
COLOR TYPES

Height	Weight	Temperament
18–21 in (46–54 cm)	30–44 lb (14–20 kg)	Intelligent, active

Country of origin	First use	Origins
Great Britain	Herding cattle	1960s

LANCASHIRE HEELER

Although short in the leg, the Lancashire Heeler is a strong, well-proportioned working dog with a firm, level back and an engaging personality.

• **HISTORY** This breed derives from Welsh Corgis crossed with Manchester Terriers, which imparted their coloration and vermin-catching skills.

• **REMARK** The Lancashire Heeler has strong natural herding instincts.

• **OTHER NAMES** Ormskirk Terrier.

tan coloration fades with age
tail set high and carried forward in a slight curve
firm, level back
well-spaced, erect ears
feet turn slightly outward

Height	Weight	Temperament
10–12 in (25–31 cm)	6–13 lb (3–6 kg)	Obedient, intelligent

Country of origin Great Britain	First use Herding sheep	Origins 1500s

ROUGH COLLIE

Truly spectacular in full coat, the Rough Collie is one of the most glamorous breeds in the world. It is unmistakable with its profuse mane and frill, and has a highly intelligent expression.

• **HISTORY** Essentially the same breed as the Smooth Collie (opposite), it derived from the same Scottish working collie stock. It enjoyed royal patronage when Queen Victoria kept the breed at Balmoral Castle, Scotland.

• **REMARK** The greatest of all "movie star" dogs, "Lassie," was a Rough Collie.

• **OTHER NAMES** Rough-haired Collie.

small, tipped ears
long, tapering muzzle

bushy tail
top of the skull is flat

long body
pronounced frill between forelegs

COLOR TYPES

Height 20–24 in (51–61 cm)	Weight 40–65 lb (18–30 kg)	Temperament Loyal, responsive

Country of origin Great Britain	First use Herding sheep	Origins 1500s

SMOOTH COLLIE

Easily distinguishable from its rough-coated relative (see p.108), the Smooth Collie has a short, somewhat harsh, flat coat, as well as a dense, weather-resistant undercoat. The blue merle (blue and black mixed with tan) form often shows blue coloration in the eyes.
• **HISTORY** This breed's history can be traced back to a dog called Trefoil, a tri-color collie born in 1873.
• **REMARK** The Smooth Collie has not enjoyed the popularity of the rough form.
• **OTHER NAMES** Smooth-haired Collie.

ears erect when alert, with tips hanging forward

sweet expression in almond-shaped eyes
powerful, arched neck
muscular thighs
straight, muscular forelegs

COLOR TYPES

Height 20–24 in (51–61 cm)	Weight 40–65 lb (18–29.5 kg)	Temperament Loyal, responsive

Country of origin Great Britain	First use Herding sheep	Origins 1700s

SHETLAND SHEEPDOG

Noticeably smaller in size than a Rough Collie (see p.108), this small but glamorous sheep-dog has a double coat with a distinctive frill and mane around its head.
• **HISTORY** Bred originally on the Shetland Islands off Scotland, this sheepdog is now common around the world.
• **REMARK** Affectionate with its owner, this dog does not take so readily to strangers.

small ears set close together
distinctive mane

level back
feathering on back of forelegs

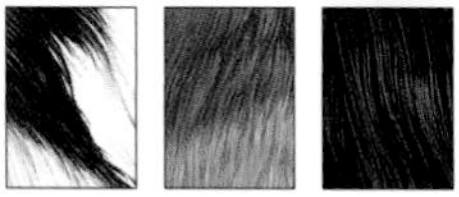

COLOR TYPES

Height 14–14½ in (35–37 cm)	Weight 14–16 lb (6–7 kg)	Temperament Active, intelligent

Country of origin	First use	Origins
Great Britain	Herding sheep	1800s

Old English Sheepdog

The immense, shaggy coat, which is the distinctive feature of this breed, requires a great deal of grooming. Thick-set and muscular, this strong, square-built dog has great symmetry and a distinctive rolling gait.

• **History** Developed from drover's dogs in the 1800s, it is probably related to shepherd's dogs found in mainland Europe, such as the Bergamasco (see p.135).

• **Remark** This breed requires plenty of exercise if it is to remain healthy and happy.

• **Other Names** Bobtail.

hair extends over eyes

small ears on side of head, hidden by hair
coat is shaggy, not curly
thick-set, compact body
strong, straight forelegs
small, round feet

COLOR TYPES

Height	Weight	Temperament
22–24 in (56–61 cm)	66 lb (30 kg)	Active, protective

Country of origin	First use	Origins
Great Britain	Droving cattle	1200 BC

CARDIGAN WELSH CORGI

The Cardigan is distinguishable from the Pembroke Welsh Corgi (below) by its long, fox's brush tail. The Cardigan's ears are also larger and more widely spaced, and the feet tend to have a more round appearance.

- **HISTORY** The Corgi is traditionally a droving dog; its small size enabled it to dodge in and bite the lower legs of cattle, forcing them to move where required.
- **REMARK** Until the 1850s, the Cardigan Welsh Corgi was the only dog known to be kept in some Welsh communities.

erect, round ears
wide skull and foxlike head
powerful, muscular neck
long body in relation to height

COLOR TYPES

Height	Weight	Temperament
10½–12½ in (27–32 cm)	25–38 lb (11–17 kg)	Active, obedient

Country of origin	First use	Origins
Great Britain	Droving cattle	1000s

PEMBROKE WELSH CORGI

In spite of its size, this bold, inquisitive dog is still powerful and has a surprisingly loud bark. Unlike the Cardigan (above), the Pembroke has only a short tail, and it is bred in a more restricted color range.

- **HISTORY** The Welsh Corgi may be related to the Swedish Vallhund (see p.132), but its precise origins are not known. Its presence has been recorded in Wales since the Domesday Book of 1086.
- **REMARK** This breed is now internationally known as the favorite pet of Queen Elizabeth II.

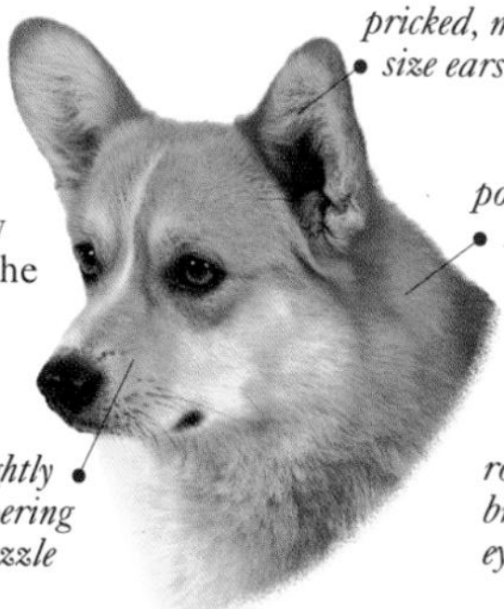
pricked, medium-size ears
powerful neck
slightly tapering muzzle

flat skull
round, brown eyes
short tail and strong hind-quarters

COLOR TYPES

Height	Weight	Temperament
10–12 in (25–31 cm)	20–26 lb (10–12.5 kg)	Active, obedient

Country of origin Australia	First use Herding cattle	Origins 1800s

AUSTRALIAN CATTLE DOG

This strong, compact dog was first developed in Australia to drive herds of cattle on long, arduous treks to market. Its key qualities are its amazing stamina, versatility, and endurance. It is essentially silent when working, controlling cattle with precision and the minimum of effort.

• **HISTORY** A number of different breeds contributed to its ancestry. The most significant of these was the dingo, the feral dog of the Aboriginal people, which was too unruly to perform the task of cattle-driving competently.

• **REMARK** This breed holds the record for canine longevity – 29 years.

• **OTHER NAMES** Australian Queensland Heeler, Blue Heeler.

broad, erect ears
prominent black nose
thick-set neck

puppies are born white, due to Dalmatian blood in ancestry

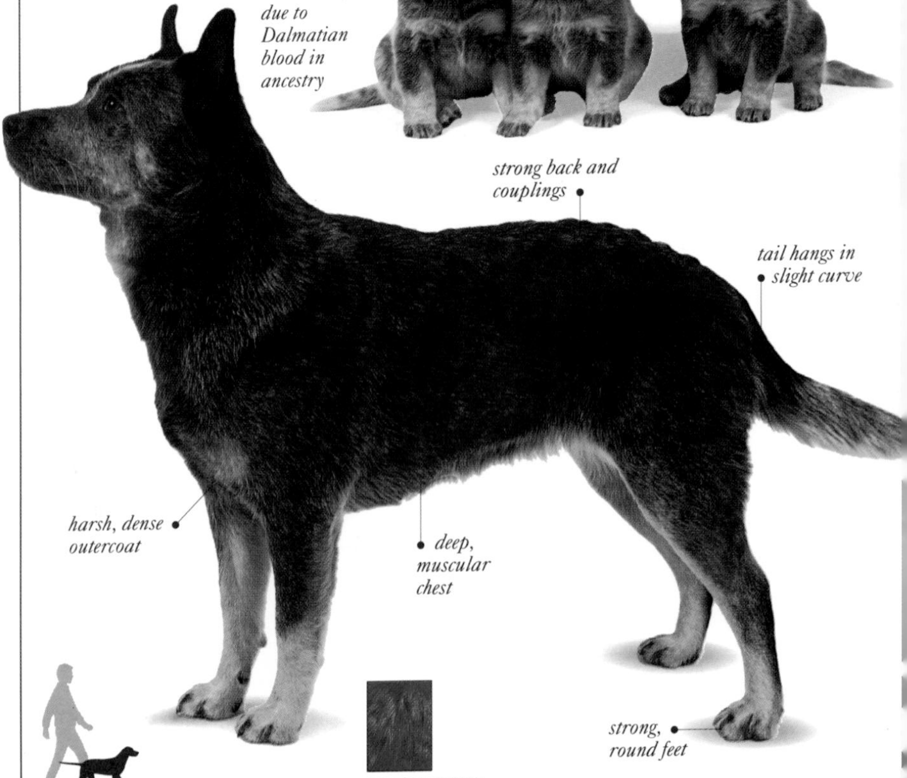
strong back and couplings
tail hangs in slight curve
harsh, dense outercoat
deep, muscular chest
strong, round feet

COLOR TYPES

Height 17–20 in (43–51 cm)	Weight 35–45 lb (16–20 kg)	Temperament Bold, determined

Country of origin Australia	First use Herding livestock	Origins 1800s

AUSTRALIAN KELPIE

The work rate of this tough little sheepdog has become a legend in its native Australia. An economical, compact body, well-muscled but lean, is supported on strong, firm-boned legs. The Kelpie has a tough, weather-resistant outercoat and a short, dense undercoat. A wide range of coat colors is seen; black dogs are sometimes known as barbs.

• **HISTORY** A New South Wales grazier called Allen imported a pair of English collies into Australia in 1870. These dogs mated on board ship and one of the offspring was bred with a local black-and-tan bitch named *Kelpie*. Her progeny became the basis of this breed, which was first exhibited in 1908.

• **REMARK** Australian Kelpies seem to have the ability to mesmerize and control sheep simply by staring at them.

• **OTHER NAMES** Kelpie, Barb.

very erect, pointed ears
lively, intelligent eyes

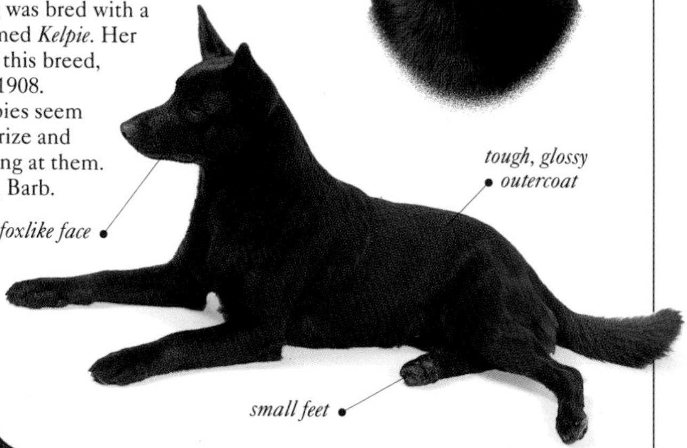
tough, glossy outercoat
foxlike face
small feet

well-developed hindquarters
powerful neck
broad chest
body slightly longer than dog is tall

COLOR TYPES

Height 17–20 in (43–51 cm)	Weight 25–45 lb (10–20 kg)	Temperament Keen, responsive

Country of origin Finland	First use Herding reindeer	Origins 1600s

FINNISH LAPPHUND

This medium-size breed is typically spitz-like in appearance, with a beautiful, fluffy coat occurring in a large range of colors.

• **HISTORY** Originally kept by the Lapp people, who have long inhabited northernmost Europe, it is probably related to the Samoyed evolved by the Samoyede tribes of the Urals.

• **REMARK** In the particolor dog, the colored area must predominate, with small and symmetrical white markings.

• **OTHER NAMES** Lapinkoira.

square skull
foxlike head
mane of longer hair evident on neck
muscular hindquarters

COLOR TYPES

Height 18–20½ in (46–52 cm)	Weight 44–47 lb (20–21 kg)	Temperament Responsive, intelligent

Country of origin Finland	First use Herding reindeer	Origins 1600s

LAPINPOROKOIRA

This herding dog has a loosely curled tail, which may be held against the thigh rather than over the back. Its body is longer than that of the Finnish Lapphund (above).

• **HISTORY** Having been kept primarily as a working breed for many years, in the 1960s a standard was at last created for the Lapinporokoira by the Finnish Kennel Club.

• **REMARK** Working dogs from the north are brought south to mate with bitches; male offspring are then sent north to herd. This helps to maintain the breed's working instinct.

• **OTHER NAMES** Lapland Reindeer Dog.

widely spaced, erect ears
coarse outercoat in wide range of colors
relatively short muzzle
long tail, well-covered with hair
soft, woolly undercoat

COLOR TYPES

Height 19–22 in (48–56 cm)	Weight 60–66 lb (27–30 kg)	Temperament Alert, responsive

Country of origin France	First use Hunting boar	Origins 1500s

Beauceron

One of the best-known sheepdogs in France, the Beauceron is somewhat reminiscent of the Dobermann (see pp.250–51) in overall appearance, but can be distinguished by its long tail and double dewclaws. In France, its ears are often cropped.

• **History** Originally used for hunting wild boar, its intelligent and adaptable nature was later employed for herding sheep, and even for carrying messages during wartime.

• **Remark** The alternative name of Bas Rouge refers to the tan markings on the legs of this breed.

• **Other Names** Bas Rouge, Berger de Beauce.

reddish tan color on lower legs
tail carried low

black nose
long muzzle

powerful neck
smooth, flat coat with fringes on flanks, legs, and tail
double dewclaws on hind legs
round feet with black nails

COLOR TYPES

Height 25–28 in (64–71 cm)	Weight 66–85 lb (30–39 kg)	Temperament Loyal, protective

Country of origin France	First use Guarding and herding stock	Origins 1200s

BRIARD

This large, muscular breed of French sheepdog is one of the oldest of northern Europe. Although a fierce and protective guardian of its flock, it is an amiable giant, easy to train, affectionate, and patient with children. One of the most unusual features of the Briard is its double dewclaws. These must always be present on the hind legs of show dogs. The muscular build of the Briard means that when running it should appear to have an effortless stride, seeming to glide over the ground. Its slightly wavy and very dry coat gives protection against the elements but needs good grooming.

• **HISTORY** The Briard is named after the French province of Brie, although the breed appears to have been kept all over France. They were used not only for herding stock, but also for guarding their charges against wolves.

• **REMARK** A number of Briards were taken to the USA after World War I, but it was not until the 1970s that the breed started to become popular in Britain.

• **OTHER NAMES** Berger de Brie.

COLOR TYPES

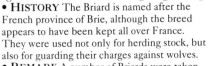

rectangular skull
strong, powerful forelegs

prominent, black nose
coat not less than 3 in (7 cm) on body

Height 23–27 in (57–69 cm)	Weight 75 lb (34 kg)	Temperament Lively, protective

hair thinly covers eyes
occasional white hairs
ears covered by long hair
slightly wavy, very dry coat

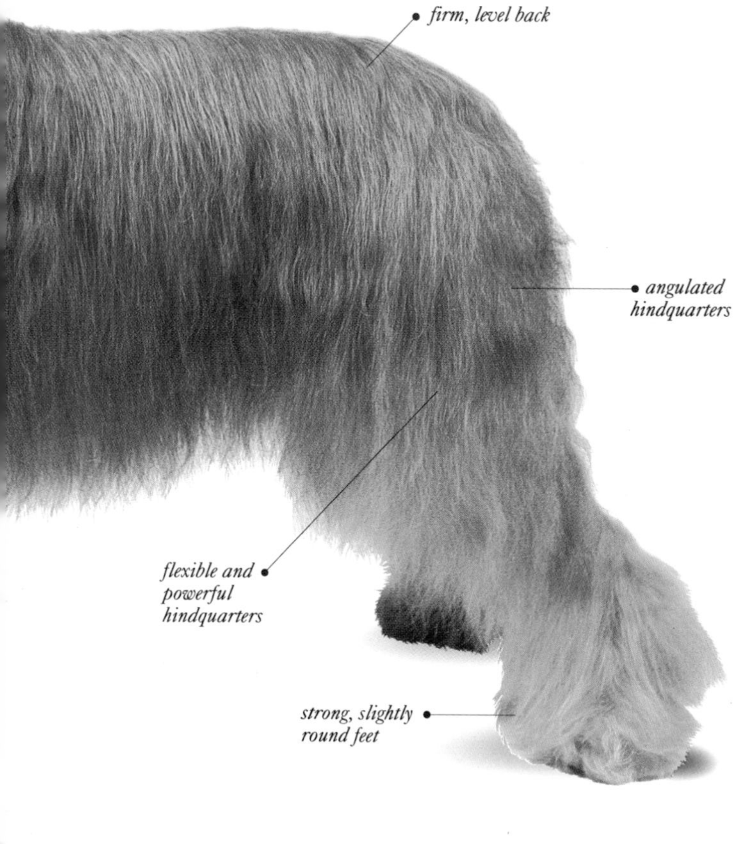
firm, level back
angulated hindquarters
flexible and powerful hindquarters
strong, slightly round feet

Country of origin	First use	Origins
France	Herding sheep	800s

Berger de Picard

This is the oldest of the French sheepdogs, and is thought to have been brought to northern France around the 9th century. In size, the Berger de Picard is about as tall as a German Shepherd, with a rough, durable outercoat and a thick, waterproof undercoat. The breed is usually fawn or gray in coloration, the white markings confined to the chest and legs.

• **History** The Celts are thought to have introduced the Berger de Picard into France. Its origins, however, are obscure, and the few that remain in France are largely working dogs. The breed is seen infrequently outside its native France.

• **Remark** Members of this breed make excellent and affectionate housedogs. They tend, however, to be a little surly and defensive of their home territory.

• **Other Names** Picardy Shepherd.

large head with powerful muzzle

tail slightly curled at tip

well-spaced, upright ears
prominent chest
muscular thighs
rough, tousled coat, never curly
solidly boned legs

COLOR TYPES

Height	Weight	Temperament
21½–26 in (55–66 cm)	50–70 lb (23–32 kg)	Lively, adaptable

Country of origin Germany	First use Herding sheep	Origins 1800s

GERMAN SHEPHERD DOG

With a slightly elongated body and a strong, muscular build, the German Shepherd ranks among the most popular breeds in the world. A versatile and enthusiastic worker, it is used in many capacities, including search and rescue and as Seeing Eye dogs. At one time, short-, long-, and wire-haired forms were recognized, but now only the short-haired form is accepted for show purposes. Occasionally, long-haired German Shepherds are still produced.

• **HISTORY** Although its working ancestry dates a great deal further back, the modern German Shepherd was first exhibited at a show in Hanover, Germany, in 1882.

• **REMARK** White coloration is not favored in this breed. Only small light markings are permitted.

• **OTHER NAMES** Deutscher Schäferhund, Alsatian.

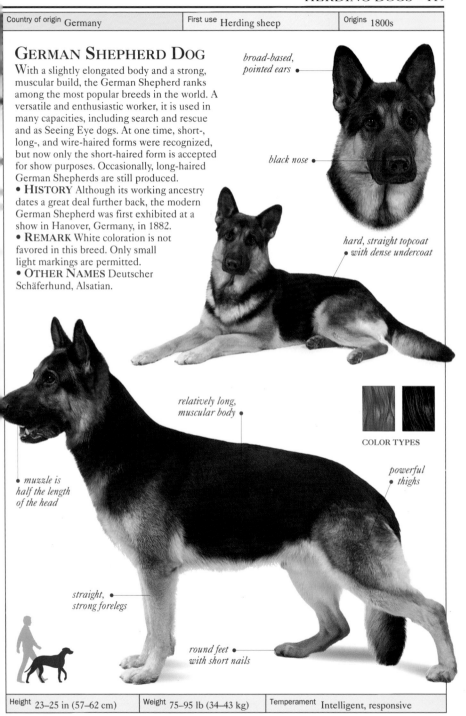

broad-based, pointed ears
black nose

hard, straight topcoat with dense undercoat

relatively long, muscular body
muzzle is half the length of the head
powerful thighs
straight, strong forelegs
round feet with short nails

COLOR TYPES

Height 23–25 in (57–62 cm)	Weight 75–95 lb (34–43 kg)	Temperament Intelligent, responsive

Country of origin Germany	First use Guarding estates	Origins 1200s

Hovawart

COLOR TYPES

This breed has a long, thick, weatherproof coat. It is lightly built with a strong physique. In appearance, the breed is similar to the Flat-coated Retriever (see p.67), but there is no direct relationship between them. Indeed, the Hovawart is not a gundog, but a traditional guardian of sheep and other domestic stock. It exhibits a highly developed protective nature and displays great loyalty.

• **History** The recent development of the Hovawart is credited to Kurt König, a German breeder. The breed was recognized by the German Kennel Club in 1936. This dog was first seen in the USA during the 1980s but is not AKC recognized.

• **Remark** The name "Hovawart" comes from the German word, *hofe-wart,* meaning "guardian of the estate."

strong, straight back
tail extends past the hocks
feathering on back of forelegs
oval feet
powerful hind legs
color of claws matches coat

Height 23–28 in (58–70 cm)	Weight 55–90 lb (25–41 kg)	Temperament Alert, protective

pendulous ears
color of nose matches coat
broad, convex forehead
long topcoat with straight or slightly wavy undercoat
dark, oval eyes
well-feathered tail, held high when excited
slightly sloping pasterns
a few white hairs are permissible at end of tail

Country of origin Germany	First use Droving cattle	Origins 1400s

GIANT SCHNAUZER

This is the largest of the three breeds of schnauzer, and also the most recent addition to the group. The Giant Schnauzer is a powerful, muscular dog. Its height at the shoulders should match its body length, giving it a rather square shape when viewed in profile.

• **HISTORY** It is likely that the Giant Schnauzer was developed from rough-coated cattle dogs that were mated with smaller schnauzers. The breed was first exhibited at a show in Munich, Germany, in 1909, under the name of the Russian Bear Schnauzer. It was also known as the Munich Schnauzer for a brief period during its early development.

• **REMARK** The top coat of the Giant Schnauzer is especially important for show purposes. It must be harsh and wiry in texture, with no tendency toward softness. About twice a year, the coat needs to be stripped to remove dead hairs.

• **OTHER NAMES** Riesenschnauzer.

round
feet with
dark nails

flat forehead

chin whiskers
and stubby
mustache
deep chest
strong, rather
square profile
muscular
forelegs

COLOR TYPES

Height 23½–27½ in (60–70 cm)	Weight 70–77 lb (32–35 kg)	Temperament Loyal, protective

Country of origin Poland	First use Herding sheep	Origins 1500s

Polish Lowland Sheepdog

This breed looks a little like the Bearded Collie (see p.106), but it is smaller. Some are born without a tail, but if a pup is born with a tail, it is docked.

- **HISTORY** After World War II, the breed was saved from extinction by a Polish veterinarian who had two dogs and six bitches that survived the war.
- **REMARK** This dog is said to have an excellent memory.
- **OTHER NAME** Polski Owczarek Nizinny.

COLOR TYPES

medium-size head
thick, shaggy coat
rectangular profile

dark nose with wide nostrils

Height 16–20 in (41–51 cm)	Weight 30–35 lb (14–16 kg)	Temperament Alert, affectionate

Country of origin Netherlands	First use Herding sheep	Origins 1700s

Schapendoes

The Schapendoes, a native of Holland, has a long, straight, powerful back. A dense, shaggy coat gives it a friendly appearance, although as a working dog it is a hardy and fearless herder and guardian of its flock.

- **HISTORY** There is now no record of the early origins of this dog. It is believed to be a very old breed with a similar descent to that of the Briard (see pp.116–17) and the Bergamasco (see p.135).
- **REMARK** The decline in sheep herding has seen this dog's numbers fall.
- **OTHER NAMES** Dutch Sheepdog.

broad skull

ears flat to head
tail raised when dog is alert
broad, deep chest

COLOR TYPES

Height 17–20 in (43–51 cm)	Weight 33 lb (15 kg)	Temperament Active, friendly

Country of origin Netherlands	First use Herding stock	Origins 1700s

DUTCH SHEPHERD DOG

A keen, alert expression graces the finely chiseled face of this hardworking and agile herding dog. The Dutch Shepherd is officially recognized as having three distinctly different coat types: long-haired, rough-haired, and short-haired. It occurs in various shades of brindle, such as yellow, red, and blue, and its coloration lightens as it grows older.

• **HISTORY** It is likely that this dog is descended from the Groenendael, one of the Belgian shepherd dog breeds (see p.126), and, apart from coloration, the two breeds are judged by the same standard.

• **REMARK** Short-tailed pups are often born, but these are not acceptable for show purposes.

• **OTHER NAMES** Hollandse Herdershond.

long, parallel, well-muscled forelegs
medium-length muzzle with prominent nostrils

triangular, erect ears, set high on head
slightly sloping rump
broad, deep chest
when resting, tail hangs down with tip slightly upward
arched toes with rounded shape to forefeet

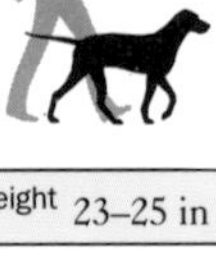

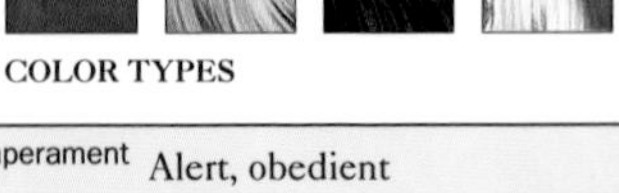

COLOR TYPES

Height 23–25 in (58–64 cm)	Weight 66 lb (30 kg)	Temperament Alert, obedient

Country of origin Netherlands	First use Improving dog stocks	Origins 1900s

SAARLOOS WOLFHOUND

Unmistakably similar to a wolf in appearance, this dog still retains a strong pack instinct and needs firm handling as a result, due in particular to its large size and strong-willed nature.

• **HISTORY** This powerful breed was developed in the Netherlands by Leendert Saarloos, who noted that contemporary dogs had become weakened with hip dysplasia and similar conditions. He resolved to rectify the situation and created this breed by crossing a German Shepherd Dog back to a wolf.

• **REMARK** Saarloos died in 1969, just six years before his breed was accepted by the Dutch Kennel Club.

erect ears, broad at base and pointed at tips

almond-shaped, intelligent eyes
long, well-muscled back
ruff of longer hair may be evident around neck
short and very dense coat

slightly domed skull
skull tapers down to nose, with only a slight stop
prominent, dark nose

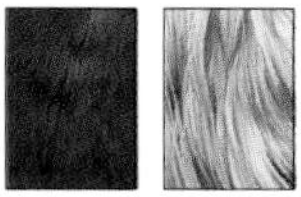

COLOR TYPES

Height 27½–29½ in (70–75 cm)	Weight 79–90 lb (36–41 kg)	Temperament Shy, independent

Country of origin	First use	Origins
Belgium	Herding stock	1200s

GROENENDAEL

Its characteristic black coat easily distinguishes the Groenendael from the other three breeds typically grouped under the general heading of Belgian shepherd dogs (see pp.126–29). These dogs are all of a similar type, differing only in terms of their coloration and coat length.

• **HISTORY** The breeding of the Groenendael began by chance in about 1890. Nicholas Rose, owner of the Belgian Café du Groenendael, bred a black puppy, and obtained another. This pair formed the basis of the breed.

• **REMARK** In the USA the AKC recognizes these Belgian breeds as three separate breeds; the Belgian Sheepdog, the Belgian Malinois, and the Belgian Tevuren.

• **OTHER NAMES** Chien de Berger Belge.

long head
round forefeet

slightly elongated neck

moderately harsh, long, straight outercoat
ruff around neck
males have longer coats than females
thick, springy soles
strong, short pasterns

Height	Weight	Temperament
22–26 in (56–66 cm)	62 lb (28 kg)	Obedient, loyal

Country of origin	First use	Origins
Belgium	Herding and guarding stock	1200s

LAEKENOIS

This is considered to be the rarest of the Belgian shepherd dogs, and it is still not widely recognized outside of its homeland. It can be immediately identified by its coat, which is rough and wiry, although not actually curly.

• **HISTORY** This breed was the favorite of Queen Henrietta of Belgium, and was named after the Château de Laeken where she lived. The breed was recognized in Belgium in 1897.

• **REMARK** The Laekenois served not only to guard sheep, but also linen. Linen making was an important industry in the vicinity of Bloom, near Antwerp, where the breed originated. The Lakenois guarded linen that was left in the fields to be bleached by the sun.

• **OTHER NAMES** Lackense, Chien de Berger Belge.

black shading
on muzzle

dark shading
on tail

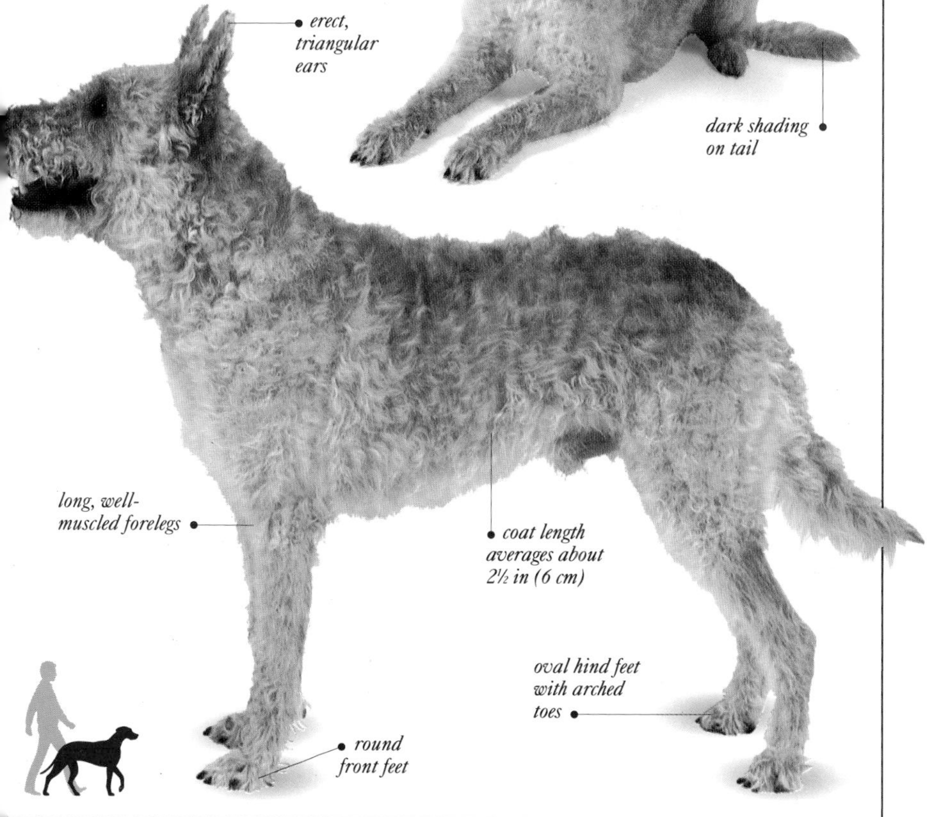
erect,
triangular
ears
long, well-
muscled forelegs
coat length
averages about
2½ in (6 cm)
oval hind feet
with arched
toes
round
front feet

Height	Weight	Temperament
22–26 in (56–66 cm)	62 lb (28 kg)	Obedient, loyal

Country of origin Belgium	First use Herding stock	Origins 1890s

TERVUREN

This member of the Belgian shepherd dog group is identical to the better-known Groenendael (see p.126) apart from its coat coloration. As a distinguishing feature, much emphasis is placed on the coloration – each of the Tervuren's hairs has a dark tip, creating an impression of blackening on the back, ribs, and shoulders, especially on a mature male. The bitch has a shorter coat than the dog.

• **HISTORY** The Tervuren was developed under the guidance of Professor Reul at the Belgian School of Veterinary Science in 1891.

• **REMARK** Sharing the same origins as all the Belgian shepherds, this robust breed's particularly close relationship with the Groenendael is demonstrated when the mating of two Groenendaels occasionally results in the birth of a Tervuren pup.

• **OTHER NAMES** Belgian Tervuren, Chien de Berger Belge.

brownish eyes and black eyelids
scissor bite

hair shorter on face than on body
long, straight topcoat; dense undercoat
long, well-muscled forelegs
well-muscled, powerful hindquarters

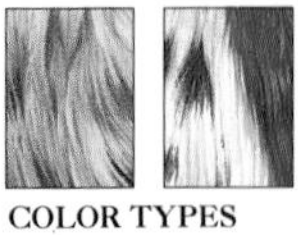

COLOR TYPES

Height 22–26 in (56–66 cm)	Weight 62 lb (28 kg)	Temperament Obedient, loyal

Country of origin Belgium	First use Herding stock	Origins 1200s

MALINOIS

The Malinois is the only Belgian shepherd dog with a short coat. It is also reputedly the oldest form, originating from the vicinity of Malines in Belgium.

• **HISTORY** Ironically, it was only when the working value of this hardy dog declined, at the end of the last century, that interest was rekindled in it.

• **REMARK** The breed obtains its full adult coloration by the time that it is 18 months old.

• **OTHER NAMES** Belgian Malinois, Chien de Berger Belge.

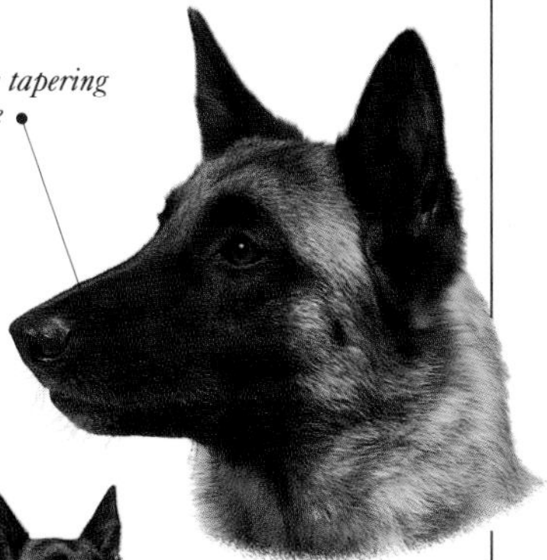
slightly tapering muzzle

thicker hair on neck
black shading on ears and muzzle preferred
neck broadens close to shoulders
hindquarters fringed with longer hair
deep, low chest
medium-length tail
short hair on lower legs
forefeet round in shape

COLOR TYPES

Height 22–26 in (56–66 cm)	Weight 62 lb (28 kg)	Temperament Obedient, loyal

Country of origin Belgium	First use Herding cattle	Origins 1600s

Bouvier des Flandres

The protective nature of this breed is reflected in its formidable appearance, and accentuated by its very impressive eyebrows, beard, and mustache. Despite this rugged appearance, the Bouvier des Flandres makes an excellent pet. It is good with children and always vigilant. Although by no means lazy, this amiable giant is quite content with moderate exercise.

• **History** The ancestry of this breed is unclear, but by the 1800s several distinct types could be found on the Flanders plain. Three forms survived until 1965, when they were finally amalgamated under one standard. A breed club was founded in Belgium in 1922.

• **Remark** Renowned for their bravery and loyalty, this dog was in active service during World War I, carrying messages and locating wounded troops.

• **Other Names** Belgian Cattle Dog.

triangular ears
bushy eyebrows
harsh beard

large head
beard and mustache

white star on chest permissible
short, round, compact feet
coat length about 2½ in (6 cm), with unkempt appearance

Height 23–27 in (58–69 cm)	Weight 59½–88 lb (27–40 kg)	Temperament Alert, responsive

hair feels coarse to the touch, and is dry and matte

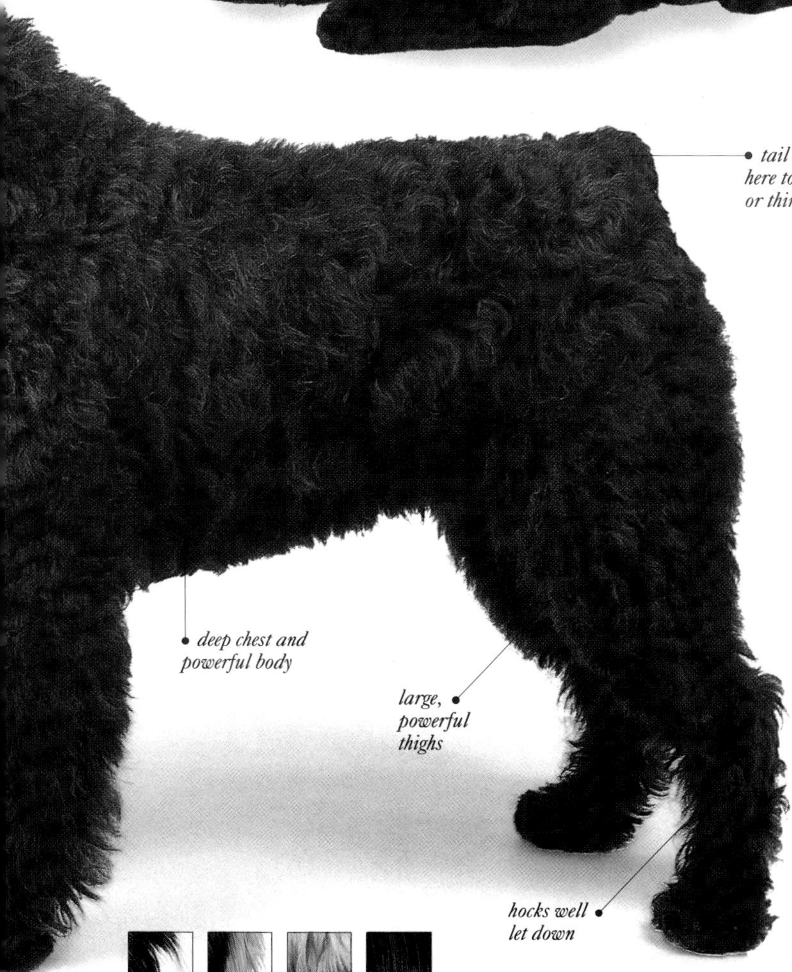
powerful neck muscles
tail docked here to second or third joint
deep chest and powerful body
large, powerful thighs
hocks well let down

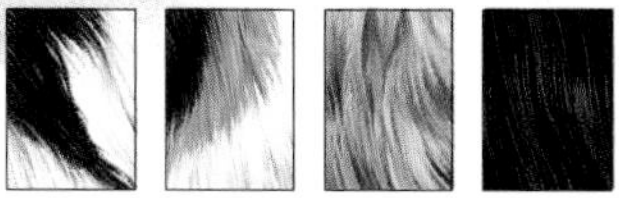

COLOR TYPES

Country of origin Sweden	First use Herding cows, ratting	Origins 500s

SWEDISH VALLHUND

Although small, the Swedish Vallhund is powerfully built with masses of energy. The breed bears a striking resemblance to the Welsh Corgi (see p.111), apart from its coat, which tends to be of more subdued coloration. In its native Sweden the main role of the Vallhund is herding.

• **HISTORY** The breed was recognized by the Swedish Kennel Club in 1948.

• **REMARK** There is some argument about whether the Vallhund is the ancestor or the descendant of the corgi breeds.

• **OTHER NAMES** Väsgötaspets.

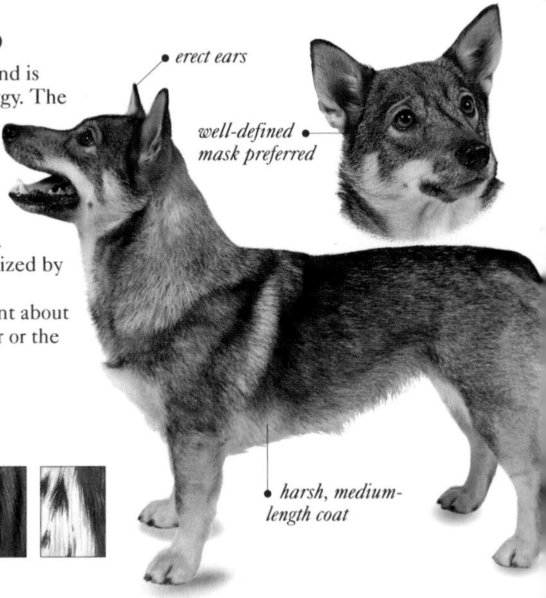
erect ears
well-defined mask preferred
harsh, medium-length coat

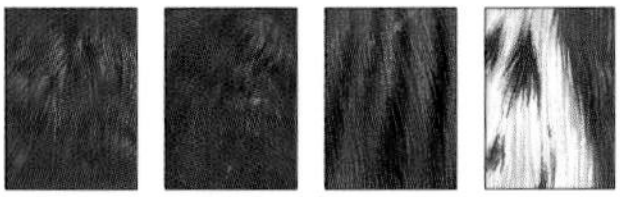

COLOR TYPES

Height 12–14 in (31–35 cm)	Weight 25–35 lb (11–15 kg)	Temperament Responsive, affectionate

Country of origin Iceland	First use Herding, pulling sleds	Origins 1800s

ICELAND DOG

This small dog has an elongated muzzle, a thick, medium-length coat, and carries its tail in a curve on its back. Although similar to other members of the spitz family, the Iceland Dog is more of a herder than a hunter.

• **HISTORY** It is thought that the Iceland Dog was first introduced to Iceland by the Norwegians, who refer to the breed as the Friaar Dog. It may share common ancestry with the Greenland Dog (see p.244).

• **REMARK** The breed came close to extinction at the turn of the century, due to an epidemic of distemper. It was saved by the efforts of Icelandic and English breeders.

• **OTHER NAMES** Icelandic Sheepdog, Friaar Dog.

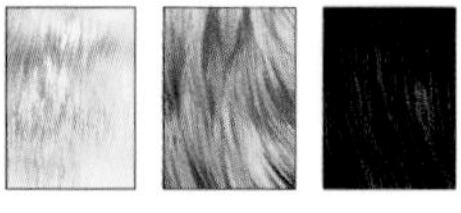

COLOR TYPES

black masking often present
widely spaced ears
thick coat carried close to body
slender legs

Height 12–16 in (31–41 cm)	Weight 20–30 lb (9–14 kg)	Temperament Lively, tough

Country of origin	Hungary	First use	Herding sheep	Origins	900s

PULI

The highly distinctive coat of this sturdy breed is traditionally corded, although in the USA recently there has been a tendency to show Pulis with coats in the wooly form.

• **HISTORY** Of uncertain origin, the Puli may have descended from the ancient Tibetan Dog. Kept in Hungary as sheepdogs, the highly obedient Pulis have since been employed successfully as police dogs.

• **REMARK** Each of the Puli's cords has to be groomed separately.

• **OTHER NAMES** Hungarian Puli.

cords can reach to the ground on adult dogs

domed head has shorter hair

COLOR TYPES

Height	14–19 in (36–48 cm)	Weight	20–40 lb (9–18 kg)	Temperament	Responsive, obedient

Country of origin	Hungary	First use	Herding cattle	Origins	1600s

PUMI

Bred from the Puli, and since crossed with Pomeranians or possibly poodles, this dog has lost the corded coat of its Hungarian ancestor. Instead, the coat is long, thick, and curly. The distinctive curl of the tail is complemented by a similar tendency in the ears.

• **HISTORY** The Pumi was first developed for driving cattle and as a watchdog. Recently, it has become popular as a companion both in its homeland and further afield.

• **REMARK** It is quite vocal, especially near strangers.

upright ears curl over at tips
tail is high set and curls forward

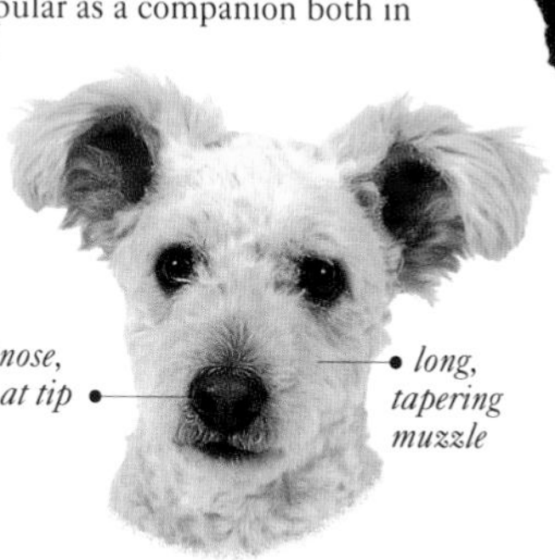
pointed nose, narrow at tip
long, tapering muzzle

COLOR TYPES

Height	13–19 in (33–48 cm)	Weight	18–29 lb (8–13 kg)	Temperament	Alert, energetic

Country of origin Former Yugoslavia	First use Guarding flocks	Origins 1600s

ISTRIAN SHEEPDOG

The iron-gray coloration of this dog, offset by darker shadings, is quite striking. The coat itself is dense and harsh, offering good protection against the elements.

• **HISTORY** Originating in Karst, in the north of the former Yugoslavia, this flock guardian is related to the Illyrian Sheepdog (below).

• **REMARK** Although now scarce in its homeland, international interest in the breed started to develop in the late 1970s.

• **OTHER NAMES** Karst Sheepdog, Krasky Ovcar.

V-shaped ears lie flat to the head
powerful chest
tapering tail covered with hair
compact, round feet

dark mask
straight back

Height 20–24 in (51–61 cm)	Weight 58–88 lb (26–40 kg)	Temperament Loyal, reserved

Country of origin Former Yugoslavia	First use Herding sheep	Origins 1200s

ILLYRIAN SHEEPDOG

The Illyrian Sheepdog shares the main physical characteristics of the Istrian Sheepdog (above), but it has more variation in coat coloration than that of its near relative.

• **HISTORY** This breed developed in Illyria, the area that is present-day Bosnia and Albania. The dog's precise origins are unknown.

• **REMARK** The Illyrian was first exported to the USA in 1975 and has proved to be popular.

• **OTHER NAMES** Sarplaninac, Sar Planina.

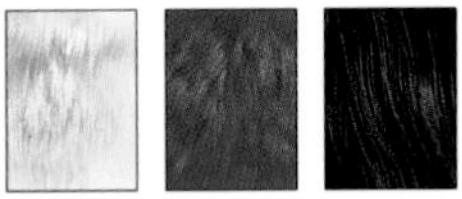
COLOR TYPES

pendant ears set high on head
dense, medium-length coat
bushy, scimitar-shaped tail
powerful, straight legs
feathering on underparts and legs
powerful hind legs

Height 22–24 in (56–61 cm)	Weight 55–80 lb (25–37kg)	Temperament Reserved, independent

Country of origin	First use	Origins
Italy	Guarding livestock	100 BC

BERGAMASCO

The distinctly corded coat of this sheepdog is not only effective protection against the elements, but it also made it harder for wolves to inflict injuries in the days when such attacks were likely in its native Italy. Coloration may be all shades of gray, with white markings (if present) comprising no more than 20 percent of the entire coat area.

• **HISTORY** This breed is named after the Bergamo region of Italy, where the stock is believed to have originated as a working sheepdog. Its precise ancestry is unknown, but it began to win major Italian dog shows in 1949 and has since become internationally popular.

• **REMARK** A thick, naturally oily undercoat protects the skin.

• **OTHER NAMES** Cane da Pastore Bergamasco.

hair forms long, wavy, strong flocks

broad skull, slightly domed between the ears
triangular ears
tail tapers to a point

facial hair is finer textured
natural parting in middle of back
well-muscled body
thick tail, carried low
oval feet with well-arched toes

Height	Weight	Temperament
22–24 in (56–61 cm)	57–84 lb (26–38 kg)	Loyal, intelligent

Country of origin Spain	First use Herding livestock	Origins 1700s

Catalan Sheepdog

Bearing some similarity to the Bearded Collie (see p.106), the Catalan Sheepdog has a prominent beard and mustache and is about the same size as an English Springer Spaniel (see p.66). Developed in the region of Catalonia in northeast Spain, two distinct forms arose, differing in coat length. The short-coated version, sometimes described as Gos d'Atura Cerda, is now very scarce. Traditionally, the ears of this sheepdog were cropped to make it appear more ferocious.

• **History** The area in which the Catalan Sheepdog evolved has a strong French influence, and this suggests a possible relationship with French dog breeds. However, nothing certain has been recorded about its origins.

• **Remark** Dogs of this adaptable breed acted as messengers and guard dogs in the Spanish Civil War.

• **Other Names** Gos d'Atura Catala.

long hair extends from top of head down the face
broad ribcage emphasizes muscular body shape

prominent, dark nose
large, thick tail set low on back

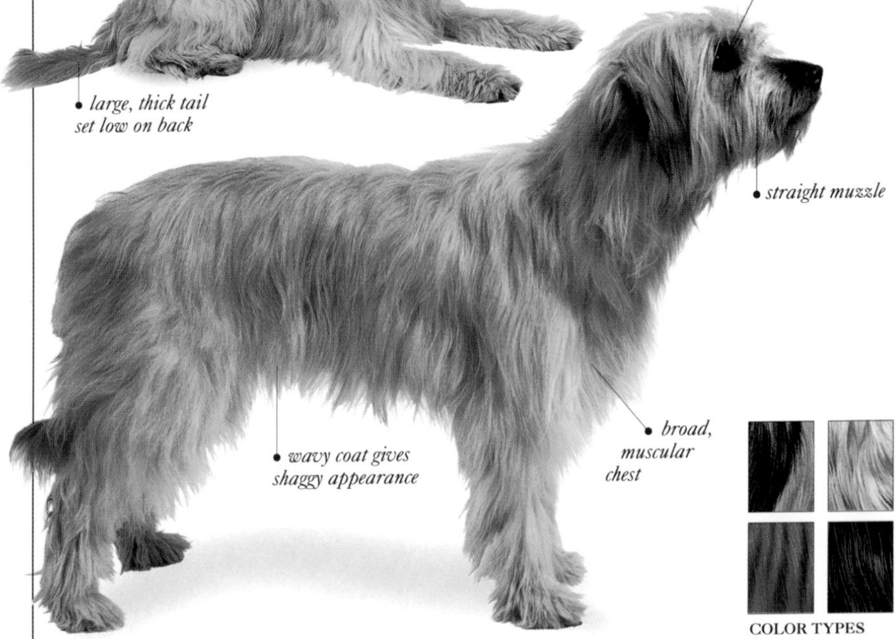
dark eyes
straight muzzle
wavy coat gives shaggy appearance
broad, muscular chest
COLOR TYPES

Height 18–20 in (46–51 cm)	Weight 40 lb (18 kg)	Temperament Brave, forceful

Country of origin Portugal	First use Herding	Origins 1800s

PORTUGUESE SHEEPDOG

This medium-size sheepdog can be variable in height, but the majority are taller than 18 in (45 cm). Its similarity to the Briard (see pp.116–17) is reflected by the presence of the hind dewclaws and a similar coat, although the Portuguese Sheepdog lacks an undercoat. Its facial expression has led to it being called the "monkey dog" in its homeland. It works not only with sheep, but is also used to guard horses, pigs, and other livestock.

- **HISTORY** Dogs of this general type have been used for working purposes for many years, but only since 1930 has their appearance become standardized. They may have originated from crossings between Pyrenean Sheepdogs and Briards, or even Catalan Sheepdogs.
- **REMARK** With a reputation for intelligence and devotion to duty, these dogs are well able to locate stock that has strayed from the herd.
- **OTHER NAMES** Cão da Serra de Aires.

dark nostrils
ears hang straight down sides of head

well-defined stop

broad head
thick "eye-brows" above dark eyes
long, slightly wavy coat
beard and mustache of long hair
powerful, prominent chest

Height 16–22 in (41–56 cm)	Weight 26–40 lb (12–18 kg)	Temperament Active, independent

HOUNDS

ORIGINALLY BRED for hunting, these medium-size dogs usually have short bicolor or tricolor coats and an athletic build. Some are bred for stamina and some for pace. They may be divided broadly into sight hounds, such as the Afghan (see p.202), and scent hounds, such as the Bloodhound (see pp.166–67), depending on their hunting technique. Some breeds are still kept solely for working purposes and may be unknown outside their local area. Hounds do not always adjust well to an urban life-style and need plenty of space for exercise. They are friendly by nature, but their hunting instincts are so strong that training them to return can pose problems.

Country of origin USA	First use Hunting deer	Origins 1700s

CATAHOULA LEOPARD DOG

This compact, well-muscled, workmanlike dog is used for a variety of purposes besides hunting. Its general appearance substantiates its affirmed hound ancestry. As a stock animal, it excels at rounding up and driving unruly cattle and pigs.

• **HISTORY** Named after the Parish of Catahoula, Louisiana, its precise ancestry is not known. It is, however, highly valued for herding semi-wild cattle and pigs found in the region.

• **REMARK** The Catahoula Leopard Dog was adopted as the state dog of Louisiana in 1979.

• **OTHER NAMES** Catahoula Hog Dog.

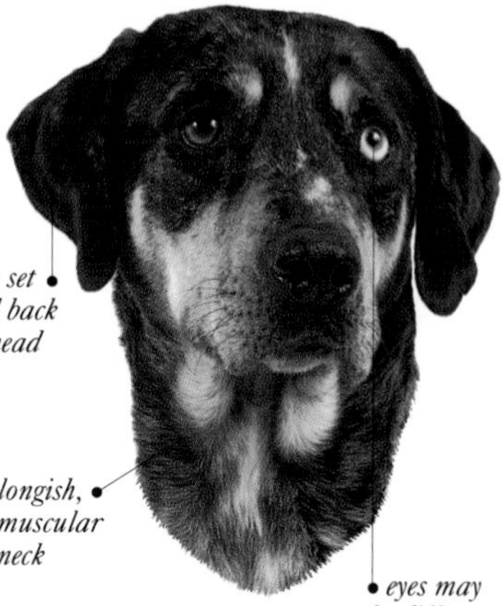
ears set well back on head
longish, muscular neck
eyes may be different colors

round tips to ears
short, dense coat

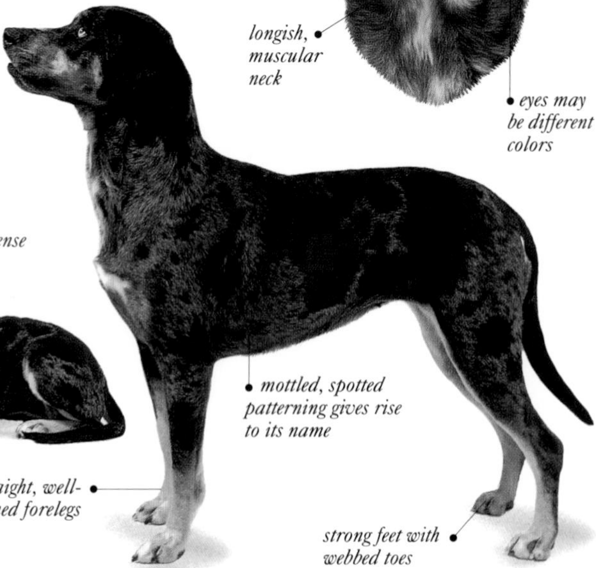
mottled, spotted patterning gives rise to its name
straight, well-boned forelegs
strong feet with webbed toes

COLOR TYPES

Height 20–26 in (51–66 cm)	Weight 40–50 lb (18–23 kg)	Temperament Affectionate, protective

Country of origin USA	First use Hunting bears	Origins 1700s

PLOTT HOUND

A long, curving tail held high and outsize ears characterize this sturdy breed. Tenacious and strong, this hound tracks game over considerable distances. Since it occasionally finds itself pitched against a cornered bear at the end of the trail, its bravery is prized as much as its tremendous stamina.

• **HISTORY** This hound is named after the Plott family, who developed the breed over several generations from their home in the USA, after emigrating from Germany in 1750.

• **REMARK** This hardy hound is still kept for hunting today.

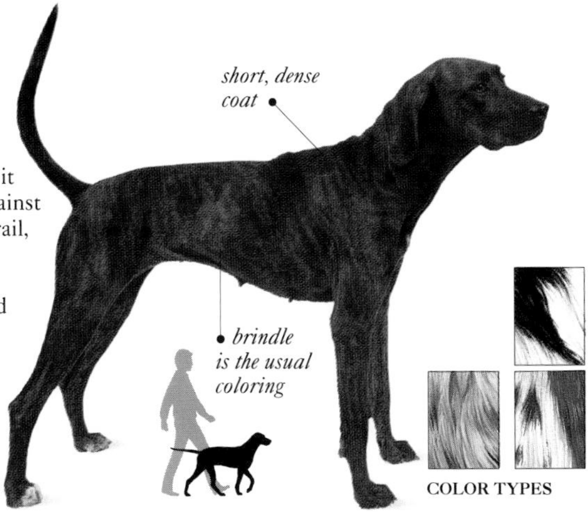
short, dense coat
brindle is the usual coloring

COLOR TYPES

Height 20–24 in (51–61 cm)	Weight 45–55 lb (20–25 kg)	Temperament Responsive, active

Country of origin USA	First use Hunting raccoons	Origins 1900s

BLUETICK COONHOUND

The distinctive blue appearance of this hound is the result of heavy black ticking in white areas of its coat. The Bluetick is actually tricolor, its coat being a combination of black, tan, and white.

• **HISTORY** Development of the Bluetick Coonhound began in the early 1900s. It is descended from French hounds, such as the Grand Bleu de Gascogne (see pp.170–71) which were brought to America during the early days of colonization. These were crossed with other hunting breeds, such as the Bloodhound.

• **REMARK** The Bluetick is described as having a "cold nose," referring to its ability to follow an old trail left by the animal being pursued.

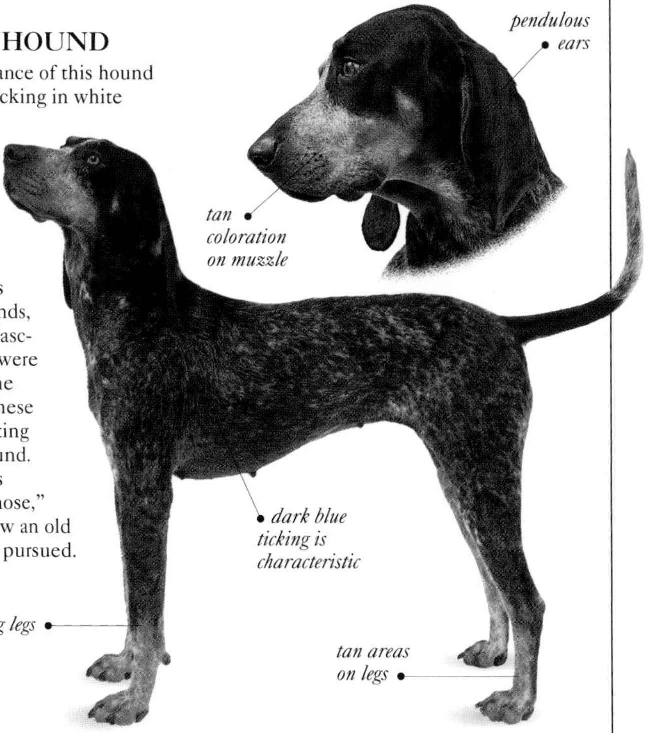
pendulous ears
tan coloration on muzzle
dark blue ticking is characteristic
long legs
tan areas on legs

Height 20–27 in (51–69 cm)	Weight 45–80 lb (20–36 kg)	Temperament Active, alert

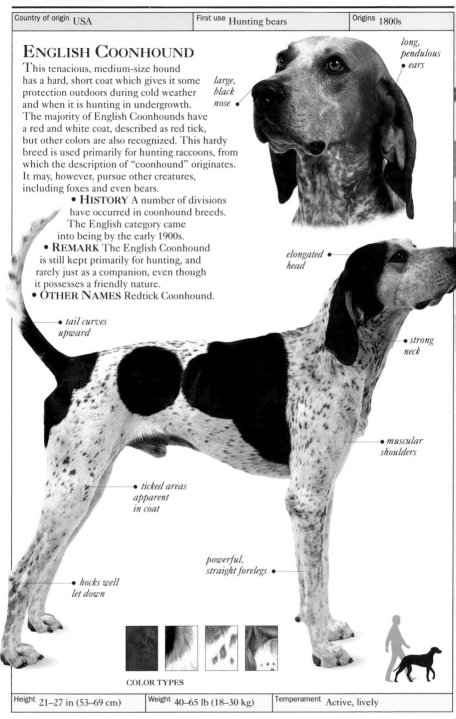

Country of origin USA	First use Hunting bears	Origins 1800s

English Coonhound

This tenacious, medium-size hound has a hard, short coat which gives it some protection outdoors during cold weather and when it is hunting in undergrowth. The majority of English Coonhounds have a red and white coat, described as red tick, but other colors are also recognized. This hardy breed is used primarily for hunting raccoons, from which the description of "coonhound" originates. It may, however, pursue other creatures, including foxes and even bears.

large, black nose
long, pendulous ears

• **History** A number of divisions have occurred in coonhound breeds. The English category came into being by the early 1900s.

• **Remark** The English Coonhound is still kept primarily for hunting, and rarely just as a companion, even though it possesses a friendly nature.

• **Other Names** Redtick Coonhound.

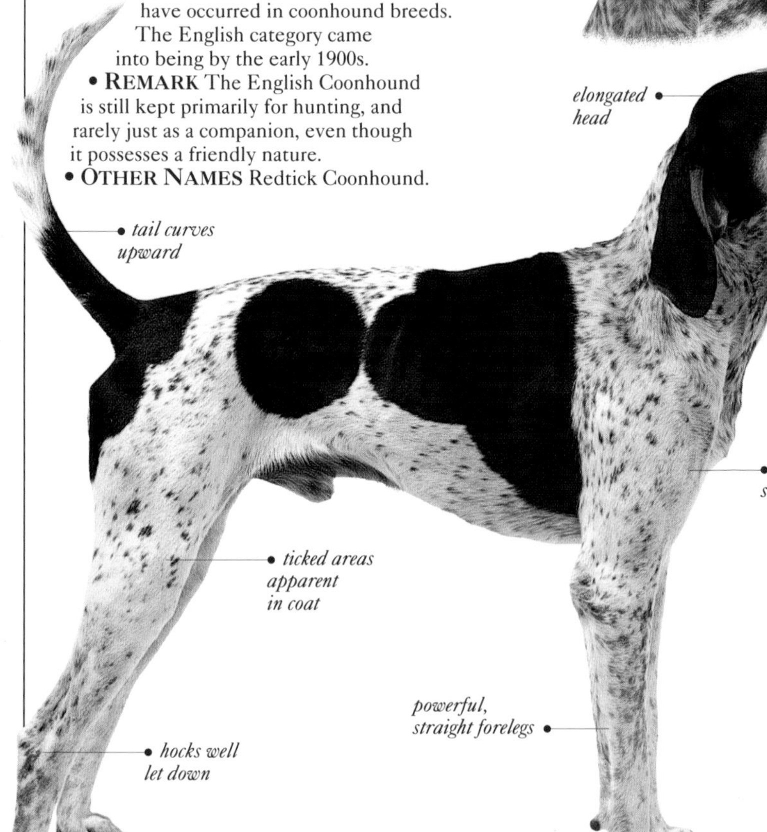
elongated head
tail curves upward
strong neck
muscular shoulders
ticked areas apparent in coat
powerful, straight forelegs
hocks well let down

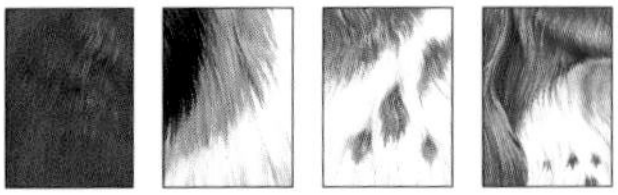

COLOR TYPES

Height 21–27 in (53–69 cm)	Weight 40–65 lb (18–30 kg)	Temperament Active, lively

Country of origin	First use	Origins
USA	Hunting raccoons	1700s

REDBONE COONHOUND

Immediately distinguishable by its mainly red coat, this is the only solid-colored coonhound. Some individuals do have small traces of white, either on the feet or chest, but this is not penalized in show dogs. This good-natured, medium-size hound is becoming increasingly popular throughout the USA.

• **HISTORY** Hounds with this coloration have been documented in the USA for more than 200 years. Earlier examples of this breed had larger areas of white on their coats than are seen in dogs today.

• **REMARK** This type of hound was probably named after an early breeder, Peter Redbone, who lived in Tennessee.

pendulous ears

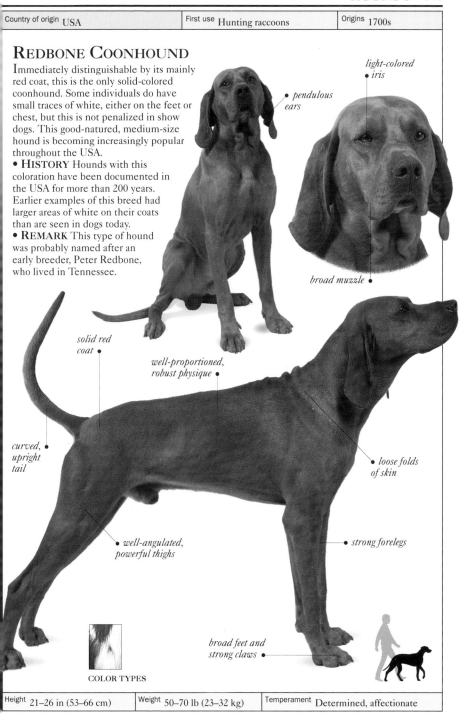

light-colored iris
broad muzzle

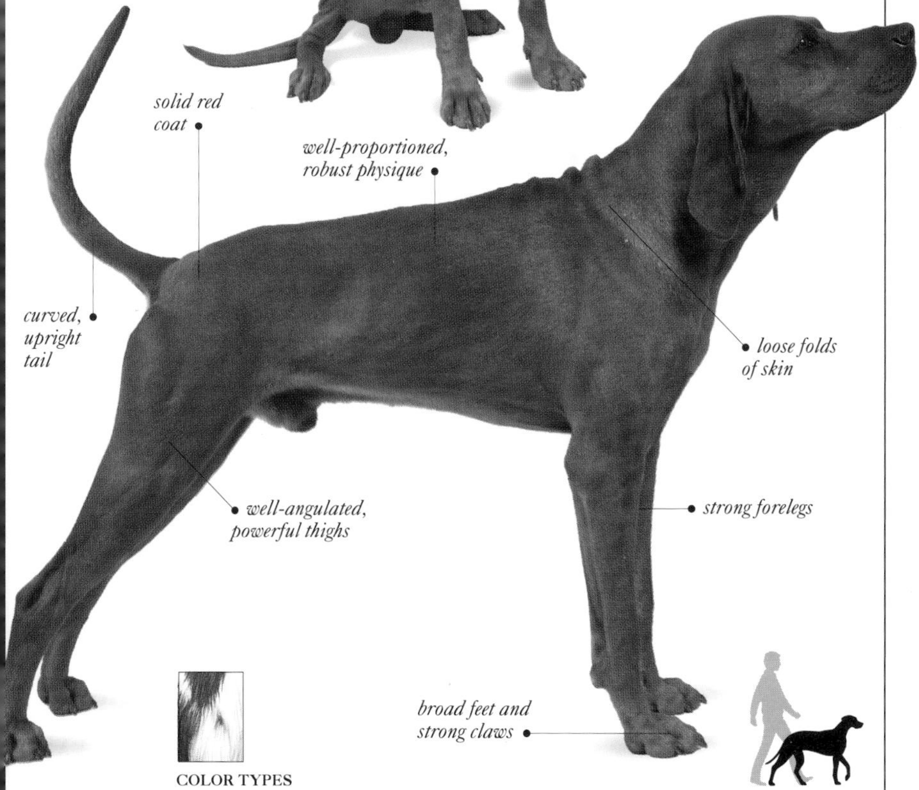
solid red coat
well-proportioned, robust physique
curved, upright tail
loose folds of skin
well-angulated, powerful thighs
strong forelegs
broad feet and strong claws

COLOR TYPES

Height	Weight	Temperament
21–26 in (53–66 cm)	50–70 lb (23–32 kg)	Determined, affectionate

Country of origin USA	First use Hunting raccoons	Origins 1700s

Black and Tan Coonhound

This breed was developed from foxhound and, probably, bloodhound stock. It is predominantly black in color, with tan markings comprising 10 to 15 percent of the coat. Occasional white areas around the chest are also still seen. Although good-natured, the Black and Tan Coonhound is a tenacious tracker once it is on the scent. Hunters recognize their dogs by their individual calls.

• **History** The origins of this dog lie in the USA, and can be traced back to the 1700s. In 1900, it was the first of the coonhounds to be recognized as a distinctive breed.

• **Remark** It is often referred to as a "treeing hound," since it forces the raccoon to take refuge in a tree.

• **Other Names** American Black and Tan Coonhound.

long, drooping ears
black nails
powerful toes

small tan area above each eye, shaped like a pumpkin seed
skin fits loosely over body

Height 23–27 in (58–69 cm)	Weight 55–75 lb (25–35 kg)	Temperament Determined, lively

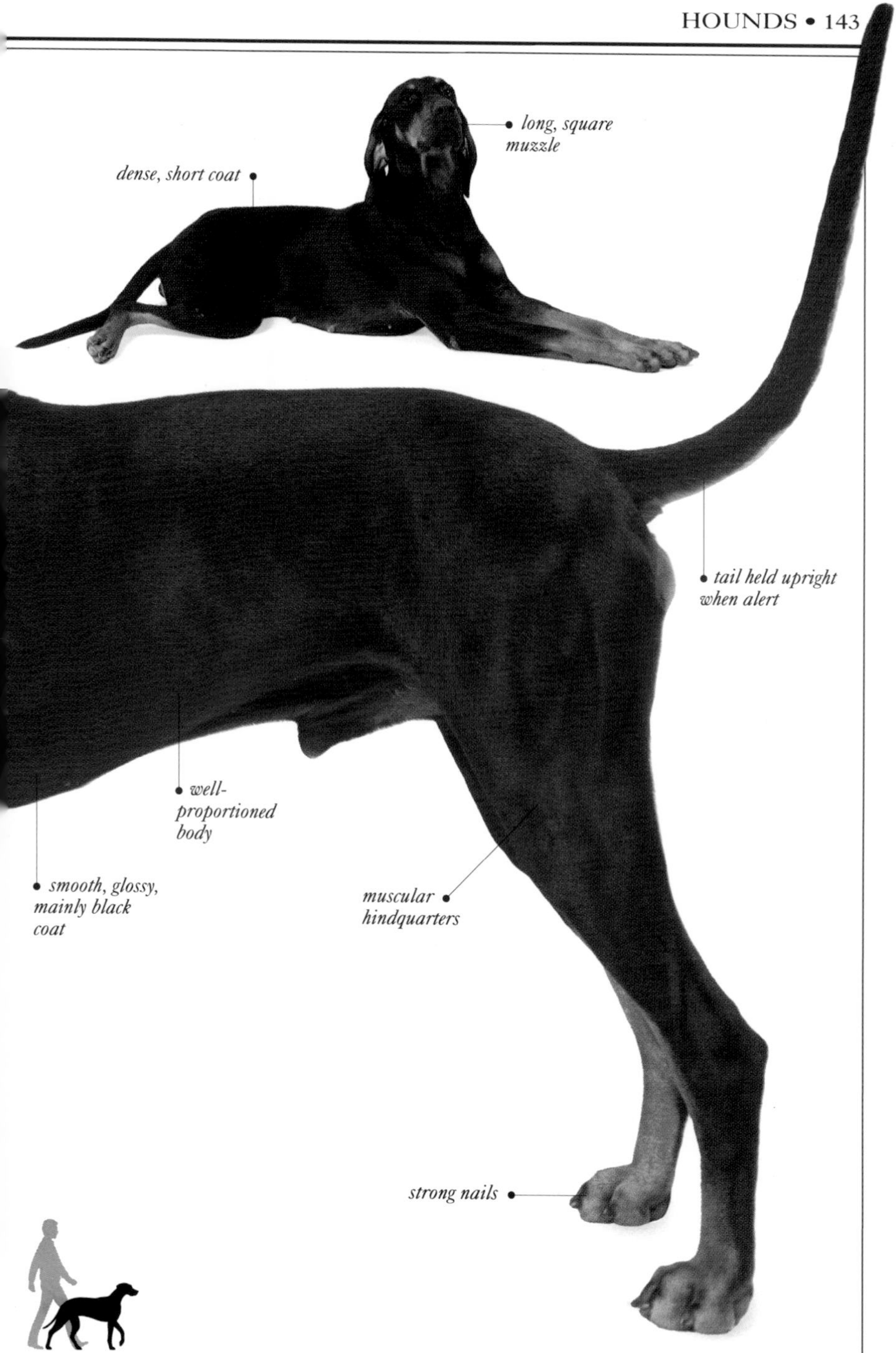
long, square
muzzle
dense, short coat
tail held upright
when alert
well-
proportioned
body
smooth, glossy,
mainly black
coat
muscular
hindquarters
strong nails

Country of origin USA	First use Hunting raccoons	Origins 1800s

Treeing Walker Coonhound

This coonhound is lighter and faster than other similar breeds. The tricolor dog is preferred, although bicolors do exist. Tan-and-white Treeing Walkers are not described as "red" to avoid confusion with the Redbone Coonhound (see p.141).

• **History** Descended from English Foxhounds, the development of this coonhound involved a dog stolen in the 1800s. This dog, named Tennessee Lead, added speed and treeing ability.

• **Remark** This dog is still used for hunting raccoons and opossums.

broad ears hang down back of head
tricolor patterning

long, thin muzzle
very open nostrils

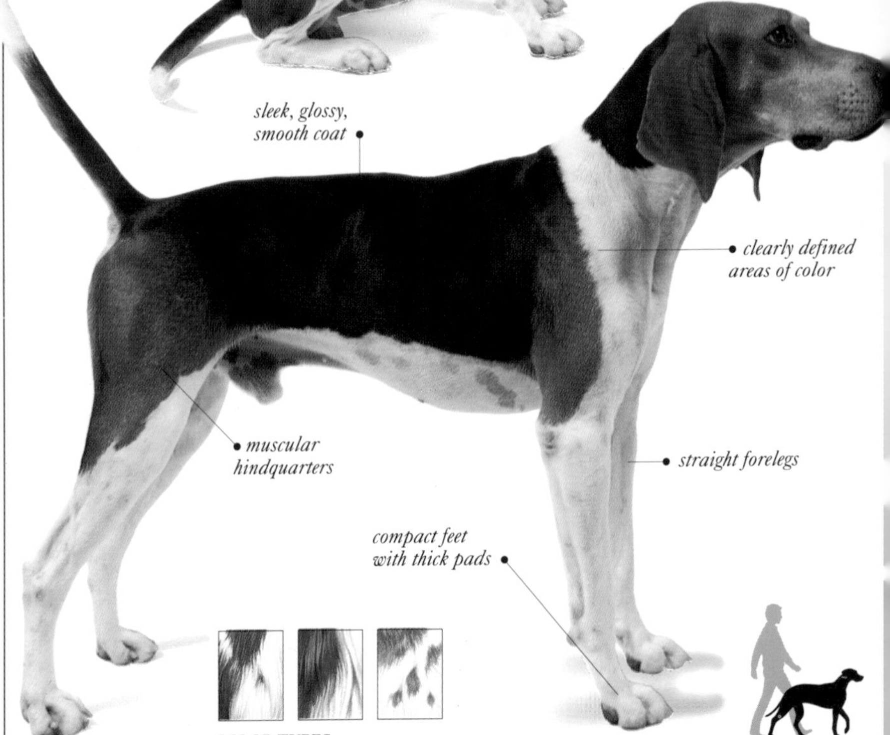
sleek, glossy, smooth coat
clearly defined areas of color
muscular hindquarters
straight forelegs
compact feet with thick pads

COLOR TYPES

Height 20–27 in (51–69 cm)	Weight 50–70 lb (23–32 kg)	Temperament Lively, intelligent

Country of origin	First use	Origins
USA	Hunting foxes	1700s

American Foxhound

Bred for greater pace, the American Foxhound is lighter-boned than its English relative (see p.147), is lighter in weight, and has a keener sense of smell. Its short coat is close and hard and is acceptable in any color combination, although the tricolored form is the one most often seen in the show ring.

• **History** The ancestry of the American Foxhound can be traced back to English hounds imported to North America in 1650 by a Mr. Robert Brooke. A century later, these were crossed with French hounds sent by General Lafayette to George Washington.

• **Remark** The songlike voice of the American Foxhound has been recorded and incorporated into some popular music.

medium-length ears, broad and straight

sloping, muscular shoulders
deep chest

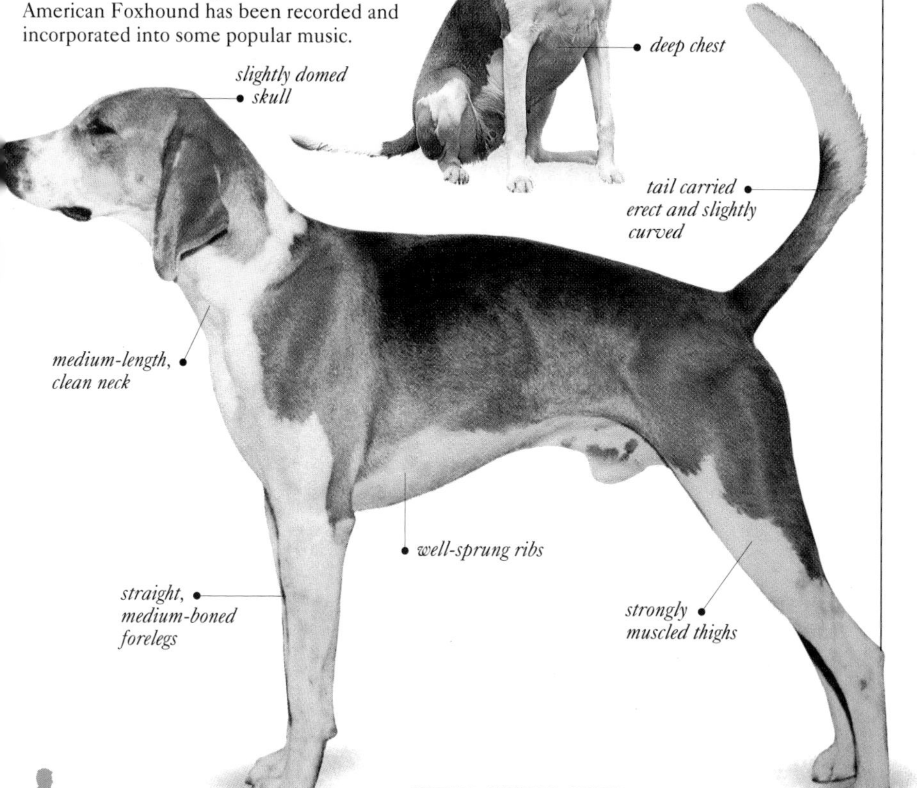
slightly domed skull
tail carried erect and slightly curved
medium-length, clean neck
well-sprung ribs
straight, medium-boned forelegs
strongly muscled thighs

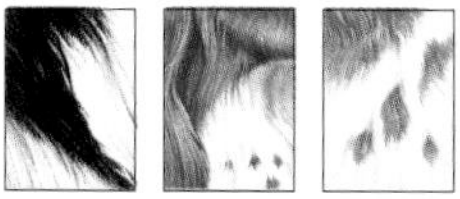
COLOR TYPES

Height	Weight	Temperament
21–25 in (53–64 cm)	65–75 lb (30–34 kg)	Active, friendly

Country of origin Great Britain	First use Hunting rabbits and hares	Origins 1800s

BASSET HOUND

The Basset Hound and bassets in general are characterized by their short legs. Relative to its size, however, the Basset Hound is the heaviest-boned dog of any breed. Both bi- and tricolor markings are acceptable.

• **HISTORY** Ironically, whereas most basset breeds originated in France, the Basset Hound itself was developed in Britain toward the end of the last century.

• **REMARK** The name is derived from the French word *bas*, meaning "low."

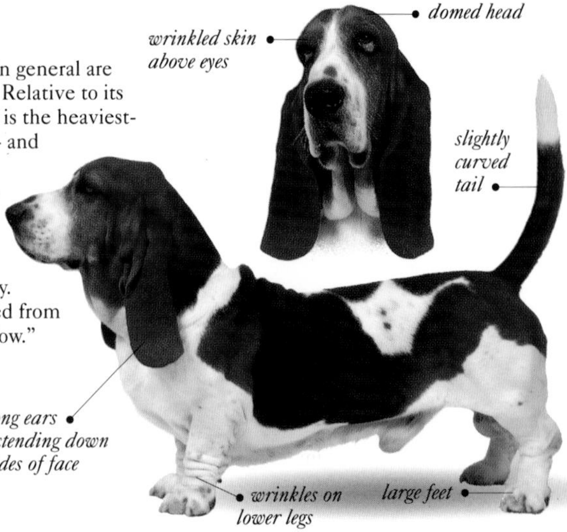
domed head
wrinkled skin above eyes
slightly curved tail
long ears extending down sides of face
wrinkles on lower legs
large feet

COLOR TYPES

Height 13–15 in (33–38 cm)	Weight 40–60 lb (18–27 kg)	Temperament Independent, active

Country of origin Great Britain	First use Hunting rabbits and hares	Origins 1300s

BEAGLE

This sturdy and compact hound has medium-length legs, and is traditionally used to hunt hares. Working in packs, it pursues its quarry by scent, and displays remarkable stamina and tenacity.

• **HISTORY** The Beagle probably evolved from small foxhounds. Today it is still kept for hunting purposes, although it also makes an affectionate and playful pet.

• **REMARK** A miniature form, the Pocket Beagle, standing about 10 in (25 cm) high, was popular up to World War I.

• **OTHER NAMES** English Beagle.

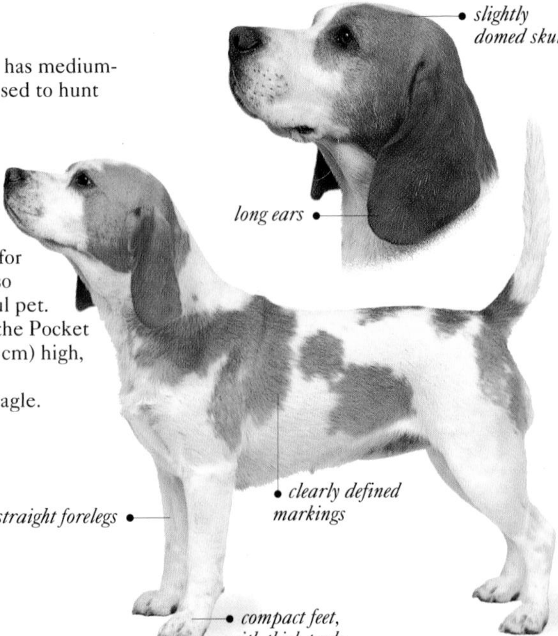
slightly domed skull
long ears
clearly defined markings
straight forelegs
compact feet, with thick pads

COLOR TYPES

Height 13–16 in (33–41 cm)	Weight 18–30 lb (8–14 kg)	Temperament Lively, friendly

Country of origin Great Britain	First use Hunting foxes	Origins 1700s

English Foxhound

The traditional English Foxhound is a solid, well-built animal, with stamina an essential ingredient in its development. Foxhounds live in packs, the members of the pack always being counted in pairs, known as couples, rather than singly. This breed is still kept almost entirely for hunting, and is unlikely to be seen regularly at dog shows.

• **HISTORY** This dog was bred from the St. Hubert Hound, originally brought to Great Britain by the Normans after the invasion of 1066. The records of the Association of Masters of Foxhounds reveal that in 1880 there were 140 packs and 7,000 English Foxhounds in Great Britain.

• **REMARK** This breed is invariably friendly and affectionate.

• **OTHER NAMES** Foxhound.

broad skull
level back
color and markings highly variable between individuals

long, but never thick, neck
solid base to tail
deep girth leaves plenty of room for heart
very powerful hindquarters
large space from end of ribs to hindquarters to give good stride length and pace
strong, straight forelegs
round, catlike feet with toes close together

COLOR TYPES

Height 23–27 in (58–69 cm)	Weight 55–75 lb (25–34 kg)	Temperament Active, friendly

Country of origin Great Britain	First use Hunting deer	Origins 800s

DEERHOUND

Although similar to the Irish Wolfhound (see pp.162–63), the Deerhound is of a sleeker, lighter build, reflecting the contribution of greyhound stock to its ancestry. This is perhaps most obviously apparent in terms of its head shape, the muzzle clearly tapering along its length. Dark blue-gray tends to be the color most favored today, but one of the oldest colors still seen is sandy red, with black areas on both the muzzle and the ears.

• **HISTORY** The Deerhound was originally developed in Scotland to hunt deer. However, the introduction of the gun for hunting led to a decline in numbers, but it is still valued as a companion dog.

• **REMARK** The Deerhound's shaggy coat offers excellent protection against the elements.

• **OTHER NAMES** Scottish Deerhound.

head broadest at the ears
dark eyes with black rims
small ears preferred, kept folded back at rest

tapering muzzle
harsh, wiry, shaggy coat
softer coat on underparts and head
long, tapering tail almost reaching the ground
ears have a soft, glossy appearance, and feel like a mouse's coat

COLOR TYPES

Height 28–30 in (71–76 cm)	Weight 80–100 lb (36–45 kg)	Temperament Gentle, active

Country of origin Great Britain	First use Otter hunting	Origins 1000s

OTTER HOUND

The coat, with its two distinct layers, is the chief feature of this breed. There is a rough outercoat, which feels hard to the touch, and a much shorter, woolly undercoat, which offers the dog protection when it enters the water.
• **HISTORY** This ancient breed probably evolved from foxhounds and other hunting dogs. It was formerly a pack hound.
• **REMARK** Like its traditional quarry, the otter, the Otter Hound has declined in numbers since the last half of the 19th century.

large, hairy head

long, pendulous ears

long, square muzzle
high-set tail
well-muscled, lean physique
coat up to 6 in (15 cm) long over back
straight, solid-boned legs
coat has slightly oily texture
large feet with webbing between toes

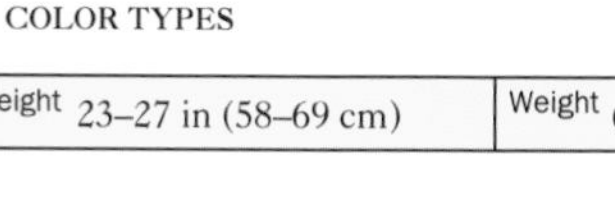

COLOR TYPES

Height 23–27 in (58–69 cm)	Weight 65–120 lb (30–55 kg)	Temperament Athletic, independent

Country of origin Great Britain	First use Coursing hares	Origins 3000 BC

GREYHOUND

The Greyhound kept for the show ring tends to be slightly larger and heavier than its famous racing counterpart, but it is, nevertheless, still built for acceleration and speed. Both forms are muscular and athletic in build, with a deep chest which provides excellent lung capacity. Few other breeds today are available in such a wide range of coat colors, including particolor combinations.

• **HISTORY** The best evidence is that Greyhound stock originated in the Middle East, for similar dogs are represented on Egyptian tombs dating back nearly 5,000 years. An early British manuscript confirms that the breed had reached Britain by AD 900.

• **REMARK** Although gentle dogs by nature, they do have a tendency to chase cats and small dogs, so they are best muzzled if allowed off the leash. They do not require a lot of exercise, a brief run being ideal.

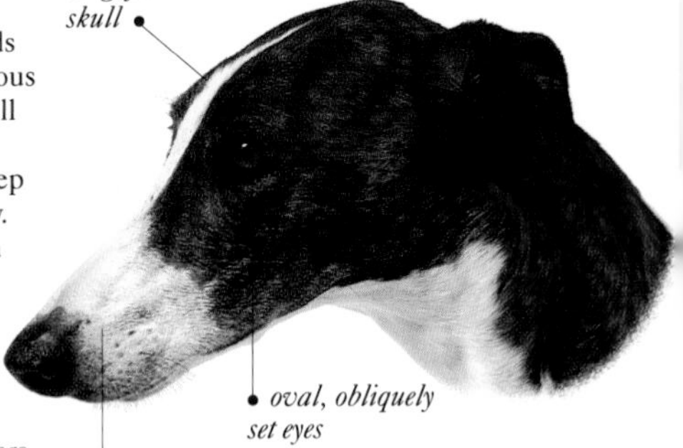
long, flat skull
oval, obliquely set eyes
long, sharp muzzle

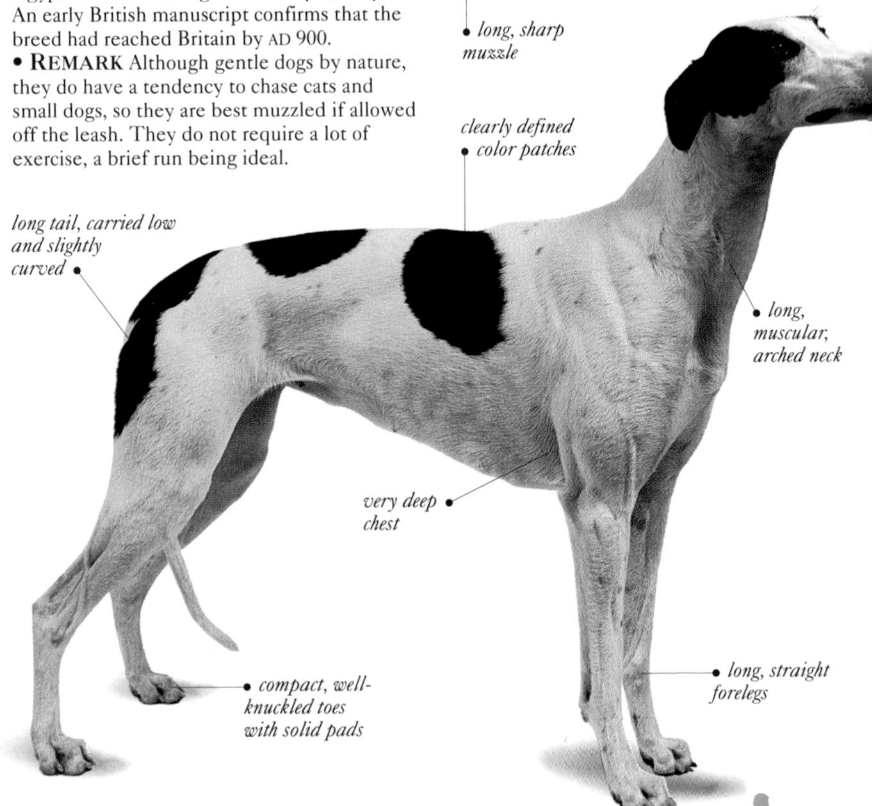
clearly defined color patches
long tail, carried low and slightly curved
long, muscular, arched neck
very deep chest
compact, well-knuckled toes with solid pads
long, straight forelegs

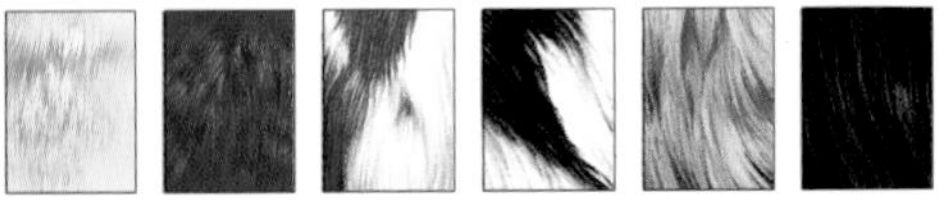

COLOR TYPES

Height 27–30 in (69–76 cm)	Weight 60–70 lb (27–32 kg)	Temperament Lively, friendly

Country of origin	First use	Origins
Great Britain	Racing	1800s

WHIPPET

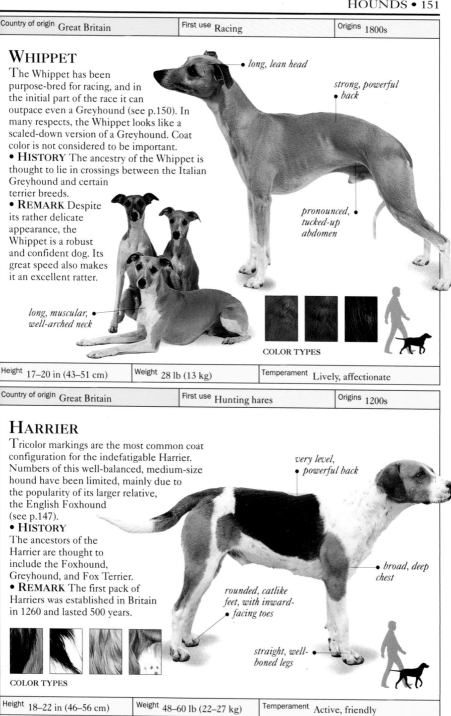

long, lean head
strong, powerful back
pronounced, tucked-up abdomen

The Whippet has been purpose-bred for racing, and in the initial part of the race it can outpace even a Greyhound (see p.150). In many respects, the Whippet looks like a scaled-down version of a Greyhound. Coat color is not considered to be important.

• **HISTORY** The ancestry of the Whippet is thought to lie in crossings between the Italian Greyhound and certain terrier breeds.

• **REMARK** Despite its rather delicate appearance, the Whippet is a robust and confident dog. Its great speed also makes it an excellent ratter.

long, muscular, well-arched neck

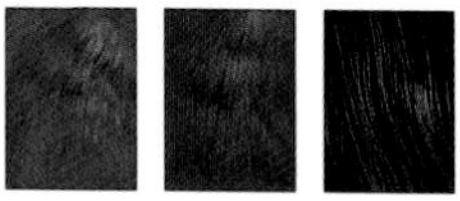

COLOR TYPES

Height	Weight	Temperament
17–20 in (43–51 cm)	28 lb (13 kg)	Lively, affectionate

Country of origin	First use	Origins
Great Britain	Hunting hares	1200s

HARRIER

Tricolor markings are the most common coat configuration for the indefatigable Harrier. Numbers of this well-balanced, medium-size hound have been limited, mainly due to the popularity of its larger relative, the English Foxhound (see p.147).

• **HISTORY** The ancestors of the Harrier are thought to include the Foxhound, Greyhound, and Fox Terrier.

• **REMARK** The first pack of Harriers was established in Britain in 1260 and lasted 500 years.

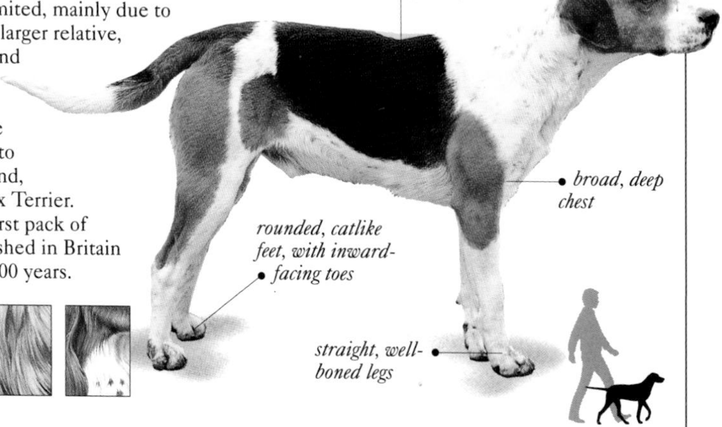
very level, powerful back
broad, deep chest
rounded, catlike feet, with inward-facing toes
straight, well-boned legs

COLOR TYPES

Height	Weight	Temperament
18–22 in (46–56 cm)	48–60 lb (22–27 kg)	Active, friendly

Country of origin Norway	First use Hunting rabbits	Origins 1800s

DUNKER

This sleek, lightly built, yet powerful hound has a poised, elegant appearance. Its thick, short coat is usually tan-colored with a unique blue-marbled or black splotchy saddle. It is an extremely hardy breed, able to withstand extremes of cold, and adapts well to any terrain.

• **HISTORY** To create the Dunker, Norwegian breeder Wilhelm Dunker crossed a Russian Harlequin Hound with reliable scent hounds, producing a dog that could hunt rabbits by scent rather than sight. It has yet to become popular outside of its homeland.

• **REMARK** A merle gene from the Harlequin Hound gave the Dunker its distinctive mottled saddle marking.

• **OTHER NAMES** Norwegian Hound.

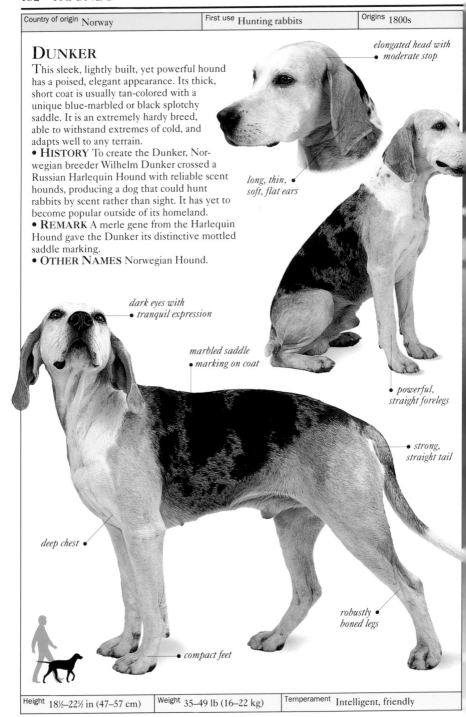

elongated head with moderate stop
long, thin, soft, flat ears
powerful, straight forelegs

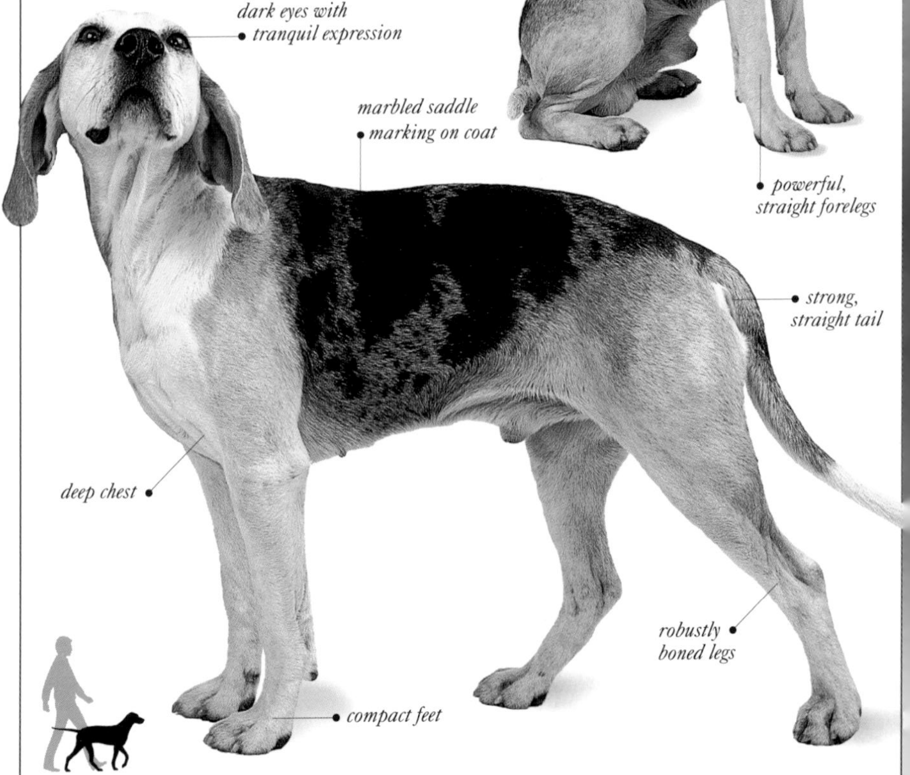
dark eyes with tranquil expression
marbled saddle marking on coat
strong, straight tail
deep chest
robustly boned legs
compact feet

Height 18½–22½ in (47–57 cm)	Weight 35–49 lb (16–22 kg)	Temperament Intelligent, friendly

Country of origin Norway	First use Tracking game	Origins 1800s

HALDENSTÖVARE

This Norwegian scent hound has a distinctive tricolor coat that is predominantly white, with black and tan markings on particular areas of the body. It is the largest of the four recognized stövare breeds.

• **HISTORY** Named after the city of Halden in southeastern Norway, not far from the Swedish border, it resulted from crossing local hounds with Swedish, German, and British hound stock.

• **REMARK** Like other Norwegian hounds, it is not a pack dog and makes a fine pet.

• **OTHER NAMES** Halden Hound.

pendant ears

straight muzzle with black nose

dome-shaped skull
long, thick tail carried low
long, curved neck
deep chest
oval feet with strong toes

Height 20–25 in (51–64 cm)	Weight 51–64 lb (23–29 kg)	Temperament Active, affectionate

Country of origin	First use	Origins
Norway	Hunting small game	1800s

HYGENHUND

This solid breed is often described as "short coupled" because it has a relatively short, compact body. The Hygenhund has been bred in several coat colors, but the yellow variety with white markings tends to be most common.

- **HISTORY** The Hygenhund was developed by a Norwegian enthusiast, F. Hygen, using Hölsteiner hounds from Germany crossed with various Scandinavian hounds.
- **REMARK** Developed for stamina, the Hygenhund tends to hunt singly with its owner.
- **OTHER NAMES** Hygenhound.

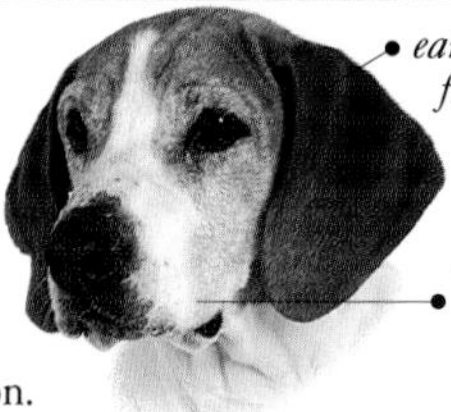

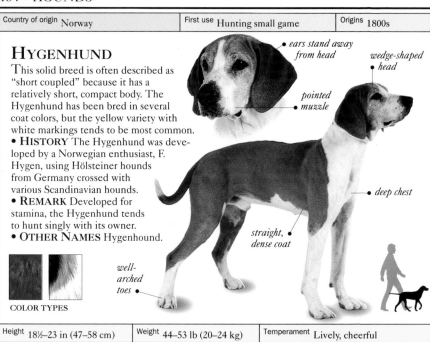

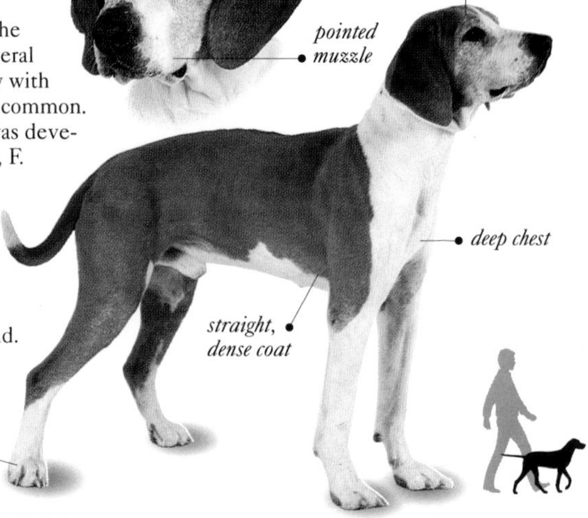
ears stand away from head
wedge-shaped head
pointed muzzle
deep chest
straight, dense coat
well-arched toes

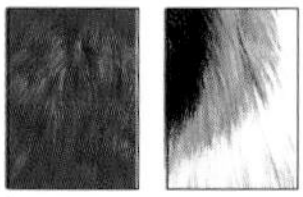

COLOR TYPES

Height	Weight	Temperament
18½–23 in (47–58 cm)	44–53 lb (20–24 kg)	Lively, cheerful

Country of origin	First use	Origins
Finland	Hunting small game	1700s

FINNISH HOUND

This relatively large hound is longer than it is tall. It has a narrow head with a prominent nose, and large, pendulous ears, which give it a rather charming appearance. It is also a nimble and very energetic hunter.

- **HISTORY** This breed has a mixed ancestry. A variety of English, Swiss, German, and Scandinavian hounds have contributed to its development.
- **REMARK** The Finnish Hound is a keen hunter in summer but prefers the hearth in winter.
- **OTHER NAMES** Suomenajokoira.

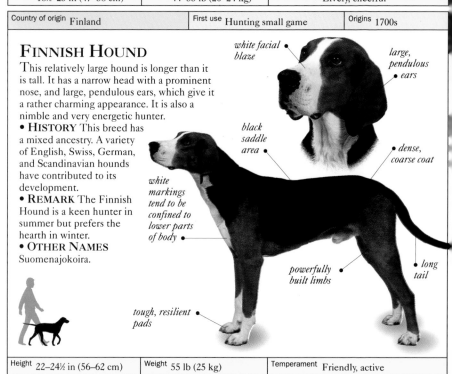

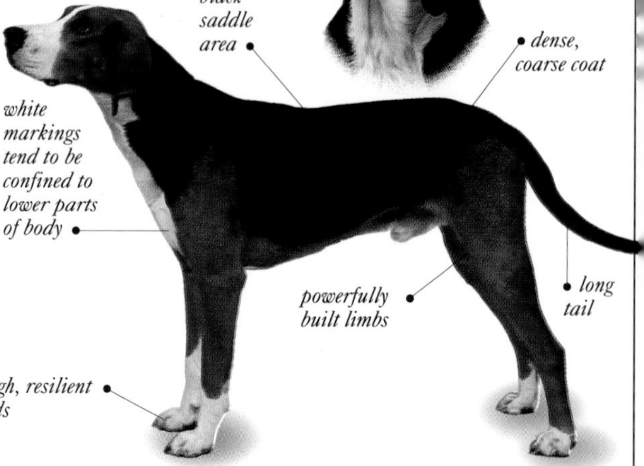
white facial blaze
large, pendulous ears
black saddle area
dense, coarse coat
white markings tend to be confined to lower parts of body
powerfully built limbs
long tail
tough, resilient pads

Height	Weight	Temperament
22–24½ in (56–62 cm)	55 lb (25 kg)	Friendly, active

Country of origin	First use	Origins
Sweden	Scenting and hunting game	1900s

DREVER

The long body and relatively short legs of the Drever give this breed a distinctly rectangular shape. White markings are an important feature and should be present on the face, neck, chest, and feet, as well as on the tip of the tail. The Drever can be recognized by its loud bark, which enables it to be tracked, even through woodland where its stature may conceal its presence.

• **HISTORY** Crossings of Westphalian and Danish Dachsbrackers gave rise to the Drever.

• **REMARK** These dogs have become popular in Canada.

• **OTHER NAMES** Swedish Dachsbracker.

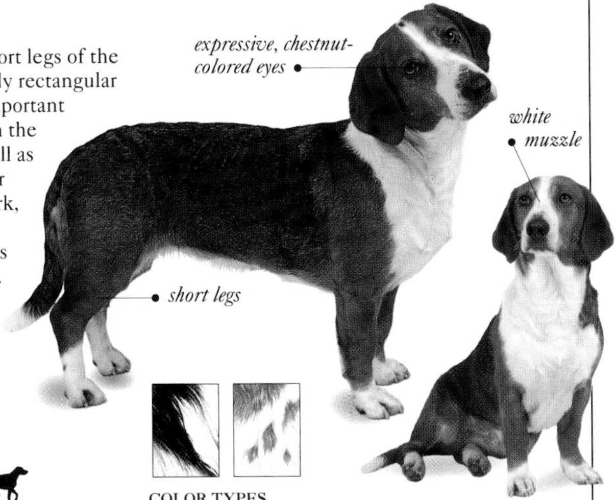
expressive, chestnut-colored eyes
white muzzle
short legs

COLOR TYPES

Height	Weight	Temperament
11½–16 in (29–41 cm)	33 lb (15 kg)	Alert, affable

Country of origin	First use	Origins
Sweden	Hunting foxes and hares	1200s

SCHILLERSTÖVARE

The light build of this hound gives it considerable pace and it is regarded as the fastest of all Swedish breeds. The Schillerstövare has a thick undercoat which provides insulation, allowing it to work in deep snow, hunting foxes and snow hares.

• **HISTORY** This breed was developed by Per Schiller from a combination of Swedish hounds and scent hounds from Switzerland, Germany, and Austria.

• **REMARK** The Schillerstövare was represented at the first Swedish dog show, held in 1886.

• **OTHER NAMES** Schiller Hound.

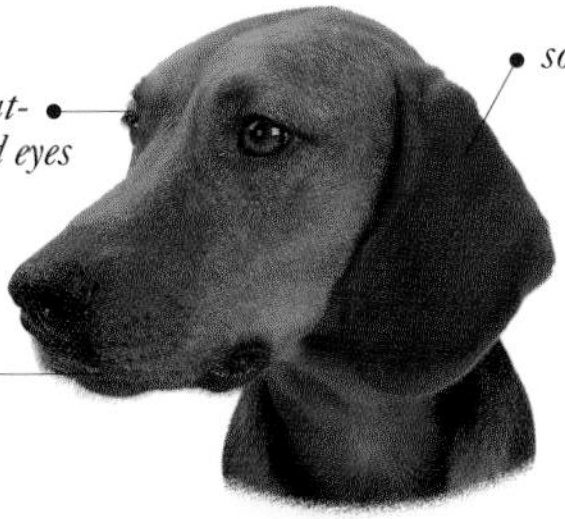
chestnut-colored eyes
soft ears
lips fit tightly to jaw

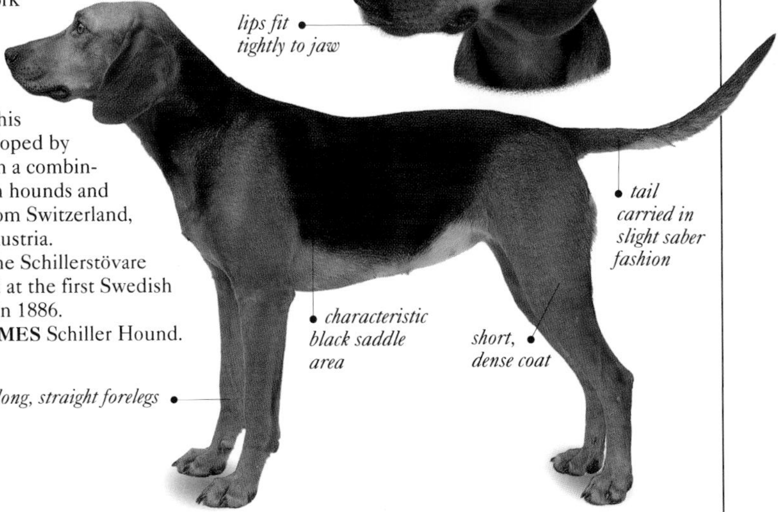
tail carried in slight saber fashion
characteristic black saddle area
short, dense coat
long, straight forelegs

Height	Weight	Temperament
21–22 in (53–57 cm)	40–53 lb (18–24 kg)	Active, enthusiastic

Country of origin Sweden	First use Tracking game	Origins 1800s

HAMILTONSTÖVARE

This well-built hound has plenty of stamina and will follow a scent with single-minded determination, no matter what the terrain or weather conditions. Well able to hunt in the thick snow of its native Sweden, the Hamiltonstövare's baying call indicates its position to the hunters when it is out of sight.

• **HISTORY** A.P. Hamilton, founder of the Swedish Kennel Club, was responsible for the development of this hound. His breeding program was based on English Foxhounds and Harriers, which were crossed with German hounds, including the now-extinct Holstein Hound, and Hanover Hounds.

• **REMARK** When this sturdy breed was first introduced into Britain in 1968, it was initially referred to simply as the Swedish Foxhound.

• **OTHER NAMES** Hamilton Hound.

long, rectangular head

black nose
short, dense, double coat
white tip to tail

ears lie flat against sides of head
powerful body
deep chest
white markings on feet, as well as on muzzle and chest
tail carried low

Height 20–24 in (51–61 cm)	Weight 50–60 lb (23–27 kg)	Temperament Courageous, active

Country of origin Sweden	First use Hunting foxes and hares	Origins 1200s

SMÅLANDSSTÖVARE

This compact, fox- and hare-hunting dog is the shortest and most heavily built of all the Swedish stövare breeds. Docking of the tail is not permitted in this breed, but many Smålandsstövares are born with tails that are unusually short for a hound. Coat color is invariably black with tan markings on the muzzle, eyebrows, and lower parts of the legs, and occasionally with white flashes on the tips of the tail and feet. The coat itself is thick, smooth, and glossy and needs very little attention in terms of grooming.

• **HISTORY** Originating in Småland, central Sweden, this breed of hound was recognized by the Swedish Kennel Club in 1921. An early breeder, Baron von Essen, had a preference for the short-tailed individuals that were sometimes born, and helped to establish this characteristic in the breed. The basic form of this dog may date back to the Middle Ages.

• **REMARK** This dog requires lots of exercise.

• **OTHER NAMES** Smålands Hound.

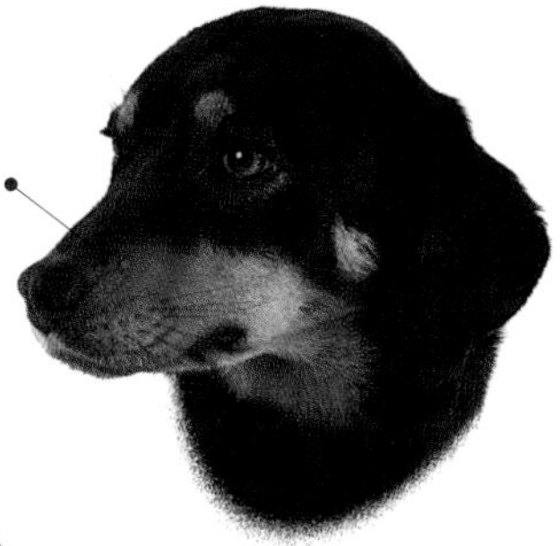
blunt muzzle

thick, smooth, glossy coat

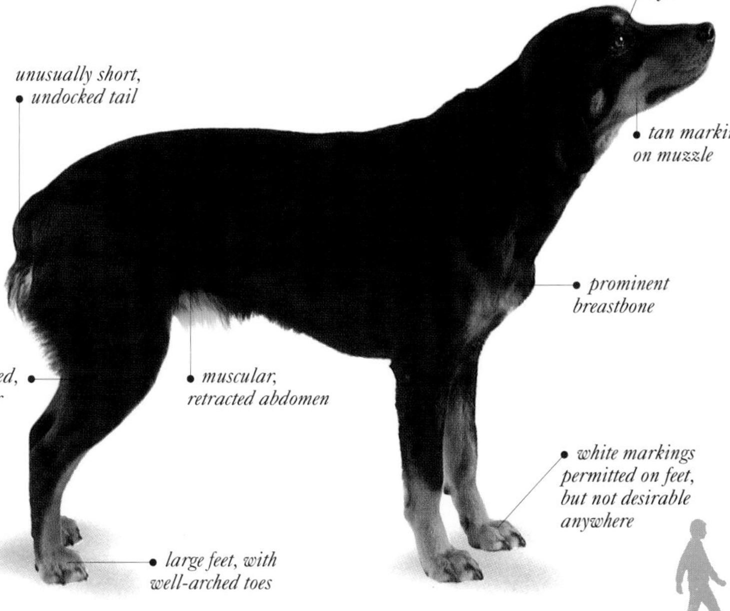
dark, tranquil eyes
unusually short, undocked tail
tan markings on muzzle
prominent breastbone
well-boned, muscular legs
muscular, retracted abdomen
white markings permitted on feet, but not desirable anywhere
large feet, with well-arched toes

Height 18–20 in (46–50 cm)	Weight 33–40 lb (15–18 kg)	Temperament Active, enthusiastic

Country of origin Germany	First use Flushing badgers	Origins 1900s

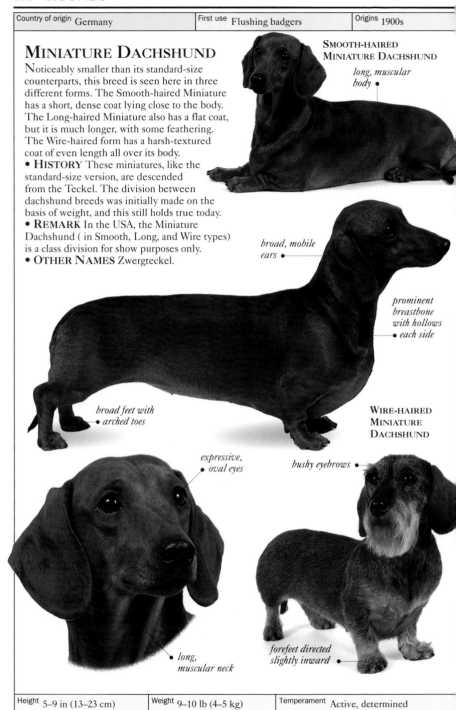

MINIATURE DACHSHUND

Noticeably smaller than its standard-size counterparts, this breed is seen here in three different forms. The Smooth-haired Miniature has a short, dense coat lying close to the body. The Long-haired Miniature also has a flat coat, but it is much longer, with some feathering. The Wire-haired form has a harsh-textured coat of even length all over its body.

• **HISTORY** These miniatures, like the standard-size version, are descended from the Teckel. The division between dachshund breeds was initially made on the basis of weight, and this still holds true today.

• **REMARK** In the USA, the Miniature Dachshund (in Smooth, Long, and Wire types) is a class division for show purposes only.

• **OTHER NAMES** Zwergteckel.

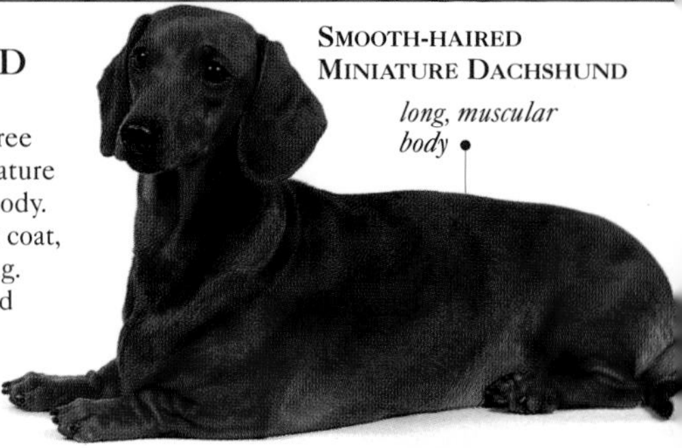
long, muscular body

SMOOTH-HAIRED MINIATURE DACHSHUND

broad, mobile ears
prominent breastbone with hollows each side
broad feet with arched toes

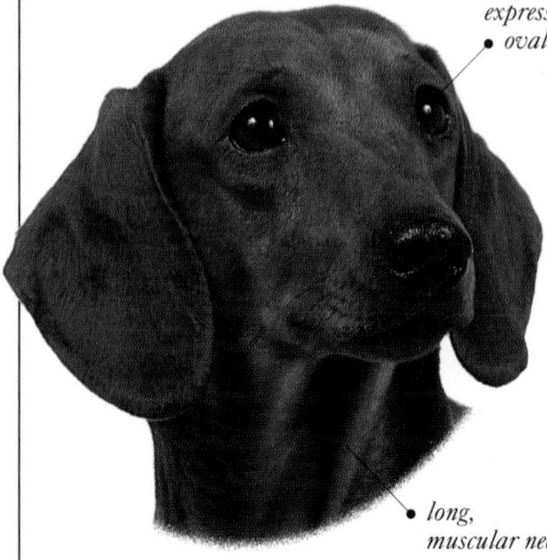
expressive, oval eyes
long, muscular neck

WIRE-HAIRED MINIATURE DACHSHUND

bushy eyebrows
forefeet directed slightly inward

Height 5–9 in (13–23 cm)	Weight 9–10 lb (4–5 kg)	Temperament Active, determined

Long-haired Miniature Dachshund

COLOR TYPES

feathering on tail
oat longest
n neck and
nderparts
hind feet smaller than forefeet

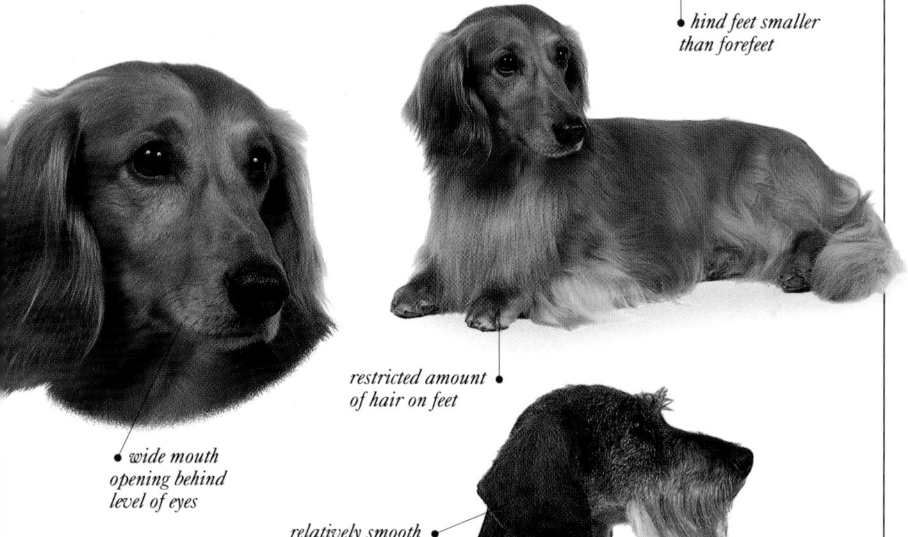
restricted amount of hair on feet
wide mouth opening behind level of eyes

relatively smooth hair on ears
round, broad rump
long neck

Country of origin Germany	First use Tracking game	Origins 1700s

Hanoverian Mountain Hound

Relatively heavy in build, with short legs, this hound is often used to track an animal that has been wounded but not killed outright. It often sports a distinctive black mask.

• **History** Developed by gamekeepers around Hanover in Germany, this breed descends from heavy tracking hounds crossed with lighter ones, such as the Haidbracke.

• **Remark** This breed is still mainly kept as a working dog, and is highly valued for its fine nose.

• **Other Names** Hannoverscher Schweisshund.

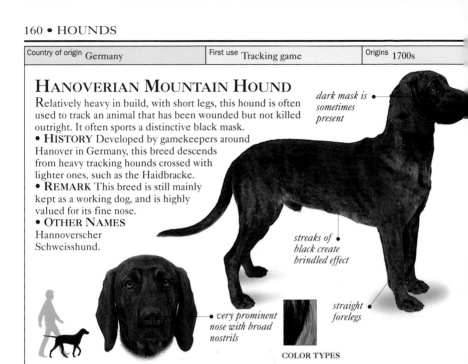

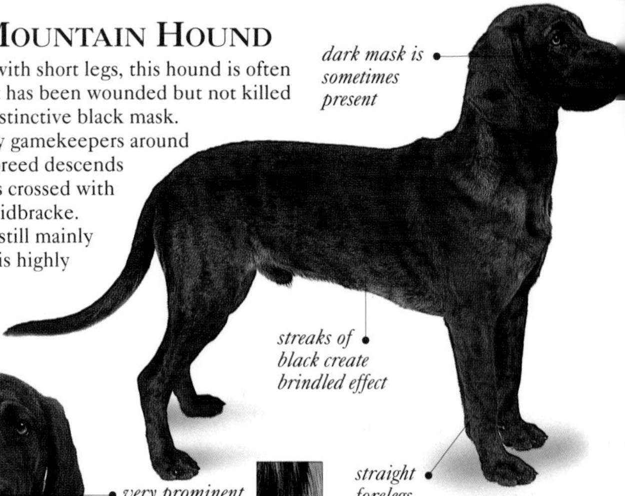
dark mask is sometimes present
streaks of black create brindled effect
straight forelegs

very prominent nose with broad nostrils

COLOR TYPES

Height 20–24 in (51–61 cm)	Weight 84–99 lb (38–44 kg)	Temperament Calm, loyal

Country of origin Germany	First use Tracking game	Origins 1800s

Bavarian Mountain Hound

Rather shorter and lighter in build than similar breeds (above), this hound is highly valued for its tracking ability. It will continue on the trail until a wounded animal is found, rather than leaving it injured.

• **History** As its name suggests, this hound evolved in Bavaria in Germany, probably from crossings between Hanoverian and Tyrolean hounds.

• **Remark** The group to which this hound belongs is described as *schweisshunden*, meaning "bloodhounds."

• **Other Names** Bayrischer Gebirgs-schweisshund.

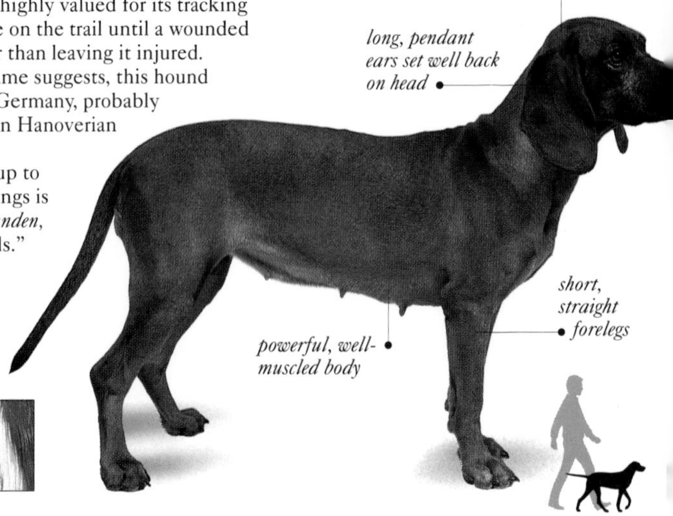
slightly domed skull
long, pendant ears set well back on head
short, straight forelegs
powerful, well-muscled body

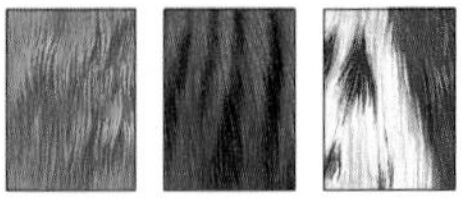
COLOR TYPES

Height 20 in (51 cm)	Weight 55–77 lb (25–35 kg)	Temperament Active, intelligent

Country of origin	First use	Origins
Poland	Hunting large game	1700s

Polish Hound

This large, heavy hound has a well-wrinkled face, a rectangular head, and powerful jaws. It is a dedicated tracker with a prominent nose and a fine voice.

• **History** The breed's origins are unknown, but it is probably related to Austrian and German breeds. The Polish Hound declined in numbers during World War II, but it has since recovered.

• **Remark** There used to be a smaller version of the Polish Hound, known as the Gonczy Polski.

• **Other Names** Ogar Polski.

noble, rectangular head

large ears hang down close to head
thick tail
deep, muscular chest
black saddle marking

wrinkles of skin on forehead
prominent black nose

Height	Weight	Temperament
22–26 in (56–66 cm)	55–71 lb (25–32 kg)	Determined, friendly

Country of origin Ireland	First use Hunting wolves	Origins 100 BC

IRISH WOLFHOUND

A true giant, the Irish Wolfhound is the tallest dog in the world. It is somewhat similar in appearance to the Deerhound (see p.148), but it is larger in overall size. Despite its size, this is a graceful dog, with a rough, wiry coat and a muscular build. The long tail is surprisingly powerful, and can cause havoc in the home when swinging back and forth. The Irish Wolfhound's temperament is excellent, but because of its size it requires training as a young pup. Minimal grooming is needed.

• **HISTORY** The Irish Wolfhound's ancestry dates back many centuries, originating from an ancient lineage of royal dogs. The extinction of the wolf in Ireland during the 1800s almost resulted in the loss of this breed. It was saved only through the efforts of a Scot, Captain George Graham.

• **REMARK** An Irish Wolfhound pup should not be taken on long walks, as these can damage its joints. Instead, it should be encouraged to run and play at its own chosen pace.

long hair over eyes
long, slightly pointed muzzle

coat longer and more wiry under jaw

small ears
powerful thighs
rough and hardy coat

Height 28–35 in (71–90 cm)	Weight 90–120 lb (40–55 kg)	Temperament Gentle, friendly

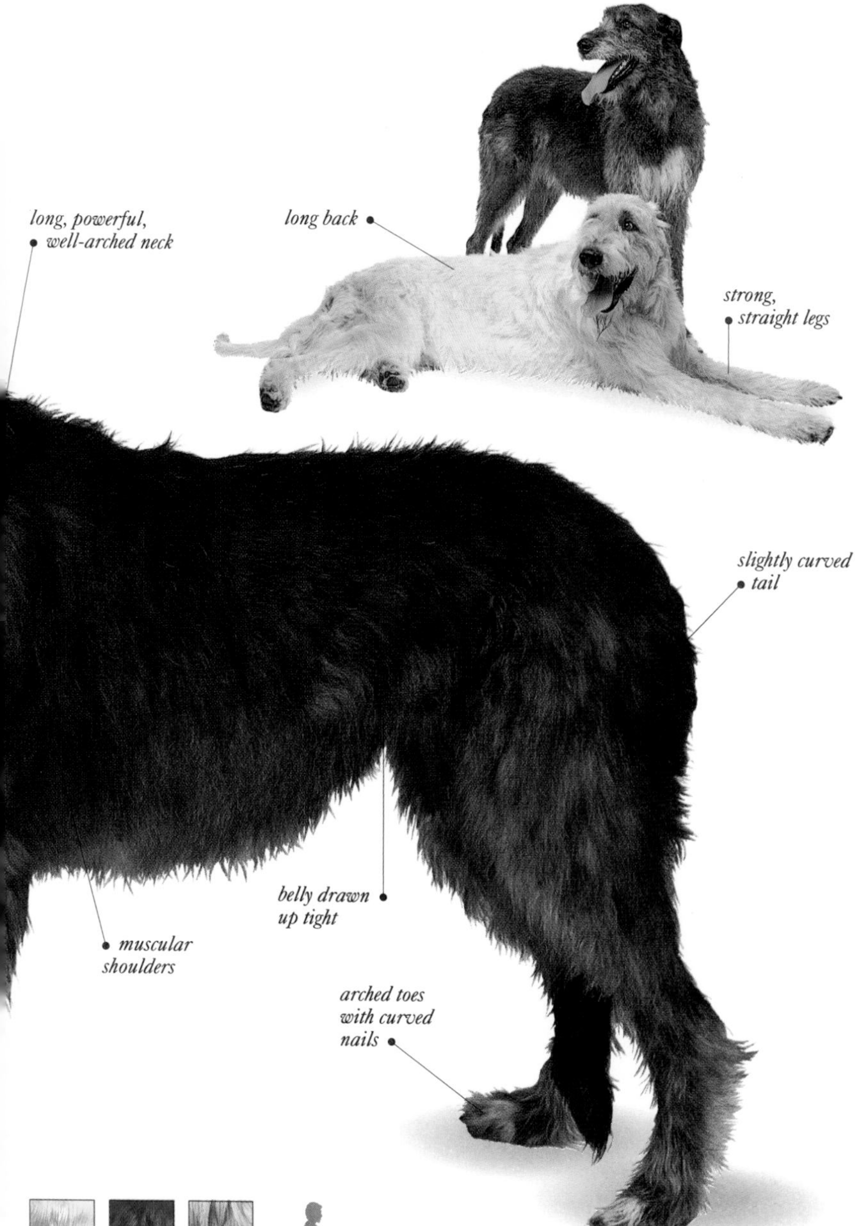
long, powerful, well-arched neck
long back
strong, straight legs
slightly curved tail
belly drawn up tight
muscular shoulders
arched toes with curved nails

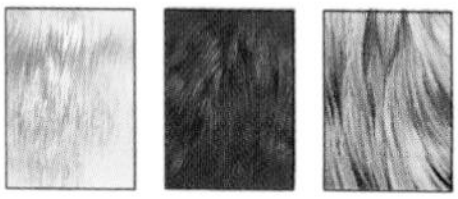

COLOR TYPES

Country of origin Ireland	First use Hunting hares	Origins 1500s

KERRY BEAGLE

Mostly black and tan in coloration, although mottled and tricolor forms are not unknown, the Kerry Beagle is a substantially larger animal than the Beagle (see p.146). This dashing hound is close-coated, has a deep muzzle, and medium-length, unfolded ears. Essentially a pack dog, the Kerry Beagle is as yet unrecognized as a breed, even in Ireland, in spite of its long history and unmistakeable appearance.

• **HISTORY** Although the ancestry of the Kerry Beagle is obscure, it is thought the breed descended from a larger, deer-hunting hound. Its appearance also suggests that its development could have involved the Bloodhound.

• **REMARK** The breed is now used mainly for hunting small game and fowl.

• **OTHER NAMES** Pocadan.

broad skull
heavy muzzle

long, straight ears

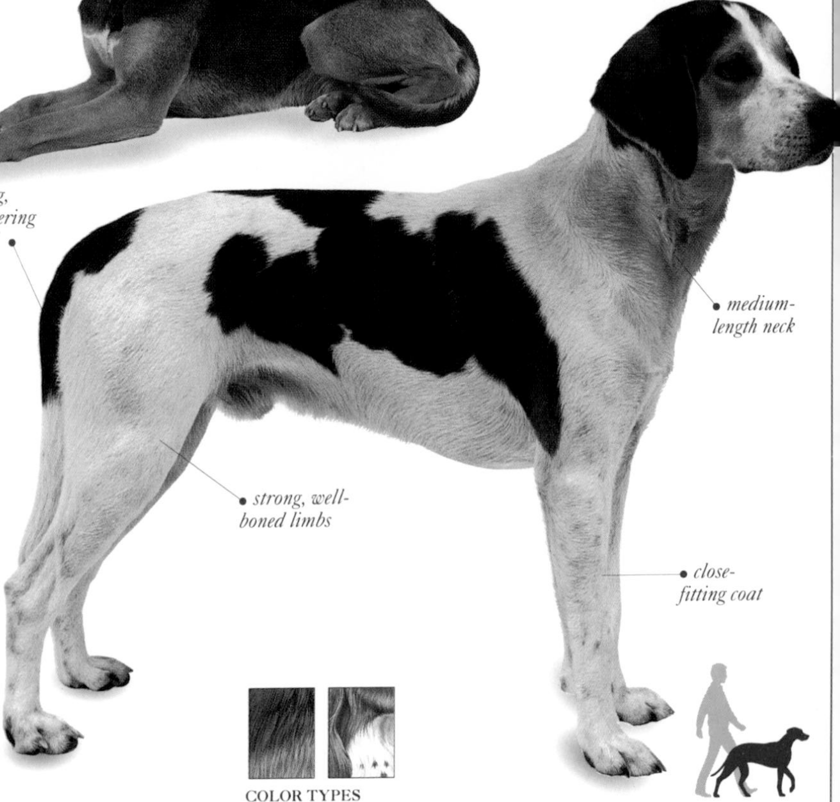
long, tapering tail
medium-length neck
strong, well-boned limbs
close-fitting coat

COLOR TYPES

Height 22–26 in (56–66 cm)	Weight 45–60 lb (20–27 kg)	Temperament Active, friendly

Country of origin Ireland	First use Coursing hares	Origins 1600s

LURCHER

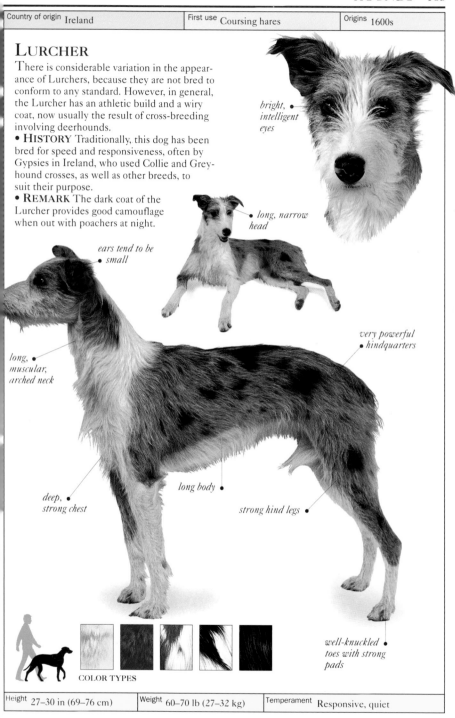

There is considerable variation in the appearance of Lurchers, because they are not bred to conform to any standard. However, in general, the Lurcher has an athletic build and a wiry coat, now usually the result of cross-breeding involving deerhounds.

• **HISTORY** Traditionally, this dog has been bred for speed and responsiveness, often by Gypsies in Ireland, who used Collie and Greyhound crosses, as well as other breeds, to suit their purpose.

• **REMARK** The dark coat of the Lurcher provides good camouflage when out with poachers at night.

bright, intelligent eyes

long, narrow head

ears tend to be small
long, muscular, arched neck
very powerful hindquarters
long body
deep, strong chest
strong hind legs
well-knuckled toes with strong pads

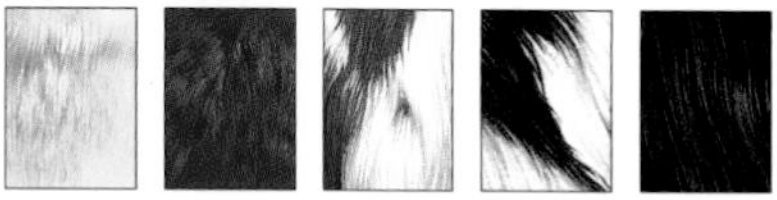

COLOR TYPES

Height 27–30 in (69–76 cm)	Weight 60–70 lb (27–32 kg)	Temperament Responsive, quiet

Country of origin	First use	Origins
Belgium	Tracking scent	800s

Bloodhound

The most famous scent hound in the world, the Bloodhound is also the largest. The folds of loose skin apparent on its face and neck create the familiar mournful expression, which belies the breed's lively and active nature. In spite of its ferocious image, this dog is very friendly toward people. It has a very distinctive, melodious voice that cannot be ignored.

• **History** The likely ancestor of today's Bloodhound is the ancient St. Hubert's Hound. It was supposedly brought back to Europe by soldiers who had been fighting in the Crusades.

• **Remark** This indomitable hound has incredible tracking skills and has proved itself capable of following a trail over 14 days old. This dog has been known to pursue a scent with its relentless, swinging stride for 138 miles (220 kilometers). Evidence discovered by a Bloodhound has been used in some court cases.

• **Other Names** St. Hubert's Hound.

dark brown or hazel eyes

thin, soft ears tend to curl inward and backward
long tail tapers to a point

long, narrow head with pronounced occipital peak
characteristic dewlap

Height	Weight	Temperament
23–27 in (58–69 cm)	80–90 lb (36–41 kg)	Determined, responsive

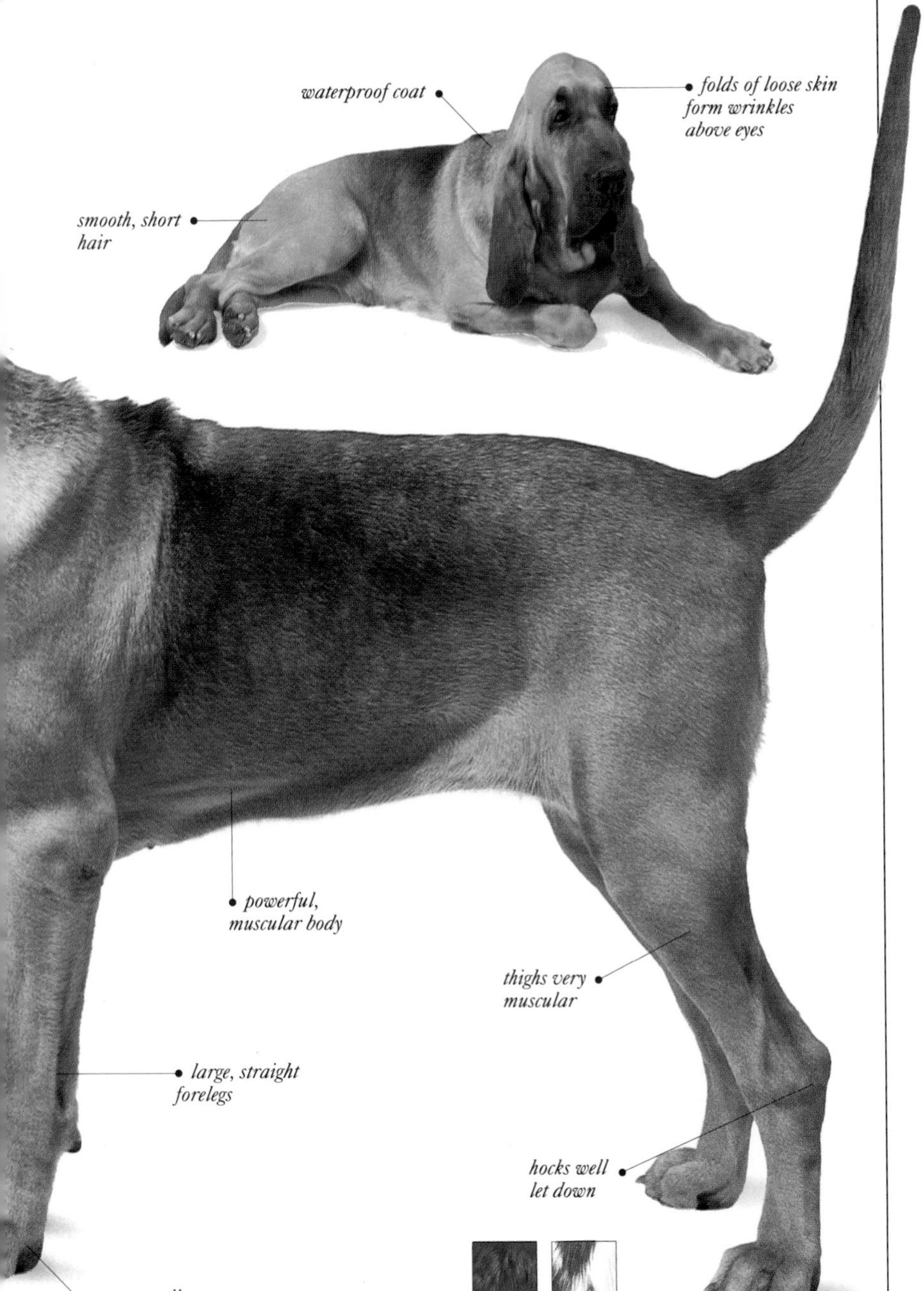
waterproof coat
folds of loose skin form wrinkles above eyes
smooth, short hair
powerful, muscular body
thighs very muscular
large, straight forelegs
hocks well let down
strong, well-knuckled feet

COLOR TYPES

Country of origin France	First use Tracking large game	Origins 1800s

BILLY

A large hound, with distinctive pale coloration, the Billy has a surprisingly musical call, which is often heard when packs are in pursuit of their quarry. The head is fine and lean, with a square muzzle and a prominent stop. Although not a heavy dog, a pack of Billys is nevertheless powerful enough for their favorite quarry, deer, and more than a match for wild boar, which they still track in France today.

• **HISTORY** The Billy is named after the home of the breeder who created them – Monsieur Gaston Hublot de Rivault, who lived at the Château de Billy, in Poitou. He used mainly bicolor Céris hounds and the now-extinct Montemboeuf, another bicolor breed. Foxhounds and the Larye, with its keen nose, have also contributed to its lineage.

• **REMARK** Just two Billys survived World War II. These dogs were used by the son of the breed's founder to save these large hounds from extinction.

slightly domed skull and moderate-length head
upper lip extends down over lower jaw

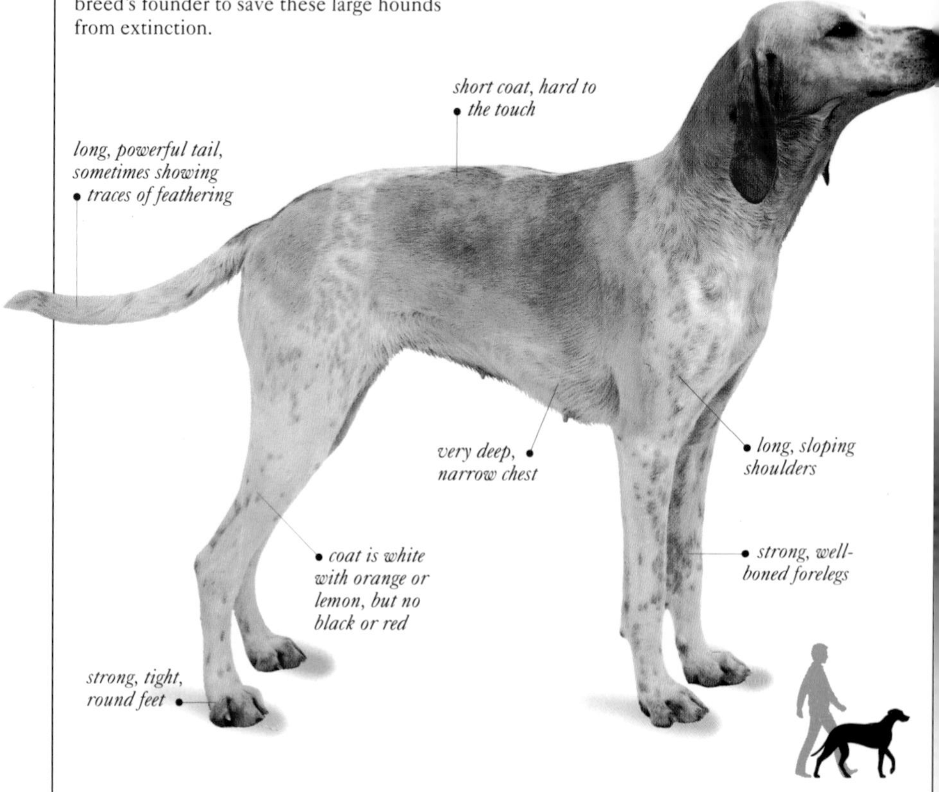
short coat, hard to the touch
long, powerful tail, sometimes showing traces of feathering
very deep, narrow chest
long, sloping shoulders
coat is white with orange or lemon, but no black or red
strong, well-boned forelegs
strong, tight, round feet

Height 24–26 in (61–66 cm)	Weight 55–66 lb (25–30 kg)	Temperament Intelligent, active

Country of origin France	First use Hunting small game	Origins 1800s

BASSET FAUVE DE BRETAGNE

Overall, the body shape of the Basset Fauve de Bretagne is typical of basset breeds – long relative to its height, with slightly crooked legs and a long face. The coat, however, is quite different, having neither the rough texture of the Basset Griffon Vendéen (see p.175), nor the smoothness of the Basset Artésian Normand (see p.173).

• **HISTORY** This breed was developed from the larger Griffon Fauve de Bretagne crossed with other bassets. It retains the solid coloration of its relative, sometimes with a single white spot on the chest or neck, although this is not encouraged.

• **REMARK** Traditionally, these dogs hunted small game in packs of four.

• **OTHER NAMES** Tawny Brittany Basset.

dark, open nose
oval ears set level with eyes and pleated at base

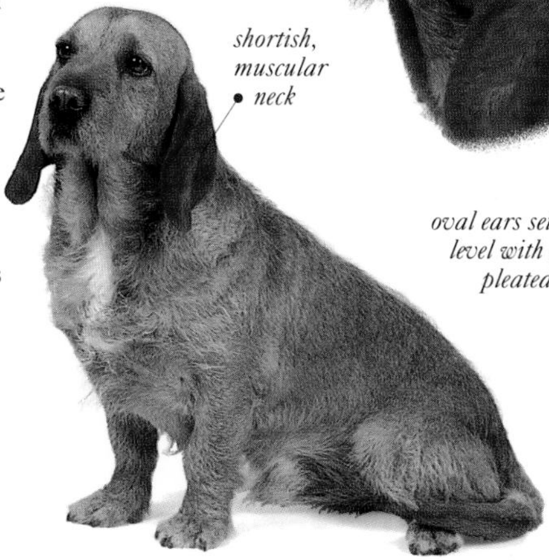
shortish, muscular neck

lively eyes
shortish, flat coat, hard and coarse
any white mark on chest to be discouraged
thick tail, tapering toward point
prominent breastbone
typical, slightly crooked legs, but can be straight

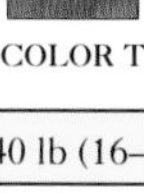

COLOR TYPES

Height 13–15 in (33–38 cm)	Weight 36–40 lb (16–18 kg)	Temperament Lively, friendly

Country of origin France	First use Hunting deer and wild boar	Origins 1300s

GRAND BLEU DE GASCOGNE

Considered by many hound enthusiasts to be the most majestic and aristocratic of the French breeds, the Grand Bleu de Gascogne is large and powerful. It was developed in the old French provinces of Guyenne and Gascony, in the dry and hot Midi region of southwestern France. Not especially quick in terms of pace, it displays prodigious stamina. Its characteristic mottled appearance is shared with other hounds from the area.

• **HISTORY** The origins of the Grand Bleu de Gascogne are not known for sure, but it is certainly an ancient breed. This dog was originally used to hunt wolves, a task it performed until the latter years of the last century. The breed first appeared in the USA in the late 1700s.

• **REMARK** Although it is not recognized by the AKC, this hound is found in the USA more often than anywhere else in the world.

• **OTHER NAMES** Large Blue Gascony Hound.

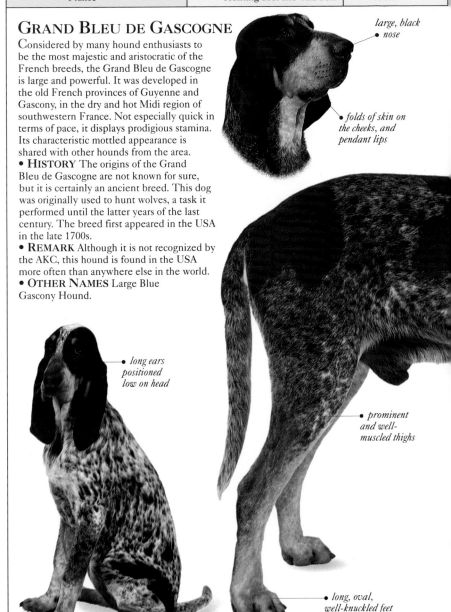

large, black nose
folds of skin on the cheeks, and pendant lips

long ears positioned low on head

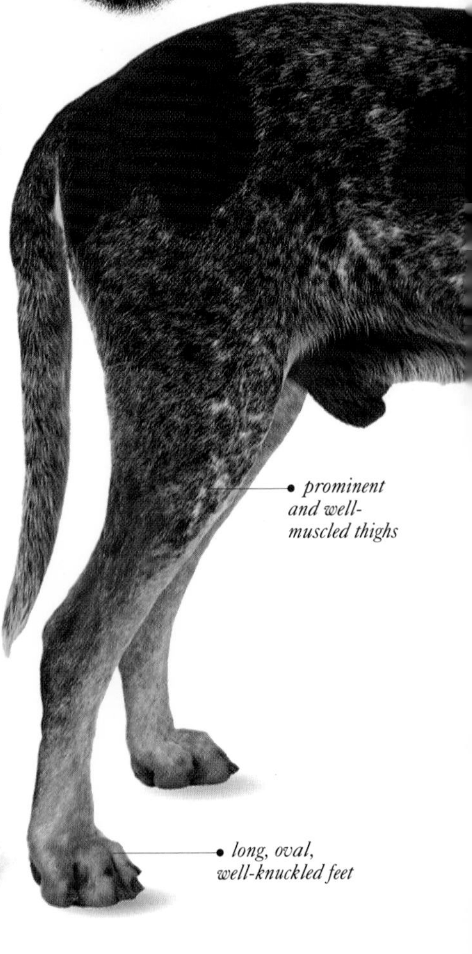
prominent and well-muscled thighs
long, oval, well-knuckled feet

Height 25–28 in (64–71 cm)	Weight 71–77 lb (32–35 kg)	Temperament Active, friendly

light tan markings above both eyes, creating a "four-eyed" impression
elongated head with convex skull
ears curl inward
long, powerful forelegs
dense mottling on weather-resistant coat
slightly sloping pasterns
strong, black claws

Country of origin France	First use Hunting hares	Origins 1500s

CHIEN D'ARTOIS

This small, well-muscled, tricolor scent hound is one of the original breeds of French hunting dog. It is the fore-runner of many of the later breeds of hound still seen today.

• **HISTORY** This dog is named after the French province of Artois, where it was developed by crossing hounds and pointing breeds. Later infusions of British gundog blood almost resulted in the original breed's total disappearance. However, the numbers of pure Artois are now slowly recovering in France.

• **REMARK** This breed specializes in small game animals such as hares.

• **OTHER NAMES** Briquet.

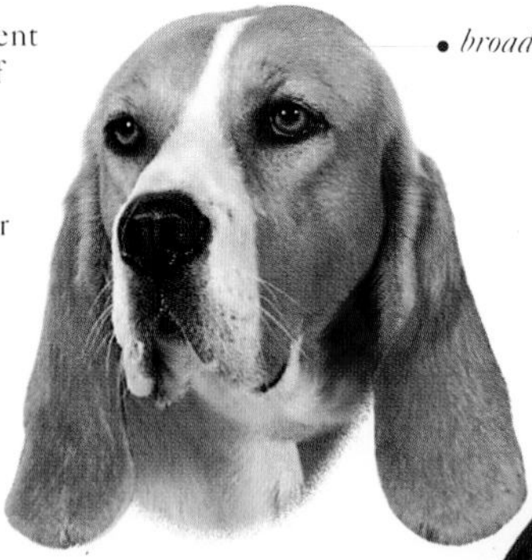
broad skull
long, broad, flat ears set on level with eyes

long tail carried in sicklelike curve
long, powerful neck
fine, short hairs make up a close-fitting coat

slightly creased facial skin
square muzzle and black nose
distinct saddlelike marking

Height 20½–23 in (52–58 cm)	Weight 40–53 lb (18–24 kg)	Temperament Lively, friendly

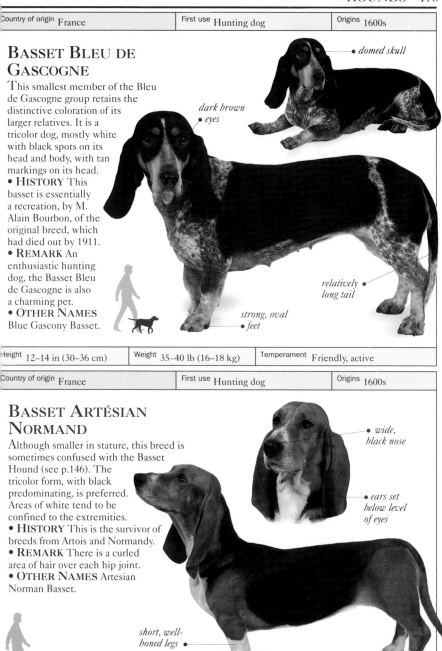

Country of origin	First use	Origins
France	Hunting dog	1600s

Basset Bleu de Gascogne

domed skull

This smallest member of the Bleu de Gascogne group retains the distinctive coloration of its larger relatives. It is a tricolor dog, mostly white with black spots on its head and body, with tan markings on its head.

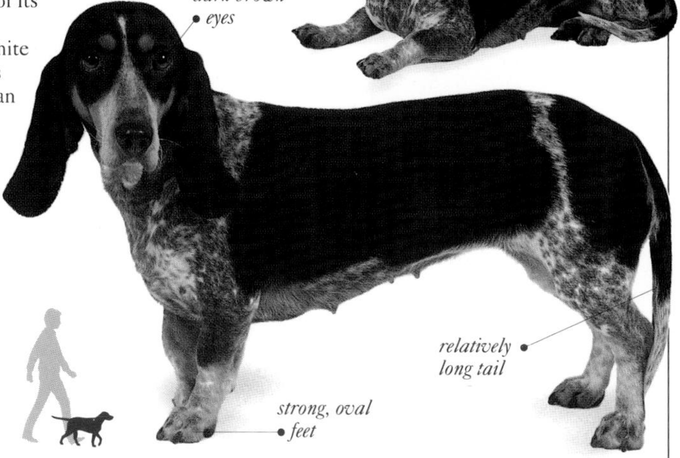
dark brown eyes
relatively long tail
strong, oval feet

• **History** This basset is essentially a recreation, by M. Alain Bourbon, of the original breed, which had died out by 1911.

• **Remark** An enthusiastic hunting dog, the Basset Bleu de Gascogne is also a charming pet.

• **Other Names** Blue Gascony Basset.

Height	Weight	Temperament
12–14 in (30–36 cm)	35–40 lb (16–18 kg)	Friendly, active

Country of origin	First use	Origins
France	Hunting dog	1600s

Basset Artésian Normand

Although smaller in stature, this breed is sometimes confused with the Basset Hound (see p.146). The tricolor form, with black predominating, is preferred. Areas of white tend to be confined to the extremities.

• **History** This is the survivor of breeds from Artois and Normandy.

• **Remark** There is a curled area of hair over each hip joint.

• **Other Names** Artesian Norman Basset.

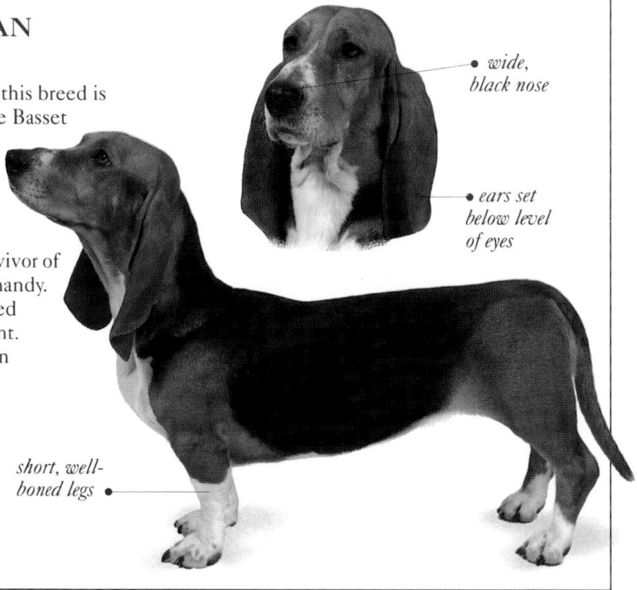
wide, black nose
ears set below level of eyes
short, well-boned legs

Height	Weight	Temperament
10–14 in (25–36 cm)	33 lb (15 kg)	Active, gentle

Country of origin France	First use Hunting roe deer	Origins 1800s

GRAND GASCON-SAINTONGEOIS

Compared with hounds seen in other countries, the Grand Gascon-Saintongeois is a large dog, with exaggeratedly long ears. It has loose folds of skin around the head and neck. Ticking is evident in its fine, short, white coat. This dog has a black mask and head, with black often extending down on to its shoulders. A smaller version of this breed, the Petit Gascon-Saintongeois, is identical in all respects except height.

• **HISTORY** This breed was created by Baron de Virelade as a result of crossing the Gascon Bleu, Saintongeois, and Ariègeois breeds.

• **REMARK** Although a popular pack hound in France, the breed is unknown in other countries.

• **OTHER NAMES** Virelade.

very pronounced occipital peak
long, conical, pendulous ears
clear tan markings restricted to head

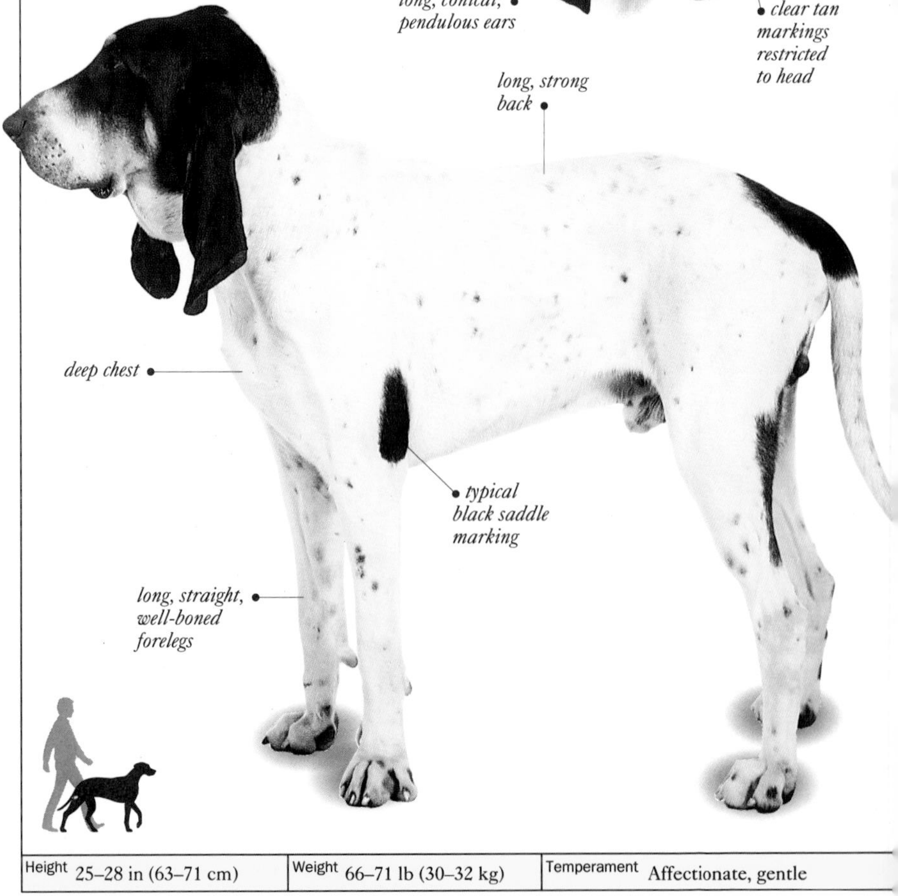
long, strong back
deep chest
typical black saddle marking
long, straight, well-boned forelegs

Height 25–28 in (63–71 cm)	Weight 66–71 lb (30–32 kg)	Temperament Affectionate, gentle

Country of origin France	First use Coursing hares	Origins 1700s

Grand Basset Griffon Vendéen

This form of the Basset Griffon Vendéen differs from its smaller relative only in size. White is often the predominant color in bi- and tricolor forms. It is an active dog and is valued for hunting rabbits and hares.

• **HISTORY** Both basset forms are descended from the Grand Griffon Vendéen (see p.176).

• **REMARK** The Grand Basset Griffon Vendéen can be very affectionate, yet has an independent nature.

• **OTHER NAMES** Large Vendéen Griffon.

GRAND BASSET GRIFFON VENDÉEN
PETIT BASSET GRIFFON VENDÉEN
solid-boned forelegs

ears attach below eye level
tail tapers along its length
wide, deep chest with rounded ribs
legs straighter than most bassets
large, powerful feet

COLOR TYPES

Height 15–16½ in (38–42 cm)	Weight 40–44 lb (18–20 kg)	Temperament Affectionate, independent

Country of origin France	First use Hunting boar	Origins 1400s

Grand Griffon Vendéen

The Grand Griffon Vendéen is either white or wheaten, with various other color markings. This dog adapts well to land or water, having a rough, wiry outercoat and a thick undercoat. Its head is slightly elongated, and its nose is well developed. It has a mustache of longer hair above its lips.

• **History** Originating in the district of Vendée in France, its ancestors are the St. Hubert Hound (see pp.184–85), the Bracco Italiano (see p.101), and the Griffon Nivernais (see p.177).

• **Remark** Excitable at the start of a hunt, this hound may tire before the quarry is in the bag. It is an excellent dog for the part-time hunter.

• **Other Names** Large Vendéen Griffon.

large, dark eyes

large black nose and mustache
straight, well-muscled back
tail carried in a saberlike curve
ears shaped like an elongated oval
firm, well-boned legs
strong chest

wiry coat must never be woolly

long hair covers feet

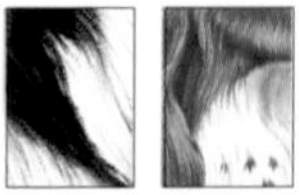
COLOR TYPES

Height 23½–26 in (60–66 cm)	Weight 66–77 lb (30–35 kg)	Temperament Lively, friendly

Country of origin	First use	Origins
France	Hunting small game	1600s

Briquet Griffon Vendéen

This smaller relative of the Grand Griffon Vendéen (left) has a short head and low-set ears. It has a dense, bushy double coat, in solid or mixed colors.

• **History** This hound shares a common ancestry with the Grand Griffon Vendéen but, instead of hunting boars and wolves, the Briquet's more likely quarry will be rabbits.

• **Remark** This breed works either in a pack or as a solitary hunter.

• **Other Names** Medium Vendéen Griffon.

large, black nose with facial whiskers
solid bone structure
thick-soled feet

COLOR TYPES

narrow, pendulous ears

Height	Weight	Temperament
19–22 in (48–56 cm)	53 lb (24 kg)	Energetic, lively

Country of origin	First use	Origins
France	Hunting large game	1200s

Griffon Nivernais

The Griffon Nivernais is a tall, light-framed dog, not unlike the Spinone (see p.100) and the Otter Hound (see p.149). It has a bushy, slightly unkempt appearance. The coat hair is long and hard, and usually gray or fawn in color.

• **History** This is an ancient breed descended from the now-extinct Chien Gris de St. Louis.

• **Remark** This hound was developed specifically to hunt wild boar and bear.

• **Other Names** Chien de Pays.

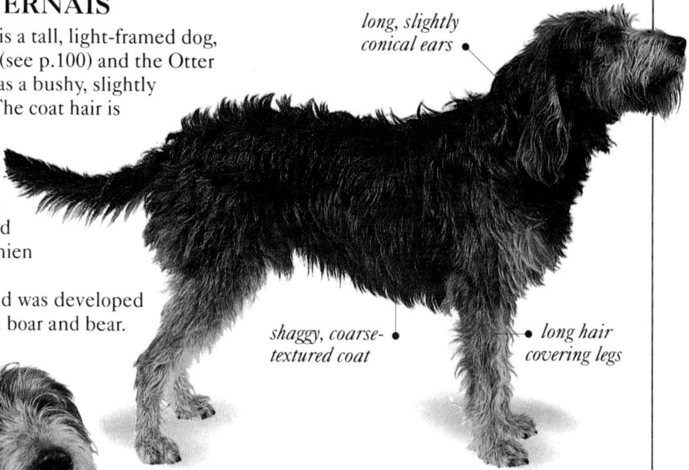
long, slightly conical ears
shaggy, coarse-textured coat
long hair covering legs

broad, prominent muzzle

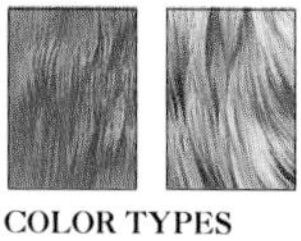

COLOR TYPES

Height	Weight	Temperament
21–24 in (53–62 cm)	50–55 lb (23–25 kg)	Active, lively

Country of origin France	First use Hunting rabbits	Origins 1500s

Petit Bleu de Gascogne

In spite of its name, the Petit Bleu de Gascogne is a relatively large breed of hound. Although a relative of the Petit Griffon Bleu de Gascogne (right), it can be distinguished by its ears, which are folded rather than flat, and larger in size. It is also slightly taller in the leg and of a heavier build, and has a smoother, shorter coat.

• **History** Selective breeding, essentially from the Grand Bleu de Gascogne (see pp.170–71), which led to a reduction in its size, underlies the development of this breed of dog. It originated in the province of Gascony, close to the Pyrenees in the southwest of France.

• **Remark** The Petit Bleu de Gascogne is highly prized in its homeland for its ability to hunt rabbits and hares.

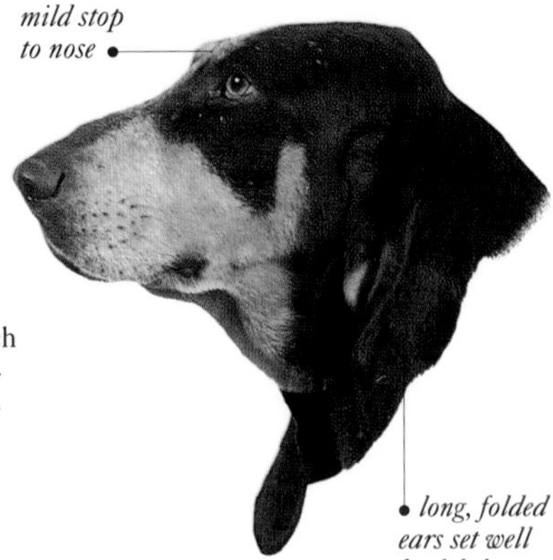
mild stop to nose
long, folded ears set well back below eye level

characteristic tan markings above eyes
straight, well-muscled back
refined, narrow head
tail tapers along its length, finishing in a point
oval feet

Height 19–23 in (48–58 cm)	Weight 40–46 lb (18–21 kg)	Temperament Proud, tenacious

Country of origin	First use	Origins
France	Hunting hares	1700s

PETIT GRIFFON BLEU DE GASCOGNE

The rough, wiry nature of the coat of this breed sets it apart from the other Bleu de Gascogne breeds. However, it still retains the characteristic coloration of the group, with the tan areas confined essentially to the head, as is the solid black coloration. The rest of the body should ideally appear bluish, resulting from the roaning of black and white hairs in the coat.

• **HISTORY** Of uncertain origin, the Petit Griffon Bleu de Gascogne is described as having a "rustic appearance," which reflects the involvement of the Petit Bleu de Gascogne and wire-haired griffons in its ancestry.

• **REMARK** This good-natured breed is considered to rank among the rarest of all of today's French hounds.

eyebrows must not obscure eyes
long ears lying unfolded, close to face

long, straight back
close, harsh coat – never curly or woolly
oval feet with firm toes
coat denser on thighs

Height	Weight	Temperament
17–21 in (43–52 cm)	40–42 lb (18–19 kg)	Diligent, friendly

Country of origin	First use	Origins
France	Hunting small game	1970s

ANGLO-FRANCAIS DE PETITE VÉNERIE

slightly domed skull

This is the smallest of the three Anglo-Francais breeds. Generally, this scent hound's coat is colored tan and white, black and white, or a combination of white, black, and tan. Although compact, it has an athletic, well-muscled body, a head that is slightly small in relation to its body size, low-set ears, and a well-developed nose.

• **HISTORY** This is a "hound in the making," so its line is not yet fixed. The dominant influences so far are French hounds and the Beagle (see p.146). A preliminary standard was first drawn up in 1978.

• **REMARK** Of all the Anglo-Francais breeds, the Petite makes the best house dog.

• **OTHER NAMES** Small French-English Hound.

medium-length, pendulous ears
tail carried erect when dog is alert
compact, well-muscled neck
broad chest
short, smooth coat, but wire-haired individuals are not unknown
straight forelegs

Height	Weight	Temperament
18–22 in (46–56 cm)	35–44 lb (16–20 kg)	Reserved, willing

Country of origin France	First use Hunting wolves	Origins 1200s

Griffon Fauve de Bretagne

The Griffon Fauve de Bretagne is mainly distinguished by its coat, which is very coarse-textured, without being too long. Coloration varies through shades of fawn to brownish red; black is not a permitted color. This well-muscled dog has a slightly elongated muzzle, either a black or a brown nose, and long, pendulous ears terminating in a point. This is an excellent pack hound, but it is virtually unknown outside its native France.

• **History** This ancient breed of hound was very well known during the Middle Ages in France. It reached its peak of popularity during the 1800s.

• **Remark** In recent years, fears were expressed that the breed standard was becoming diluted. Very strict qualifications are now set for all show dogs.

• **Other Names** Tawny Brittany Griffon.

narrow skull

COLOR TYPES

very stiff, coarse coat, never curly
elongated muzzle
long tail
longer hair on chest
stout, well-boned legs
hard, narrow feet

Height 20–22 in (51–56 cm)	Weight 44 lb (20 kg)	Temperament Active, courageous

Country of origin France	First use Hunting deer and hares	Origins 1600s

PORCELAINE

The magnificent white coat of the Porcelaine is the inspiration for this breed's name, which in French means literally "porcelain." It is a solid white coat composed of very short, fine-textured hairs, although orange-colored markings may be present, especially on the ears. Its head is finely formed, its ears are long, and its build is light but well muscled.

• **HISTORY** This is thought to be the oldest of the French scent hounds, evolved from the now-extinct Montaimboeuf. The breed died out during the French Revolution but was re-created in the mid-1800s by Swiss enthusiasts.

• **REMARK** The Porcelaine has an excellent sense of smell and a fine, musical voice.

• **OTHER NAMES** Chien de Franche-Comte.

finely chiseled head

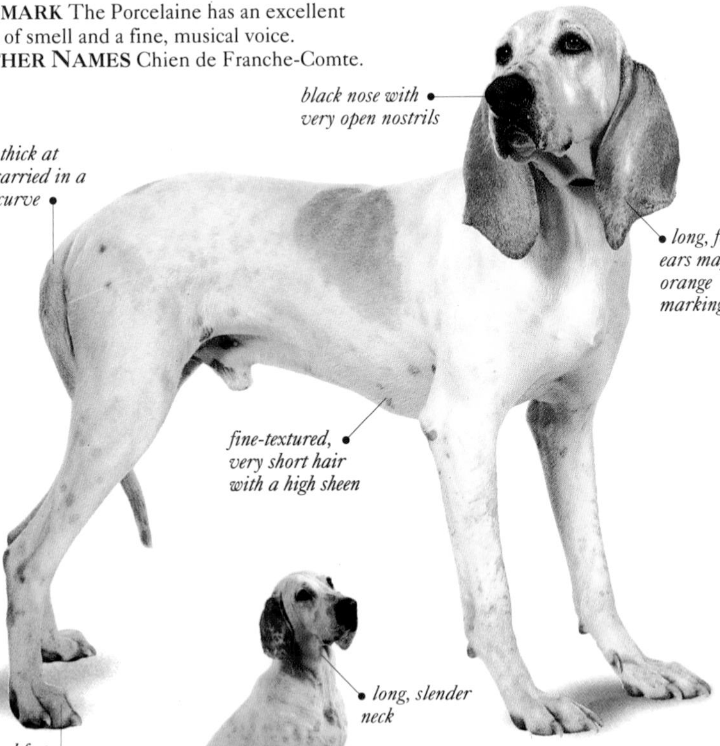
black nose with very open nostrils
tail is thick at base, carried in a slight curve
long, folded ears may have orange markings
fine-textured, very short hair with a high sheen
broad feet with well-arched toes

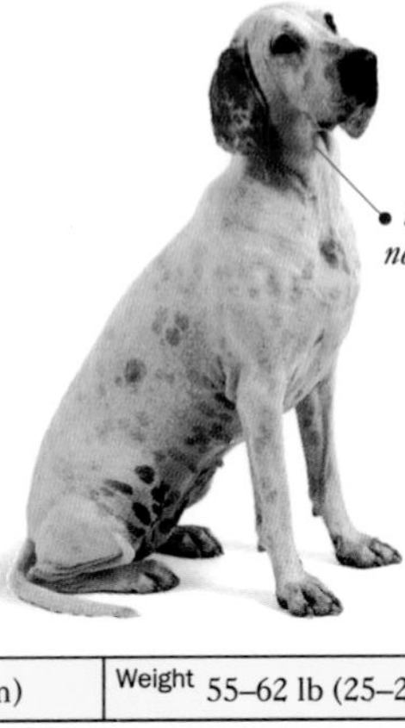
long, slender neck

Height 22–23 in (56–58 cm)	Weight 55–62 lb (25–28 kg)	Temperament Active, friendly

Country of origin	First use	Origins
Switzerland	Hunting small game	1500s

JURA LAUFHUND: BRUNO

This hound, from the Jura region of western Switzerland close to the French border, is characterized by the absence of white markings in its coat. Otherwise, the Bruno Jura is similar to laufhunds from other regions. It can be distinguished immediately from the St. Hubert form (see pp.184–85) by its less massive head and generally more refined appearance.

• **HISTORY** The laufhund is thought to descend from the old, heavier, French breeds, of which only smooth-haired forms survive.

• **REMARK** This breed retains a strong hunting instinct and requires plenty of exercise to remain in good condition.

• **OTHER NAMES** Jura Hound.

broad, round skull

long, broad back
large, black, saddle-shaped marking on back
ears set low on head, and folded
round feet with hard pads

large, black nose with broad nostrils

COLOR TYPES

Height	Weight	Temperament
18–23 in (46–58 cm)	34–44 lb (15–20 kg)	Lively, determined

Country of origin Switzerland	First use Hunting game	Origins 1500s

JURA LAUFHUND: ST. HUBERT

Although the black-and-tan coloration of this hound suggests a close affinity with the Bruno Jura Laufhund (see p.183), it is somewhat different in appearance. It tends to be of heavier build, with wrinkled skin on its forehead, reminiscent of a Bloodhound. The black markings may take the form of a saddle over the back, or they may be more widespread, typically on the head and legs, contrasting with tan areas.

• **HISTORY** The St. Hubert is thought to have a close relationship with the now-extinct St. Hubert Hound of France. This Swiss breed is certainly derived from French stock.

• **REMARK** The word *laufhund* means "walking dog". A keen tracker, it bays loudly when following a scent. This laufhund has plenty of stamina and is used to hunt a variety of game, ranging from small hares and foxes to larger animals such as deer.

• **OTHER NAMES** Jura Hound.

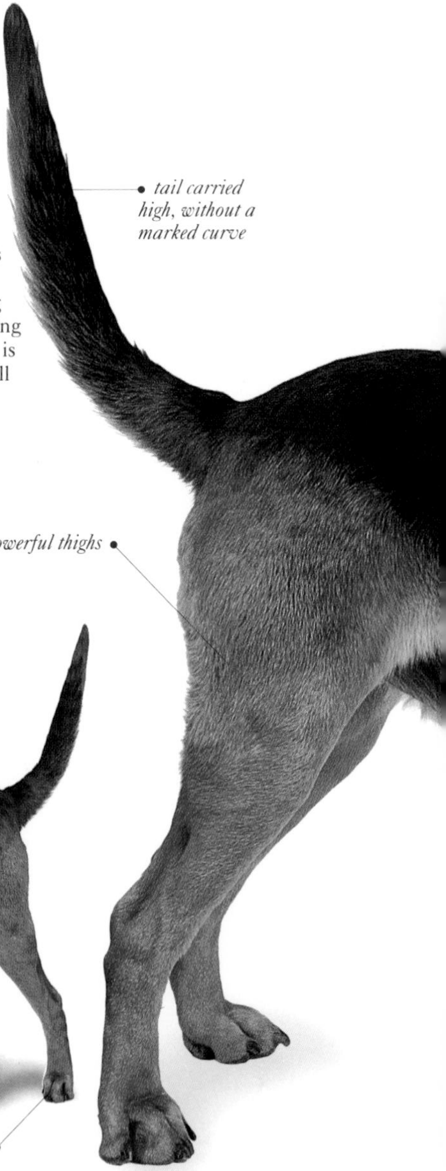
tail carried high, without a marked curve
powerful thighs

relatively long, straight back
rounded feet

Height 46–58 cm (18–23 in)	Weight 15–20 kg (34–44 lb)	Temperament Active, friendly

wrinkled skin
on forehead
prominent black nose
with wide nostrils
folds of loose skin
evident on back
long,
pendant ears
heavy, massive,
domed skull
deep
ribcage
strong,
straight forelegs
pronounced
dewlap
strong, dark
nails

Country of origin Hungary	First use Hunting small game	Origins 800s

HUNGARIAN GREYHOUND

This elegant breed of greyhound is long-legged, lean, and closely resembles the Greyhound proper (see p.150), although it is somewhat smaller in stature. The head and muzzle are wide for a dog that relies on sight rather than scenting ability. Its coat is short and coarse, and solid colors and brindles are acceptable.

• **HISTORY** This is an ancient breed which accompanied the fierce Magyar people into central Europe in the 10th century.

• **REMARK** This breed is not well-known outside of its native Hungary and is rarely seen at shows.

• **OTHER NAMES** Magyar Agár.

ears folded back
wide muzzle
elongated head
prominent breastbone
short, sleek, coarse textured coat
long, fine-boned limbs
long, thin tail, curled at end

COLOR TYPES

Height 25–27½ in (64–70 cm)	Weight 49–68 lb (22–31 kg)	Temperament Active, affectionate

Country of origin Switzerland	First use Hunting in Alpine regions	Origins 1000s

BERNER LAUFHUND

This breed of hound has a narrow head and long, folded ears. Its body is long but not heavy, with strong, well-boned legs. The Berner Laufhund's soft undercoat is covered with a harder, tricolor outercoat.

• **HISTORY** These hounds have been used by Swiss Alpine hunters for about 900 years.

• **REMARK** The formation of the Swiss Hound Club in 1931 is largely responsible for the preservation of this breed.

• **OTHER NAMES** Bernese Hound.

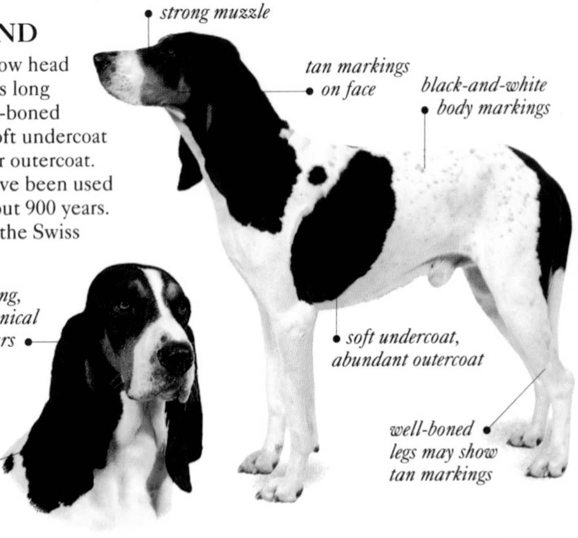
strong muzzle
tan markings on face
black-and-white body markings
soft undercoat, abundant outercoat
well-boned legs may show tan markings
long, conical ears
thick, powerful neck

Height 18–23 in (46–58 cm)	Weight 34–44 lb (15–20 kg)	Temperament Active, responsive

Country of origin	First use	Origins
Switzerland	Hunting small game	1500s

Schweizer Laufhund

The bicolor appearance of this hound serves to distinguish it from other related Swiss breeds. White predominates in the coat, offset against yellowish orange, orange, or even red markings, which are large in extent, although occasional small spots of color are not penalized in the show ring. The Schweizer Laufhund is a talented tracker and has a powerful voice, which is invariably heard whenever a scent trail is located.

- **HISTORY** This breed originated close to the Franco-Swiss border and is related to the French breeds found in that region.
- **REMARK** The shorter-legged version of this breed, known as the Schweizer Neiderlaufhund, has identical coat coloration.
- **OTHER NAMES** Swiss Hound.

well-defined stop
large, black nose with broad nostrils
long ears set well back on head

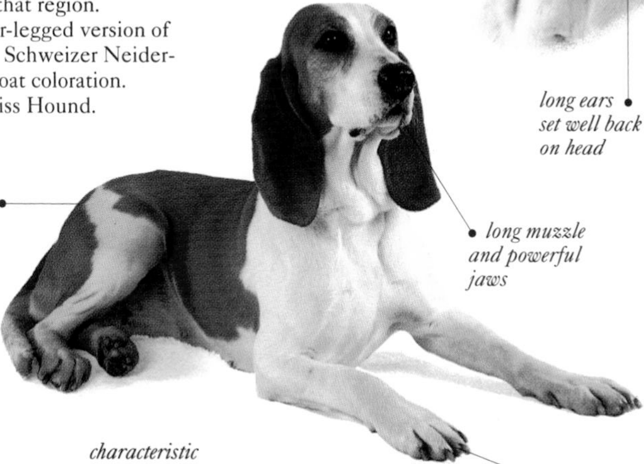
coat either short and smooth or doubled with rough-haired appearance
long muzzle and powerful jaws
round feet with tough pads and hard nails

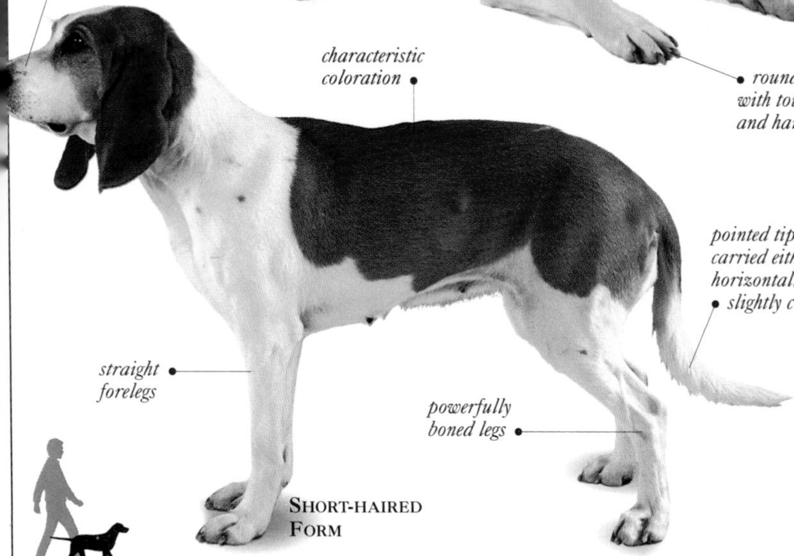
bridge of nose slightly arched
characteristic coloration
pointed tip to tail, carried either horizontally or slightly curved
straight forelegs
powerfully boned legs

Short-haired Form

COLOR TYPES

Height	Weight	Temperament
18–23 in (46–58 cm)	34–44 lb (15–20 kg)	Active, friendly

Country of origin Switzerland	First use Hunting large game	Origins 1500s

LUZERNER LAUFHUND

The Luzerner Laufhund is generally similar to the other four breeds of laufhund that have been developed in Switzerland. This breed, however, is characterized by a distinctive tricolor appearance. The pronounced black ticking over the white areas of the coat gives rise to an impression of blue coloration. There is a short-legged form of this breed, known as the Luzerner Neiderlaufhund, which stands no more than 16½ in (42 cm) tall.

• **HISTORY** The similarity between the Luzerner and French breeds, as well as their geographical proximity, indicate a close ancestral relationship. Its precise origins are unknown, however.

• **REMARK** This breed has excellent tracking abilities, and it gives voice with a very distinctive bark whenever a fresh scent is located.

• **OTHER NAMES** Lucernese Hound.

narrow skull
prominent black nose

long, pendulous, folded ears
heavy ticking in coat, offset against black and tan areas

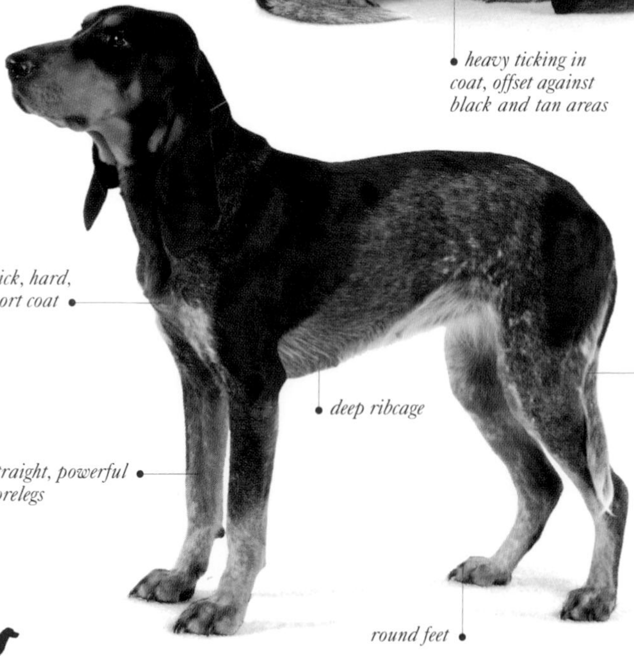
thick, hard, short coat
deep ribcage
tapering tail never held erect
straight, powerful forelegs
round feet

Height 18–23 in (46–58 cm)	Weight 34–44 lb (15–20 kg)	Temperament Active, friendly

Country of origin	First use	Origins
Former Yugoslavia	Tracking and hunting game	1000 BC

Balkan Hound

This obedient hound is black and tan, typically with a distinctive black saddle, flat head, and black marks over the eyes. It is particularly muscular in the shoulders and limbs. A diligent, determined hunter, the Balkan Hound works in packs and is used to hunt game ranging from hares to wild boars.

• **History** The Balkan hound's ancestors are thought to have been brought to the Balkan region from Egypt by Phoenicians in about 1000 BC.

• **Remark** Despite its undoubted tracking skills in many different terrains, the Balkan Hound is still not widely known.

• **Other Names** Balkanski Gonic.

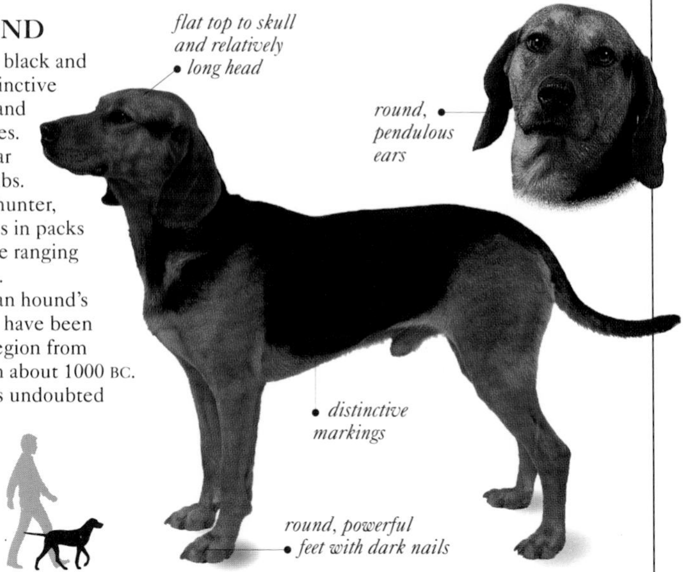
flat top to skull and relatively long head
distinctive markings
round, pendulous ears
round, powerful feet with dark nails

Height	Weight	Temperament
17–21 in (43–53 cm)	44 lb (20 kg)	Active, responsive

Country of origin	First use	Origins
Former Yugoslavia	Hunting small game	1700s

Posavac Hound

The coat of this stocky hound tends to be predominantly red in color. Other colors, such as yellow and fawn, are less common.

• **History** The Posavac probably shares a common origin with other similar breeds that originated in the former Yugoslavia, their ancestors having been introduced via the ports of the Adriatic coast.

• **Remark** Exercise is absolutely essential for this active hound.

• **Other Names** Posavski Gonic.

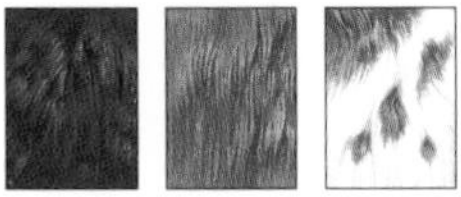

COLOR TYPES

pendulous ears with round tips
white markings tend to be confined to underparts
relatively short legs

thick, hard coat

Height	Weight	Temperament
17–23 in (43–59 cm)	35–45 lb (16–20 kg)	Active, alert

Country of origin Former Yugoslavia	First use Hunting	Origins 1700s

YUGOSLAVIAN MOUNTAIN HOUND

This particular breed of hound, of the many that have originated within the borders of the former country of Yugoslavia, can be recognized by its black-and-tan coloration. The Yugoslavian Mountain Hound has a smooth, coarse-textured, thick outercoat and a very full undercoat, making it ideal for the harsh mountain terrain and thick bushland in which it normally hunts.

• **HISTORY** This is certainly an old breed whose ancestors may have been brought to the Adriatic by the Phoenicians. Selective breeding in different parts of the region has given rise to the diversity of hound breeds seen there today.

• **REMARK** A keen sense of smell, an athletic build, and a good voice make this an excellent hunting dog.

• **OTHER NAMES** Jugoslavenski Planinski Gonic.

broad head
powerful muzzle

long, tapering tail

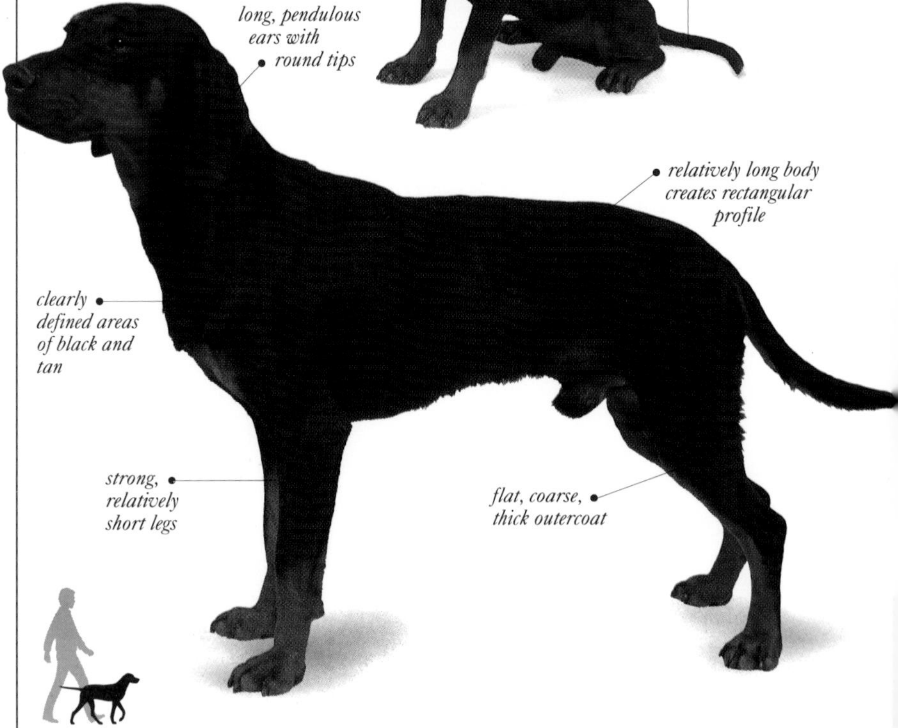
long, pendulous ears with round tips
relatively long body creates rectangular profile
clearly defined areas of black and tan
strong, relatively short legs
flat, coarse, thick outercoat

Height 18–22 in (46–56 cm)	Weight 44–55 lb (20–25 kg)	Temperament Active, friendly

Country of origin Former Yugoslavia	First use Hunting small game	Origins 1800s

YUGOSLAVIAN TRICOLORED HOUND

The coloration of this short-haired breed of hound distinguishes it from the Yugoslavian Mountain Hound (opposite). Tan markings are prominent here, offset against black; a white area is evident at the front of the dog, sometimes extending down to its underparts. This breed is very localized in distribution and is most common in the southern parts of what was formerly Yugoslavia. Even here, however, it has become quite a rare sight in recent years.

• **HISTORY** A combination of sight and scent hound stock, as has been used in other Yugoslavian hounds, underlies this dog's breeding history.

• **REMARK** Although a devoted hunter, this breed is very adaptable and enjoys human companionship.

• **OTHER NAMES** Jugoslavenski Tribarvni Gonic.

white facial blaze
prominent black nose

muscular ears hang down sides of face

black tends to dominate in coat
white tip on tail
prominent white area on front
powerful thighs
white areas on feet and legs
solid, thick pads

Height 18–22 in (46–56 cm)	Weight 44–55 lb (20–25 kg)	Temperament Active, obedient

Country of origin Italy	First use Hunting game	Origins 100s

ITALIAN HOUND

Strong and powerfully built, this hound has a long, tapering muzzle, which is convex when seen in profile, sloping downward to the nose. Its lips are black at the edges.

• **HISTORY** This breed is descended from the early sight hounds, which were probably introduced to Italy by the Phoenicians, and scent hounds from Europe. During the Renaissance it was a popular hunting dog and has recently undergone a further revival in Italy.

• **REMARK** A rough-coated form, known as Segugio Italiano a Pelo Forte, is identical in all respects other than coat type.

• **OTHER NAMES** Segugio Italiano.

low-set, long, folded ears
sickle-shaped tail
thick, very short, shiny coat

COLOR TYPES

Height 20½–23 in (52–58 cm)	Weight 40–62 lb (18–28 kg)	Temperament Docile, active

Country of origin Italy	First use Hunting small game	Origins c.1000 BC

CIRNECO DELL'ETNA

This elegant, athletic Sicilian sight hound also hunts by scent. It is smaller than similar Mediterranean island breeds.

• **HISTORY** The Cirneco dell'Etna is probably descended from ancestral sight-hound stock acquired in Egypt and traded in the Mediterranean by the Phoenicians.

• **REMARK** Surprisingly, this breed is internationally less well known than either the similar Ibizan Hound (see p.194) or the Pharaoh Hound (see p.193).

• **OTHER NAMES** Sicilian Greyhound.

broad, stiff, triangular ears
long, straight forelegs

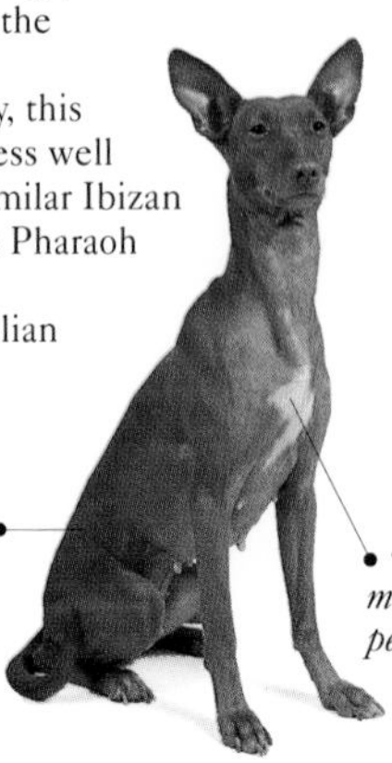
short, smooth coat
white marking permitted

Height 16½–19½ in (42–50 cm)	Weight 18–26 lb (8–12 kg)	Temperament Friendly, alert

Country of origin Malta	First use Hunting rabbits	Origins 1000 BC

Pharaoh Hound

The large, upright ears and the tan coloration of this hound immediately attract attention. It bears a striking likeness to depictions of the Egyptian god Anubis, whose task it was to act as guide for the souls of the dead. Although it is a sight hound, it also tracks its quarry by scent.

• **HISTORY** Ancestors of the Pharaoh Hound are thought to have been brought to Malta by Phoenician traders. Here they remained in a relatively pure state, first attracting attention overseas only during the late 1960s.

• **REMARK** Without adequate exercise, these dogs rapidly become overweight.

• **OTHER NAMES** Kelb Tal-fenek.

broad base to ears, which are very mobile
amber-colored eyes

slightly arched, long, muscular neck
long, lean face
white area on chest, called "the star"
white-tipped, tapering tail, reaching just below hocks
short, glossy coat
white markings may be present on feet
firm, well-knuckled feet

Height 21–25 in (53–64 cm)	Weight 45–55 lb (20–25 kg)	Temperament Affectionate, intelligent

Country of origin Spain	First use Hunting rabbits	Origins 3000BC

IBIZAN HOUND

Using large ears, this hound hunts by means of sound as well as sight. It is quite tall and, compared with other fast-paced hunting dogs, relatively stocky. Variable coloration helps distinguish it from Pharaoh Hounds (see p.193).

• **HISTORY** Images of hounds similar to the Ibizan have been found in Egypt, and date back some 5,000 years. Some were probably taken from there to the island of Ibiza.

• **REMARK** This is a sensitive and loyal dog.

• **OTHER NAMES** Podenco Ibicenco.

ears erect when alert

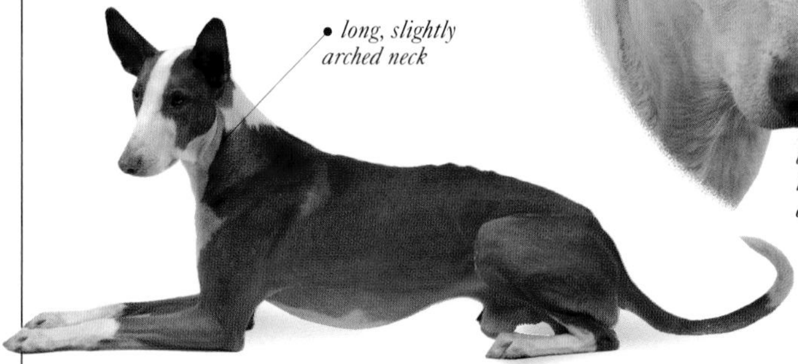
long, slightly arched neck

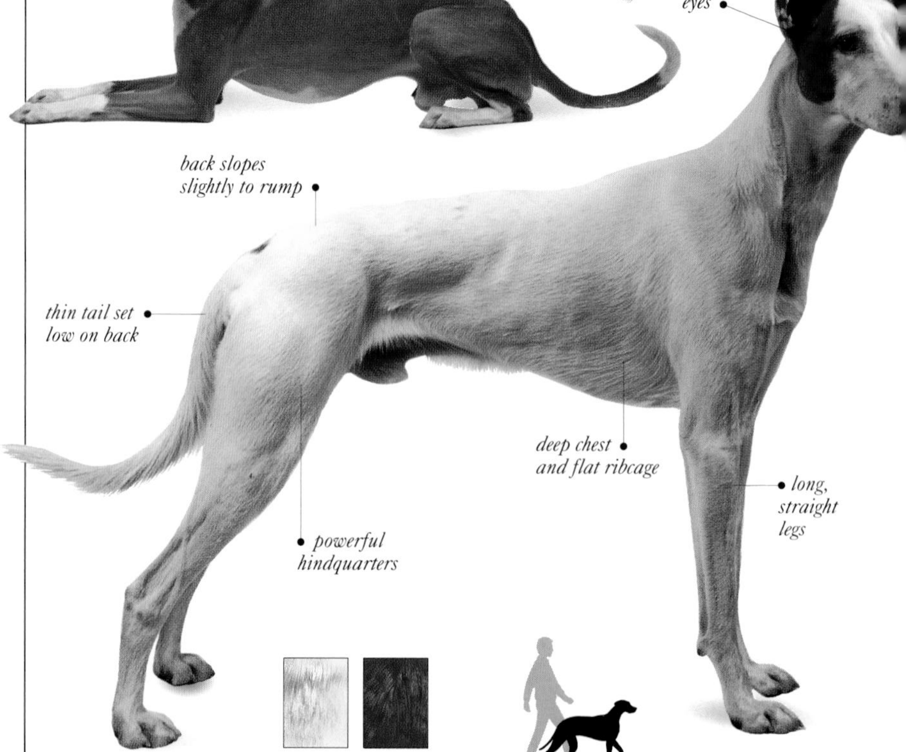
base of ears level with eyes
back slopes slightly to rump
thin tail set low on back
deep chest and flat ribcage
long, straight legs
powerful hindquarters

COLOR TYPES

Height 22½–27½ in (57–70 cm)	Weight 42–55 lb (19–25 kg)	Temperament Alert, adaptable

Country of origin Spain	First use Tracking game	Origins 500s

SABUESO ESPAÑOL

The similarity in appearance of the Sabueso Español and the mastiff breeds indicates that this is an ancient dog. There are two forms of this breed: the de Monte (shown here) weighs about 55 lb (25 kg), stands 22 in (56 cm) high, and has a hard, white coat with red or black patches; the Lebrero form is smaller, standing no more than 20 in (51 cm) high, and is usually of a more uniform red color.

• **HISTORY** Thought to have been introduced to the region by the Phoenicians, this breed has changed little within the confines of the Iberian Peninsula.

• **REMARK** This is still a hunting dog. It does not generally make a good house dog or pet.

• **OTHER NAMES** Spanish Hound.

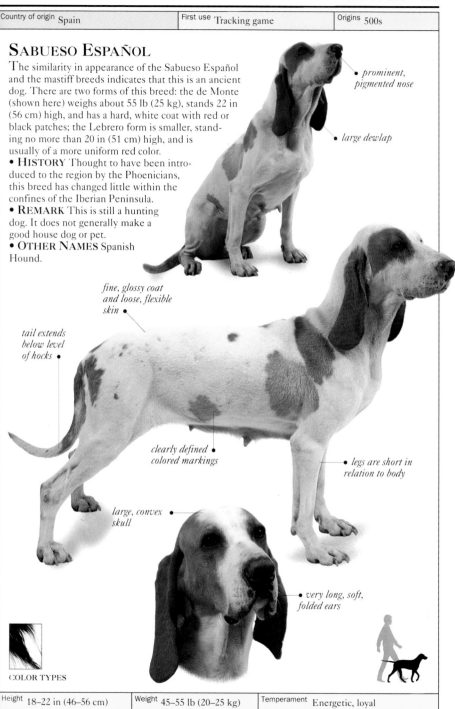

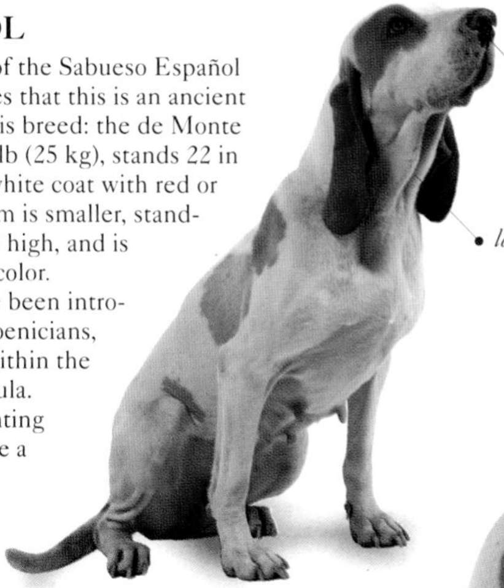
prominent, pigmented nose
large dewlap

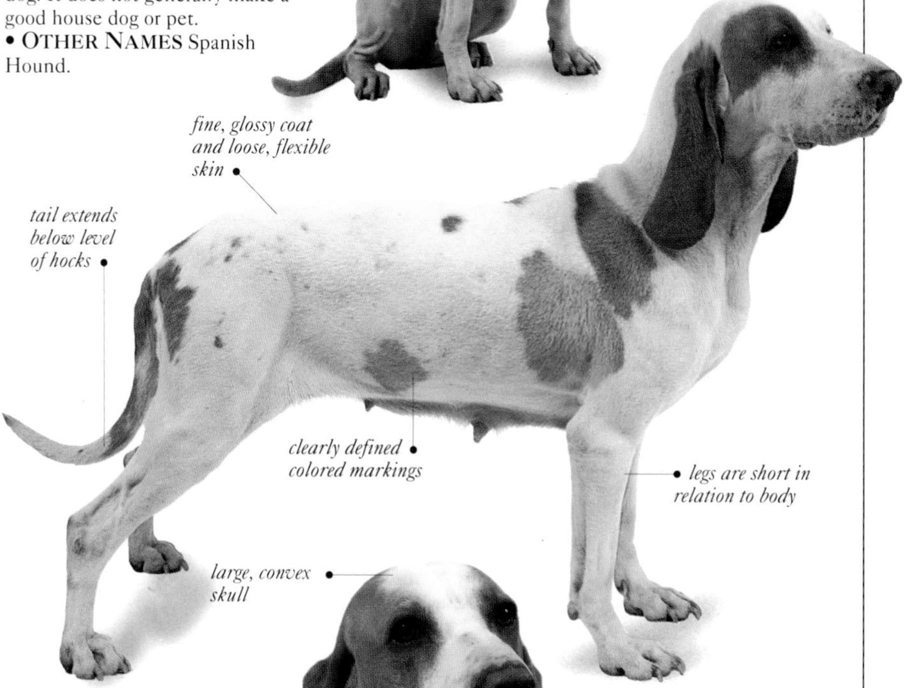
fine, glossy coat and loose, flexible skin
tail extends below level of hocks
clearly defined colored markings
legs are short in relation to body

large, convex skull
very long, soft, folded ears

COLOR TYPES

Height 18–22 in (46–56 cm)	Weight 45–55 lb (20–25 kg)	Temperament Energetic, loyal

Country of origin Spain	First use Hunting game, racing	Origins 600 BC

Spanish Greyhound

With the unmistakable outline of a greyhound, this dog is built for speed. It is a little smaller than the Greyhound itself, however (see p.150), which it otherwise resembles in appearance. The stop is also more pronounced and its build generally sturdier. Crosses with Greyhounds have produced a breed known locally in Spain as the Galgo Inglés-Español, which is used for racing.

• **HISTORY** The early origins of the Spanish Greyhound are not clear, but it is of ancient lineage and was documented in Roman times.

• **REMARK** As a racing dog, this breed is not as swift as the Greyhound itself.

• **OTHER NAMES** Galgo Español.

Smooth-haired Form

dark, expressive, oval eyes

pronounced stop
low-set rose ears

Wire-haired Form

long, narrow head
slightly arched, powerful loin
long, muscular, elegantly arched neck
tall, straight forelegs
well-bent stifles
very long, relatively slender tail carried low

COLOR TYPES

Height 26–28 in (66–71 cm)	Weight 60–66 lb (27–30 kg)	Temperament Active, friendly

Country of origin Portugal	First use Flushing game, ratting	Origins 1800s

PODENGO PORTUGUESO PEQUEÑO

The Pequeño is sometimes described as resembling a sturdy Chihuahua (see p.41), but there seems to be no ancestral link between the two breeds. The Pequeño is in fact a miniature sight hound, a well-proportioned little dog, with a body longer than it is tall, a convex skull, a straight muzzle, and a lively, intelligent expression.

• **HISTORY** It appears that this breed was derived from the Podengo Portugueso Medio, and it, too, is bred in both wire-haired and smooth-haired forms.

• **REMARK** This enthusiastic breed sometimes works with its larger cousins. It enters warrens and flushes out rabbits, leaving them to be captured by the other dogs. It is also a very talented ratter and an affectionate and popular house pet.

• **OTHER NAMES** Small Portuguese Hound.

triangular, mobile ears
tail carried erect when dog is alert
short, coarse coat

convex skull

SMOOTH-HAIRED FORM

medium-length, shaggy coat

straight muzzle

WIRE-HAIRED FORM

COLOR TYPES

Height 8–12 in (20–31 cm)	Weight 11–13 lb (5–6 kg)	Temperament Lively, affectionate

Country of origin Portugal	First use Hunting small game	Origins 1600s

Podengo Portugueso Medio

Both smooth-haired and wire-haired forms of the Medio are bred, with fawn and white coloration tending to predominate, although yellow and black forms with white markings are also seen. This medium-size hound is powerful for its size, and is muscular, agile, and an extremely efficient hunter of small game, either singly or working with other dogs.

• **History** The sight hounds of northern Africa were probably used in the development of the Podengo breeds, although it is thought that this medium-size version descended directly from the Podengo Portugueso Grande, and is, therefore, of more recent origin.

• **Remark** Of all the Podengo breeds, the Medio is the most popular in Portugal, being thought of as neither too small nor too large, and able to adapt readily to a domestic lifestyle.

• **Other Names** Medium Portuguese Hound.

ears naturally upright and directed forward

Wire-haired Form

powerful, muscular neck
tail erect when dog is alert
straight muzzle
coat is coarse-textured in both forms

Smooth-haired Form

arched eyebrows

COLOR TYPES

Height 15–22 in (39–56 cm)	Weight 35–44 lb (16–20 kg)	Temperament Lively, alert

Country of origin Iran	First use Hunting gazelle	Origins 3000 BC

SALUKI

In terms of appearance, the Saluki is unmistakable – slim, high-stepping, and elegant. It has a relatively short coat with significantly longer hair on both its ears and tail. Feathering is also present on the thighs and at the back of the legs. For all its elegance, the Saluki possesses devastating acceleration, which, in its homeland, enables it to outpace gazelles, one of the fastest of all antelopes.

• **HISTORY** Images of dogs similar to the contemporary Saluki have been found on ancient Egyptian tombs dating back more than 5,000 years, but the breed's name is thought to derive from the city of Saluk, which is now part of Yemeni territory.

• **REMARK** Care should be taken when exercising these hounds in areas where they might encounter cats or small dogs.

• **OTHER NAMES** Gazelle Hound.

long, narrow head
long, mobile ears hang close to sides of head

black or liver-colored nose
smooth, silky coat
powerful hips
long, naturally curved tail
long, muscular, and supple neck
well-boned, straight forelegs
feathering present on backs of legs
inner toes longer than outer toes
COLOR TYPES

Height 22–28 in (56–71 cm)	Weight 44–66 lb (20–30 kg)	Temperament Active, friendly

Country of origin Russia	First use Hunting wolves	Origins 1200s

Borzoi

Built on lines of speed and grace, this beautiful sight hound was traditionally used to course wolves. This required not only pace, but also intelligence and considerable bravery on the part of the dog. These qualities are clearly reflected in the Borzoi's proud, aristocratic bearing. Sensitive and aloof in temperament, it is nevertheless, faithful and protective toward its owner.

• **History** The ancestry of the Borzoi is inextricably linked with Russian royalty. Popular as gifts, they were sent to Britain's Princess Alexandra in 1842, and were exhibited at the first Crufts Dog Show in 1891.

• **Remark** The name "Borzoi" derives from the Russian word *borzii*, meaning swift.

• **Other Names** Russian Wolfhound.

long, powerful jaws

hair is longer over chest, neck, and thighs

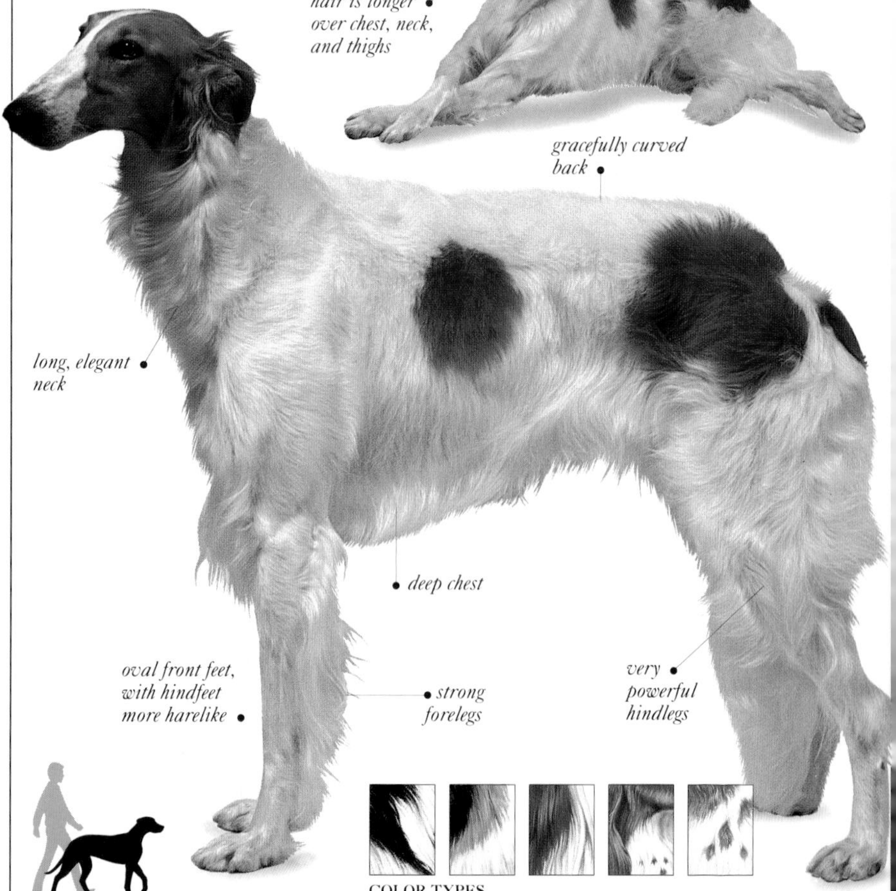
gracefully curved back
long, elegant neck
deep chest
oval front feet, with hindfeet more harelike
strong forelegs
very powerful hindlegs

COLOR TYPES

Height 27–31 in (69–79 cm)	Weight 75–105 lb (35–48 kg)	Temperament Active, intelligent

Country of origin Mali	First use Hunting gazelles	Origins 1000s

AZAWAKH

With an exceedingly athletic appearance, the Azawakh is exceptionally fast, being able to reach speeds of 40 mph (64 kph), and displays considerable stamina. The breed's slender head is characterized by the presence of distinctive swellings on the sides of its face.

- **HISTORY** The Azawakh was developed by the Tuareg people of the southern Sahara to slow down gazelles and other game animals, thus allowing riders to overtake and kill them.
- **REMARK** This breed is slowly finding homes in other countries throughout the world.
- **OTHER NAMES** Tuareg Sloughi.

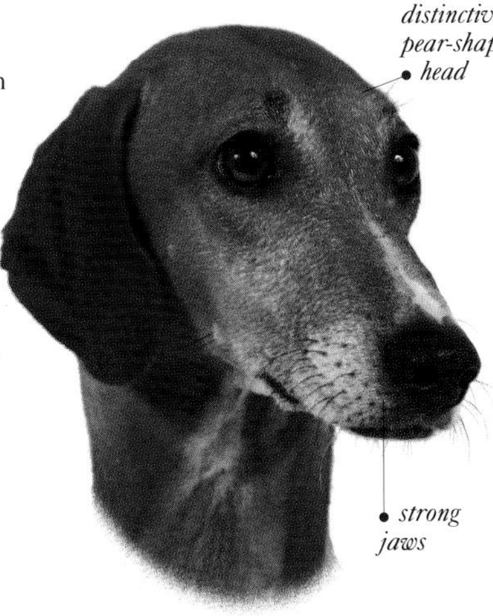
distinctive, pear-shaped head
strong jaws

pendant ears hang down neck
long, elegant back
elongated, muscular neck
deep, powerful chest with well-sprung ribs
very short, soft coat
long, powerful legs
long, muscular thighs
relatively small feet

Height 23–29 in (58–74 cm)	Weight 37–55 lb (17–25 kg)	Temperament Independent, alert

Country of origin	First use	Origins
Afghanistan	Hunting gazelles and wolves	1600s

AFGHAN HOUND

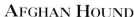

The elegant appearance of the Afghan, with its long, silky coat, has attracted many people to this breed. Such styling, however, is possible only by dedicated grooming. The length of the coat has been greatly developed by selective breeding over about the last 50 years. In motion, the Afghan Hound is high-stepping, giving the impression of springing over the ground with its coat flowing behind.

• **HISTORY** This hound was first seen in Europe in the late 1800s, when it was brought back by soldiers returning from the Afghan War. At that time there were a number of localized forms – some were larger, for example – but such distinctions have disappeared in contemporary bloodlines.

• **REMARK** This athletic hound requires plenty of exercise. It may tend to run off too readily – perhaps a reflection of its hunting past.

• **OTHER NAMES** Tazi.

long skull

long, silky hair covering eyes
prominent hip bones
dense covering of long hair on feet
long, straight legs
large, strong forefeet

COLOR TYPES

Height	Weight	Temperament
25–29 in (64–74 cm)	50–60 lb (23–27 kg)	Lively, active

Country of origin	First use	Origins
Morocco	Guarding flocks	6000 BC

SLOUGHI

The build of the Sloughi has led to debate that it is merely a smooth-coated form of Saluki (see p.199), modified by crossings with other similar breeds. That aside, the Sloughi is a striking dog, slenderly built, with fine, well-defined musculature and rather sad, dark eyes.

- **HISTORY** This breed's origins lie in North Africa, where ancient drawings and carvings depict similar dogs. Earlier, its ancestors probably came from the region of present-day Saudi Arabia.
- **REMARK** Although used as a flock guardian and hunter in its homeland, it can occasionally be seen in the show ring in Britain and the USA.
- **OTHER NAMES** Arabian Greyhound.

large, dark eyes
well-defined bone structure

medium-length, pendant ears, with slightly round tips
long, lean neck with folds of skin at the throat
hard, smooth coat consisting of tough, fine hair
abdomen is well tucked up
very straight, well-boned forelegs
long, thin tail with slight curve at end

Height	Weight	Temperament
24–28½ in (61–72 cm)	45–60 lb (20–27 kg)	Active, friendly

Country of origin Japan	First use Hunting boar and deer	Origins 1700s

KAI DOG

The fiercely loyal Kai Dog is a powerfully built animal with strong legs that makes it well suited to hunting in its mountainous Japanese homeland. It is invariably brindled in coloration. The red form is known as Aka-Tora, the medium is called Chu-Tora, and the black brindle form is Kuro-Tora.

• **HISTORY** The name of this breed originates from part of central Japan that is now in the prefecture of Yamanashi. The Kai was first seen in the USA in 1951, but it did not become established here at this stage.

• **REMARK** Kai Dog pups are usually born solid black in color. Their distinctive brindle coloring develops only as they grow and mature.

• **OTHER NAMES** Tora Dog.

triangular, pricked ears directed slightly forward

ears are larger than on other medium-size Japanese breeds
thick, muscular neck
thick tail set high and curled over the back
deep, muscular chest
straight, well-muscled forelegs
well-arched, tightly closed toes

small, dark brown eyes
harsh, straight outercoat with soft, thick undercoat

COLOR TYPES

Height 18–23 in (46–58 cm)	Weight 35–40 lb (16–18 kg)	Temperament Determined, independent

Country of origin South Africa	First use Hunting lions	Origins 1800s

RHODESIAN RIDGEBACK

Dignified and formidable, the Ridgeback derives its name from the distinctive ridge of hair which grows, contrary to the direction of the rest of the coat, in a tapering line along the middle of its back. It shares the color as well as the heart of the lion that was once its quarry.

• **HISTORY** Developed by the Boers in the late 19th century, its standard was fixed in Rhodesia (now Zimbabwe) in 1922. In the hunt for lions it was renowned for its great stamina and surprising agility. Nowadays it is used as a guard dog and makes a loyal and affectionate family pet.

• **REMARK** The breed's unique ridge of hair is thought to have been inherited from the now extinct Hottentot Dog.

• **OTHER NAMES** African Lion Hound.

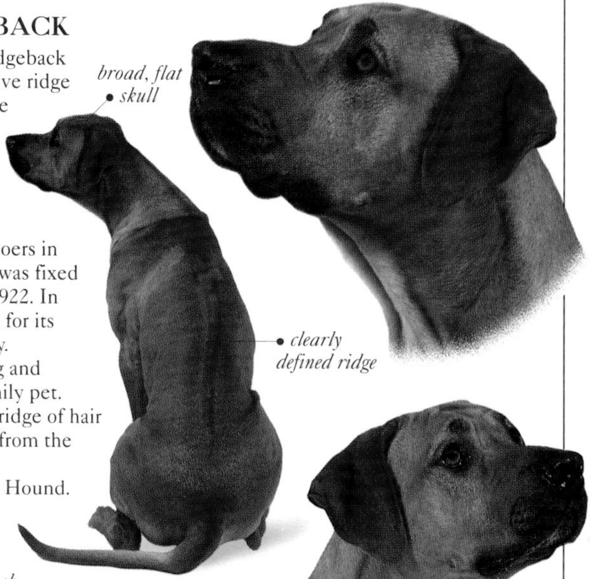
broad, flat skull
clearly defined ridge

strong, tapering tail
short, sleek coat
long, muscular neck
powerful hindquarters
trace of white permitted on chest
strong, deep chest
compact, well-arched toes

Height 24–27 in (61–69 cm)	Weight 65–85 lb (30–39 kg)	Temperament Friendly, obedient

TERRIERS

MOST OF THE DOGS in this group are relatively small in size, but, despite this, they are usually spirited and independent. Although many terriers were originally kept on farms, often as rat catchers, they have made the transition to household pets quite readily, to the extent that a number of them rank among the best-known breeds in the world. Their alert and curious nature, and their tendency to explore underground, means that the are more inclined to dig than othe breeds, and they have an alarmin tendency to disappear down rabbi holes when out for a walk. As a result they are not true lapdogs, although the do make loyal companions. Terriers ar usually lively, alert, and extremel plucky. They do not always get on wel together, however, and enjoy ever opportunity to run around on their own

Country of origin	First use	Origins
USA	Hunting rats	1930s

AMERICAN TOY TERRIER

This small, attractive terrier shows a clear relationship to the Smooth Fox Terrier (see p.216). The tricolored form with white predominating in the coat is favored in the show ring. A popularizing feature is the American Toy Terrier's smooth, short coat, which is extremely easy to care for and groom.

- **HISTORY** The American Kennel Club recognized this breed in 1936. Crosses with English Toy Terriers and Chihuahuas have refined its features.
- **REMARK** These terriers have been trained to assist handicapped people around the home.
- **OTHER NAMES** Toy Fox Terrier, Amertoy.

white blaze often present

close-set ears
tail is traditionally docked
square body shape
straight, lightly boned forelegs
oval, compact feet

Height	Weight	Temperament
10 in (25 cm)	4½–7 lb (2–3 kg)	Lively, alert

Country of origin USA	First use Dogfighting	Origins 1800s

AMERICAN PIT BULL TERRIER

This is probably the most feared and legislated-against dog in the world today. The breed exudes power, with a broad, slab-like head, immensely strong jaws, and a thickly muscled neck and body. To house the Pit Bull's fearsome jaws the face is particularly wide between its cheeks.

• **HISTORY** This terrier was bred specifically for dogfighting and it is still used for this purpose today, although illegally. The breed descends from Staffordshire Bull Terriers crossed with bulldogs.

• **REMARK** In the UK, ownership is legally restricted to registered, neutered dogs only.

• **OTHER NAMES** Pit Bull Terrier, American Pit Bull.

thick-boned, slablike head
wide face
extremely muscular jaws

small, cropped ears
slightly long back in relation to height
powerful hindquarters
round, often black, eyes
very broad, muscular chest
thick, hard, short coat
white markings typically cover less than 80 percent of body

COLOR TYPES

Height 18–22 in (46–56 cm)	Weight 50–80 lb (23–36 kg)	Temperament Tenacious, fearless

Country of origin USA	First use Baiting bulls	Origins 1800s

AMERICAN STAFFORDSHIRE TERRIER

This breed resembles its English ancestor, the Staffordshire Bull Terrier (see p.212), although it is taller, heavier, and generally more substantial. This dog is very powerful, but not usually ill-disposed toward people.

• **HISTORY** The American Kennel Club first granted recognition of the American Staffordshire Terrier as a separate breed in 1936.

• **REMARK** The close similarity in appearance of this breed to the notorious American Pit Bull Terrier (see p.207) has not served to enhance its reputation recently.

broad head with powerful jaw muscles
ears may be cropped
tail appears short in relation to body
smooth, short coat

COLOR TYPES

Height 17–19 in (43–48 cm)	Weight (18–23 kg) 40–50 lb	Temperament Intelligent, determined

Country of origin USA	First use Baiting bulls, ratting	Origins 1800s

BOSTON TERRIER

Although descended from bull-baiting dogs, the Boston Terrier today, with its broad, flat head without wrinkles, large, round eyes, and sweet expression, is a well-tempered and patient companion dog. Brindle and white are the preferred coat colors. The breed is grouped into three categories, depending on weight.

• **HISTORY** The Boston Terrier can be traced back to crosses involving bulldogs and terriers in the city of Boston some time in the 1800s.

• **REMARK** The broad head of this dog can lead to problems, pups sometimes becoming trapped in the birth canal.

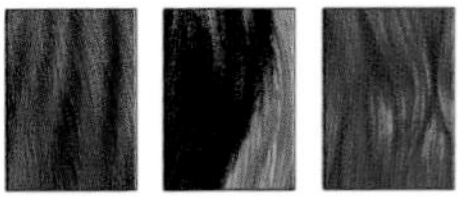
COLOR TYPES

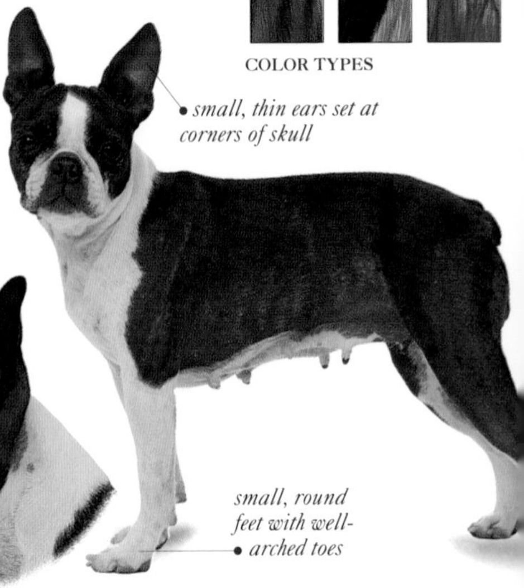
small, thin ears set at corners of skull
small, round feet with well-arched toes

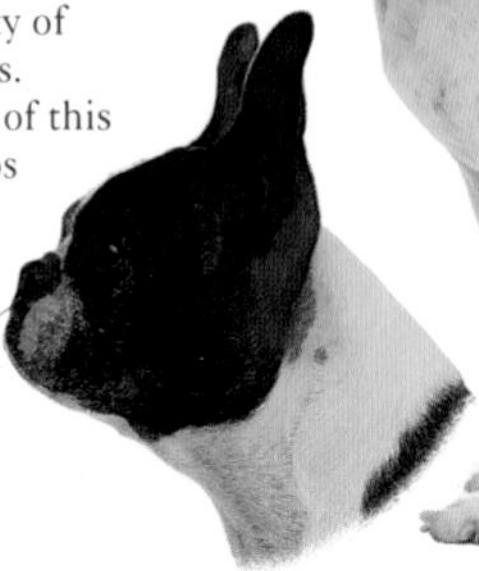
large, round, intelligent, dark eyes

Height 15–17 in (38–43 cm)	Weight 10–25 lb (4.5–11.5 kg)	Temperament Intelligent, lively

Country of origin Great Britain	First use Hunting badgers and otters	Origins 1800s

Airedale Terrier

The largest of all the terriers, the Airedale is a distinctive combination of black and tan in color. Its wiry coat is dense and waterproof.

• **History** This hardy breed evolved in southern Yorkshire, England. It is descended from an old type of terrier crossed with an Otter Hound.

• **Remark** The coat is shed twice a year and should be stripped on these occasions.

• **Other Names** Waterside Terrier, Bingley Terrier.

long, flat skull
tops of ears extend above line of skull
deep chest
black saddle extends over top of tail and neck
small, round feet

Height 22–24 in (56–61 cm)	Weight 44–50 lb (20–23 kg)	Temperament Intelligent, responsive

Country of origin Great Britain	First use Hunting badgers and rats	Origins 1800s

Bedlington Terrier

Lithe and graceful, with a lamblike appearance, the Bedlington Terrier is unlikely to be confused with any other breed. In spite of its gentle appearance, however, it is tough and hardy.

• **History** Wire-coated terriers crossed with Whippets (see p.151) and Dandie Dinmonts (see p.213) laid the foundations for the breed.

• **Remark** The coat requires regular trimming.

• **Other Names** Rothbury Terrier.

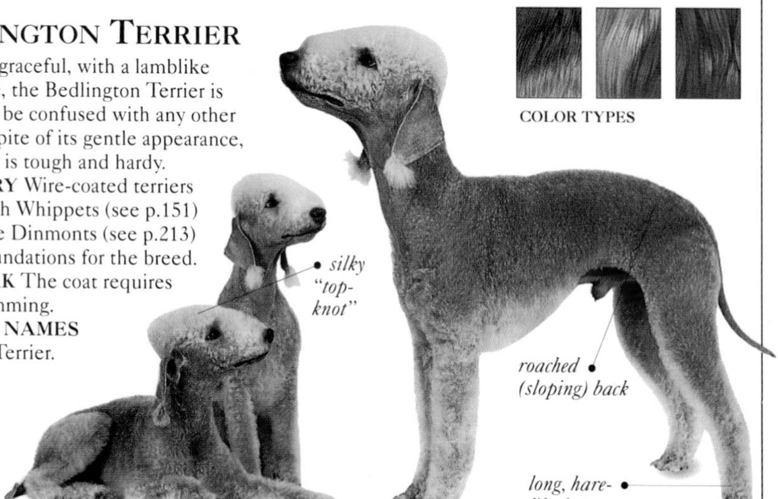

COLOR TYPES
silky "top-knot"
roached (sloping) back
long, hare-like feet

Height 15–17 in (38–43 cm)	Weight 17–23 lb (8–10 kg)	Temperament Alert, affectionate

Country of origin Great Britain	First use Ratting and rabbiting	Origins 1800s

ENGLISH TOY TERRIER

A miniature form of the Manchester Terrier (below), it can be distinguished primarily by its size and the erect carriage of the ears. Coloration is a vital feature of this breed, comprised of jet black and rich chestnut markings. Thin black lines, described as "penciling," are present on the toes and pasterns.

• **HISTORY** This compact breed was developed from crossing the now extinct Black and Tan Terrier with the Italian Greyhound (see p.50).

• **REMARK** The ears are never cropped.

• **OTHER NAMES** Toy Manchester Terrier.

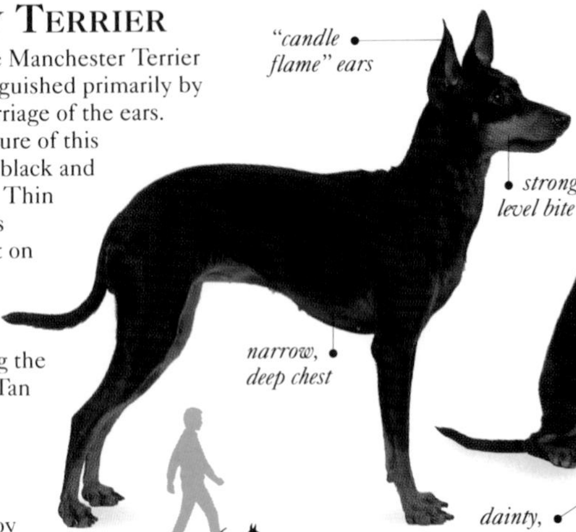
"candle flame" ears
strong, level bite
narrow, deep chest

dainty, arched feet

Height 10–12 in (25–30 cm)	Weight 6–8 lb (3–4 kg)	Temperament Lively, alert

Country of origin Great Britain	First use Ratting and rabbiting	Origins 1500s

MANCHESTER TERRIER

Evidence of Whippet (see p.151) is visible in this breed's elegant, roach back and the relatively straight shape of the nose.

• **HISTORY** The Manchester Terrier used to show great variation in size; miniature versions became popular in the latter part of the last century, when the breed was first introduced to North America.

• **REMARK** A Manchester Terrier called Billy took just 6 minutes and 13 seconds to kill 100 rats in a contest held during the late 1800s.

• **OTHER NAMES** Black and Tan Terrier.

tan spots above eyes
tan markings should reach sides of nose

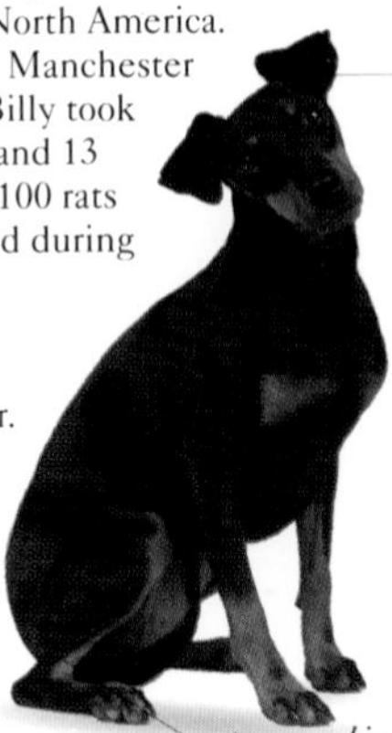
small, V-shaped ears
tan markings on legs

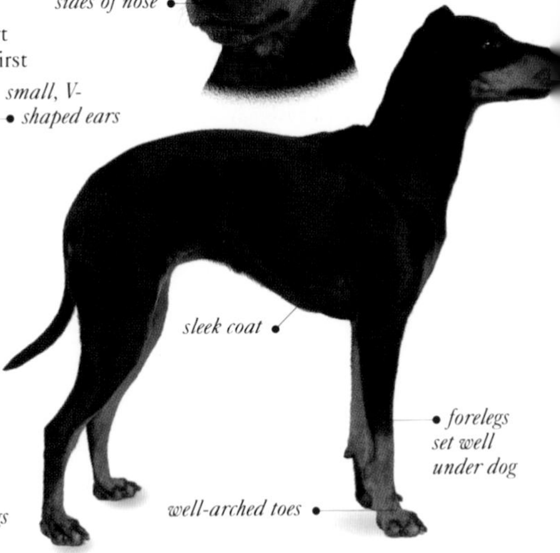
sleek coat
forelegs set well under dog
well-arched toes

Height 15–16 in (38–41 cm)	Weight 12–22 lb (5–10 kg)	Temperament Lively, attentive

Country of origin	First use	Origins
Great Britain	Hunting rats	1700s

BORDER TERRIER

The Border is one of the smallest of the terriers, standing only 10 in (25 cm) high. It is still able to keep up with horses when out fox hunting, while its narrow body allows it to go to earth without difficulty. Its coat is durable enough to withstand the weather on the border between Scotland and England. It is capable of confronting a fox or even the much tougher badger.

• **HISTORY** There is evidence of dogs similar to the Border Terrier in the 18th century. The name is thought to come from the then famous Border Hunt.

• **REMARK** A Border Terrier Club was established in 1921 and the breed is now widely distributed throughout the world.

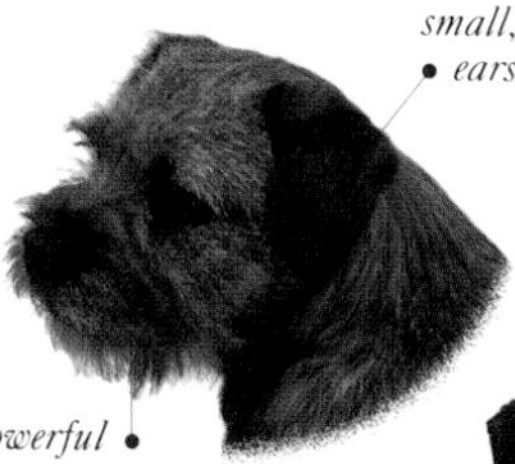
small, V-shaped ears
powerful jaws

otterlike head
moderately short tail
deep, narrow body
muscular hindquarters

COLOR TYPES

Height	Weight	Temperament
10 in (25 cm)	11½–15½ lb (5–7 kg)	Plucky, alert

Country of origin	First use	Origins
Great Britain	Hunting rats	1800s

NORWICH TERRIER

This is one of the native terrier breeds of Norfolk, England, a region traditionally rich in game. The Norwich is readily distinguishable from the Norfolk Terrier (see p.214) by its alert, pricked ears. The coat is generally short and smooth on the head and ears. For its size, it is a powerful dog, with a tight-lipped mouth and a scissor bite.

• **HISTORY** In the 19th century, the Norwich Terrier was the mascot of the students at Cambridge University, England.

• **REMARK** Tail docking is now optional in the case of this breed.

erect, pointed ears

slightly round, wide skull
strong neck
short, powerful legs and round feet

COLOR TYPES

Height	Weight	Temperament
10 in (25 cm)	11–12 lb (5–5.5 kg)	Alert, friendly

Country of origin	First use	Origins
Great Britain	Baiting bulls, ratting	1800s

Miniature Bull Terrier

This breed is the smallest surviving version of the Bull Terrier (see p.239) and is still a strong reminder of its larger relative. The head is almost flat at the top of the skull and curves down to the tip of its powerful muzzle.

- **History** Common during the 1800s, its popularity waned until quite recently.
- **Remark** The Miniature Bull Terrier delights in human company, but tends to be less tolerant toward other dogs.

small, thin ears
muscular neck
short, flat, glossy coat
powerful hindlegs

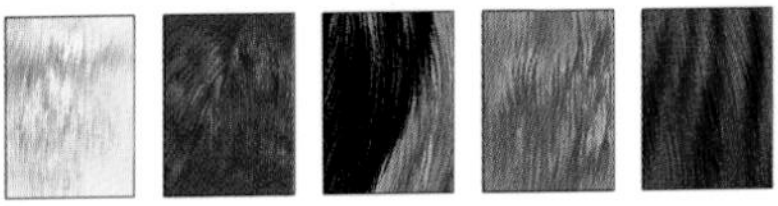

COLOR TYPES

Height	Weight	Temperament
10–14 in (25–35 cm)	24–33 lb (11–15 kg)	Fearless, determined

Country of origin	First use	Origins
Great Britain	Dog fighting, ratting	1800s

Staffordshire Bull Terrier

This smooth-coated breed gives the appearance of power and strength coupled with agility and athleticism. Coat coloration is very varied.

- **History** This powerful terrier originates from the county of Staffordshire, England, and its ancestry displays crossings with the Bulldog and a variety of terrier breeds.
- **Remark** Although bred originally for dog fighting, its loyalty and devotion is legendary.

rose, or half-pricked, ears
well-sprung ribs
deep chest

COLOR TYPES

Height	Weight	Temperament
14–16 in (36–41 cm)	24–38 lb (11–17 kg)	Plucky, strong-willed

Country of origin	First use	Origins
Great Britain	Hunting badgers and rats	1600s

Dandie Dinmont Terrier

Distinguished by its topknot of hair, this small terrier also has an unusual texture to its coat. This occurs because of a combination of hard and soft hair, which creates a crisp texture over much of the body. The underparts, however, are predominantly soft-haired.

• **HISTORY** This very old breed was probably developed by crossing Scottish and Skye Terriers.

• **REMARK** It is named after a character in Sir Walter Scott's novel *Guy Mannering*.

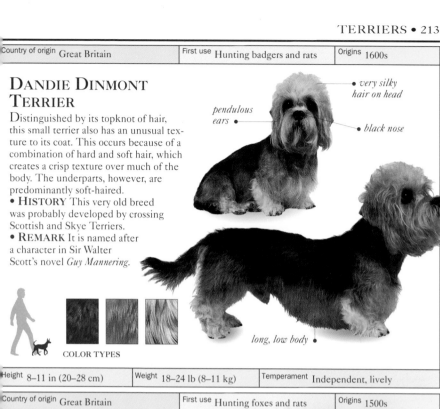

very silky hair on head
pendulous ears
black nose
long, low body

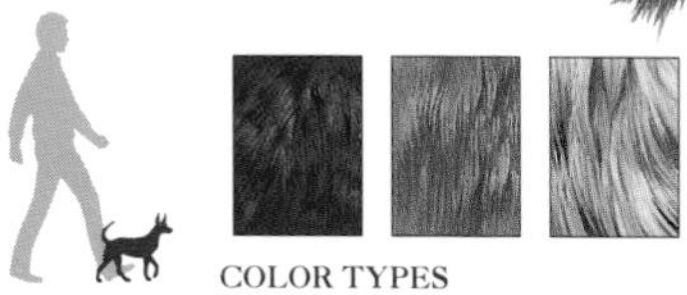
COLOR TYPES

Height	Weight	Temperament
8–11 in (20–28 cm)	18–24 lb (8–11 kg)	Independent, lively

Country of origin	First use	Origins
Great Britain	Hunting foxes and rats	1500s

Cairn Terrier

Lively and fearless, this shaggy terrier is well adapted to working outdoors and possesses a dense, double-layered, water-resistant coat. The head of a Cairn is broader and not as long as that of other terrier breeds, and the jaw is surprisingly powerful for a dog of this size.

• **HISTORY** The breed name was changed to Cairn Terrier only after 1909, before which it was called the Short-haired Skye Terrier. Cairn Terriers were originally used to drive foxes and other animals from rocky retreats. The breed was introduced into the USA in 1913.

• **REMARK** The Cairn Terrier is an excellent swimmer.

small, erect ears
strong, level jaw
forefeet larger than hind feet

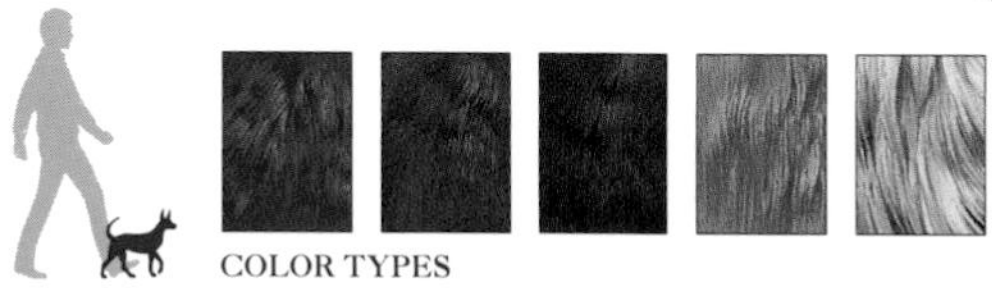
COLOR TYPES

Height	Weight	Temperament
10–12 in (25–30 cm)	13–16 lb (6–7.5 kg)	Bold, alert

Country of origin Great Britain	First use Ratting, killing vermin	Origins 1700s

LAKELAND TERRIER

Square-framed and solidly built, with a wiry, waterproof double coat, this sturdy terrier is equally content on the slopes of its Lake District ancestral home, in the north of England, as it is in the family home.

• **HISTORY** There used to be several strains of this terrier, known under a variety of names. They were grouped in 1912.

• **REMARK** Stingray of Derrybach, a Lakeland Terrier, was best in show at Crufts in 1967, and at the National Westminster Show, New York, in 1968.

small, V-shaped ears
tail set high and usually docked
straight, well-boned forelegs

broad muzzle
relatively narrow chest

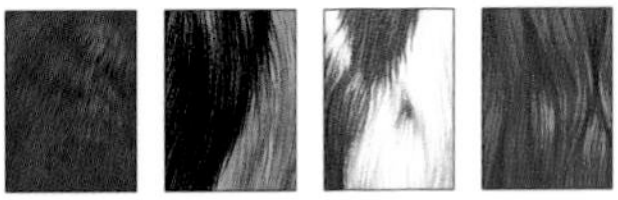

COLOR TYPES

Height 13–15 in (33–38 cm)	Weight 15–17 lb (7–8 kg)	Temperament Brave, hardy

Country of origin Great Britain	First use Ratting	Origins 1800s

NORFOLK TERRIER

The Norfolk is distinguishable from its close relative, the Norwich Terrier (see p.211), by its drop ears, which are folded forward. Its outer- coat is hard and wiry, and there is a thick undercoat beneath. White markings on the coat are considered an undesirable feature.

• **HISTORY** The Norfolk and Norwich Terrier breeds were inextricably linked until 1964, when the two breeds finally received separate recognition. They both seem to have developed as farm terriers in their East Anglian homeland in England.

• **REMARK** The British Kennel Club accepts "scars from fair wear and tear" in the breed's standard.

broad, and slightly round skull
ears drop forward, close to cheeks

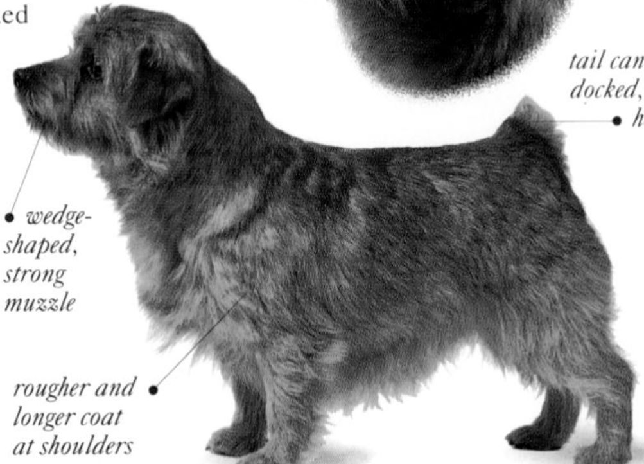
tail can be docked, as here
wedge-shaped, strong muzzle
rougher and longer coat at shoulders

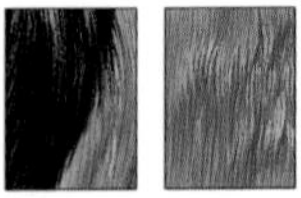

COLOR TYPES

Height 10–10¼ in (25–26 cm)	Weight 11–12 lb (5–5.5 kg)	Temperament Alert, friendly

Country of origin	First use	Origins
Great Britain	Going to ground and ratting	1800s

PARSON JACK RUSSELL TERRIER

This active, robust, and well-known terrier has a predominantly white coat, which can occur in three forms: smooth-, broken-, and rough-coated. The Parson Jack Russell is a standardized variety.

• **HISTORY** The Reverend Jack Russell (nicknamed "the Hunting Parson"), from Devon, England, is credited with developing this breed.

• **REMARK** While not recognized by the AKC, the United Kennel Club recognized the breed in 1991.

strong neck
tail docked to 4 in (10 cm)

muscular hind legs

white blaze is common

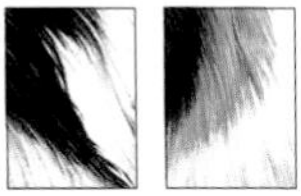

COLOR TYPES

Height	Weight	Temperament
14 in (35 cm)	16–18 lb (7–8 kg)	Alert, lively

Country of origin	First use	Origins
Great Britain	Hunting foxes	1700s

WIRE FOX TERRIER

Similar to the smooth-coated breed (see p.216) in all but coat type, the Wire Fox Terrier should have a coat with a dense and wiry texture, without any traces of curls. It is actually double-layered, with a softer undercoat.

• **HISTORY** Breeds of terrier that are now extinct, notably the Wire-haired Terrier, contributed to the development of this dog.

• **REMARK** It takes considerable time to prepare the coat for show purposes.

short, level back
straight forelegs

dark, round eyes
ears fold forward toward cheeks

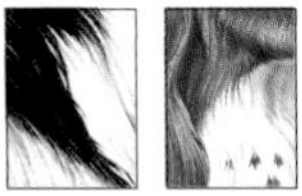

COLOR TYPES

Height	Weight	Temperament
15½ in (39 cm)	16–18 lb (7–8 kg)	Alert, determined

Country of origin Great Britain	First use Flushing foxes	Origins 1700s

Smooth Fox Terrier

Less well-known than its wire-haired relative (see p.215), the Smooth Fox Terrier is an easily recognized breed, with its short back and long, tapering muzzle. Its distinctive, short tail is set high and carried gaily. This dog is lively and alert, and will take any amount of exercise.

• **History** The origins of this terrier are not clear, although it was first recorded about 20 years after the appearance of the wire-haired form. The breed standard has not altered significantly in terms of type since 1876, except that today's dogs are somewhat lighter than their ancestors.

• **Remark** White coloring should always predominate in the coat of this terrier.

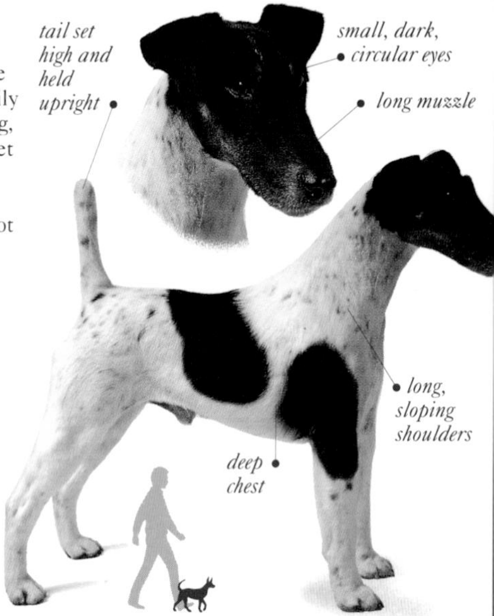
tail set high and held upright
small, dark, circular eyes
long muzzle
long, sloping shoulders
deep chest

COLOR TYPES

Height 15½ in (39 cm)	Weight 16–18 lb (7–8 kg)	Temperament Alert, determined

Country of origin Great Britain	First use Hunting rats	Origins 1800s

Welsh Terrier

Often confused with the Lakeland Terrier (see p.214), the Welsh Terrier can be distinguished by its broader head and distinctive coloration. Black and tan is preferred, but black, grizzle, and tan is also permitted, provided there is no black penciling on the toes.

• **History** The old Black and Tan Terrier contributed to the ancestry of this breed. It was first recognized by the Kennel Club in Britain in 1886, and was introduced to the USA two years later.

• **Remark** It needs hand-stripping twice a year for show purposes.

flat top to head
small ears
long, sloping shoulders
powerful, muscular thighs
hard, wiry, thick coat
small, cat-like feet

COLOR TYPES

Height 14–15½ in (36–39 cm)	Weight 20–21 lb (9–10 kg)	Temperament Active, playful

Country of origin	First use	Origins
Great Britain	Going to ground	1800s

Scottish Terrier

This energetic terrier has a distinctive appearance because of its elongated head shape. In addition, it has longer hair on its forehead, creating the impression of eyebrows.

• **History** Although the Scottish Terrier breed dates back many years, it was not until 1882 that an official standard was drawn up.

• **Remark** The coat of this terrier lies close to the ground. Mud sticking to it can be brushed out quite easily once it has dried.

• **Other Names** Aberdeen Terrier.

distinctive eyebrows
erect, pointed ears
long head with large nose
thick tail
powerful hind-quarters
harsh, wiry, dense outer-coat

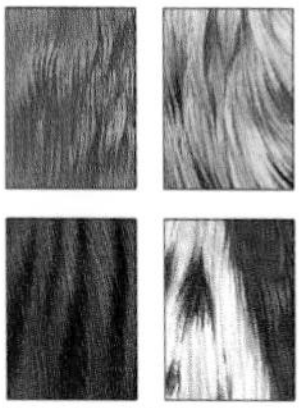

COLOR TYPES

Height	Weight	Temperament
10–11 in (25–28 cm)	19–23 lb (8.5–10.5 kg)	Active, assertive

Country of origin	First use	Origins
Great Britain	Hunting foxes and badgers	1600s

Skye Terrier

The long, trailing coat of the Skye Terrier needs plenty of grooming to stay immaculate. The hair covering the head is shorter and softer than elsewhere on the body and forms a veil over the forehead and eyes. The front feet, when visible, are large and point directly forward. A small white area on the chest may be noticeable on some individuals.

• **History** Bred in the isolation of the Scottish Isle of Skye, in the Inner Hebrides, these terriers were developed to hunt foxes and badgers.

• **Remark** It may take up to three years for the coat of a young Skye Terrier to develop to its full extent.

long, powerful head
ears are usually pricked but can be dropped

long, level back
strong hindquarters
softer, shorter hair on head

COLOR TYPES

Height	Weight	Temperament
9–10 in (23–25 cm)	19–23 lb (8.5–10.5 kg)	Loyal, lively

Country of origin Great Britain	First use Hunting rabbits	Origins 1700s

PATTERDALE TERRIER

Although small in size, the Patterdale Terrier is a brave and tenacious working dog, with a short, coarse, weatherproof coat of black, black-and-tan, brown, or red coloration. This stocky, well-built dog retains the terrier's love of hunting.

• **HISTORY** Originating in the north of England, the breed is named after the Cumbrian village of Patterdale, where it was popular.

• **REMARK** These lively dogs need plenty of exercise.

• **OTHER NAMES** Black Fell Terrier.

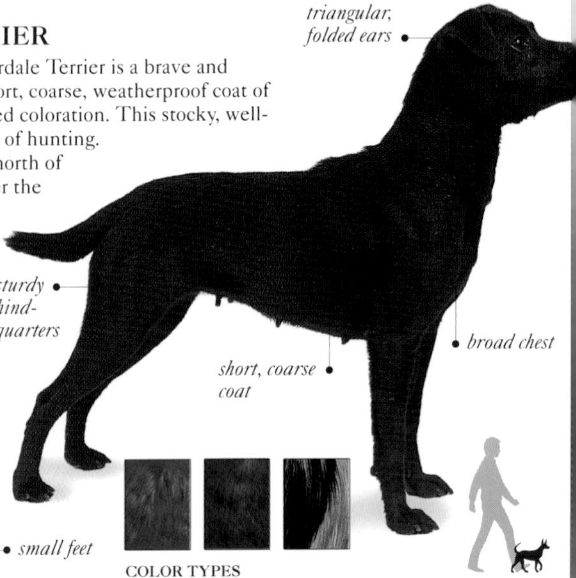
triangular, folded ears
sturdy hind-quarters
broad chest
short, coarse coat

straight back
small feet

COLOR TYPES

Height 12 in (30 cm)	Weight 11–13 lb (5–6 kg)	Temperament Brave, enthusiastic

Country of origin Great Britain	First use Hunting rats	Origins 1800s

WEST HIGHLAND WHITE TERRIER

As its name implies, this terrier from the Western Highlands of Scotland is pure white in coloration. Its face is a little foxlike in appearance, and there is a pronounced stop to the muzzle.

• **HISTORY** It is likely that all the Scottish terriers descended from a common ancestry in what was then a sparsely populated part of Great Britain. The dogs were first shown as Poltalloch Terriers – bred in a village of this name for over sixty years by a Colonel Malcolm.

• **REMARK** The thick coat needs a lot of attention.

slightly domed skull
naturally short tail, not docked
very pointed, small, erect ears
hindfeet smaller than forefeet

powerful muzzle

Height 10–11 in (25–28 cm)	Weight 15–22 lb (7–10 kg)	Temperament Active, assertive

Country of origin Great Britain	First use Hunting rats	Origins 1800s

YORKSHIRE TERRIER

Apart from its diminutive size, the most distinctive feature of this active terrier is its coat, which is steely blue in coloration with areas of golden tan on the head, silky in texture, and sufficiently long to reach the ground. When seen walking, the Yorkshire Terrier can give the impression of being mounted on wheels, because its feet may not be visible.

• **HISTORY** Developed by the miners of the West Riding area of Yorkshire, this terrier is the result of relatively recent crosses of the Skye, Dandie Dinmont, and Maltese Terriers.

• **REMARK** This is recognized as a toy breed in the USA. Newborn Yorkshire Terriers are black in color.

• **OTHER NAMES** Broken-haired Scottish Terrier.

small, flat-topped head
perfectly straight, silky body hair

dark, sparkling eyes
short, level back
rich, bright tan-colored hair on chest

medium-length muzzle
very long hair on muzzle
straight limbs

short, very rich, deep-tan hair on ears
round feet

Height 9 in (23 cm)	Weight Less than 7 lb (3 kg)	Temperament Intelligent, confident

Country of origin	First use	Origins
Great Britain	Hunting badgers and otters	1850s

SEALYHAM TERRIER

Although small, no more than 12 in (30 cm) high, the Sealyham has powerful jaws, a muscular neck, and strong legs. Its coat is long and coarse, usually white or yellowish white in color. The coat must be stripped by hand every six months to remove dead hair.

• **HISTORY** This strong, determined terrier is named after the village of Sealyham, Wales, where it originated. The first breed club was established there in 1908.

• **REMARK** Having been bred to hunt badgers, the Sealyham has kept its bold disposition and active temperament.

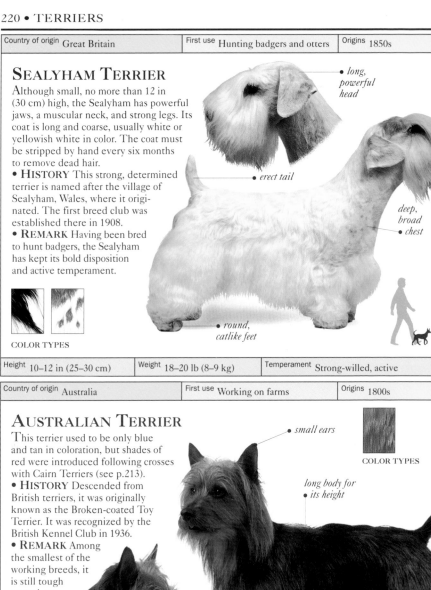

long, powerful head
erect tail
deep, broad chest
round, catlike feet

COLOR TYPES

Height	Weight	Temperament
10–12 in (25–30 cm)	18–20 lb (8–9 kg)	Strong-willed, active

Country of origin	First use	Origins
Australia	Working on farms	1800s

AUSTRALIAN TERRIER

This terrier used to be only blue and tan in coloration, but shades of red were introduced following crosses with Cairn Terriers (see p.213).

• **HISTORY** Descended from British terriers, it was originally known as the Broken-coated Toy Terrier. It was recognized by the British Kennel Club in 1936.

• **REMARK** Among the smallest of the working breeds, it is still tough enough to tackle snakes.

COLOR TYPES

small ears
long body for its height
hard, straight hair
distinctive ruff

Height	Weight	Temperament
10 in (25.5 cm)	12–14 lb (4–7 kg)	Feisty, dutiful

Country of origin Australia	First use Companion	Origins 1800s

SILKY TERRIER

A compact and lightly built dog of Australian origin, the Silky has typical terrier characteristics. Straight, silky body hair forms a natural parting along its level, moderately long back; the ears are pricked and alert.

• **HISTORY** The Silky Terrier was developed during the late 1800s from British terriers, notably the Yorkshire Terrier (see p.219), and the Australian Terrier (see p.220).

• **REMARK** This dog was developed strictly as a companion dog.

• **OTHER NAMES** Australian Silky Terrier, Sydney Silky.

skull broad between the ears
erect ears
wedge-shaped skull
moderately long, level back
silky hair may be 6 in (15 cm) long on the back
small cat-like feet

Height 9 in (23 cm)	Weight 8–11 lb (4–5 kg)	Temperament Spirited, friendly

Country of origin Germany	First use Hunting rats and small game	Origins 1800s

GERMAN HUNTING TERRIER

The cheeks of this relatively large terrier are full, the jaw powerful, and the teeth strong. Its dense coat is usually black or chocolate with tan markings, or it may be pure red. Both wire-haired and smooth-haired forms are found.

• **HISTORY** Despite being developed in Bavaria, its ancestry consists entirely of British terrier breeds, including Welsh and Fox Terriers.

• **REMARK** This breed is still strictly a working dog, renowned for its fine nose.

• **OTHER NAMES** Deutscher Jagdterrier.

short, thick tail
triangular, folded ears
powerful jaws and muzzle
well-muscled legs
large feet

COLOR TYPES

Height 16 in (41 cm)	Weight 20–22 lb (9–10 kg)	Temperament Keen, tenacious

Country of origin Germany	First use Hunting rats	Origins 1800s

GERMAN PINSCHER

Often bearing the black-and-tan markings of its relative, the Doberman Pinscher (see p.250), the German, or Standard, Pinscher is, however, also seen in dark brown and various shades of fawn. It has the same elegance of bearing and cleanness of line as the Doberman Pinscher, albeit without that dog's musculature and aura of barely restrained power.

• **HISTORY** This native of Germany may be related to the Black and Tan Terrier, as are the Doberman and Miniature Pinschers (see p.223), although it has never achieved the international popularity of the other two breeds.

• **REMARK** This breed is large for a terrier and is often used as a general farm hand.

• **OTHER NAMES** Standard Pinscher.

cropped ears are erect
well-arched toes

natural, folded position of ears
well-muscled neck
tail traditionally docked
deep chest
well-defined color markings
well-boned forelegs

COLOR RANGE

Height 16–19 in (41–48 cm)	Weight 25–35 lb (11–16 kg)	Temperament Alert, intelligent

Country of origin	First use	Origins
Germany	Hunting rodents	1600s

AFFENPINSCHER

A foreshortened muzzle, pronounced stop, large round eyes, erect ears, and flyaway head and facial hair combine to give this little terrier a unique, impish appearance. The coat is longer on some parts of the body than others.

• **HISTORY** There is no precise record of the Affenpinscher's ancestry, although it contributed to the development of the Brussels Griffon.

• **REMARK** Although small, this breed makes an excellent watchdog. It is recognized as a toy breed in the USA.

domed skull
blunt, short muzzle
distinct mustache
straight, well-boned forelegs
rough, harsh-textured coat

Height	Weight	Temperament
10 in (25 cm)	7–8 lb (3–3½ kg)	Alert, quiet

Country of origin	First use	Origins
Germany	Hunting rats	1800s

MINIATURE PINSCHER

This square-shaped, high-spirited terrier is sturdy, athletic, and able to outjump dogs far larger than itself. One of its most distinctive features is its hackney gait (characterized by pronounced flexion of the knee).

• **HISTORY** This ancient breed descended from traditional native German terriers. The breed became standardized in 1895.

• **REMARK** This breed was known as the Reh Pinscher due to its resemblance to small roe deer (*reh* in German). It is recognized as a toy breed in the USA.

• **OTHER NAMES** Reh Pinscher, Zwergpinscher.

large, erect ears
narrow, tapering muzzle
very dark eyes
short, smooth coat, hard to the touch
powerful hindquarters

Height	Weight	Temperament
10–12 in (25–30 cm)	8–10 lb (4–5 kg)	Lively, alert

Country of origin Germany	First use Ratting	Origins 1400s

MINIATURE SCHNAUZER

This dog has the general appearance and all the appealing features of its full-size brethren (see p.122) – bushy eyebrows, bristly, stubby mustache, and chin whiskers. It is very nearly square in profile, with a straight and level back and well-developed thighs. The ears may be cropped in the USA.

• **HISTORY** This miniature form of schnauzer is thought to have evolved from crossings of the Standard Schnauzer and Affenpinschers. The breed was first seen in Britain in 1928. Its diminutive size makes it an excellent ratter.

• **REMARK** The coat of this terrier must be stripped at least twice a year and regularly groomed to remove dead hairs. Its whiskers and longer hair should be combed every day.

• **OTHER NAMES** Zwegschnauzer.

prominent black nose and wide nostrils

strong, straight back, slightly higher at shoulders than hindquarters
forelegs appear straight from every angle

dark, oval eyes set beneath bushy eyebrows

V-shaped ears, high on head, hanging forward to temples

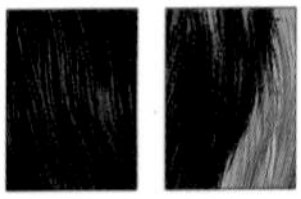

COLOR TYPES

Height 13–14 in (33–36 cm)	Weight 13–15 lb (6–7 kg)	Temperament Lively, very friendly

Country of origin Germany	First use Watchdog, companion	Origins 1945

KROMFOHRLÄNDER

Of powerful build, this attractive terrier has been bred in a wire-coated form, which is the most common, and in a less popular, straight-haired form. Its coloration, a combination of white and tan in various shades, is a significant feature. There is often a tan area on the head, and another on the back which forms a saddle-type patch.

• **HISTORY** At the end of World War II, American soldiers entering the town of Siegen in Westphalia, Germany, brought with them a tawny-colored dog of griffon type. They gave it to a local resident called Frau Schleifenbaum, and it mated with a terrier. Frau Schleifenbaum decided to form a breed from the resulting puppies.

• **REMARK** The Kromfohrländer was first recognized by the German Kennel Club in 1953.

balanced markings are desirable
muzzle tapers along its length

STRAIGHT-HAIRED FORM

ears are positioned high on head
medium-length coat

dark, oval eyes
straight, sturdy front legs

WIRE-HAIRED FORM

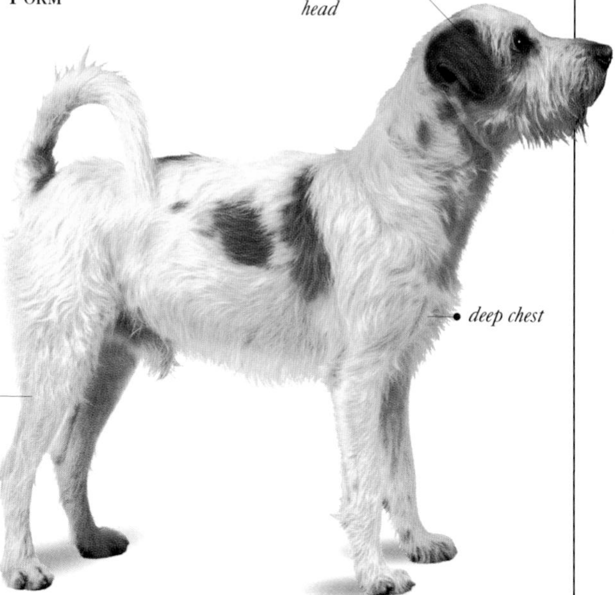
wedge-shaped head
deep chest
strong hind legs

Height 15–17 in (38–43 cm)	Weight 26 lb (12 kg)	Temperament Affectionate, alert

Country of origin Ireland	First use Watchdog	Origins 1700s

IRISH TERRIER

Of unmistakable terrier appearance, with a harsh coat, the long-legged Irish Terrier is somewhat reminiscent of the larger Airedale (see p.209). It has an active, lively nature. Good-tempered toward people, it is not generally well disposed toward other dogs.

• **HISTORY** Crossings involving the old Black and Tan and Wheaten Terriers may have laid the foundations of this breed, which originated in County Cork, Ireland. Standardization occurred only in 1879 when a breed club was established.

• **REMARK** Hand clipping of the coat is required to maintain the graceful outline of these terriers.

• **OTHER NAMES** Irish Red Terrier.

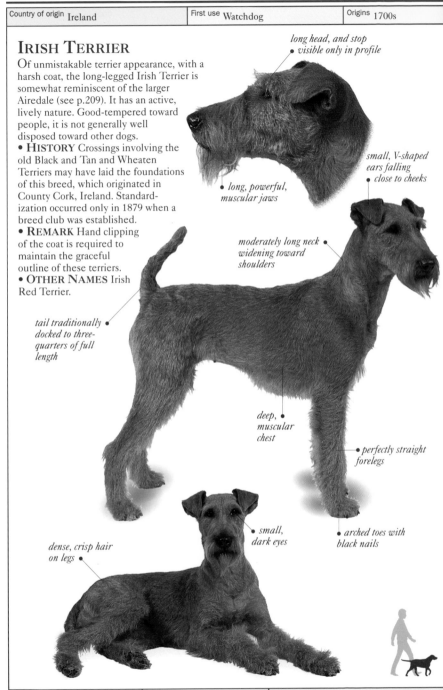

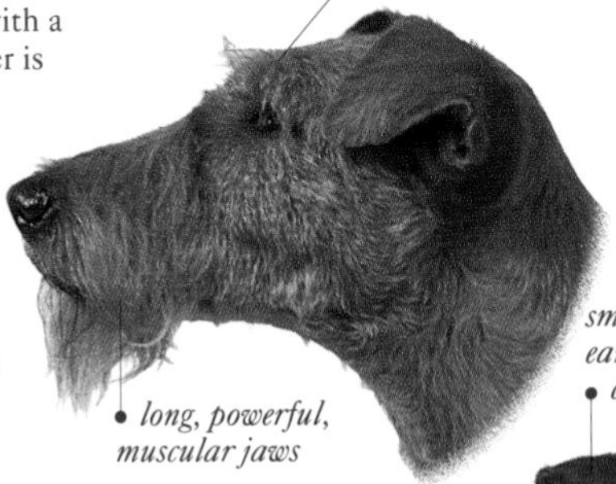
long head, and stop visible only in profile
long, powerful, muscular jaws

small, V-shaped ears falling close to cheeks
moderately long neck widening toward shoulders
tail traditionally docked to three-quarters of full length
deep, muscular chest
perfectly straight forelegs
arched toes with black nails

small, dark eyes
dense, crisp hair on legs

Height 18–19 in (46–48 cm)	Weight 25–27 lb (11–12 kg)	Temperament Determined, friendly

Country of origin Ireland	First use Herding cattle, ratting	Origins 1700s

SOFT-COATED WHEATEN TERRIER

This terrier has a distinctive coat, which is not shed. It needs thorough grooming daily to prevent matting. The coat color is described as "wheaten," because it should match the color of ripening wheat. Whitish or reddish tones are not acceptable. Pups may have darker markings on their coats, however, which should disappear by two years of age. The adult coat hangs either in loose waves or in large, light curls.

• **HISTORY** This is believed to be the oldest terrier breed in Ireland, most common in the vicinity of Kerry (where it gave rise to the Kerry Blue Terrier) and Cork, but its precise origins are unknown. When working, the Soft-coated Wheaten Terrier is an adept badger- and otter-hunter.

• **REMARK** Training requires a little effort, but the results are worth it.

long hair on head falls forward over eyes
tight, black lips

large, black nose

V-shaped, folded ears
moderately long, strong, muscular neck
upright, docked tail, set high on back
square muzzle with strong jaws
strong, muscular thighs
powerful feet with black toenails
deep chest

Height 18–19 in (46–48 cm)	Weight 35–45 lb (16–20 kg)	Temperament Lively, loyal, energetic

Country of origin	First use	Origins
Ireland	Hunting vermin	1700s

Glen of Imaal Terrier

The body of this terrier is relatively long compared with its height, and its coat is of medium length. It is both agile and silent when working, factors that allow it to strike its quarry unexpectedly.

• **History** This dog is named after the Glen of Imaal in County Wicklow, Ireland, where it was first recognized in 1933.

• **Remark** This is a hardy, working terrier breed, well able to deal with badgers as well as the more typical terrier fare, such as rats.

round, brown eyes
harsh outercoat
strong feet with round pads
front feet turn out slightly

ears back when relaxed

Height	Weight	Temperament
14 in (36 cm)	35 lb (16 kg)	Determined, brave

Country of origin	First use	Origins
Ireland	Hunting vermin	1800s

Kerry Blue Terrier

The appearance of pups of this breed differs greatly from that of adult dogs because they are born with black coats. It can take up to 18 months before young dogs acquire the characteristic blue adult coloration. Dark points may also be seen in adult dogs.

• **History** Originating in County Kerry, in the southwest of Ireland, this terrier is thought to be descended from Welsh, Bedlington, and Soft-coated Wheaten Terrier stock.

• **Remark** The silky coat of these terriers is not shed and needs daily attention.

V-shaped ears hang forward on head
tail set high and carried erect
long, lean head with powerful jaws
straight forelegs
small, round feet with black nails

Height	Weight	Temperament
18–19 in (46–48 cm)	33–37 lb (15–17 kg)	Determined, friendly

Country of origin Belgium	First use Hunting vermin	Origins 1800s

BRUSSELS GRIFFON

There is considerable confusion over the nomenclature of this dog, which is shown as one breed in North America and the UK, but which is separated into three types in Europe. The Brussels Griffon can be distinguished from the Belgian Griffon by its red coloration, although both have long coats. By contrast, the Petit Brabancon has a short coat.

• **HISTORY** It is thought that the Affenpinscher may have been involved in the ancestry of this dog. Other breeds, such as the Pug, may also have played a part in its development.

• **REMARK** The ears of this dog are commonly cropped in North America, and its tail is docked.

• **OTHER NAMES**
Griffon Belge.

PETIT BRABANCON

semi-erect, small, high-set ears
short coat

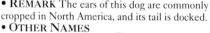

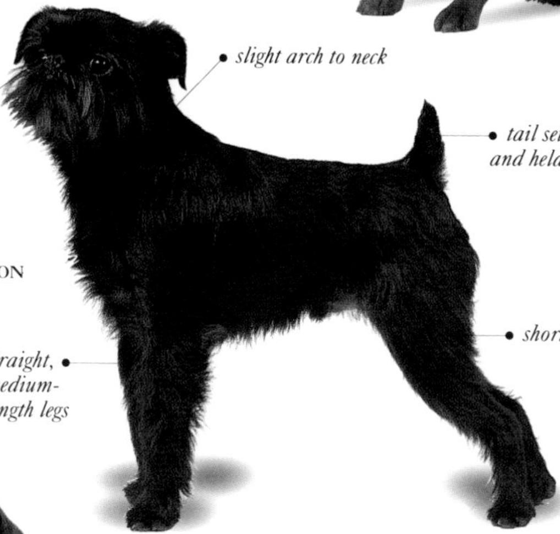
slight arch to neck
very dark, large, round eyes
tail set high and held erect
short, tight coat
straight, medium-length legs

BELGIAN GRIFFON

BRUSSELS GRIFFON

head is large in relation to body
harsh, wiry coat with no hint of a curl

COLOR TYPES

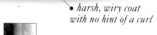

Height 7–8 in (18–20 cm)	Weight 6–12 lb (2.5–5.5 kg)	Temperament Lively, obedient

Country of origin Austria	First use Ratting, watchdog	Origins 1800s

Austrian Pinscher

This small dog displays typical pinscher characteristics. Seen from the front, it has a very broad chest, suggesting greater width than height.

• **History** Although related to other European terrier breeds, it has never been particularly common outside Austria.

• **Remark** The Austrian Pinscher proves to be an alert and noisy guardian, but is often given to persistent barking.

• **Other Names** Österreichischer Kurzhaariger Pinscher.

small ears, sometimes pricked
very broad, powerful chest
fringes of hair on belly
muscular legs

COLOR TYPES

Height 14–20 in (36–51 cm)	Weight 26–40 lb (12–18 kg)	Temperament Bold, alert

Country of origin Czechoslovakia	First use Watchdog	Origins 1940s

Cesky Terrier

Sporting a distinctive, silky coat, and a fine beard and eyebrows, this graceful little terrier is robust and agile. It has a long head with a large nose.

• **History** This loyal breed was developed by the Czechoslovakian geneticist, Dr. F. Horàk. It was officially recognized in 1963.

• **Remark** The Cesky is good with children and makes a fine watchdog. It is now becoming popular in the USA.

• **Other Names** Czesky, Bohemian Terrier.

long head
coat is clipped
sturdy legs
profuse beard
silky coat

COLOR TYPES

Height 10–14 in (25–36 cm)	Weight 12–18 lb (5.5–8 kg)	Temperament Good-natured, obedient

WORKING DOGS

THE DIVERSITY IN APPEARANCE of the many breeds of working dogs reflects the variety of tasks they have performed throughout history. For thousands of years, man has exploited the dog's powerful territorial instinct to protect his own property from intruders. This basic function was mythologized by the Ancient Greeks in the form of Cerberus, the fearsome guardian at the gates of Hades. But the dog has other, more specialized, functions: seeing for the blind; hearing for the deaf; rescuing the injured; transporting humans and cargo across Arctic terrain. As humans made ready to enter the Space Age, they sent the dog before them to prepare the way.

Country of origin	First use	Origins
USA	Guarding farms, fighting	1700s

AMERICAN BULLDOG

This powerful dog is thought to be similar to the old form of 16th-century British bulldog, a breed used for bullbaiting. The head of the American Bulldog is large, and the neck and shoulders hugely muscled.

• **HISTORY** Settlers brought the original bulldog stock from Britain, and their versatility as hunters and farm dogs ensured their popularity in the USA.

• **REMARK** The American Bulldog is still very much a working dog and so there is a wider variation in height and weight than there is with its British counterpart which has become a companion and show breed.

• **OTHER NAMES** Old Country Bulldog.

long, square skull

very powerful jaws

thick, powerful neck and shoulders
short, shiny, hard coat
angulated, parallel hindlegs
straight, well-muscled forelegs
more than half the coat should be white, with patches of color

COLOR TYPES

Height	Weight	Temperament
19–28 in (48–71 cm)	65–130 lb (30–58 kg)	Bold, lively

Country of origin	First use	Origins
USA	Baiting bulls, guard dog	1900s

OLDE ENGLISH BULLDOGGE

This powerfully built, medium-size, mastiff-type dog is the result of American breeders' attempts to produce a traditional image of the old-style English Bulldog, while eliminating breed weaknesses such as breathing difficulties.

• **HISTORY** This form of dog is said to be the result of a breeding program carried out by David Leavitt in Pennsylvania and involving Bullmastiffs (see p.238), the Bulldog itself (see p.39), American Bulldogs (see p.231), and American Pit Bull Terriers (see p.207).

• **REMARK** Although this is a large, fierce-looking dog, the aim of the breeding program has been to produce a determined and courageous dog, yet one that is not aggressive.

powerful, broad, mastiff-type head
semipendulous flews
double-folded dewlap

short, broad muzzle with prominent stop
thick, powerful neck
well-boned, straight forelegs

rose or button-style ears
short, close coat

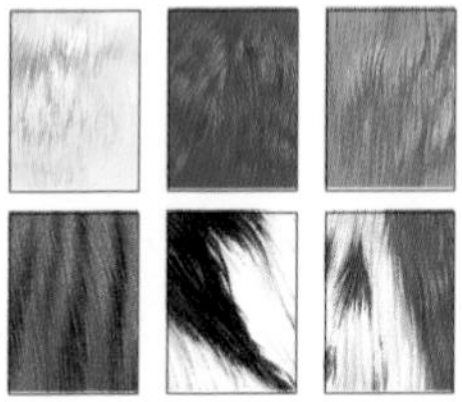
COLOR TYPES

Height	Weight	Temperament
20–25 in (51–64 cm)	65–105 lb (29.5–48 kg)	Bold, friendly

Country of origin	First use	Origins
USA	Pulling sleds	1900s

CHINOOK

The tawny coloration is characteristic of this breed. Seen from the side, it has a square profile, emphasizing its great strength. The thick, double coat of the Chinook becomes thinner during the hot summer months.

• **HISTORY** Developed as a sled dog by breeder Arthur Walden, the Chinook was derived from crossings involving Eskimo Dogs (see p.239), smooth-coated St. Bernards (see p.273), and Belgian Shepherds (see p.128).

• **REMARK** Fewer than 200 known individuals of this breed exist today.

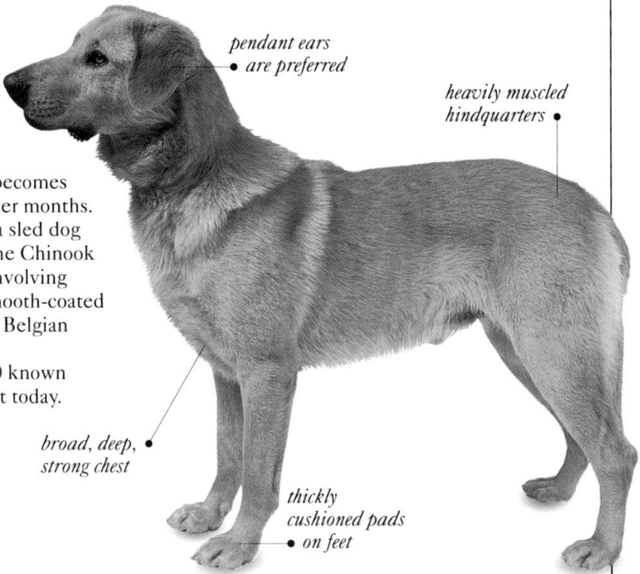
pendant ears
are preferred
heavily muscled
hindquarters
broad, deep,
strong chest
thickly
cushioned pads
on feet

Height	Weight	Temperament
21–26 in (53–66 cm)	65–90 lb (29.5–41 kg)	Strong, determined

Country of origin	First use	Origins
USA	Herding, hunting	1000 BC

CAROLINA DOG

This dog is similar in appearance to other pariah-type dogs, such as the Dingo, seen in other parts of the world. The Carolina Dog has a dense, yellowish gold coat and a strong, prominently boned head and face.

• **HISTORY** This breed could be similar to the earliest types of dog seen in North America. Formerly kept by Native Americans, the Carolina Dog is now best known in the southern states of the USA.

• **REMARK** Some Carolina Dogs are semiwild, but pups can easily be trained to herd stock or hunt small prey.

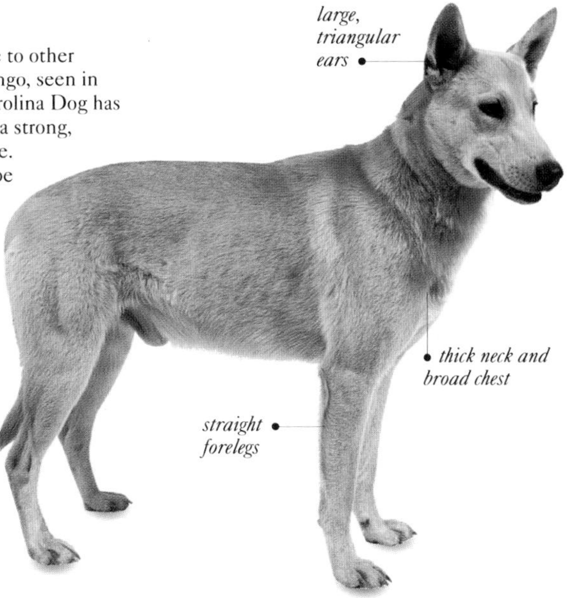
large,
triangular
ears
thick neck and
broad chest
straight
forelegs
tail reaches to
level of hocks

Height	Weight	Temperament
22 in (56 cm)	30–40 lb (13.5–18 kg)	Active, reserved

Country of origin USA	First use Pulling sleds	Origins 3000 BC

Alaskan Malamute

Powerful and strong, this northern dog was developed for stamina rather than speed, unlike some of the smaller breeds from this part of the world. Its dense, double-layered coat affords excellent protection from the often severe elements, having coarse outer guard hairs over a thick, oily, woolly undercoat. The length of the guard hairs varies, becoming longest over the shoulders and in the vicinity of the neck, as well as down the back. The color ranges from light gray through intermediate shades to black, or from gold through shades of red to liver.

• **History** The breed is named after the Malhemut tribe, an Inuit people who lived in northwestern Alaska. They were nomadic, and the dogs were used to haul their possessions between locations.

• **Remark** Due to its size and considerable strength, firm training from an early age is essential. It still retains something of a pack instinct, which may lead to outbreaks of aggressive behavior when it is in the company of other dogs. However, by nature it is friendly and affectionate to people.

powerful hindquarters
moderately ben
stifles
broad, strong hocks

large, prominent muzzle
weather-resistant double coat
tough, thick pads

Height 23–28 in (58–71 cm)	Weight 85–125 lb (39–57 kg)	Temperament Active, exuberant

ears are small in relation to size of head
brown, almond-shaped eyes which may be lighter in red or white dogs
powerful neck
body is somewhat longer than dog's height
broad jaws with large teeth
longer guard hairs around shoulders and neck
white coloration dominates lower part of body
strong, deep chest
large, compact feet

Country of origin Great Britain	First use Guard dog	Origins 1000 BC

MASTIFF

This grand, ancient breed is powerfully built, well-boned, and extremely muscular. The Mastiff is renowned for its great courage and guarding instincts. Its massive size is an important feature of this dog, combined with a symmetrical, well-knit frame. The head should appear square when viewed from any angle. In spite of its ferocious appearance, the Mastiff is responsive and docile in temperament, although it is a reliable guardian which does not take kindly to intruders.

• **HISTORY** Mastiffs were documented in Britain at the time of the Roman invasion: Julius Caesar acknowledged their bravery in battle. Later, at the Battle of Agincourt in 1415, Sir Peers Legh's body was guarded by his Mastiff as the battle raged. On returning to England, it reputedly started the famous Lyme Hall bloodline. Mastiffs nearly died out during World War II, but have since recovered in number.

• **REMARK** Renowned for its intelligence, this breed requires plenty of human contact. Potential owners should therefore have a great deal of time for their dog. The Mastiff also requires lots of space and exercise.

broad skull with flat forehead
large, round feet

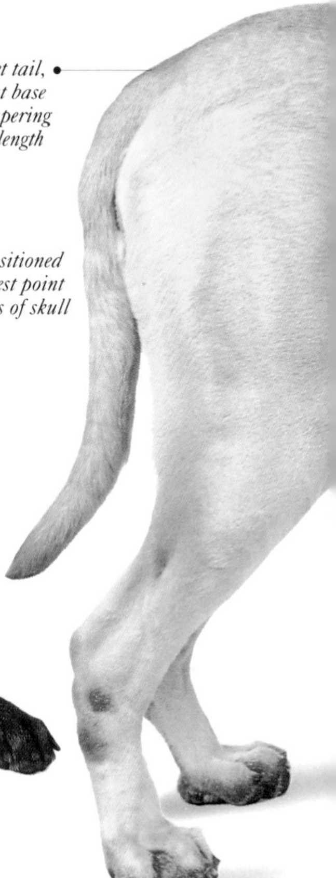
high-set tail, wide at base and tapering along length

ears positioned at highest point on sides of skull
square head
short, close-lying coat

Height 27½–30 in (70–76 cm)	Weight 175–190 lb (79–86 kg)	Temperament Loyal, alert

very powerful hindquarters
forehead wrinkles when attention is excited
ears lying flat and close to cheeks
very muscular and slightly arched neck
great depth in the flanks, emphasizing the powerful build
strong, straight legs
black hair extends over the muzzle, nose, and around the eyes, irrespective of the dog's coloration

Country of origin Great Britain	First use Guarding estates	Origins 1800s

BULLMASTIFF

The powerful, active Bullmastiff can easily be distinguished from the Mastiff (see pp.236–37) by its smaller size and its more compact face. The American Bullmastiff tends to be more Mastiff-like than its British counterpart. Originally, dark-colored brindle was the favored coloration, but today fawns and reds are popular.

• **HISTORY** Crossings between mastiffs and bulldogs gave rise to the Bullmastiff, which is sometimes known as "the gamekeeper's dog." It was bred specifically to accompany gamekeepers on their rounds, being able to track well and having sufficient size and strength to tackle and overpower a poacher.

• **REMARK** As is the case with other large breeds, pups may seem clumsy and uncoordinated when very young. Once mature, there should be no evidence of awkwardness in the way they move.

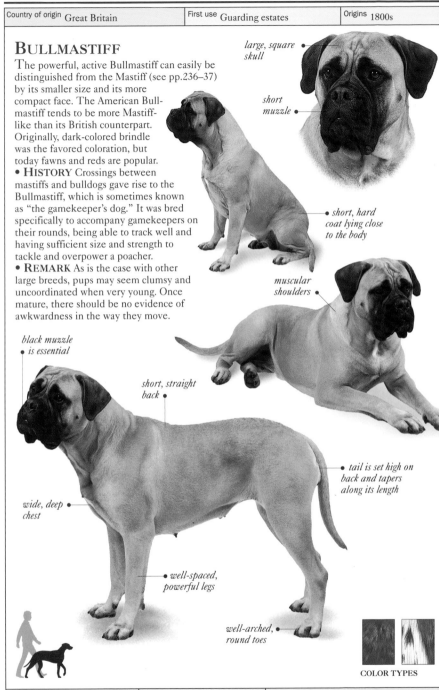

large, square skull
short muzzle

short, hard coat lying close to the body

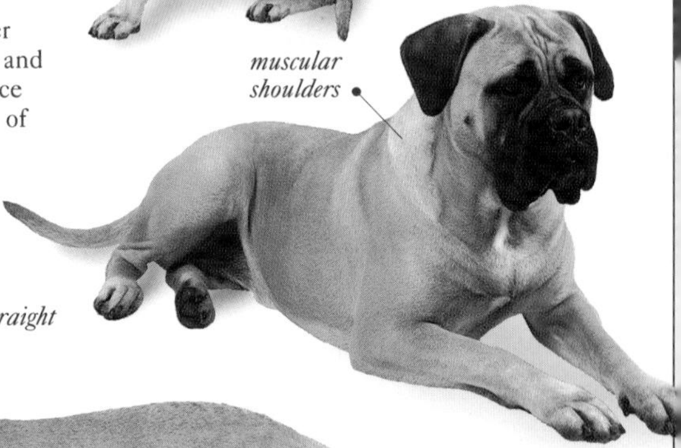
muscular shoulders

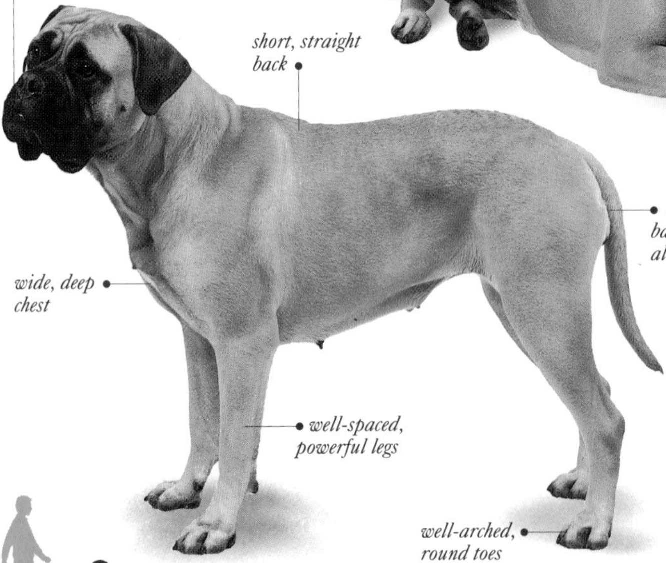
black muzzle is essential
short, straight back
tail is set high on back and tapers along its length
wide, deep chest
well-spaced, powerful legs
well-arched, round toes

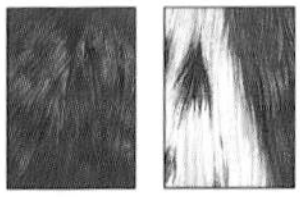

COLOR TYPES

Height 25–27 in (64–69 cm)	Weight 90–130 lb (41–59 kg)	Temperament Loyal, fearless

Country of origin Great Britain	First use Baiting bulls	Origins 1800s

BULL TERRIER

This sturdy breed is characterized by a long, oval head with no stop; small, triangular eyes; thin, erect ears; and tight-fitting coat over a large-boned, muscular body.

• **HISTORY** This breed was developed from crosses with the bulldog and Old English Terrier.

• **REMARK** It may not get along with other dogs. The breed is recognized as a terrier in the USA.

• **OTHER NAME** English Bull Terrier.

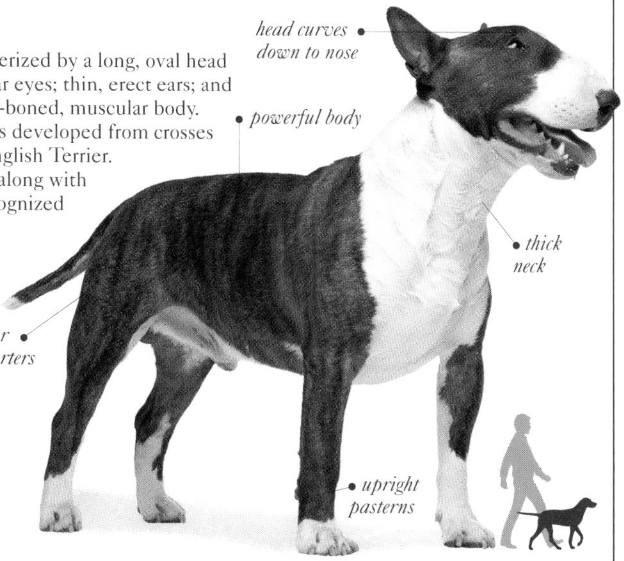
head curves down to nose
powerful body
thick neck
muscular hindquarters
upright pasterns

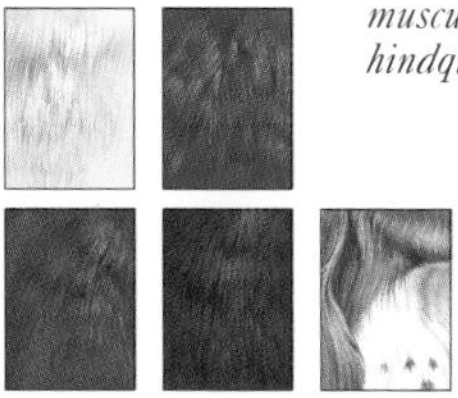

COLOR TYPES

Height 21–22 in (53–56 cm)	Weight 52–62 lb (24–28 kg)	Temperament Fearless, determined

Country of origin Canada	First use Hunting, pulling sleds	Origins 1000 BC

ESKIMO DOG

This dog originated in the lands of the Arctic. It is seen in a variety of colors, with upright ears and a long tail that curls down over its back. Its dense coat affords it some protection in temperatures that fall far below freezing.

• **HISTORY** This breed provided a vital lifeline for Arctic peoples before mechanized transport.

• **REMARK** Firm training is essential for this dog.

• **OTHER NAMES** Husky, Esquimaux.

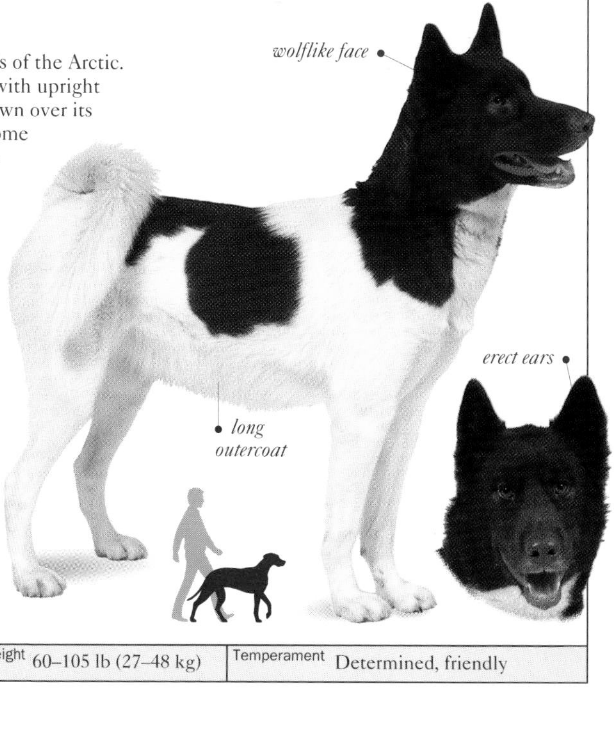
wolflike face
erect ears
long outercoat

COLOR TYPES

Height 20–27 in (51–69 cm)	Weight 60–105 lb (27–48 kg)	Temperament Determined, friendly

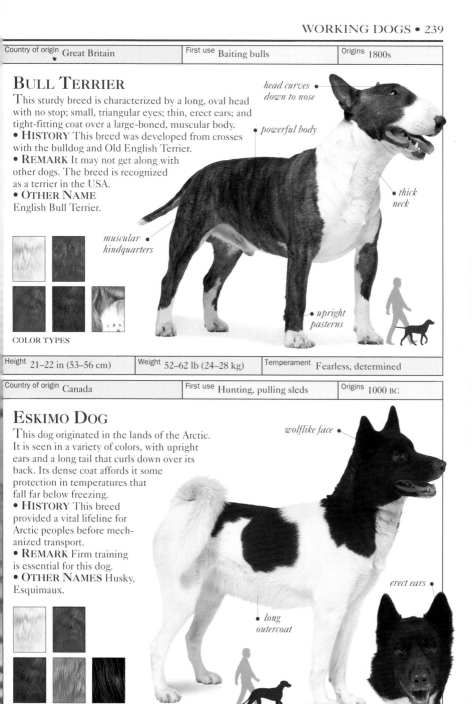

Country of origin Canada	First use Helping fishermen	Origins 1700s

NEWFOUNDLAND

As a pup, this massive, imposing dog actually looks like a bear cub. In spite of its size, the adult Newfoundland is usually gentle and affectionate. However, it can prove to be a loyal household guard if necessary. Its distinctive, oily coat is highly water-resistant and falls back naturally into place if groomed against the lie of the fur.

• **HISTORY** The earliest Newfoundland originated in northeastern Canada. It is thought to be descended from dogs brought by European colonists, although Native North Americans may have had mastiff-type dogs.

• **REMARK** This dog once helped fishermen haul in their nets.

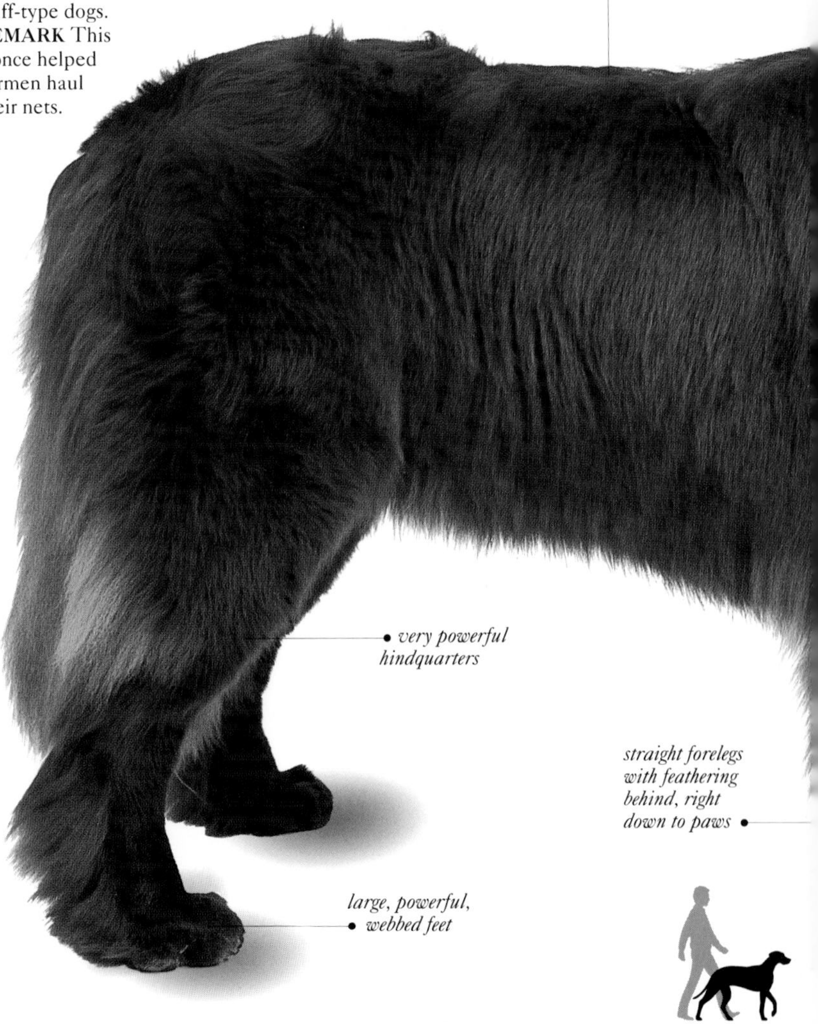
coat is flat, quite coarse, and dense
very powerful hindquarters
straight forelegs with feathering behind, right down to paws
large, powerful, webbed feet

Height 26–28 in (66–71 cm)	Weight 110–150 lb (50–68 kg)	Temperament Responsive, docile

small, dark brown, wide-set eyes
short, square muzzle
dull black coloration
broad and massive skull
small, close-lying ears
strong neck

Country of origin	First use	Origins
Argentina	Hunting pumas and jaguars	1920s

Dogo Argentino

One of the few breeds developed in South America, the Dogo Argentino is a powerful dog, invariably white in color. It has a strong, square head indicative of mastiff origins. Notorious for its aggressive, fearless nature, it was originally used to pursue big cats in its homeland. It is, nevertheless, reputedly trustworthy with people and exceptionally loyal.

• **History** The breed is descended from the Old Fighting Dog, which originated in Spain. Crosses with other breeds, most notably the Boxer (see p.255), took place under the guidance of the breed's founder, Dr. Antonio Martinez, to produce a more obedient temperament.

• **Remark** This dog is banned in Great Britain due to concerns about its temperament.

• **Other Names**
Argentinian Mastiff.

ears are invariably cropped
broad jaws

short, sleek coat
relatively long tail

long, straight forelegs
traces of pigment on skin may be visible through hair
powerful hind legs

Height	Weight	Temperament
24–27 in (61–69 cm)	80–100 lb (36–45 kg)	Bold, brave

Country of origin Brazil	First use Hunting big game	Origins 1800s

Fila Brasileiro

The result of the combination of powerful mastiff stock with the Bloodhound (see pp.166–167), the Fila Brasileiro displays distinctive folds of skin on its huge head, which extend on to the neck. Further links with the Bloodhound can be detected from its unerring sense of smell and elongated muzzle.

- **History** Aggression was first bred into the Fila Brasileiro for bringing down wild cats and for controlling cattle.
- **Remark** This fearsome breed was also used for tracking down escaped slaves.
- **Other Names** Brazilian Mastiff.

prominent dewlap

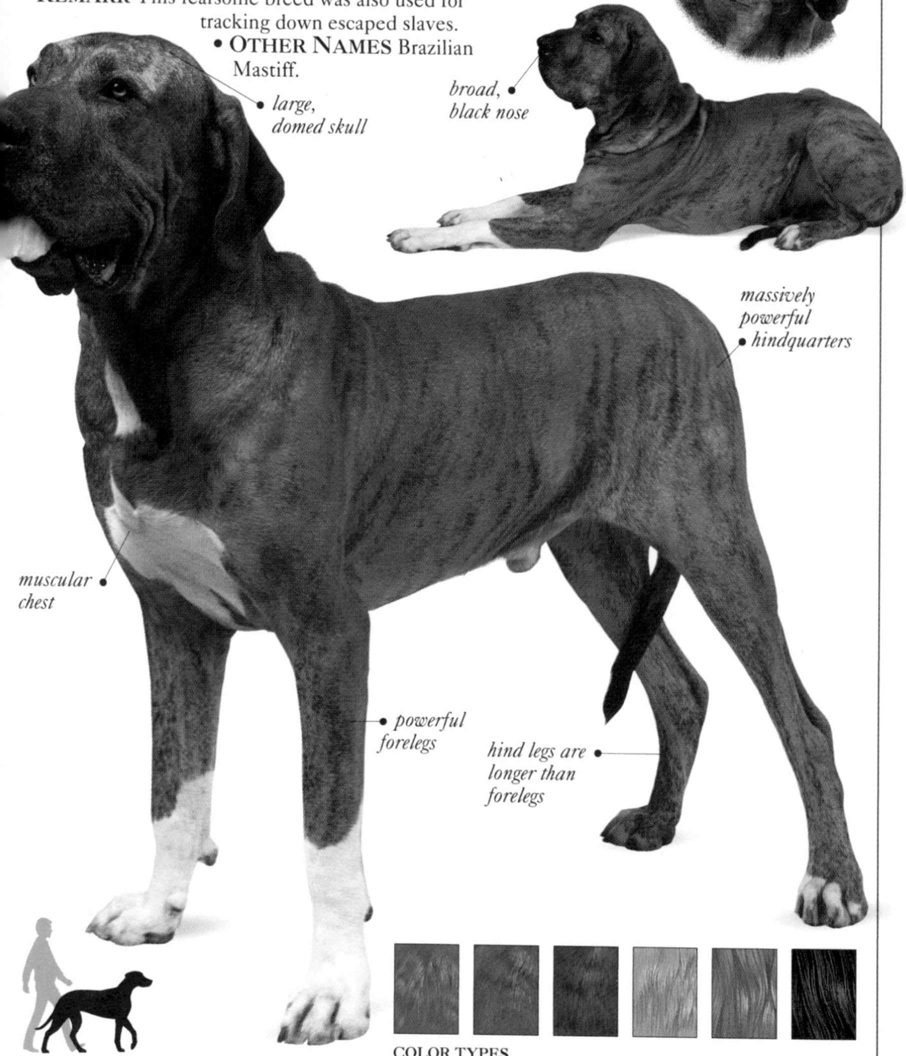
broad, black nose
large, domed skull
massively powerful hindquarters
muscular chest
powerful forelegs
hind legs are longer than forelegs

COLOR TYPES

Height 24–30 in (61–76 cm)	Weight 90–110 lb (41–50 kg)	Temperament Bold, aggressive

Country of origin Greenland	First use Pulling sleds	Origins 1500s

Greenland Dog

The Greenland Dog is generally taller than the Eskimo Dog (see p.239), but slightly lighter and shorter in the back. So close is the relationship between these breeds, however, that they are judged to the same standard in some countries.

• **History** Thought by some to be descended from Arctic wolves, this dog is superbly adapted to survival in the harsh conditions found in that region. Many local forms of this type of dog were bred in the Arctic regions before mechanized transportation was introduced.

• **Remark** As a hunter, the Greenland can track the breathing holes of seals in the ice.

• **Other Names** Grønlandshund, Grünlandshund.

broad, wedge-shaped head
large, well-spread feet

strong jaws

small, triangular ears
large, bushy tail curls to one side over back
broad chest
color is highly variable between individuals
straight, powerful forelegs

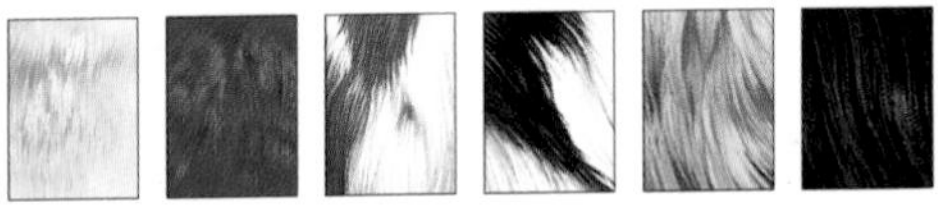

COLOR TYPES

Height 22–25 in (56–64 cm)	Weight 66–70 lb (30–32 kg)	Temperament Affectionate, independent

Country of origin	First use	Origins
Norway	Hunting elk	1000s

NORWEGIAN ELKHOUND

Bred as a specialist hunter of elk, this dog is large and powerfully built. Its heavily muscled body is compact, giving it a rather stocky appearance, an impression that is reinforced by a dense covering of gray hair. A black form also exists (below).

• **HISTORY** Skeletons of Stone Age dogs closely resembling Elkhounds have been unearthed in Scandinavia.

• **REMARK** This is a very friendly dog and makes an excellent companion.

• **OTHER NAMES** Norsk Elghund (Grå), Elkhound.

gray coat with black tips
tightly curled tail
powerful hindquarters
large, dark eyes
well-boned legs
darker hair on muzzle

Height	Weight	Temperament
19–21 in (49–52 cm)	44–50 lb (20–23 kg)	Alert, friendly

Country of origin	First use	Origins
Norway	Hunting elk	1000s

BLACK NORWEGIAN ELKHOUND

This dog is the black form of the more common gray Norwegian Elkhound (above). Apart from its comparative rarity, it is essentially the same dog, except a little smaller and lighter.

• **HISTORY** The Norwegian Elkhounds are thought to have changed little since they first became human companions over a thousand years ago.

• **REMARK** It can scent an elk over a distance of several miles.

• **OTHER NAMES** Norsk Elghund (Sort).

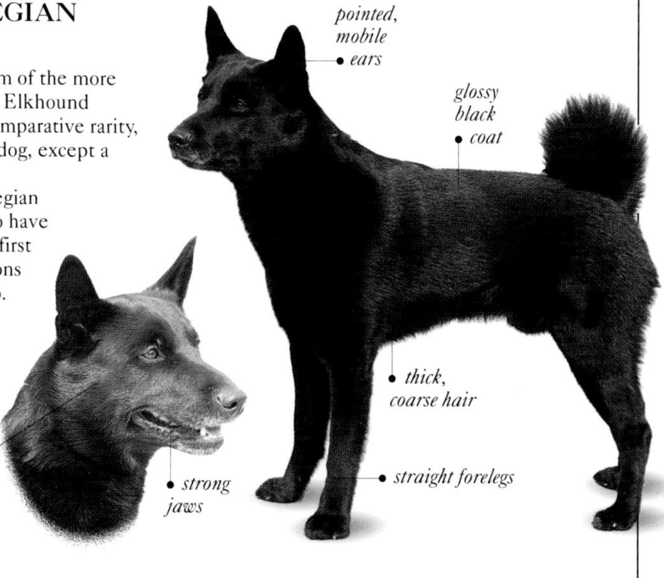
pointed, mobile ears
glossy black coat
thick, coarse hair
conical head
strong jaws
straight forelegs

Height	Weight	Temperament
18–20 in (46–51 cm)	40 lb (18 kg)	Alert, friendly

Country of origin Norway	First use Hunting puffins	Origins 1500s

LUNDEHUND

A neat, compact build characterizes this strong and industrious breed. Its specialized breeding has resulted in well-developed feet, additional toes, and extra joints to aid it in its traditional job of scaling cliff faces in search of puffins. This very agile dog can bend its head horizontally backward almost to touch its back.

• **HISTORY** The breed was used for centuries along the coasts of Norway. The Lundehund went into decline, however, along with the popularity of puffin hunting, and at one point there were only 50 individuals known to exist.

• **REMARK** The Lundehund can close its ears to keep out water.

• **OTHER NAMES** Norwegian Puffin Dog.

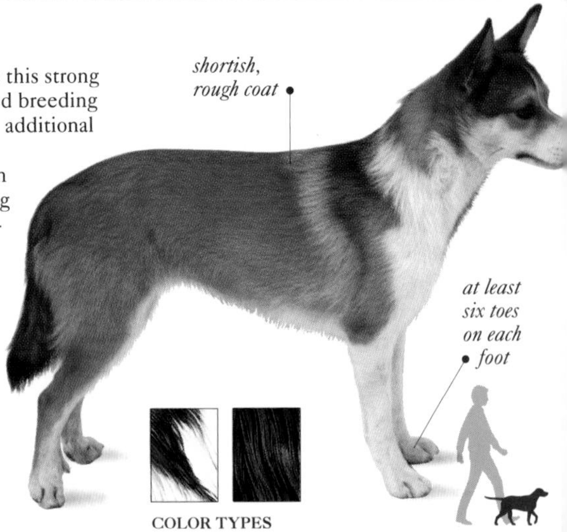
shortish, rough coat
at least six toes on each foot

COLOR TYPES

Height 12–15½ in (31–39 cm)	Weight 13–14 lb (6 kg)	Temperament Lively, alert

Country of origin Norway	First use Herding stock	Origins 800s

NORWEGIAN BUHUND

This dog shows typical spitz characteristics, as do many northern European breeds. It has erect, pointed ears, a powerful, stocky body, and a tail curling up and forward over its body.

• **HISTORY** The Buhund was developed primarily for farm work, undertaking a variety of tasks. Its herding instinct is so ingrained that it will even round up chickens.

• **REMARK** The name comes from the Norwegian word *bu*, meaning "shed," or "stall."

• **OTHER NAMES** Norsk Buhund.

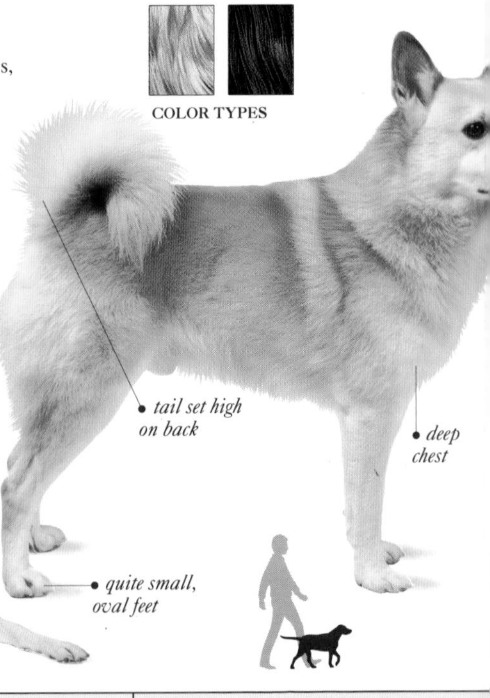
COLOR TYPES
tail set high on back
deep chest
quite small, oval feet

short, dense outercoat

Height 17–18 in (43–46 cm)	Weight 53–58 lb (24–26 kg)	Temperament Brave, companionable

Country of origin Finland	First use Hunting birds and game	Origins 1800s

Finnish Spitz

An alert, pointed face and a reddish brown or red-gold coloration give this member of the spitz family a distinctly foxlike appearance.

• **HISTORY** A standard for the Finnish Spitz was established in 1812. Originally, the dog was used for hunting birds and small game.

• **REMARK** In contests, dogs bark to indicate the presence of game and are marked on the number of barks per minute, which can be as many as 160.

• **OTHER NAMES** Suomenpystykorva, Finsk Spets.

dark, almond-shaped eyes
plumed tail curves forward and around the thigh
deep chest and strong, straight forequarters
round feet

outer coat is longer and coarser on shoulders

Height 15–20 in (38–51 cm)	Weight 31–35 lb (14–16 kg)	Temperament Lively, vocal

Country of origin Finland	First use Hunting large game	Origins 1600s

Karelian Bear Dog

Robust and lively, this breed has very distinctive coloration – predominantly black, with white markings on its face, neck, chest, abdomen, feet, and tail.

• **HISTORY** This breed was named after the Karelia province of Finland. It was first recognized by the Finnish Kennel Club in 1935.

• **REMARK** After a decline in the 1960s, it is now increasing in numbers worldwide.

• **OTHER NAMES** Björnhund, Karjalankarhukoira.

wedge-shaped head
fully arched tail preferred, though bobtails do exist
characteristic white tip on tail
strong chest
thick, tall, round paws
white blaze on face

Height 18–23 in (48–58 cm)	Weight 44–50 lb (20–23 kg)	Temperament Brave, determined

Country of origin Sweden	First use Hunting elk	Origins 1000s

Swedish Elkhound

This is the largest and most powerful of the elkhound-type breeds native to Scandinavia. The Swedish Elkhound has an elongated, rather narrow head, and this, combined with a straight muzzle, gives it a slightly foxlike appearance. The coat of this breed consists of a long, hard outercoat and a dense, woolly, much softer, undercoat.

• **History** The forebears of the Swedish Elkhound may have accompanied Stone Age people in the Scandinavian region of the world. Certainly this specific breed has been known for centuries, even though it was not officially recognized by the Swedish Kennel Club until 1946.

• **Remark** Best known in the Jämtland area of Sweden, the Swedish Elkhound is designed for living in cold climates.

• **Other Names** Jämthund.

large, erect, pointed ears
small, dark eyes

broad, muscular shoulders
tail curls tightly over back and rests on one side
deep, powerful chest
heavily muscled hind legs
hard, long outercoat over woolly undercoat

Height 23–25 in (58–64 cm)	Weight 66 lb (30 kg)	Temperament Friendly, alert

Country of origin	First use	Origins
Sweden	Herding reindeer	1800s

SWEDISH LAPPHUND

This medium-size dog shows typical spitz characteristics in terms of its foxlike facial appearance and dramatically curving tail. It is protected from the cold of its homeland by a dense, woolly, double coat.

• **HISTORY** The ancestors of this breed were kept by the Lapps to herd reindeer, although they have since been adapted to herding sheep. The breed was officially recognized in Sweden in 1944.

• **REMARK** This dog tends to be solid in color, although individuals with white markings are seen and not penalized.

• **OTHER NAMES** Lapplandska Spets.

short, erect ears
dark, chestnut-colored eyes
plumed tail hangs forward
harsh, thick coat
feathering on legs and body

COLOR TYPES

Height	Weight	Temperament
17½–19½ in (44–49 cm)	44 lb (20 kg)	Lively, alert

Country of origin	First use	Origins
Sweden	Hunting birds	1600s

NORRBOTTENSPETS

The Norrbottenspets is one of the smaller spitz breeds, distinguishable from other spitzes by its relatively short coat, which is dense and stands away from the body. Its ears are pointed and erect, its muzzle is pointed, and its eyes are alert and lively.

• **HISTORY** The breed was close to extinction in 1948, but enthusiasts sought out the last few remaining dogs and bitches and started a successful breeding program.

• **REMARK** The Norbottenspets was once widely kept in Sweden as a hunting dog.

• **OTHER NAMES** Pohjanpystykorva, Nordic Spitz.

erect, triangular ears
short, stand-off coat
any colored areas must be well defined
straight, muscular forelegs
white is the dominant color

COLOR TYPES

Height	Weight	Temperament
16–17 in (41–43 cm)	26–33 lb (12–15 kg)	Quiet, affectionate

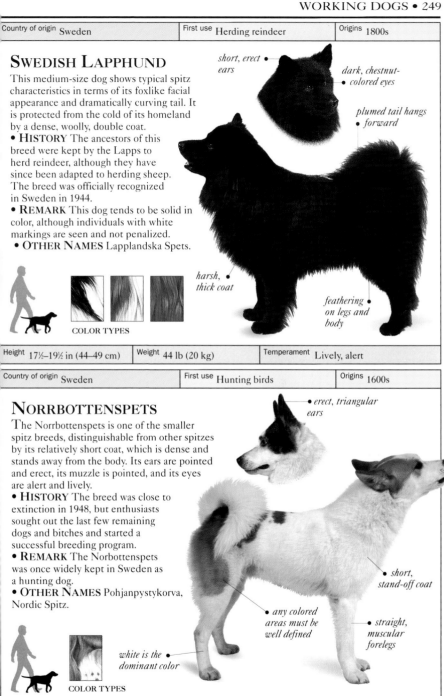

Country of origin Germany	First use Guard dog	Origins 1800s

DOBERMANN

This medium-size mastiff breed has a sculpted, elegant appearance. It is sleek, well-muscled, and powerful, and is usually black and tan in coloration. The Dobermann is a bold, alert dog with a great deal of stamina.

• **HISTORY** This breed of dog was developed by a German tax collector, Ludwig Dobermann, to act as a deterrent against thieves and muggers, as well as aggrieved taxpayers. He used a variety of breeds, including the German Shepherd Dog, Rottweiler, German Pinscher, and Manchester Terrier.

• **REMARK** The Dobermann once had a particular reputation for aggression. Although this has now been curbed to a great extent, firm training is still necessary from puppyhood.

• **OTHER NAMES** Dobermann Pinscher.

flat top to skull
lean, relatively long neck

almond-shaped eyes, no lighter than coat color
powerful jaws and well-filled face

Height 25½–27 in (65–69 cm)	Weight 66–88 lb (30–40 kg)	Temperament Bold, fearless

small ears set high on head – sometimes naturally erect, or may be cropped
sharply defined markings

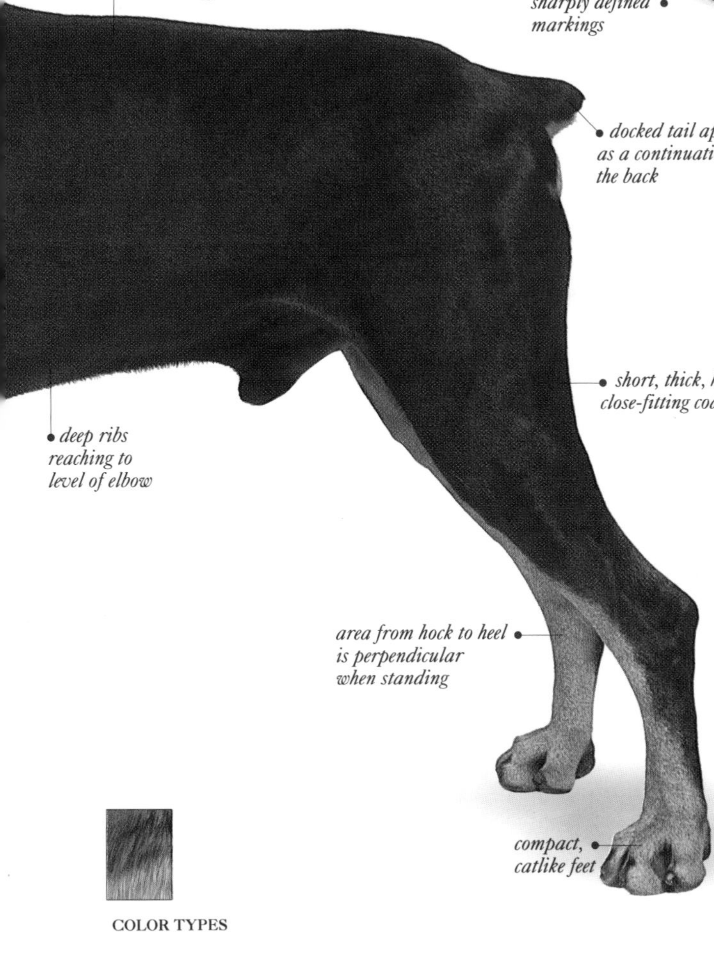
square body shape and short, firm back
docked tail appears as a continuation of the back
short, thick, hard, close-fitting coat
deep ribs reaching to level of elbow
area from hock to heel is perpendicular when standing
compact, catlike feet

COLOR TYPES

Country of origin Germany	First use Hunting large game	Origins 2000 BC

GREAT DANE

A gentle giant, the Great Dane combines enormous size and strength with equal portions of dignity and elegance. It has a long, well-chiseled face with a distinctive, intelligent expression. It comes in a variety of colors including black, blue, brindle, fawn, and a striking harlequin. The breed is often seen with cropped ears in North America, giving the dog a more fearsome appearance that belies its naturally affectionate disposition.

- **HISTORY** Of ancient origin, the Great Dane was developed in Germany and is believed to have inherited its grace and agility from crossings with greyhounds.
- **REMARK** Renowned for its tolerance toward children, clean in its habits, and easy to groom, the Great Dane makes an excellent family pet for those who have the space and can afford to pay for this gigantic dog's equally huge food bill.
- **OTHER NAMES** Deutsche Dogge.

wide, blunt nose with characteristic ridge

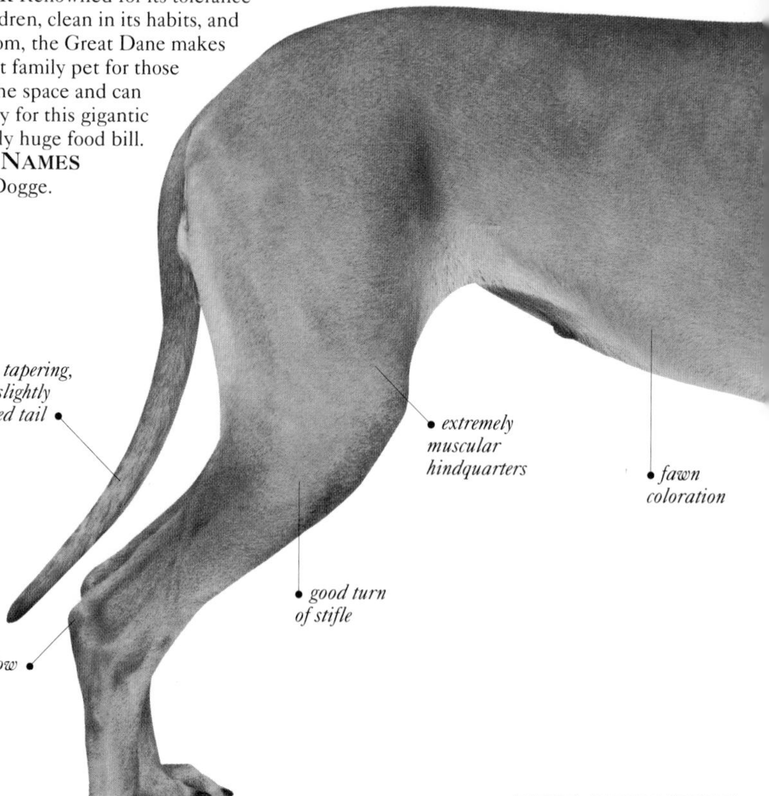
long, tapering, and slightly curved tail
extremely muscular hindquarters
fawn coloration
good turn of stifle
hocks set low

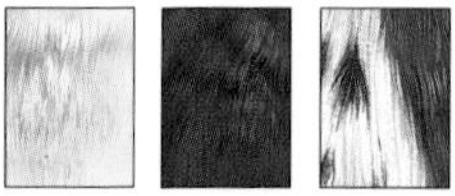

COLOR TYPES

Height 30–32 in (76–81 cm)	Weight 100–120 lb (45–55 kg)	Temperament Alert, lively

long, flat skull
ears set high and folded forwards
round, fairly deep-set eyes
very deep, strong chest with well-sprung ribs
short coat is dense and sleek
harlequin coloration

Country of origin Germany	First use Retrieving from water	Origins 1400s

STANDARD POODLE

This is the largest of the three breeds of poodle. An elegantly proportioned, squarely built dog, the Standard Poodle is a highly regarded retriever of game from rivers and marshland. The hair is clipped (as shown here), to provide warmth around its ankle joints, while the mane improves buoyancy.

• **HISTORY** Originating in Germany, the modern poodle is likely to have descended from the now rare French water dog, the Barbet (see p.95).

• **REMARK** As a working dog, its profuse coat used to hinder movement in the water, hence the need for clipping.

• **OTHER NAMES** Barbone, Caniche.

COLOR TYPES

moderately round skull
tight-fitting lips

coat color must be solid
long, straight muzzle

strong, well-proportioned neck
docked tail is set high and carried erect
muscular hind legs
straight, parallel forelegs
deep chest with well-sprung ribs

Height 15 in (38 cm)	Weight 45–70 lb (20.5–32 kg)	Temperament Intelligent, lively

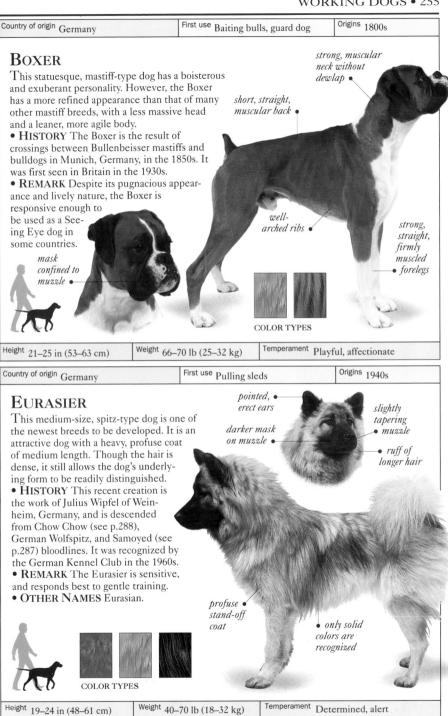

Country of origin	First use	Origins
Germany	Baiting bulls, guard dog	1800s

BOXER

This statuesque, mastiff-type dog has a boisterous and exuberant personality. However, the Boxer has a more refined appearance than that of many other mastiff breeds, with a less massive head and a leaner, more agile body.

• **HISTORY** The Boxer is the result of crossings between Bullenbeisser mastiffs and bulldogs in Munich, Germany, in the 1850s. It was first seen in Britain in the 1930s.

• **REMARK** Despite its pugnacious appearance and lively nature, the Boxer is responsive enough to be used as a Seeing Eye dog in some countries.

strong, muscular neck without dewlap
short, straight, muscular back
well-arched ribs
strong, straight, firmly muscled forelegs

mask confined to muzzle

COLOR TYPES

Height	Weight	Temperament
21–25 in (53–63 cm)	66–70 lb (25–32 kg)	Playful, affectionate

Country of origin	First use	Origins
Germany	Pulling sleds	1940s

EURASIER

This medium-size, spitz-type dog is one of the newest breeds to be developed. It is an attractive dog with a heavy, profuse coat of medium length. Though the hair is dense, it still allows the dog's underlying form to be readily distinguished.

• **HISTORY** This recent creation is the work of Julius Wipfel of Weinheim, Germany, and is descended from Chow Chow (see p.288), German Wolfspitz, and Samoyed (see p.287) bloodlines. It was recognized by the German Kennel Club in the 1960s.

• **REMARK** The Eurasier is sensitive, and responds best to gentle training.

• **OTHER NAMES** Eurasian.

pointed, erect ears
darker mask on muzzle
slightly tapering muzzle
ruff of longer hair

profuse stand-off coat
only solid colors are recognized

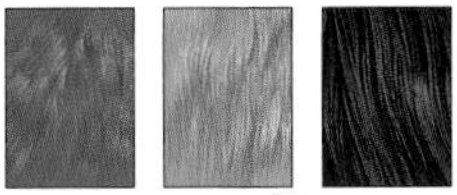

COLOR TYPES

Height	Weight	Temperament
19–24 in (48–61 cm)	40–70 lb (18–32 kg)	Determined, alert

Country of origin	First use	Origins
Germany	Helping fishermen	1800s

LANDSEER

This dog closely resembles the Newfoundland (see pp.240–41), but differs most notably in its coloration. Black areas should be prominent on the back and rump, as well as the head, where only a small white blaze is present. In some countries, including Great Britain and the USA, the Landseer is registered only as a color form of the Newfoundland.

• **HISTORY** In the early 1800s, Newfoundlands varied a great deal in appearance. Gradually, two types evolved in mainland Europe. The traditional form is larger, with a short muzzle and a predominantly black coat. The taller Landseer is lighter, has a longer head, and a distinctive slightly curly coat.

• **REMARK** The artist Sir Edwin Landseer (1802–73) gave his name to the new breed. Portraying contemporary Newfoundland dogs in his painting *Off to the Rescue*, he established the credentials for the Landseer.

even, black markings on body

medium-length, dense coat

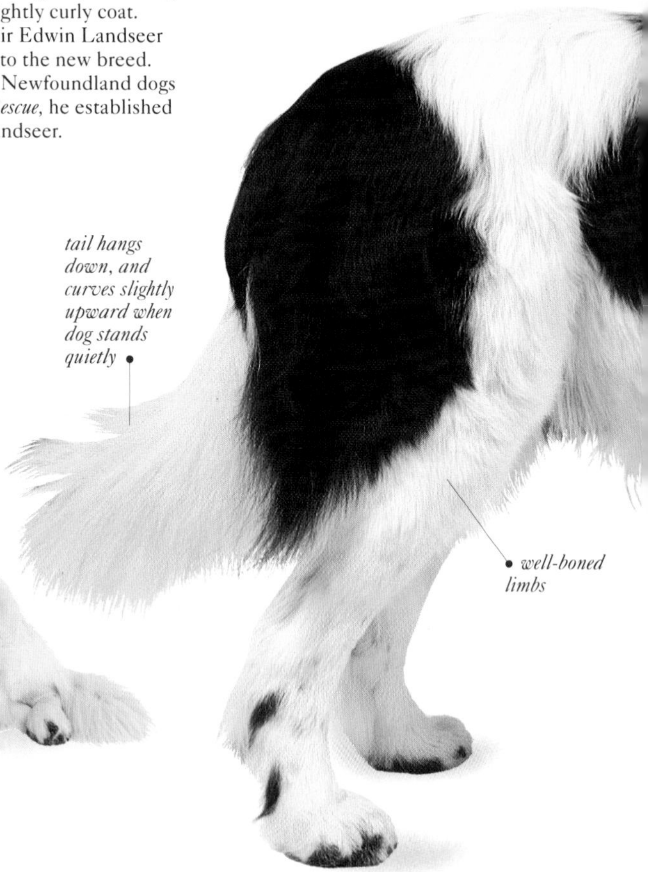
tail hangs down, and curves slightly upward when dog stands quietly
well-boned limbs

Height	Weight	Temperament
26–28 in (66–71 cm)	110–150 lb (50–68 kg)	Alert, friendly

massive head
strong, powerful neck
short hair on face
narrow, white blaze
large feet for swimming
huge, powerful jaws

Country of origin Germany	First use Symbolic mascot	Origins 1800s

Leonberger

This large, friendly dog displays many of the characteristics of the breeds that contributed to its ancestry, most notably the Newfoundland (see pp.240–41), from whom it inherited its love of water, and the St. Bernard (see p.273). Other breeds, such as the Great Swiss Mountain Dog (see p.272), were probably involved as well. Only very restricted areas of white are permitted in the Leonberger at present.

• **History** In the 1840s, Heinrich Essig, the Mayor of Leonberg, Germany, set out to create a breed of dog that resembled the dog featured on the town's crest. Not surprisingly it was named the Leonberger.

• **Remark** This breed has a natural love of water and has proved outstanding as a water rescue dog. Its coat is waterproof and it has webs between its toes.

black mask on
face is preferred

broad, square
muzzle
distinctive mane
at throat and chest

dark points
permissible
on coat
round feet with
webbed toes

Height 26–31½ in (65–80 cm)	Weight 75–110 lb (34–50 kg)	Temperament Intelligent, friendly

well -feathered ears
forehead must not be wrinkled
light yellow to red-brown coloration
underside of tail may be slightly lighter in color than coat

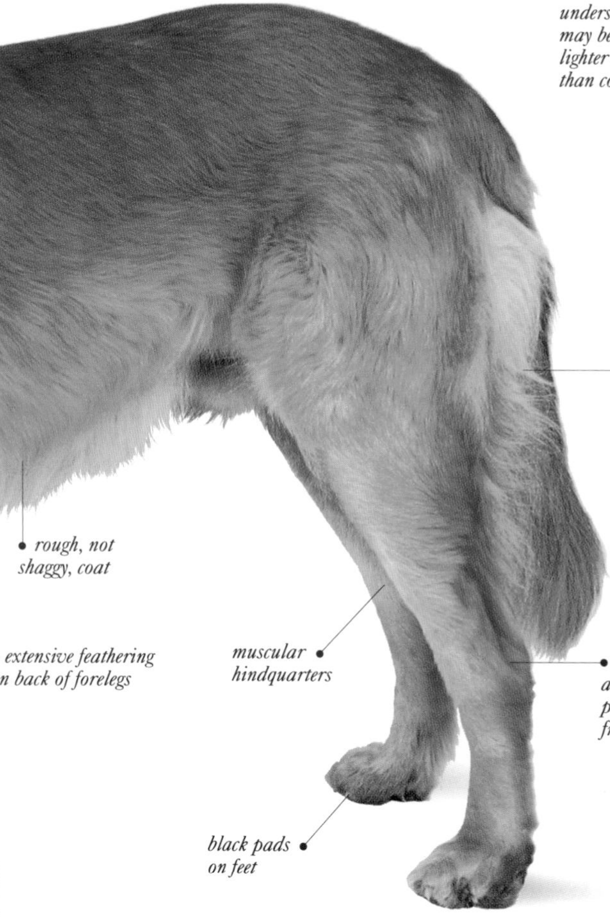
bushy tail, never held high
rough, not shaggy, coat
extensive feathering on back of forelegs
muscular hindquarters
hind legs are well angulated, appearing parallel when viewed from behind
black pads on feet

COLOR TYPES

Country of origin Germany	First use Driving cattle, guard dog	Origins 1800s

ROTTWEILER

Enormously powerful and muscular, this breed has a calm, self-assured expression which reflects a tranquil temperament. Its coloration is black, with distinctive symmetrical tan markings. It is responsive to training and an enthusiastic worker.

• **HISTORY** The Rottweiler was developed in the German town of Rottweil, where it was used as a butcher's dog, for droving, and for guarding cattle. Now one of the top five most popular dogs in the USA, this breed came close to extinction in the early 19th century.

• **REMARK** Irresponsible mishandling has given this breed a reputation for viciousness.

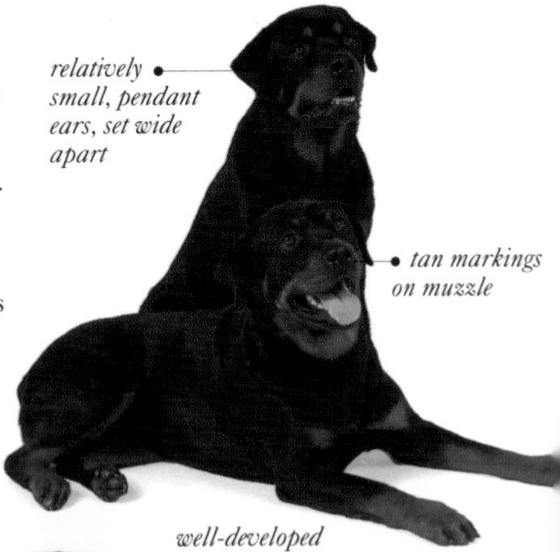
relatively small, pendant ears, set wide apart
tan markings on muzzle

skull broad between the ears
arched forehead
well-developed occipital bone
customarily docked tail
broad, deep chest with well-sprung ribs
broad, powerful hindquarters
hind feet larger than front
forward-sloping pasterns

Height 23–27 in (58–69 cm)	Weight 90–110 lb (41–50 kg)	Temperament Protective, determined

Country of origin Poland	First use Guarding flocks	Origins 1700s

OWCZAREK PODHALANSKI

Although large and heavy, this sheepdog breed is surprisingly quick and agile. The usual coloration is solid white, although cream is also found, and both straight-haired and wavy-haired forms occur. This sturdy animal is well able to withstand the severe winter weather of its native Poland.

• **HISTORY** Received wisdom claims the Italian Bergamasco (see p.135) as this breed's ancestor, but its more likely forebears would seem to be the very similar sheepdog breeds of neighboring Czechoslovakia and Hungary.

• **REMARK** A placid nature is one of the key characteristics of this breed, and individuals prone to irritability are likely to be disqualified from the show ring. The Owczarek has recently been adopted for military and police duties in North America.

• **OTHER NAMES** Tatra Mountain Sheepdog.

large, broad skull
dogs have shorter bodies than bitches
feathering on tail

hair on head and muzzle is shorter than body hair
strong neck
heavily boned forelegs
white- or cream-colored, thick, dense coat
large, thick-soled feet

Height 24–34 in (61–86 cm)	Weight 100–150 lb (45–68 kg)	Temperament Independent, friendly

Country of origin Belgium	First use Guard dog on barges	Origins 1500s

SCHIPPERKE

The Schipperke is relatively small for a member of the spitz family of dog breeds, but its attractive appearance has the distinctive features of this group. The outercoat is long, thick, and harsh, forming a ruff at the neck. According to the USA standard, solid black is the only acceptable color, although in other countries different colors are also permitted.

• **HISTORY** The Schipperke has always been a small breed. It was used originally as a guard dog on barges and also perhaps to encourage barge ponies to renewed efforts. Its name is thought to derive from a corruption of the Flemish word for "little bargeman."

• **REMARK** The Schipperke is recognized by the AKC as a nonsporting breed. Most Schipperke are born tailless.

very mobile, erect, triangular ears
foxlike head with pointed muzzle

short back
outer hair forms a ruff
strong hind legs
small, round, tight feet

fairly broad, flat skull with little stop
short, strong neck
straight forelegs

COLOR TYPES

Height 10–13 in (25–33 cm)	Weight 12–16 lb (5.5–7.5 kg)	Temperament Alert, loyal

Country of origin France	First use Baiting bulls	Origins 1800s

FRENCH BULLDOG

This small, compact breed has a large head and distinctive batlike ears. It has suffered less from the breeding extremes that have afflicted its English relative.

• **HISTORY** These dogs are descended from the toy bulldogs of the 19th century, some of which were taken to France.

• **REMARK** Overweight individuals may have trouble with their breathing.

• **OTHER NAMES** Bouledogue Francais.

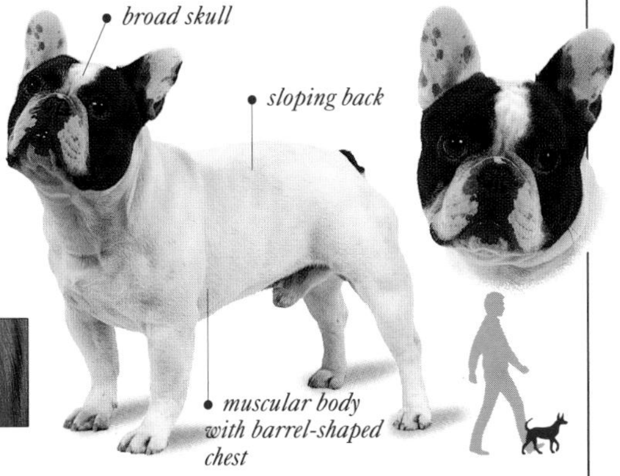
broad skull
sloping back
muscular body with barrel-shaped chest

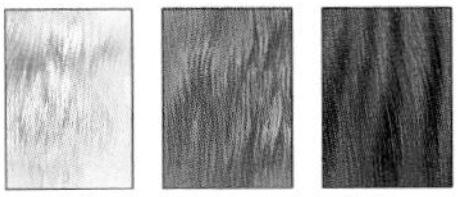

COLOR TYPES

Height 12 in (31 cm)	Weight 22–28 lb (10–13 kg)	Temperament Affectionate, playful

Country of origin France	First use Hunting game, guard dog	Origins 300s

DOGUE DE BORDEAUX

Descended from ancient mastiff stock, the Dogue de Bordeaux is a very powerful breed with a well-furrowed face and a head so massive it could be the largest in the canine world.

• **HISTORY** The sheer strength of this mastiff led to its being pitted against bulls in circus spectacles.

• **REMARK** Careful breeding has pacified these dogs. A special breeding program was established in the 1960s.

• **OTHER NAMES** French Mastiff.

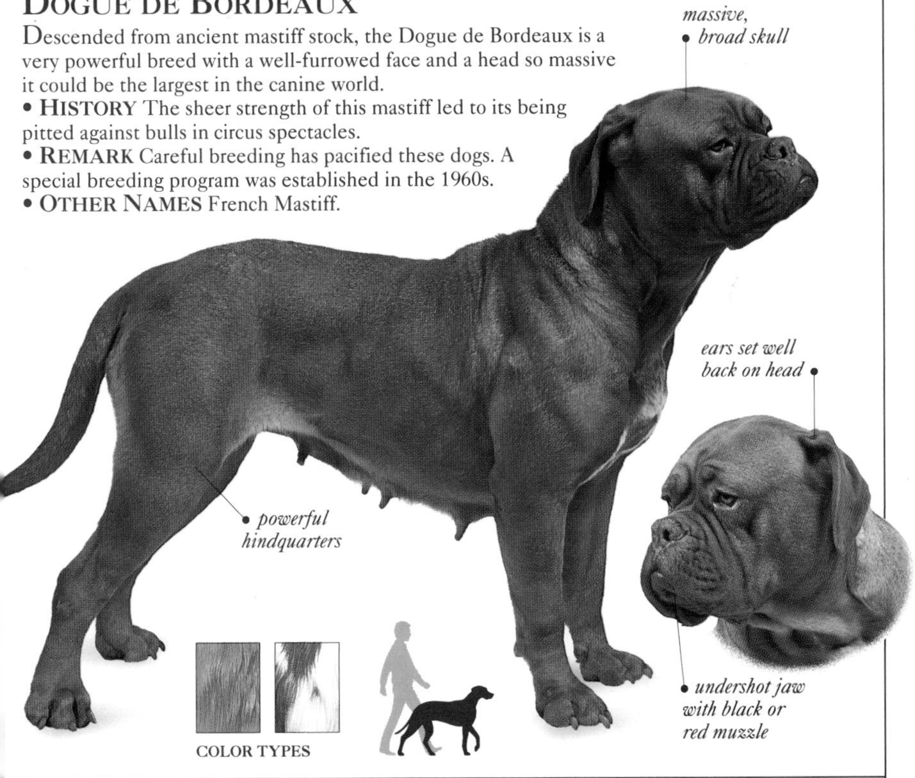
massive, broad skull
ears set well back on head
powerful hindquarters
undershot jaw with black or red muzzle

COLOR TYPES

Height 23–27 in (58–69 cm)	Weight 80–100 lb (36–45 kg)	Temperament Determined, fearless

Country of origin France	First use Guarding sheep	Origins 2000 BC

PYRENEAN MOUNTAIN DOG

Sometimes confused with the Pyrenean Mastiff (see p.278), this enormous yet elegant breed can be distinguished by the color of its markings, which may be badger, wolf gray, or pale yellow. However, it is often all white with distinctive black eye rims. The coarse coat enables it to withstand the severest climatic conditions.

• **HISTORY** Of ancient, French origin, this breed is thought to have descended from the old heavy shepherd dogs found in the Pyrenees.

• **REMARK** This giant takes three or four years to reach full maturity.

• **OTHER NAMES** Great Pyrenees, Chien des Pyrénées.

broad chest reaches just below elbows
straight, well-muscled forelegs

fairly small, triangular ears
mane of hair forms around neck

strong, slightly tapering muzzle

Height 26–32 in (65–81 cm)	Weight 90–125 lb (41–57 kg)	Temperament Watchful, loyal

thick, slightly wavy coat
almond-shaped eyes with black borders

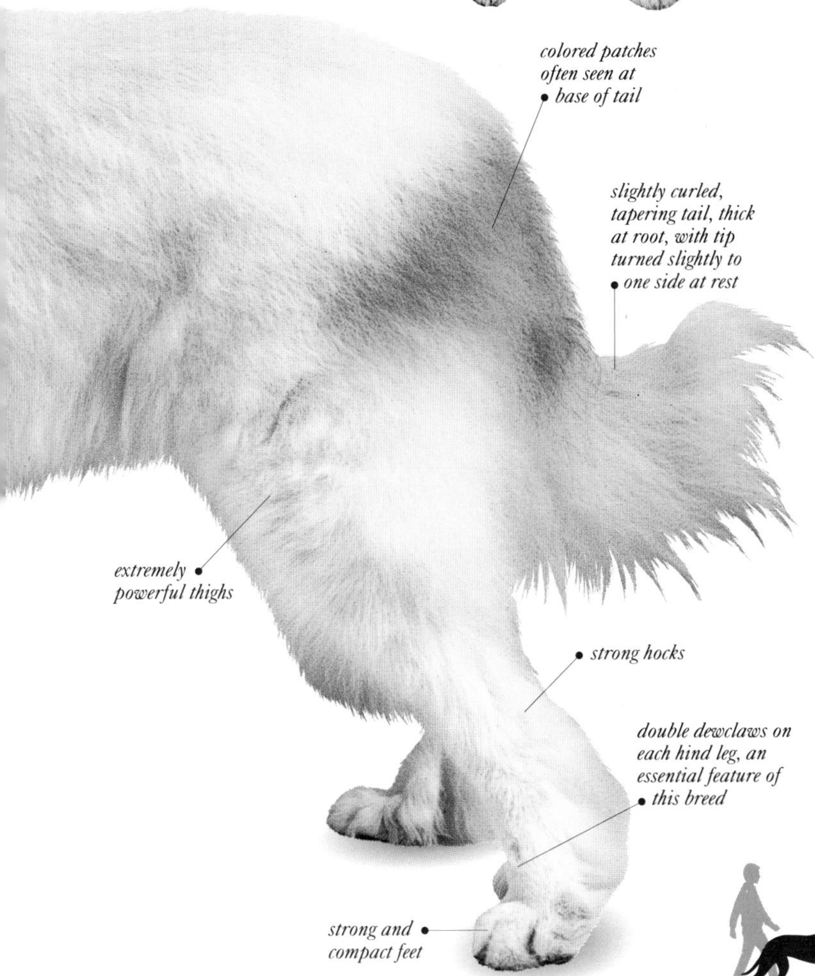
colored patches often seen at base of tail
slightly curled, tapering tail, thick at root, with tip turned slightly to one side at rest
extremely powerful thighs
strong hocks
double dewclaws on each hind leg, an essential feature of this breed
strong and compact feet

Country of origin Hungary	First use Guarding sheep	Origins 800s

Komondor

The distinctive corded coat of the Komondor reaches down to the ground. The breed is similar in appearance to its Hungarian relative, the Puli (see p.133), although it is much larger and has a thick-boned skeleton.

• **History** The Komondor is well-suited to its traditional role of guarding flocks. Its coat helps it to blend in with the sheep, until it leaps out at unsuspecting predators. Its name may derive from *komondor kedvu*, which means "somber" or "angry."

• **Remark** The coat of the Komondor is particularly demanding. It must never be brushed or combed. Instead the hair is divided into cords and trimmed to suit.

corded coat with the sensation of felt

black nose
medium-size ears
slightly arched profile to skull
adult coat starts at six to nine months; coat may take two years to become fully corded
tail extends down to hocks
large, powerful feet

Height 26–32 in (66–81 cm)	Weight 80–135 lb (36–61 kg)	Temperament Protective, loyal

Country of origin	First use	Origins
Hungary	Guarding flocks	1200s

KUVASZ

A working dog developed specifically as a flock guardian, as opposed to herder, the Kuvasz is a sturdily built dog with a medium-boned frame of beautiful proportions. Its coat is dense and must be pure white or ivory in coloration. Its ears are folded and lie close to the head, which is large without being bulky and has a round stop.

• **HISTORY** The precise ancestry of the Kuvasz is not known. Its origins lie in Tibet, from where it traveled to Hungary via Turkey. In general appearance, it is similar to the Maremma Sheepdog (see p.275), and the Pyrenean Mountain Dog (see pp.264–65), and may share a common ancestry.

• **REMARK** The Kuvasz has a natural affinity with children, is very protective, and forms a strong bond with its owner.

elongated, but not pointed, head
large black nose with open nostrils
straight muzzle

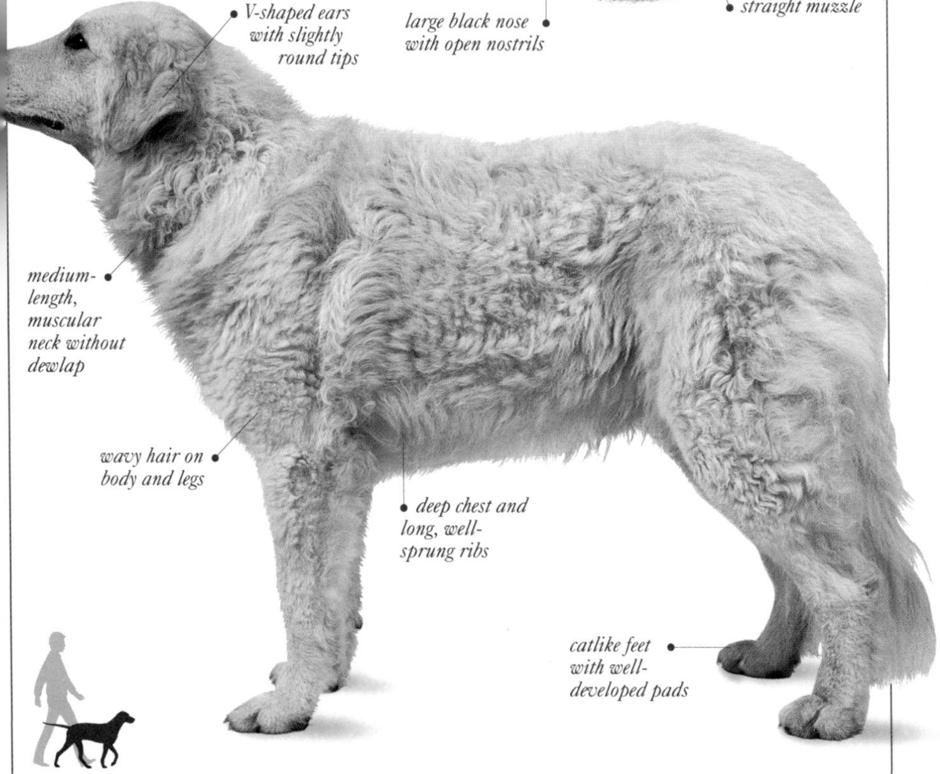
V-shaped ears with slightly round tips
medium-length, muscular neck without dewlap
wavy hair on body and legs
deep chest and long, well-sprung ribs
catlike feet with well-developed pads

Height	Weight	Temperament
22–26 in (56–66 cm)	80–110 lb (36–50 kg)	Loyal, wary

Country of origin	First use	Origins
Hungary	Guarding flocks	1800s

Mudi

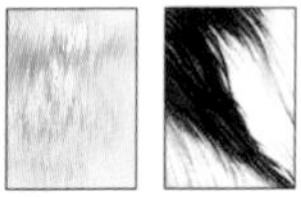

COLOR TYPES

Less well known than its older and much better established countrymen, the Puli and Komondor (see pp.133 and 266), the Mudi is a versatile flock guardian and herder. It is both heavier and taller than the Puli, and the absence of the corded coat makes caring for the Mudi easier. The coat is usually black, but white is not uncommon, and a "pepita" form exists with an even distribution of both colors throughout its coat.

• **History** The development of the Mudi seems to have been unplanned. It is a versatile and favorable blend of the ancient sheep-herding dogs of its Hungarian homeland. The breed was unknown until about one hundred years ago.

• **Remark** A good tracker and hunter, the Mudi also works well with livestock.

• **Other Names** Hungarian Mudi.

erect, triangular ears
straight, short back
coat length about 2 in (5 cm) on body
hair on muzzle and legs shorter than on body
small, round feet

Height	Weight	Temperament
14–20 in (36–51 cm)	18–29 lb (8–13 kg)	Adaptable, friendly

Country of origin	First use	Origins
Switzerland	Herding goats	500s

APPENSELL MOUNTAIN DOG

One of four breeds of Swiss mountain dogs, or sennenhunds, the Appenzeller is a hardy, well-built dog. It can be distinguished from the other similar breeds by its tail, which is typically curled back over its thigh.

• **HISTORY** This dog is thought to be descended from the now extinct Molussus.

• **REMARK** It has the unusual ability to both herd and guard livestock.

• **OTHER NAMES** Appenzeller Sennenhund.

tan markings
above each eye
characteristic, curled tail
white area on chest
well-muscled hindquarters

blaze must be present on head
symmetrical facial markings

Height	Weight	Temperament
19–23 in (48–58 cm)	50–55 lb (23–25 kg)	Lively, loyal

Country of origin	First use	Origins
Switzerland	Driving cattle	1800s

ENTELBUCH MOUNTAIN DOG

The smallest member of the sennenhund group, the Entelbuch is easily distinguished by the absence of a tail, which is docked at birth. All four sennenhunds share the same symmetrical coloration of black, tan, and white.

• **HISTORY** A native of the Swiss town of Entelbuch, this breed was traditionally used to drive cattle to market.

• **REMARK** Renowned for its gentle attitude to children, it makes a fine pet. It must be exercised regularly to prevent it from becoming obese.

• **OTHER NAMES** Entelbucher.

flat skull
V-shaped, pendant ears
powerful hindquarters
deep chest
strong hocks
white markings on feet

Height	Weight	Temperament
19–20 in (48–51 cm)	55–66 lb (25–30 kg)	Obedient, friendly

Country of origin Switzerland	First use Pulling weavers' carts	Origins 100 BC

BERNESE MOUNTAIN DOG

This is the best known of the Swiss mountain dogs, or sennenhunds, and it can be readily distinguished from the other varieties by its coat. This is long and slightly wavy in appearance, without being curly. In terms of coloration and markings, it is identical to the other forms. A white blaze on the head extending between the eyes, and a white chest marking known as a cross, are essential characteristics. White paws, ideally extending no farther than the pastern, are also preferred, as is a white tip to the tail. These affectionate and responsive dogs make good family pets if they have adequate exercise.

• **HISTORY** It is possible that crosses between native Swiss herding dogs, and guard animals brought to Switzerland by the invading Roman legions, laid the early foundations for this breed. In more recent times, Bernese Mountain Dogs have worked on farms, notably in the canton of Berne, frequently acting as draft dogs on market days by pulling carts laden with produce.

• **REMARK** This breed has established a strong following in continental Europe, but is not widely kept elsewhere in the world.

• **OTHER NAMES** Berner Sennenhund.

flat skull with slight furrow apparent
rounded, compact feet
long, sloping shoulder

markings well defined, even in pups

Height 23–27½ in (58–70 cm)	Weight 87–90 lb (40–44 kg)	Temperament Attentive, friendly

soft, silky-textured coat, with good sheen
characteristic white chest marking
compact body shape
medium-length, strong, muscular neck
broad, strong, muscular hindquarters
bushy tail can extend to just below hocks

Country of origin Switzerland	First use Pulling farmers' carts	Origins 300s

GREAT SWISS MOUNTAIN DOG

This is the largest member of the four sennenhund breeds. It has a smooth coat and distinctively long tail, which is held below the level of the back. Like the other group members, its coloration is basically black and tan, the tan areas bordered by both black and white markings. White areas form a blaze, extending down to the chest, and are also present on the toes and tip of the tail.

• **HISTORY** This dog has a long history on Swiss farms. It declined during the mid-1800s, however, and by the turn of the century had almost vanished. The few purebred individuals left were crossed with smooth-coated St. Bernards. They are now once again well established and were introduced into the USA in 1968.

• **REMARK** Despite their size, grooming their coats is easy and straightforward.

• **OTHER NAMES** Grosser Schweizer Sennenhund.

characteristic tan markings above the eyes

long tail terminates in white tip

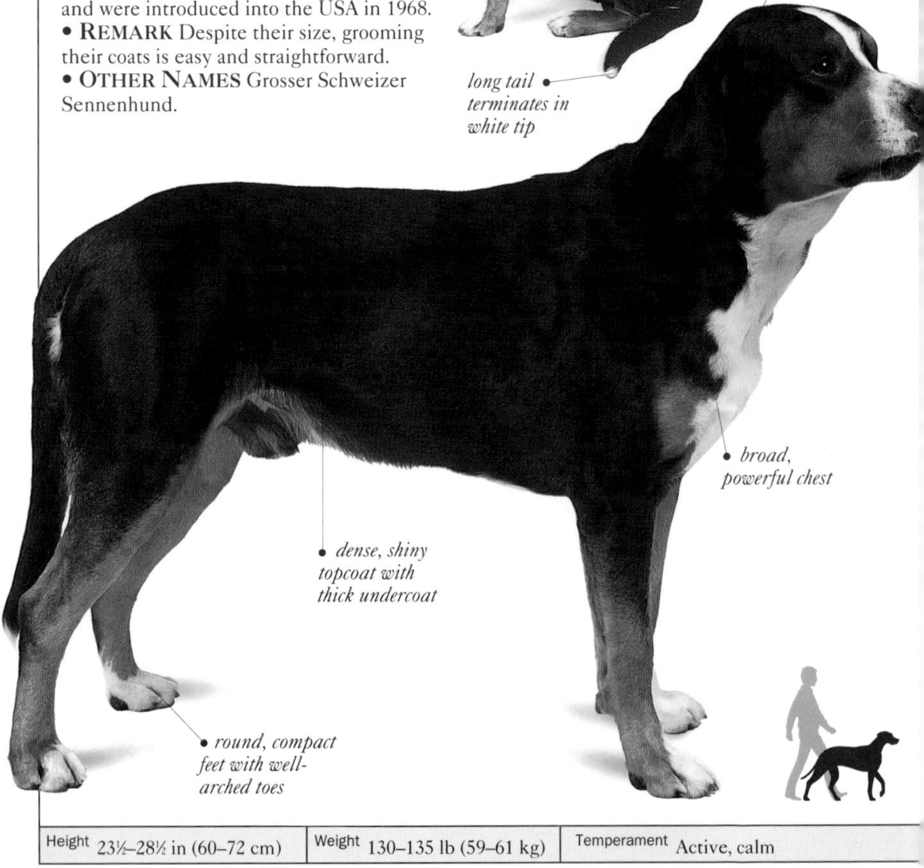
triangular ears set high on head
broad, powerful chest
dense, shiny topcoat with thick undercoat
round, compact feet with well-arched toes

Height 23½–28½ in (60–72 cm)	Weight 130–135 lb (59–61 kg)	Temperament Active, calm

Country of origin	First use	Origins
Switzerland	Searching and rescuing	1000s

St. Bernard

The St. Bernard is a dog of imposing proportions – tall, broad, massively boned, and heavy – but it is always dignified in expression and carriage. Both smooth-haired and rough-haired forms of this breed exist, white and red, or red and brownish-yellow being the most favored color combinations.

• **HISTORY** The St. Bernard is descended from the the Roman Molossus, which was the original mastiff stock introduced into the Alps by the Romans some 2,000 years ago. The first St. Bernard was bred at the Hospice of St. Bernard de Menthon about 1,000 years ago.

• **REMARK** This dog requires strong handling when out walking on a lead.

• **OTHER NAMES** St. Bernhardshund.

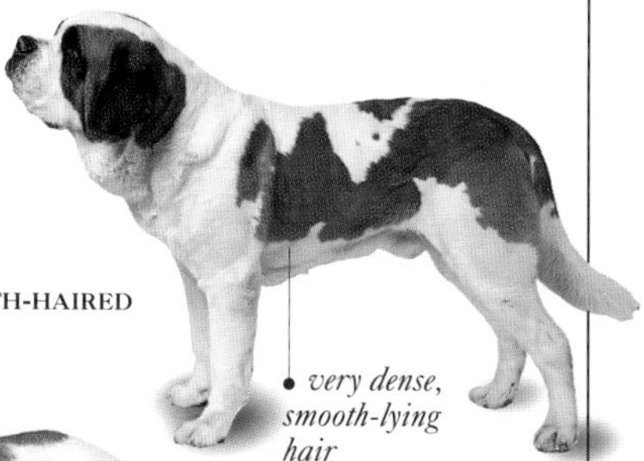
very dense, smooth-lying hair

SMOOTH-HAIRED FORM

slightly arched, massive skull
short, square muzzle

very muscular neck
deep chest
dense, flat hair
large, compact feet with strong toes

ROUGH-HAIRED FORM

Height	Weight	Temperament
24–28 in (61–71 cm)	110–200 lb (50–91 kg)	Tranquil, benevolent

Country of origin Former Yugoslavia	First use Carriage dog	Origins 1400s

DALMATIAN

A bold, spotted patterning, offset against a clear, white background, makes this perhaps the most distinctive of all dog breeds. Black-spotted Dalmatians are far more common than their liver-colored counterparts. The spots should be round in shape, clearly defined, and not overlapping. Those on the extremities should be smaller in size than elsewhere on the body. Dalmatian pups are pure white at birth and develop their spots later.

• **HISTORY** This breed originated in Dalmatia, the region after which it is named, in what was formerly the country of Yugoslavia. It became very popular as a carriage dog in the 1800s, trotting alongside horse-drawn vehicles – especially fire engines.

• **REMARK** The Dalmatian has attracted considerable attention through Dodie Smith's book *One Hundred and One Dalmatians*, which was later made into an extremely popular animated film by the Walt Disney Studios.

color of eye rims matches that of spots

sleek, glossy coat
short, hard, dense hair
round, well-arched, catlike feet

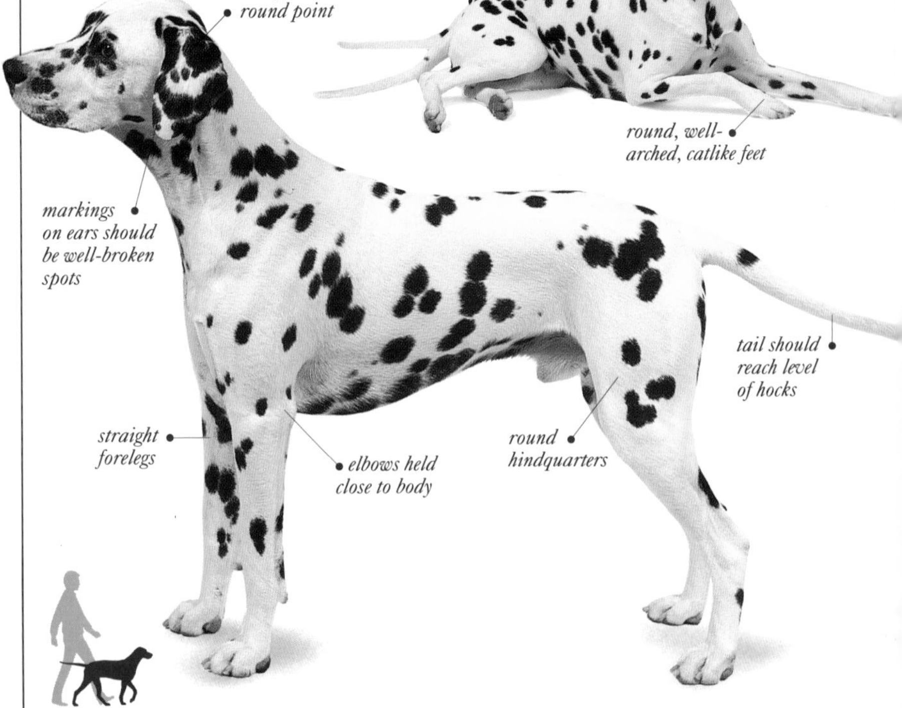
ears are set high on head and taper to a round point
markings on ears should be well-broken spots
tail should reach level of hocks
straight forelegs
elbows held close to body
round hindquarters

Height 22–24 in (56–61 cm)	Weight 50–55 lb (23–25 kg)	Temperament Quiet, alert

Country of origin Italy	First use Guarding flocks	Origins 100 BC

MAREMMA SHEEPDOG

White is the predominant color of this majestic sheepdog, sometimes with ivory or pale fawn shadings evident, notably on the ears. It is a muscular, powerful dog with a long, somewhat harsh, coat. Its head is large and bearlike.

• **HISTORY** This breed may be descended from the earliest flock guardians. They may have been kept in the Maremma and Abruzzi regions of Italy since before Roman times.

• **REMARK** This majestic breed is highly intelligent but is not easy to train, having a rather independent and aloof character.

• **OTHER NAMES** Pastore Abruzzese.

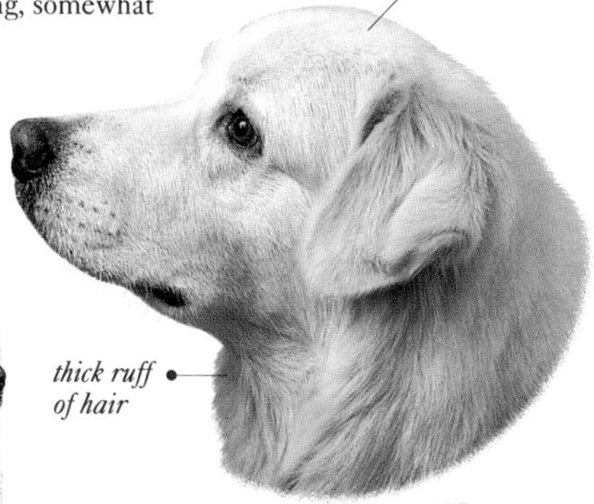
large, conical head
thick ruff of hair

tail has dense covering of hair

strong, medium-length back
large shoulders and thick legs
close-fitting, slightly wavy coat
hind feet more oval than forefeet

Height 23½–28½ in (60–73 cm)	Weight 66–100 lb (30–45 kg)	Temperament Responsive, protective

Country of origin Italy	First use Guard dog, dog fighting	Origins 100 BC

Neapolitan Mastiff

This ancient breed of dog has a slow, ponderous, bearlike gait in common with other mastiff-type breeds and a very large head. From the head, prominent dewlaps of skin extend in folds down to the neck, thus producing a multichinned appearance. In spite of its aggressive history as a fighting dog, the Neapolitan Mastiff is generally a calm, placid, and friendly animal, especially with people it knows well.

• **History** The ancestry of the Neapolitan Mastiff may extend back to the Molossus breed of Roman times. Its enormous strength has seen it used for fighting, although it has also been a guard dog and a beast of burden, pulling carts. It was only in 1946 that steps were taken, by painter Piero Scanziani, to safeguard the breed's future. He established a kennel for the breed and did much to promote its survival.

• **Remark** This huge dog is not aggressive by nature, although it will prove a loyal guardian, reflecting its mastiff ancestry.

• **Other Names** Mastino Napoletano.

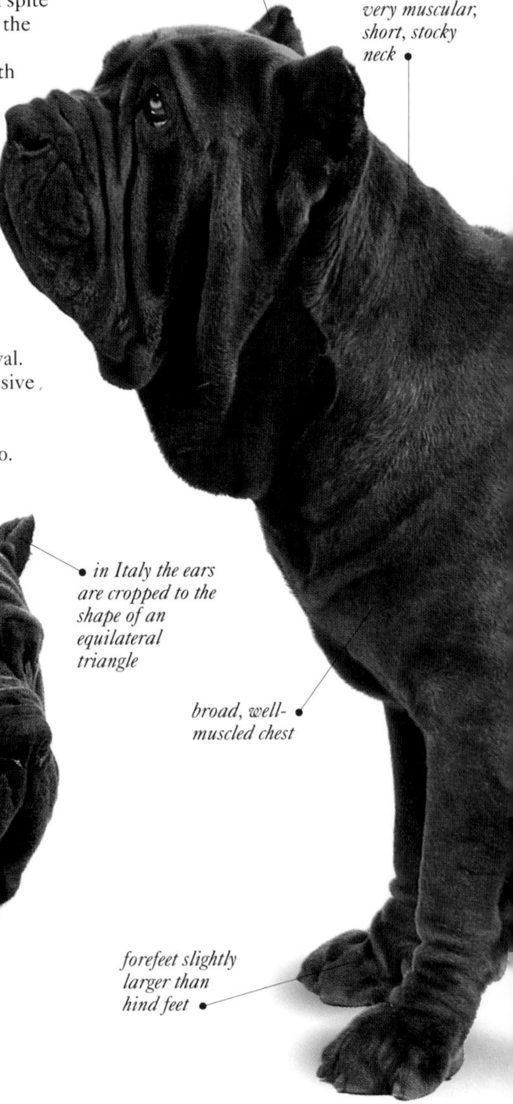
small, well-spaced ears, positioned forward on head
very muscular, short, stocky neck
broad, well-muscled chest
forefeet slightly larger than hind feet

in Italy the ears are cropped to the shape of an equilateral triangle
dewlap hanging from lower jaw to mid-point of neck

Height 26–29 in (65–75 cm)	Weight 110–150 lb (50–68 kg)	Temperament Protective, alert

broad, flat skull
deep, spherical shape to the head
long, well-sprung ribs

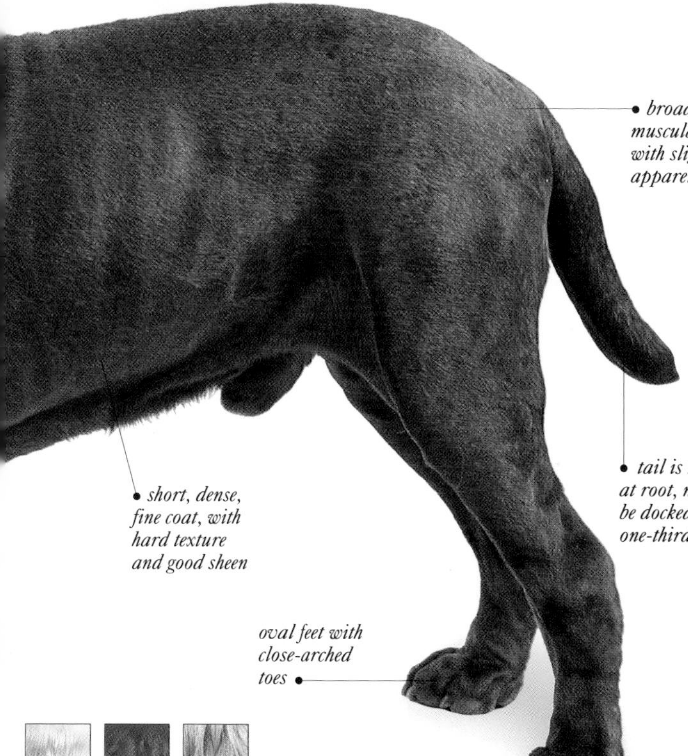
broad, muscular croup with slight slope apparent
tail is thick at root, may be docked by one-third length
short, dense, fine coat, with hard texture and good sheen
oval feet with close-arched toes

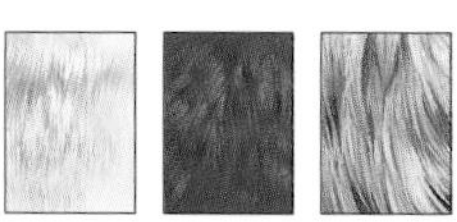
COLOR TYPES

Country of origin Spain	First use Guarding flocks	Origins 3000 BC

PYRENEAN MASTIFF

Although the Pyrenean Mastiff is slightly smaller than the Pyrenean Mountain Dog (see pp. 264–65), they share a common ancestry. The Mastiff is a robustly built, symmetrical dog with a large head, powerful neck (often with excessive dewlap), and a deep body, all supported on very sturdy legs.

• **HISTORY** Like the Pyrenean Mountain Dog, the Mastiff descended from dogs brought to Spain by early Mediterranean seafarers.

• **REMARK** For its enormous size, this breed has a small appetite and is light on its feet.

• **OTHER NAMES** Perro Mastin del Pireneo.

heavily boned, broad skull

pointed, pendulous ears
large, heavily muscled chest
thick, powerful legs
broad, thick-soled feet

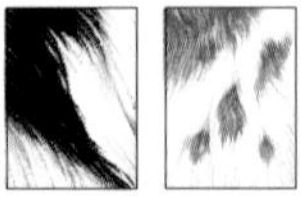

COLOR TYPES

Height 28½–34 in (72–86 cm)	Weight 120–155 lb (54–70 kg)	Temperament Responsive, alert

Country of origin Spain	First use Guarding livestock	Origins 800s

Spanish Mastiff

This breed has the typical mastiff appearance: a broad head with a relatively short muzzle, a massive chest, and a characteristic dewlap on the neck. The ears are pointed and pendulous, but are not large.

• **HISTORY** These dogs have been used to guard livestock in the hills of Spain for centuries. The origins of the breed may lie with ancient mastiff stock brought to the region by the Romans. It has only recently attracted attention from dog owners in northern Europe and in the USA.

• **REMARK** The Spanish Mastiff is essentially nonaggressive toward people, but may be combative with other dogs.

• **OTHER NAMES** Mastin Español.

clearly defined stop between eyes
broad nose

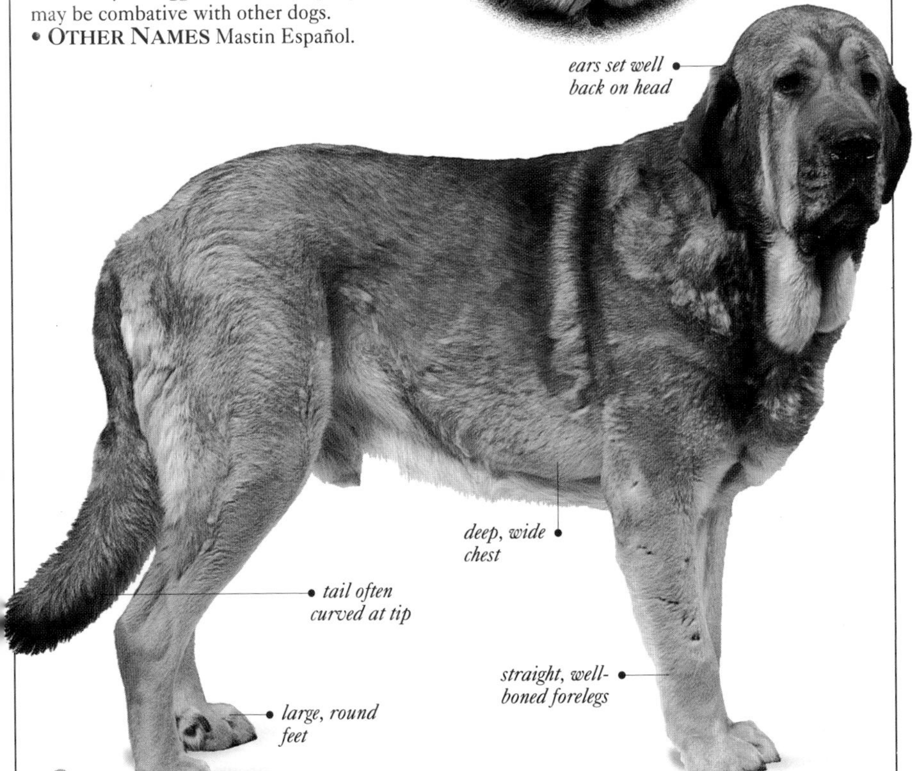
ears set well back on head
deep, wide chest
tail often curved at tip
straight, well-boned forelegs
large, round feet

COLOR TYPES

Height 26–29 in (66–74 cm)	Weight 110–135 lb (50–61 kg)	Temperament Obedient, protective

Country of origin	First use	Origins
Balearic Islands	Guarding farms	1700s

Perro de Pastor Mallorquin

A well-defined head and a tapering muzzle give this breed a distinctive appearance. The tail is long and tapering toward the tip. Both long-haired and short-haired forms exist.

• **History** The Perro de Pastor Mallorquin is native to the Balearic Islands, off the coast of Spain. It is a utility animal.

• **Remark** This dog was bred to withstand the heat of the Mediterranean sun, and can be fierce and aggressive.

• **Other Names** Ca de Bestiar.

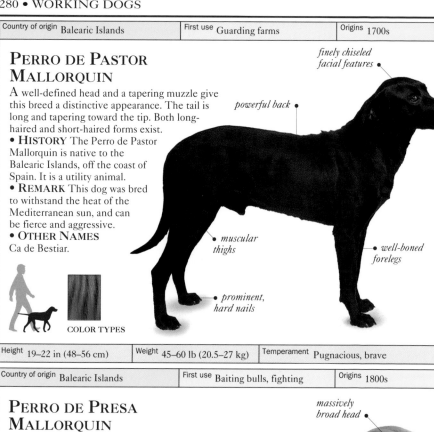

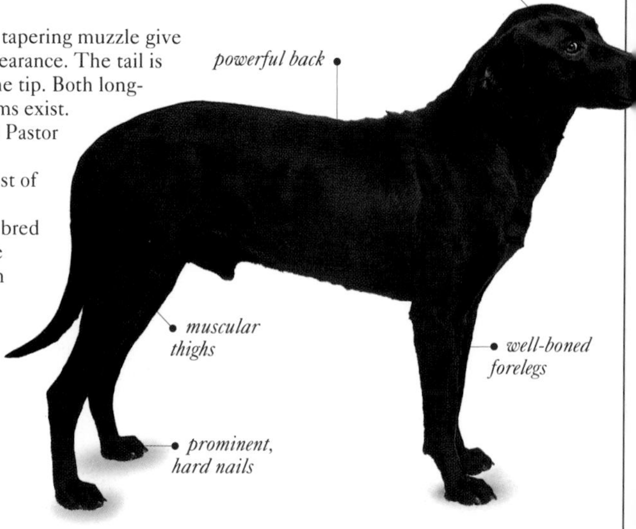
finely chiseled facial features
powerful back
muscular thighs
well-boned forelegs
prominent, hard nails

COLOR TYPES

Height	Weight	Temperament
19–22 in (48–56 cm)	45–60 lb (20.5–27 kg)	Pugnacious, brave

Country of origin	First use	Origins
Balearic Islands	Baiting bulls, fighting	1800s

Perro de Presa Mallorquin

This mastiff-type breed is fierce and formidable. It is heavily muscled with powerful, gripping jaws. The coat is very short and sleek, usually yellow in color, with patches of lighter or darker colors.

• **History** The popularity of this dog has declined with the outlawing of bull-baiting and the decline of dog fighting.

• **Remark** This breed needs firm discipline from a very early age.

• **Other Names** Ca de Bou.

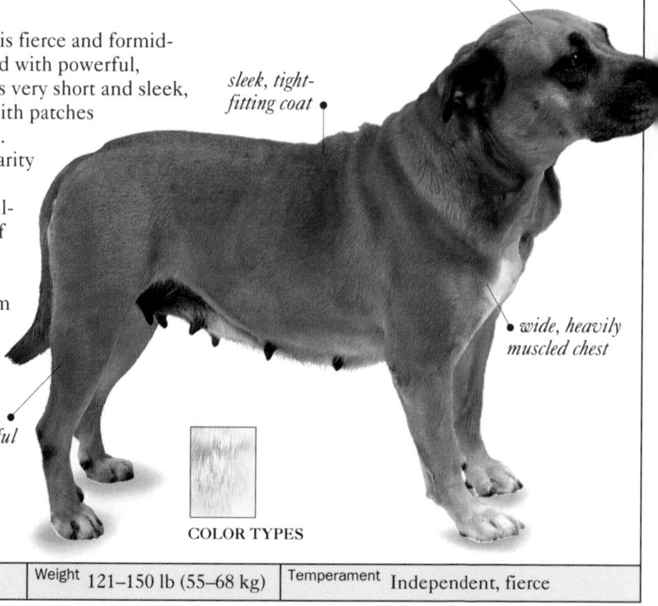
massively broad head
sleek, tight-fitting coat
wide, heavily muscled chest
sturdy, powerful legs

COLOR TYPES

Height	Weight	Temperament
23–24 in (58–61 cm)	121–150 lb (55–68 kg)	Independent, fierce

Country of origin Israel	First use Guarding livestock	Origins 2000 BC

CANAAN DOG

This medium-size, robustly made, spitz-type dog has been indigenous to the region encompassed by modern Israel for centuries. The ancestors of today's Canaan were pariah dogs, which have traditionally been domesticated to act as flock guardians, protecting the tribespeople's goats against jackals and other predators.

• **HISTORY** A program to breed these dogs so that the puppies would resemble their parents in appearance (breeding true) was begun in 1935 by a Dr. Menzel and her husband. Most of the stock seen around the world today originated in the Shaar Hagai Kennels in Jerusalem.

• **REMARK** In spite of its feral origins, this dog is easily trained.

• **OTHER NAMES**
Kelef K'naani.

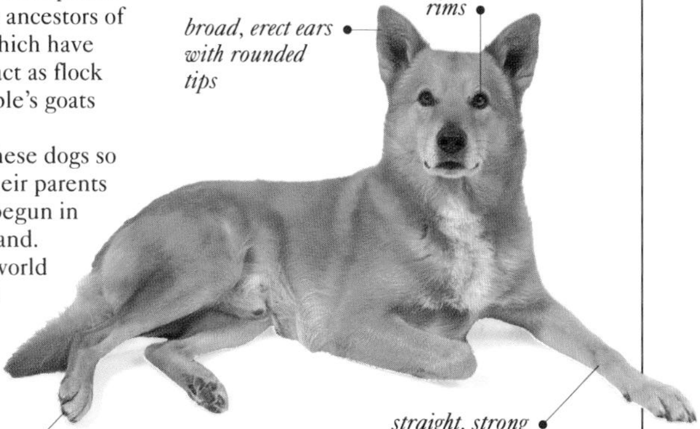
almond-shaped, dark brown rims
broad, erect ears with rounded tips
hard pads
straight, strong forelegs

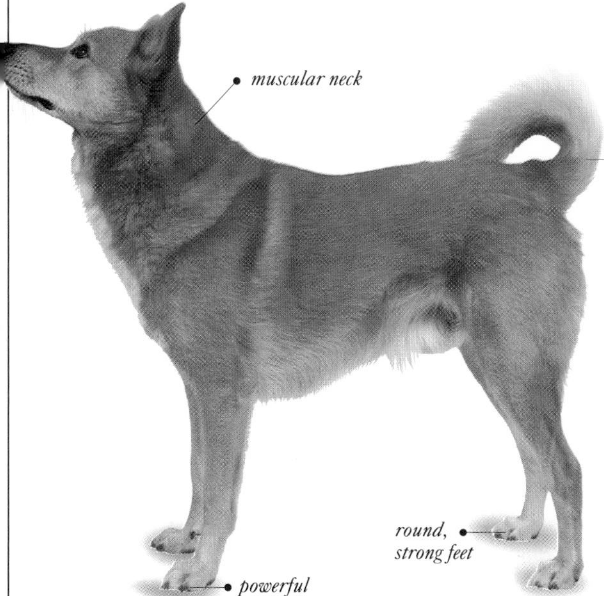
muscular neck
thick, brushlike tail curves over back
round, strong feet
powerful nails

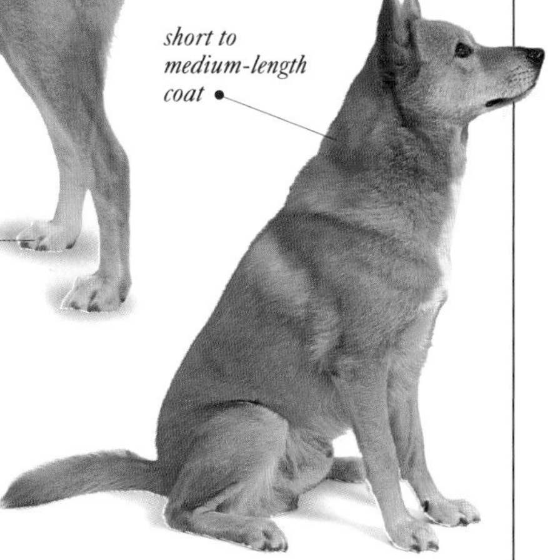
short to medium-length coat

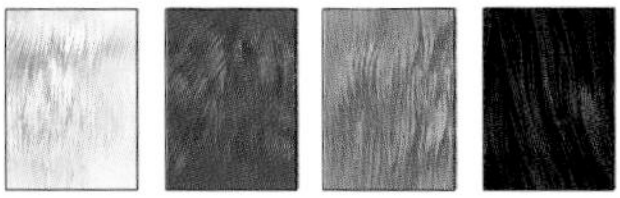

COLOR TYPES

Height 19–24 in (48–61 cm)	Weight 35–55 lb (16–25 kg)	Temperament Intelligent, resourceful

Country of origin Portugal	First use Guarding flocks	Origins 1800s

Estrela Mountain Dog

COLOR TYPES

Two distinct coat types are associated with this breed. The longer-coated form displays more abundant feathering than its smooth-coated counterpart, although a double-layered coat affords both of them excellent protection against the worst of the elements. The large size and loud bark could make them formidable opponents, but they are usually friendly dogs.

- **History** This breed is named after the Estrela region in central Portugal, where it was traditionally used as a flock guardian.
- **Remark** This is not a demonstrative animal. Like all powerful dogs, it requires thorough training.
- **Other Names** Cão da Serra da Estrela.

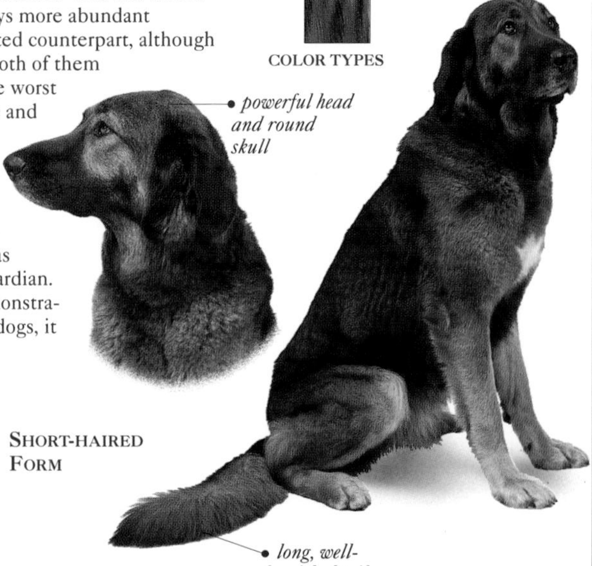
powerful head
and round
skull
long, well-
furnished tail

SHORT-HAIRED FORM

slightly sloping
croup
very
powerful
shoulders
solidly muscled,
straight legs
hind dewclaws
present

LONG-HAIRED FORM

Height 24½–28½ in (62–72 cm)	Weight 66–110 lb (30–50 kg)	Temperament Loyal, active

Country of origin	First use	Origins
Portugal	Guard dog	1800s

Rafeiro do Alentejo

This powerful dog has a body not unlike that of a St. Bernard (see p.273), but it has a head shaped like a bear's. This is the largest of the Portuguese breeds and is an imposing animal.

• **History** This breed originated in the Alentejo region of southern Portugal. The Spanish Mastiff (see p.279) may have contributed to its ancestry, along with the Estrela Mountain Dog (see p.282).

• **Remark** This dog has an aggressive nature, as well as a strong independent streak.

• **Other Names** Portuguese Watchdog.

large head with broad muzzle
longer fur around neck

long, curved tail

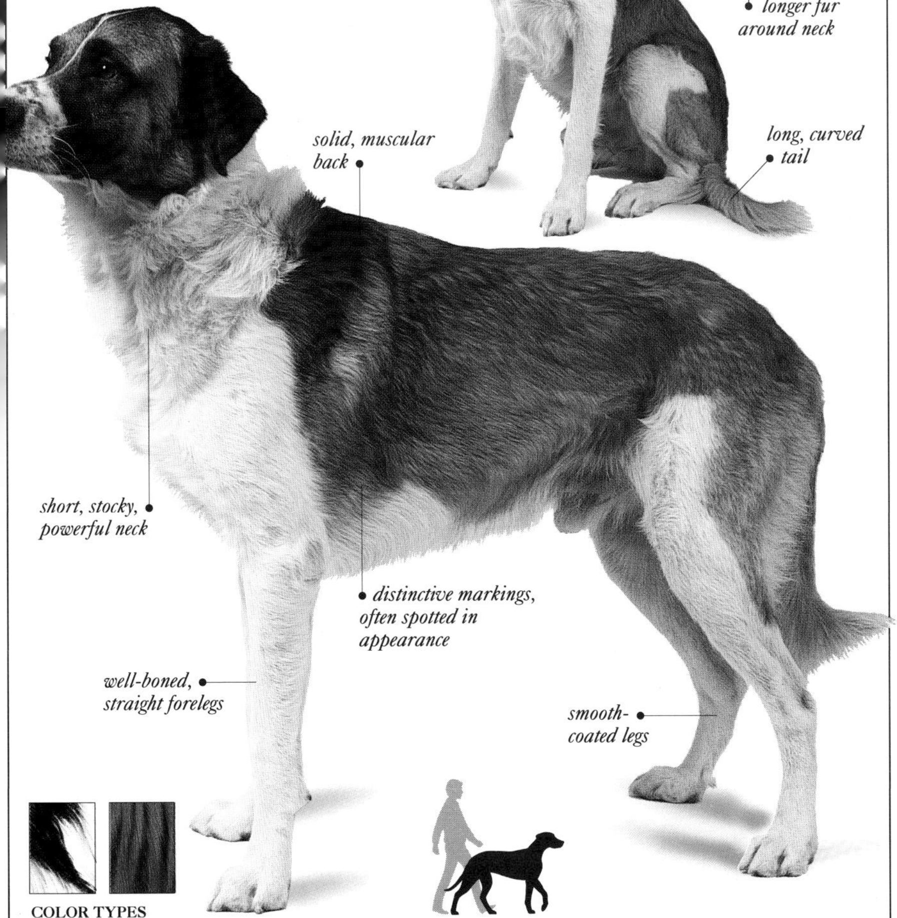
solid, muscular back
short, stocky, powerful neck
distinctive markings, often spotted in appearance
well-boned, straight forelegs
smooth-coated legs

COLOR TYPES

Height	Weight	Temperament
30 in (76 cm)	95–110 lb (43–50 kg)	Alert, independent

Country of origin	First use	Origins
Portugal	Guarding and herding flocks	1500s

PORTUGUESE CATTLE DOG

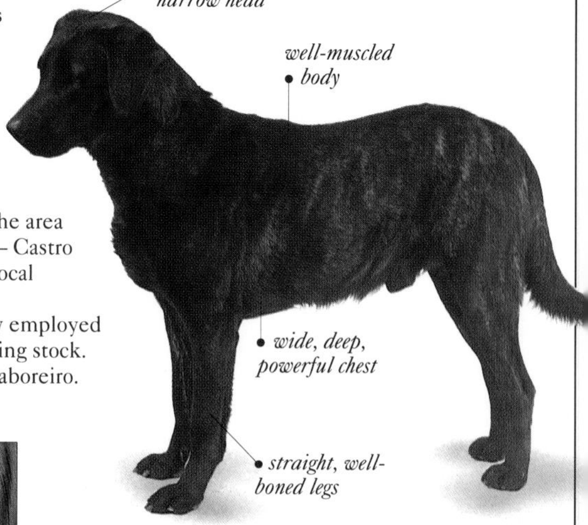
large, narrow head
well-muscled body
wide, deep, powerful chest
straight, well-boned legs

This rugged, powerfully built dog has traditionally been used as a herding animal in the rocky, less accessible parts of Portugal. Its rather long body has a strong, weatherproof, coarse outercoat over a finer, thicker undercoat, making it ideal for the often harsh conditions of this region.

• **HISTORY** The isolated nature of the area of Portugal where this dog originated – Castro Laboreiro – makes it likely that only local breeds were used in its development.

• **REMARK** This breed is still widely employed in its homeland for herding and guarding stock.

• **OTHER NAMES** Cão de Castro Laboreiro.

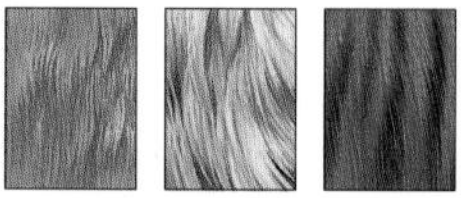

COLOR TYPES

Height	Weight	Temperament
20–24 in (51–61 cm)	50–75 lb (23–34 kg)	Alert, brave

Country of origin	First use	Origins
Russia and Finland	Hunting big game	1700s

RUSSO-EUROPEAN LAIKA

conical head
large, prominent, upright ears
tail curled (if present)
broad, powerful chest
wide, thick-soled feet

This is a powerfully built dog, characterized by its black-and-white coloration and pricked ears. If present, its tail is distinctively curled, but this breed is often born without a tail.

• **HISTORY** The Russo-European Laika evolved near the border shared by Russia and Finland. Already an intrepid moose and wolf hunter, crossings with the fearless Utchak Sheepdog widened its role to encompass bear hunting.

• **REMARK** This breed cannot be regarded as a house dog or pet.

• **OTHER NAMES** Karelian Bear Laika, Lajka Ruissisch Europaisch.

Height	Weight	Temperament
21–24 in (53–61 cm)	45–50 lb (20.5–23 kg)	Independent, brave

Country of origin Russia	First use Hunting bears	Origins 1800s

East Siberian Laika

This member of the laika family is large and squarely built and has a slightly spiky coat that stands away from the body. Its head is broad, its expression is alert, and its ears are large and erect.

• **History** This breed was used for pulling sleds, as well as for hunting such quarry as bear, elk, and reindeer.

• **Remark** Laikas were used as test animals in the early Soviet space experiments.

shorter hair on head
well-spaced, erect ears
well-arched toes
thickly muscled neck

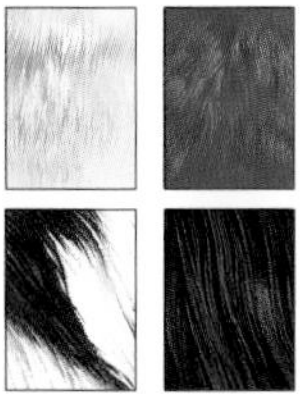

COLOR TYPES

Height 22–25 in (56–64 cm)	Weight 40–50 lb (18–23 kg)	Temperament Obedient, loyal

Country of origin Russia	First use Hunting bears	Origins 1800s

West Siberian Laika

The long legs and wolflike face of the West Siberian Laika give it an apparent lightness of bearing, which belies its power and immense endurance.

• **History** This breed is more firmly established than its East Siberian relative (above) and is certainly more numerous.

• **Remark** The strenuous life of the West Siberian Laika means that its average working span is quite short.

tightly curled tail
short, dense double coat
prominent nostrils

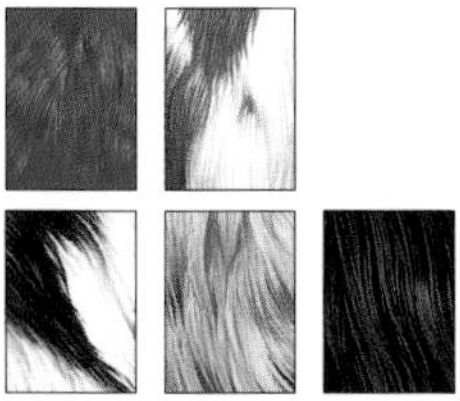

COLOR TYPES

Height 21–24 in (53–61 cm)	Weight 40–50 lb (18–23 kg)	Temperament Active, lively

Country of origin Russia	First use Pulling sleds	Origins 1800s

SIBERIAN HUSKY

Although smaller and lighter than some other breeds of sled dog, the Siberian Husky is quick and athletic, agile and strong, as well as being a tireless worker. This medium-size dog has a dense and woolly undercoat, well protected by a covering of tougher guard hairs. This gives the dog a fullness of form and provides excellent insulation against the raw cold of its Siberian homeland.

- **HISTORY** Siberian Huskies were developed by the Chukchi people of northeast Asia as their only means of transportation.
- **REMARK** Communal howling is a feature of this breed. An amazing range of coat colors and markings is permitted.
- **OTHER NAMES** Arctic Husky.

medium-size, triangular ears
almond-shaped eyes, sometimes blue

medium-length muzzle

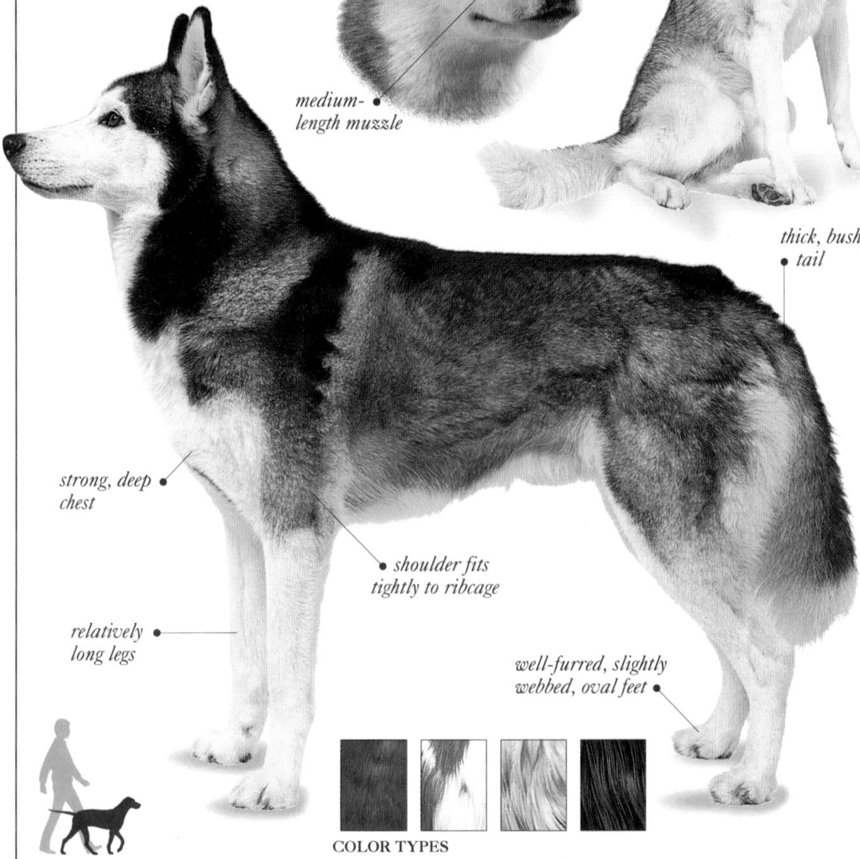
thick, bushy tail
strong, deep chest
shoulder fits tightly to ribcage
relatively long legs
well-furred, slightly webbed, oval feet

COLOR TYPES

Height 20–23½ in (51–60 cm)	Weight 35–60 lb (16–27 kg)	Temperament Dependable, energetic

Country of origin	First use	Origins
Russia	Herding reindeer	1600s

Samoyed

This far-northern breed has a very full coat, consisting of a long, weather-resistant outercoat covering an extremely dense and woolly undercoat. Samoyeds make popular and attractive pets, as well as being highly valued as sled dogs.

- **HISTORY** Today's breed is said to derive from just 12 dogs brought out of the Arctic by explorers and travelers. The basic Samoyed was developed by the once-nomadic Samoyede tribe, who now live in the Antarctic region east of the Ural Mountains.
- **REMARK** Polar explorers Scott and Amundsen both used Samoyeds.
- **OTHER NAMES** Samoyedskaja.

dark brown eyes

thick, well-spaced, rounded ears
weather-resistant coat stands away from body

broad, very muscular body
long, well-covered tail is carried over the back and to one side
solid, muscular legs
deep chest
exceedingly muscular hindquarters
cushioning of fur on feet

Height	Weight	Temperament
18–22 in (46–56 cm)	50–65 lb (23–29.5 kg)	Companionable

Country of origin	First use	Origins
China	Guard dog, pulling carts	100s

Chow Chow

The rough-coated form (shown here) is most commonly seen; its coat is profuse, thick, and straight. The smooth-coated form reveals the squarely built, hugely muscled outline of this courageous and powerful dog. The Chow Chow is bred in solid colors from tan or red through to silver-gray or black, while white is rare.

• **HISTORY** Although popular in China for at least 2,000 years, the Chow first appeared in Britain only in the late 19th century. In its homeland it was used to pull carts and as a guard dog. Its fur was also a valuable commodity, as was its flesh for human consumption.

• **REMARK** The unusual tongue of the Chow Chow is, like that of the Shar Pei (opposite), blue-black in coloration.

broad, flat skull

small ears blend with the ruff
tail set high and curved over the back
broad, deep chest
small, round, catlike feet

muzzle is broad along its length

COLOR TYPES

Height	Weight	Temperament
18–22 in (46–56 cm)	45–70 lb (20–32 kg)	Alert, independent

Country of origin	First use	Origins
China	Dog-fighting	1500s

SHAR PEI

The bristly coat of this dog is quite distinctive, but the folds of loose skin covering its body, and especially its head, giving it a permanent frown, are by far its most striking feature.

• **HISTORY** This ancient breed is thought to result from crosses between mastiffs and certain Nordic breeds. It was in danger of extinction until a Hong Kong fancier established stock in the USA and elsewhere.

• **REMARK** The loose skin was originally developed for the gruesome purpose of making the animal impossible to pin down in a dog fight.

triangular, folded ears

round tail set high on back
dark, almond-shaped eyes
relatively long, broad muzzle
strong, short neck with loose skin
deep, broad chest

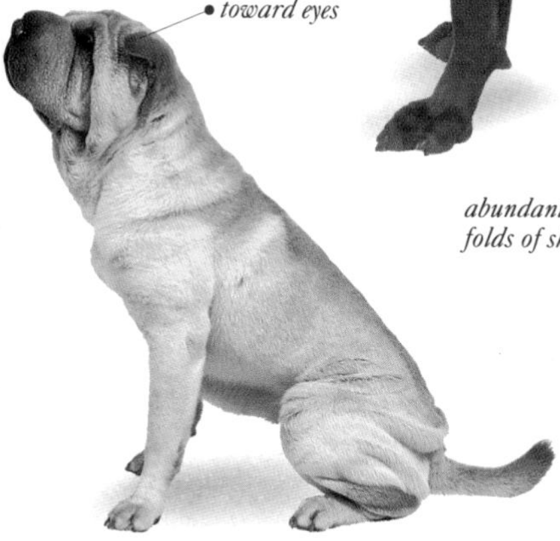
ear tips point toward eyes

abundant, loose folds of skin

SHAR PEI PUP

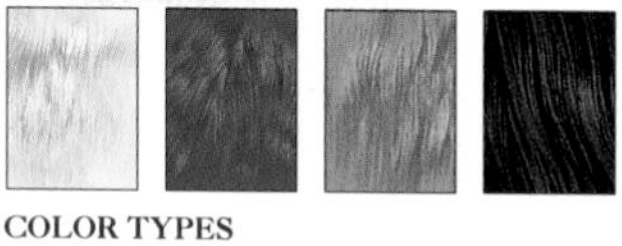

COLOR TYPES

Height	Weight	Temperament
18–20 in (46–51 cm)	35–45 lb (16–20 kg)	Independent, aloof

Country of origin Japan	First use Hunting big game	Origins 1600s

AKITA

The erect ears, and tail that curls forward over its back, indicate that the powerful Akita dog is descended from spitz stock. The head is large and broad, with a very distinctive, bearlike expression.

• **HISTORY** The Akita was developed by a Japanese nobleman living in exile in the province of Akita, on Honshu island. Here the dogs were used in pairs to hunt such dangerous quarry as bears.

• **REMARK** The Akita was officially recognized as part of Japan's national heritage in 1931.

• **OTHER NAMES** Akita Inu, Japanese Akita.

thick, tight feet with broad pads

strong, broad muzzle

erect ears carried over eyes in line with back of neck
tail is set high and curls forward
muscular hindquarters with well-developed thighs
clear, well-defined coloration
straight forelegs

COLOR TYPES

Height 24–28 in (60–71 cm)	Weight 75–110 lb (34–50 kg)	Temperament Active, independent

Country of origin Japan	First use Hunting small game	Origins 1000 BC

Shiba Inu

This dog is similar to the Akita (opposite), but it is smaller. Its name translates from the Japanese as "small dog." The keen and alert appearance is a result of its broad forehead, pointed muzzle, and triangular ears, which incline slightly forward.

• **HISTORY** The origins of the Shiba Inu breed go back more than 2,000 years in Japan, with the possibility of Chow Chow blood in its ancestry.

• **REMARK** The Shiba Inu is the most commonly kept of the native breeds in Japan.

• **OTHER NAMES** Japanese Small-size Dog, Brushwood Dog.

tapering muzzle
small, well-shaped oval eyes
short, level back
thick, sickle-shaped tail
harsh, double coat

COLOR TYPES

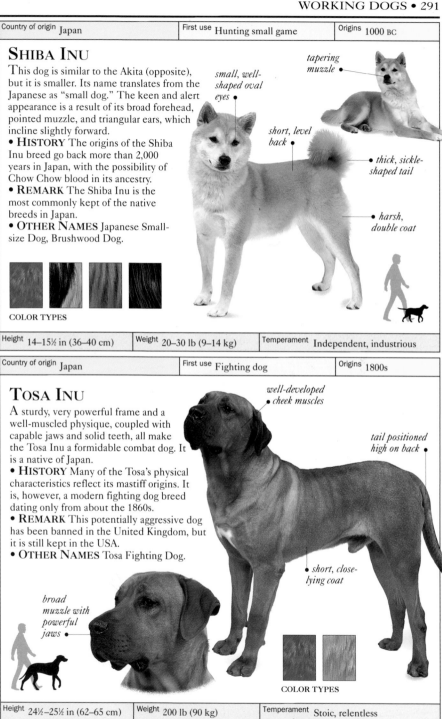

Height 14–15½ in (36–40 cm)	Weight 20–30 lb (9–14 kg)	Temperament Independent, industrious

Country of origin Japan	First use Fighting dog	Origins 1800s

Tosa Inu

A sturdy, very powerful frame and a well-muscled physique, coupled with capable jaws and solid teeth, all make the Tosa Inu a formidable combat dog. It is a native of Japan.

• **HISTORY** Many of the Tosa's physical characteristics reflect its mastiff origins. It is, however, a modern fighting dog breed dating only from about the 1860s.

• **REMARK** This potentially aggressive dog has been banned in the United Kingdom, but it is still kept in the USA.

• **OTHER NAMES** Tosa Fighting Dog.

well-developed cheek muscles
tail positioned high on back
short, close-lying coat

broad muzzle with powerful jaws

COLOR TYPES

Height 24½–25½ in (62–65 cm)	Weight 200 lb (90 kg)	Temperament Stoic, relentless

Country of origin	First use	Origins
Japan	Retrieving game, ratting	1700s

JAPANESE TERRIER

This terrier has a relatively small head and a tail that is traditionally docked quite close to the body. Its tricolor coat is distinctive: it is predominantly white, with the black and tan areas proportionately small in size, creating an attractive speckled appearance.

• **HISTORY** Descended from the Smooth Fox Terrier, which was introduced to Japan in 1702, the subsequent development of this breed centered on the cities of Kobe and Yokohama.

• **REMARK** In Japan this dog can be seen working as a water-fowl retriever.

• **OTHER NAMES** Nippon Terrier.

ears folded forward and set high on head

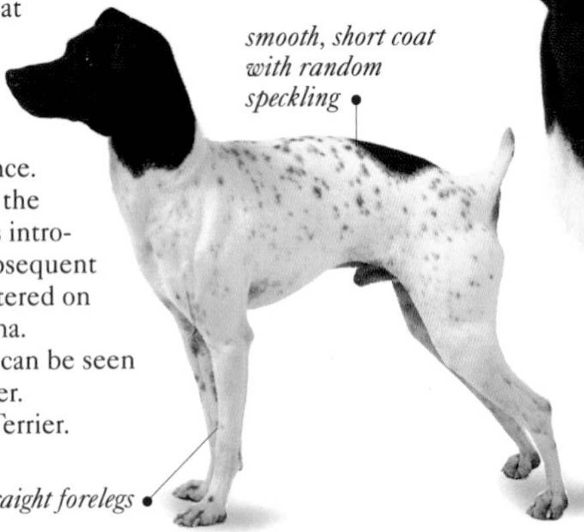
smooth, short coat with random speckling
long, straight forelegs

Height	Weight	Temperament
13 in (33 cm)	10–13 lb (4.5–6 kg)	Affectionate, adaptable

Country of origin	First use	Origins
Japan	Hunting large game	1000 BC

AINU

Resembling the Akita (see p.290), although smaller in size, the Ainu's foxlike head shape and curled tail carriage are typical spitz characteristics. This breed has an unusually fierce facial expression.

• **HISTORY** Developed in Japan by the Ainu people, this handsome breed is thought to be the oldest of all the Japanese dog breeds.

• **REMARK** Although not encouraged, a dark bluish tongue may occur, as with the Chow Chow and Shar Pei (see pp.288 and 289).

• **OTHER NAMES** Hokkaido Dog.

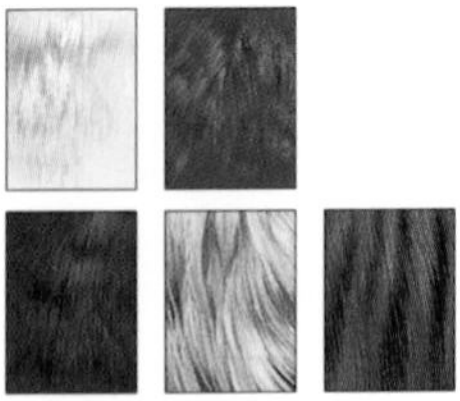

COLOR TYPES

short, broad muzzle

small, pricked ears
broad, deep chest
short, thick coat standing off from the body

Height	Weight	Temperament
18–22 in (46–56 cm)	45–65 lb (20.5–29.5 kg)	Brave, loyal

Country of origin Tibet	First use Guarding flocks	Origins 900s

TIBETAN MASTIFF

The formidable size of the Tibetan Mastiff makes it an excellent guard dog, yet it is responsive to training and is usually gentle, even with children. In Tibet it is customary for the dog to wear a red yak's-hair collar as a sign of its status.

• **HISTORY** It is possible that many of today's European mastiff breeds are descended from the Tibetan Mastiff, which spread eastward with the armies of Alexander the Great.

• **REMARK** The female Tibetan Mastiff may come into season only once rather than twice a year, as is usual with other breeds.

broad, massive head

fairly long, thick, double coat
high-set tail
sturdy legs
strong, muscular body
very large, powerful feet

COLOR TYPES

Height 24–28 in (61–71 cm)	Weight 140–180 lb (64–82 kg)	Temperament Brave, loyal

Country of origin Canary Islands	First use Dogfighting	Origins 1800s

CANARY DOG

Bearing a strong likeness to the Perro de Presa Mallorquin (see p.280), the Canary Dog is a powerfully built, square-headed, mastiff-type dog. Fawn or brindle is the usual coloration, although white markings are also seen, and the coat itself is short and rough over slightly mobile skin.

• **HISTORY** The ancestry of the Canary Dog involved crosses between the extinct Bardino Majero and the Mastiff, the latter being developed in Great Britain and introduced into the Canaries in the 1800s. The Canary Dog was developed specifically for dogfighting.

• **REMARK** Now recovering in numbers, this breed was almost extinct by the 1960s due to the banning of dogfighting in its homeland.

• **OTHER NAMES** Perro de Presa Canario.

large, powerful, square head

powerful, muscled back

slightly raised rump
blunt, broad muzzle
very broad, heavily muscled chest
short, coarse-textured coat
strong, heavily boned legs

COLOR TYPES

Height 21½–25½ in (55–65 cm)	Weight 84–106 lb (38–48 kg)	Temperament Determined, forceful

Country of origin Morocco	First use Guard Dog	Origins 1000s

AIDI

White is the preferred color for this breed, although it does occur in a variety of colors. The coat is dense and fleecelike, offering protection from the searing desert heat and freezing cold nights in the Atlas Mountains of Morocco.

• **HISTORY** The ancestors of this breed were probably introduced from Spain. It has served as guard dog and tracker, locating game that the faster Sloughi (see p.203) can then run to ground.

• **REMARK** The Moroccan Kennel Association is helping to ensure the survival of the Aidi.

• **OTHER NAMES** Chien de l'Atlas.

muscular neck
heavily plumed tail is desirable
straight, well-boned forelegs
tail extends to level of hocks

COLOR TYPES

Height 21–24 in (53–61 cm)	Weight 50–55 lb (23–25 kg)	Temperament Alert, highly strung

Country of origin New Guinea	First use None (pariah)	Origins Unknown

NEW GUINEA SINGING DOG

A dingolike appearance distinguishes this remarkable breed as a pariah. It is of medium size with a coat of various shades of red, sometimes with white markings.

• **HISTORY** This semiwild dog is native to New Guinea. It is found with tribes in both the lowlands and highlands and is prized for its distinctive, musical voice.

• **REMARK** This breed does not like prolonged handling.

broad head
plumed tail
muscular physique
white sometimes present on coat

COLOR TYPES

Height 14–15 in (35–38 cm)	Weight 18–22 lb (8–10 kg)	Temperament Aloof, unpredictable

Dog Credits

Dorling Kindersley is greatly indebted to the many owners and breeders who allowed their dogs to be photographed for this book; without their help and enthusiastic cooperation, it could not have been produced. While every effort has been made to accredit all those involved, the publisher will gladly incorporate additional information in future editions. The dogs and the names of their owners are listed in page order.

COMPANION DOGS
• 38 *Kyi Leo* D. Weber
• 39 *Toy American Eskimo* (refer to publisher)
Bulldog C. Thomas & G. Godfrey
• 40 *Cavalier King Charles* T. Boardman; Hull; *King Charles Spaniel* D. Fry
• 41 *Chihuahua* S. Lee
• 42 *Mexican Hairless* S. Corrone; H. Hernandez; Terry; L. Woods
• 43 *Peruvian Inca Orchid* C. & B. Christofferson; *Havanese* K. Olausson
• 44 *Giant German Spitz* A. Fiebich; M. Horhold; *German Spitz: Mittel* Bodimeade
• 45 *German Spitz: Klein* K. Hill & Trendle; *Pomeranian* Powell & Medcraft
• 46 *Keeshond* M.R. West; *Continental Toy Spaniel: Phalene* J. Meijer
• 47 *Papillon* Urquhart & Urquhart; *Toy Poodle* S. Riddett & Moody
• 48 *Miniature Poodle* Treagus
• 49 *Lowchen* K. Donovan
• 50 *Italian Greyhound* S. Dunning
• 51 *Bolognese* L. Stannard; *Volpino Italiano* A. Hammond
• 52 *Pekingese* Stannard
• 53 *Pug* N. Tarbitt; *Shih Tzu* J. Franks
• 54 *Chinese Crested Dog* (Hairless) Moon; (Powder Puff) S. Wrenn
• 55 *Tibetan Spaniel* J. Lilley; *Tibetan Terrier* T. & A. Medlow
• 56 *Lhasa Apso* L. Chamberlain; *Japanese Chin* J. Jolley
• 57 *Japanese Spitz* S. Jones; *Maltese* U. Campanis-Brockmann
• 58 *Bichon Frise* S.M. Dunger
• 59 *Basenji* J. Gostynska; *Coton de Tulear* P. Zinkstok & H. & R. Bonneveld

GUNDOGS
• 60 *American Cocker Spaniel* L. Pichard
• 61 *Chesapeake Bay Retriever* P. Taylor-Williams
• 62 *Clumber Spaniel* R. Furness
• 63 *Cocker Spaniel* (puppy) T. Morgan & N. Memery; (black and white) M. Robinson; (blue) P. & T. Read
• 64 *Curly-coated Retriever* A. Skingley
• 65 *English Setter* Grimsdell
• 66 *Gordon Setter* M. Justice; *English Springer Spaniel* D. & J. Miller
• 67 *Field Spaniel* G. Thwaites; *Flat-coated Retriever* A. Youens
• 68 *Golden Retriever* R.A. Strudwick; C. Carter
• 69 *Labrador Retriever* M. Prior; C. Coode
• 70–71 *Pointer* A. Morgan
• 72 *Welsh Springer Spaniel* J. Luckett-Roynon; *Sussex Spaniel* C. Mitchell
• 73 *Nova Scotia Duck Tolling Retriever* G. Flack
• 74 *Old Danish Pointer* E. Karlsson
• 75 *German Spaniel* L. Ahlsson
• 76–77 *Weimaraner* F. Thibaut
• 78 *German Wire-haired Pointer* M. J. Gorrissen-Sipos
• 79 *Small Münsterländer* G. Petterson
• 80–81 *Large Münsterländer* K. Groom
• 82 *Dutch Partridge Dog* S. Boersma; J.P.A. vd. Zanden; *Kooiker Dog* L.A. & B. Williams
• 83 *Stabyhoun* E. Vellenga; *Wetterhoun* J.P. Visser
• 84 *Irish Water Spaniel* G. Stirk
• 85 *Irish Red and White Setter* S.J. Humphreys
• 86 *Irish Setter* Napthine
• 87 *Braque St. Germain* J.P. Perdry
• 88–89 *Braque Francais* Y. Bassot
• 90 *Braque d'Auvergne* L. Ercole
• 91 *Braque du Bourbonnais* J. Regis
• 92 *Épagneul Francais* W. Klijn; G. de Moustier; *Épagneul Picard* M. & P. Lempereur
• 93 *Épagneul Breton* E. Reeves
• 94 *Épagneul Pont-Audemer* Y. Fouquer; J.P. Tougard
• 95 *Barbet* J.C. Valée
• 96 *Épagneul Bleu de Picardie* M. Debacker
• 97 *Wire-haired Pointing Griffon* T. Schmeitz; *Czesky Fousek* M. Hahné
• 98 *Hungarian Vizsla* J. Perkins
• 99 *Wire-haired Vizsla* J. & L.V. Essen
• 100 *Spinone* S. Grief
• 101 *Bracco Italiano* J. & L. Shaw
• 102 *Perdiguero de Burgos* P. Moreira
• 103 *Portuguese Water Dog* J. & R. Bussell
• 104 *Perdiguero Portugueso* Canil do Casal das Grutas

HERDING DOGS
• 105 *Australian Shepherd* Macintyre
• 106 *Bearded Collie* J. Wiggins
• 107 *Border Collie* P. Haydock; *Lancashire Heeler* S. Whybrow
• 108 *Rough Collie* V. Tame
• 109 *Smooth Collie* P. Sewell; *Shetland Sheepdog* J. Moody
• 110 *Old English Sheepdog* (adult) J.P. & C. Smith; (puppy) Anderson
• 111 *Welsh Corgi: Cardigan* T. Maddox; *Welsh Corgi: Pembroke* Davies
• 112 *Australian Cattle Dog* (adult) S. & W. Huntingdon; (puppies) S. Smyth
• 113 *Australian Kelpie* P. Rönnquist; M. Nilsson
• 114 *Finnish Lapphund* S. Bolin; (youngster) S. Dunger; *Lapinporokoira* B. Schmitt
• 115 *Beauceron* M.V. Rie
• 116–17 *Briard* (fawn) Snelling; (black) R. Bumstead
• 118 *Berger de Picard* C.V. Doorn; (brindle) J.C.P. Bormans
• 119 *German Shepherd Dog* W. & J. Petrie
• 120–21 *Hovawart* (black) K. Stenhols; (golden) A. Göranson
• 122 *Giant Schnauzer* Wilberg
• 123 *Polish Lowland Sheepdog* M. de Groot; *Schapendoes* J. Wierda-Gorter; (head) C. Roux
• 124 *Dutch Shepherd Dog* J. Pijffers; M. Vermeeren
• 125 *Sarloos Wolfhound* C. Keizer
• 126 *Belgian Shepherd Dog: Groenendael* J. Luscott
• 127 *Belgian Shepherd Dog: Laekenois* Hogarty
• 128 *Belgian Shepherd Dog: Tervuren* K. Ellis & A. McLaren
• 129 *Belgian Shepherd Dog: Malinois* S. Hughes

• **130–31** *Bouvier des Flandres* K.S. Wilberg
• **132** *Swedish Vallhund* J. Hammar; *Iceland Dog* A.S. Andersson
• **133** *Puli* M. Crowther; Butler; *Pumi* (black) P. Johansson; (gray and cream) I. Svard
• **134** *Istrian Sheepdog* M. Luttwitz; *Illyrian Sheepdog* P. Gvozenovie
• **135** *Bergamasco* B. Saraber; (puppy) M. Andreoli
• **136** *Catalan Sheepdog* M. Guasch Soler
• **137** *Portuguese Sheepdog* Borges, M. Loureiro; Canil do Magoito; Canil da Valeira; Cunha, M.L.N. Lopes; Gomez-Toldra
• **138** *Catahoula Leopard Dog* M. Neal

HOUNDS
• **139** *Plott Hound* J. M. Koons; B. L. Taylor & M. Seets; *Bluetick Coonhound* D. McCormick; R. Welch & B. Slaymon
• **140** *English Coonhound* M. Seets; J. Mantanona
• **141** *Redbone Coonhound* J. & C. Heck; C. Elburn
• **142–43** *Black and Tan Coonhound* K. & A. Shorter; D. Fentee & R. Speer Jnr.
• **144** *Treeing Walker Coonhound* L. Currens; J. Girnot & W. Haynes
• **145** *American Foxhound* A. Cannon
• **146** *Basset Hound* N. Frost; *Beagle* M. Hunt
• **147** *English Foxhound* The Berks and Bucks Draghounds
• **148** *Deerhound* D. & J. Murray
• **149** *Otter Hound* Smith
• **150** *Greyhound* J. Baylis; A. Baudon
• **151** *Whippet* Oliver; S. Horsnell
• **152** *Dunker* Almerud
• **153** *Haldenstovare* G. Lerstad
• **154** *Hygenhund* R. Langland; *Finnish Hound* T. Olkkonen; A. Vilpula
• **155** *Drever* L. Jönsson; *Schillerstövare* (refer to publisher)
• **156** *Hamiltonstövare* D. Cook
• **157** *Smålandsstövare* K. Skolmi
• **158–59** *Miniature Dachshund* (long coat) L. Mears; (smooth coat) B. Clark; (wire coat) P. Seymour
• **160** *Hanoverian Mountain Hound* I. Voegelen; *Bavarian Schweisshund* I. Voegelen
• **161** *Polish Hound* A. Marculanis
• **162–63** *Irish Wolfhound* (gray) Smith; A. Bennett
• **164** *Kerry Beagle* J. Sugrue; T. O'Shea; M. O'Sullivan; P. Daly; J. Kelly
• **165** *Lurcher* C. Labers
• **166–67** *Bloodhound* Richards
• **168** *Billy* A. Benoit
• **169** *Basset Fauve de Bretagne* N. Frost
• **170–71** *Grand Bleu de Gascogne* Braddick
• **172** *Chien d'Artois* A. Lopez; N.Bellet
• **173** *Basset Bleu de Gascogne* J. Nenmann; *Basset Artésian Normand* B. Hemmingsson
• **174** *Grand Gascon-Saintongeois* (refer to publisher)
• **175** *Grand Basset Griffon Vendéen* N. Frost & V. Philips
• **176** *Grand Griffon Vendéen* G. Lamoureux; D. Boursier
• **177** *Briquet Griffon Vendéen* D. Fabre; *Griffon Nivernais* D. Duede
• **178** *Petit Bleu de Gascogne* (refer to publisher)
• **179** *Petit Griffon Bleu de Gascogne* (refer to publisher)
• **180** *Anglo-Francais de Petite Vénerie* A. Dubois
• **181** *Griffon Fauve de Bretagne* Cann
• **182** *Porcelaine* R. Lavergme
• **183** *Jura Laufhund: Bruno* P. Guenole
• **184–85** *Jura Laufhund (St. Hubert)* M. Aigret
• **186** *Hungarian Greyhound* T. Christiansen; *Berner Laufhund* R.J. Luchtmeijer
• **187** *Schweizer Laufhund* O. Bonslet
• **188** *Luzerner Laufhund* M.B. Mervaille
• **189** *Balkan Hound* I. Vicentijevic; *Posavac Hound* Z. Marinkovic
• **190** *Yugoslavian Mountain Hound* D. Milosevic
• **191** *Yugoslavian Tricolor Hound* R. Andelkovic
• **192** *Cirneco dell'Etna* D.H. Blom
• **193** *Pharaoh Hound* J. Gostynska
• **194** *Ibizan Hound* Carter & Donnaby; F. Benecke
• **195** *Sabuesco Español* J.C. Palomo Romero
• **196** *Spanish Greyhound* J.F. Olij & J.W. Luijken; L. Rapeport
• **197** *Podengo Portugueso Pequeño* Macedo, L. Vaz; Reis, A.S. Oliveira
• **198** *Podengo Portugueso Medio* Canil G. Oleganense; Canil de Veiros; Canil do Vale do Criz
• **199** *Saluki* (black) Ziman; (grizzle) Spooner
• **200** *Borzoi* A.G.C. Simmonds
• **201** *Azawakh Hound* A.Hellblom
• **202** *Afghan Hound* R. Savage
• **203** *Sloughi* L. Vassalo
• **204** *Kai Dog* M. Malone
• **205** *Rhodesian Ridgeback* M. & J. Morris

TERRIERS
• **206** *American Toy Fox Terrier* A. Mauermann
• **207** *American Pit Bull Terrier* P. Perdue; (orange and white) T. Davis
• **208** *American Staffordshire Terrier* M. & K. Slotboom; *Boston Terrier* Barker
• **209** *Airedale Terrier* M. Swash & O. Jackson; *Bedlington Terrier* A. Yearley
• **210** *English Toy Terrier* T. Wright; *Manchester Terrier* E. Eva
• **211** *Border Terrier* Dean; *Norwich Terrier* R.W.J. Thomas
• **212** *Miniature Bull Terrier* Berry; *Staffordshire Bull Terrier* G. & B. McAuliffe
• **213** *Dandie Dinmont Terrier* P. Keevil & S. Bullock; *Cairn Terrier* K. Holmes
• **214** *Lakeland Terrier* J.C. Ruiz Mogrera; Hedges; *Norfolk Terrier* N. Kruger
• **215** *Parson Jack Russell Terrier* J.P. Wood; *Wire Fox Terrier* J. Palosaari; G. Dûring
• **216** *Smooth Fox Terrier* L. Bochese; *Welsh Terrier* G. Aalderink
• **217** *Scottish Terrier* M.L. Daltrey; *Skye Terrier* P. Bennett; (puppies) D. & J. Miller
• **218** *Patterdale Terrier* B. Nuttall; *West Highland White Terrier* S. Thompson; J. Pastor & M. Gonzalbo
• **219** *Yorkshire Terrier* H. Ridgwell
• **220** *Sealyham Terrier* D. Winsley; *Australian Terrier* R. Buch-Jorgens
• **221** *Silky Terrier* I. Schmied; *German Hunting Terrier* B. Andersson
• **222** *German Pinscher* R. & M. Collicott; Boyer
• **223** *Affenpinscher* A.J. Teasdale; *Miniature Pinscher* Gentle; A. Coull
• **224** *Miniature Schnauzer* P. Gowlett
• **225** *Kromfohrländer* (short coat) M. Schaub; (long coat) H. Hoppert
• **226** *Irish Terrier* A. Noonan & Williamson
• **227** *Soft-coated Wheaten Terrier* Hanton, Moyes, & Pettit
• **228** *Glen of Imaal Terrier* J. Withers; *Kerry Blue Terrier* Campbell
• **229** *Griffon Bruxellois* A.V. Fenn; (black) H. Bleeker & J. den Otte
• **230** *Austrian Short-haired Pinscher* I. Hartgers-Wagener; *Cesky Terrier* D. Delplanque

WORKING DOGS
• **231** *American Bulldog* S. Leclerc
• **232** *Olde English Bulldogge* (refer to publisher)
• **233** *Chinook* T.J. and G. Anderson; D. & C. Hendricks; *Carolina Dog* S. McKenzie
• **234–35** *Alaskan Malamute* Lena-Britt Egnell
• **236–37** *Mastiff* D. Blaxter; (dark brindle) B. Stoffelen-Luyten
• **238** *Bull Mastiff* J. & A. Gunn
• **239** *Bull Terrier* Youatt; *Eskimo Dog* E. & S. Hammond

• **240–41** *Newfoundland* Cutts & Galvin; (black and white) Cutts
• **242** *Dogo Argentino* Roelofs
• **243** *Fila Brasileiro* E.H. Vlietman
• **244** *Greenland Dog* M. Dragone; M. Demoor
• **245** *Norwegian Elkhound* A. Meijer; *Black Norwegian Elkhound* K. Bonaunet
• **246** *Lundehund* M. Jansson; *Norwegian Buhund* R.W.J. Thomas
• **247** *Finnish Spitz* Gatti; *Karelian Bear Dog* P. Gritsh
• **248** *Swedish Elkhound* A. Johansson
• **249** *Swedish Lapphund* R.A. Wind-Heuser; *Norbottenspets* A. Piltto
• **250–51** *Dobermann* K. le Mare; (head) B. Schellekens & S. Franquemont
• **252–53** *Great Dane* (fawn with black mask) D.J. Parish; (harlequin) N. Marriner
• **254** *Standard Poodle* E.A. Beswick
• **255** *Boxer* G. Nielsen & D. Spencer; *Eurasier* J. Bos Waaldijk
• **256–57** *Landseer* G. Cutts
• **258–59** *Leonberger* F. Inwood
• **260** *Rottweiler* Hine; T. Barnett
• **261** *Owczarek Podhalanski* G.V. Rijsewijk
• **262** *Schipperke* L. Wilson
• **263** *French Bulldog* J. Keates; *Dogue de Bordeaux* A.E. Neuteboom
• **264–65** *Pyrenean Mountain Dog* I. & W. Spencer-Brown
• **266** *Komondor* P. & M. Froome
• **267** *Kuvasz* J. Schelling; I. & H. Wallin
• **268** *Mudi* (refer to publisher)
• **269** *Appensell Mountain Dog* W. Glocker; *Entelbuch Mountain Dog* C. Fransson
• **270–71** *Bernese Mountain Dog* A. Hayden; (puppy) A. Hearne
• **272** *Great Swiss Mountain Dog* H. Hannberger
• **273** *St. Bernard* (short-haired) H. Golverdingen; (long-haired) T. Hansen
• **274** *Dalmatian* K. Goff
• **275** *Maremma Sheepdog* T. Barnes
• **276–77** *Neapolitan Mastiff* (black) A. E. Useletti; (gray) A.P. van Doremalen
• **278** *Pyrenean Mastiff* G. Marin
• **279** *Spanish Mastiff* Camps & Ritter
• **280** *Perro de Pastor Mallorquin* J. M. Martinez Alonso; *Perro de Presa Mallorquín* J.J. Calderón Ruiz; E. Lurbe; M. Calvino Breijo
• **281** *Canaan Dog* M. Macphail
• **282** *Estrela Mountain Dog* P. Olsson; E. Bentzer
• **283** *Rafeiro do Alentejo* Gomes, J. Oliveira
• **284** *Portuguese Cattle Dog* Canil do Casal da Granja; Amorim, J.M.P. de Lima; Macedo, L. Vaz; *Russo-European Laika* S. Enochsson; B. Vujasinovic
• **285** *East Siberian Laika* L. Milic; *West Siberian Laika* S. Enochsson
• **286** *Siberian Husky* S. Hull
• **287** *Samoyed* C. Fox
• **288** *Chow Chow* P. Goedgezelschap; U. Berglöf
• **289** *Sharpei* B. & C. Lilley
• **290** *Akita Inu* A. Rickard
• **291** *Shiba Inu* M. Atkinson; *Tosa Inu* F. Kappe
• **292** *Japanese Terrier* M. Delaye; *Ainu* M.G. Schippers Hasselman
• **293** *Tibetan Mastiff.* P. Rees-Jones & E. Holliday
• **294** *Perro de Presa Canario* D. Kelly; Grupo los Enanos
• **295** *Aidi* M. Bouayad (Cluc Chien Atlas); *New Guinea Singing Dog* A. Riddle; P. & F. Persky

Useful Addresses

American Kennel Club (AKC)
51 Madison Avenue, New York, NY 10010

AKC Customer Service
580 Centerview Drive, Raleigh, NC 27606

American Boarding Kennels Association
5475 Galley Road, Suite 400A,
Colorado Springs, CO 80915

United Kennel Club, Inc. (UKC)
100 East Kilgore Road, Kalamazoo,
MI 49001-5598

Dog Fancy magazine
P.O. Box 53264, Boulder, CO 80322

Dog World magazine
29 North Wacker Drive, Chicago, IL 60604

Purebred Dogs/American Kennel Gazette
c/o American Kennel Club, 51 Madison Avenue,
New York, NY 10010

Assistance Dog Institute
421 East Cotati Avenue, Cotati, CA 94931–4000

Humane Society of the United States
2100 L Street NW, Washington, DC 20037

Canadian Kennel Club
100–89 Skyway Avenue
Etobicoke, Ontario M9W 6R4

The Kennel Club
1 Clarges Street, London W1Y 8AB, UK

Australian Kennel Council
Royal Show Grounds, Epsom Road,
Ascot Vale 3032, Victoria, Australia

GLOSSARY

• **ANGULATION**
Angle formed by the meeting of bones at a joint.
• **BARREL**
Rounded chest shape.
• **BAT EARS**
Erect ears, wide at the base and round at the tips, pointing out.
• **BAY**
Call of hounds in pursuit of quarry.
• **BEARD**
Long, thick hair around the jaws.
• **BELTON**
Blue-lemon flecked coloration associated with English Setters.
• **BITE**
The positioning of the upper and lower teeth relative to each other.
• **BLAZE**
White marking running down forehead to muzzle.
• **BOBTAIL**
Closely docked tail – or missing altogether on breeds born tailless.
• **BRINDLE**
Combination of light and dark hairs, resulting in darker streaking.
• **BRISKET**
Area of the chest between the forelegs, including the breastbone.
• **BROKEN-COATED**
Rough, wire coat.
• **BRUSH**
Bushy tail.
• **BUTTERFLY NOSE**
Nose of two colors.
• **BUTTON EARS**
Semierect ears, folding over at their tips.
• **CLIP**
Type of trim, associated particularly with poodles.
• **COBBY**
Short-bodied and compact.
• **CONFORMATION**
Overall shape, resulting from combined relationship of all of a dog's physical parts.
• **COUPLING**
Region extending from the last rib to the pelvis.
• **COW-HOCKED**
Hocks point in toward each other.
• **CROP**
Removal of the tops of the ears, causing them to stand erect.
• **CROUP**
Area of back closest to tail.
• **CULOTTE**
Long hair at the back of the thighs.
• **DEW CLAW**
Claw on the inside of the legs, often removed in young puppies.
• **DEWLAP**
Pendulous, loose skin under the throat, as seen in the Bloodhound.
• **DOCK**
Shortening of the tail by cutting.
• **DOUBLE COAT**
Guard hairs protruding through softer, insulating layer beneath.
• **DROP EAR**
Ears that hang down, close to the sides of the head.
• **ELBOW**
Joint below shoulder.
• **ENTROPION**
Eye abnormality causing almost continual irritation.
• **FALL**
Hair hanging down over the face.
• **FEATHERING**
Long fringes of hair on the ears, body, legs, and tail.
• **FLEWS**
Pendulous upper lips.
• **FRILL**
Longer hair present on the lower neck and front of the chest.
• **GRIZZLE**
Bluish gray color.
• **GUARD HAIRS**
Coarser outer hairs.
• **HACKLES**
Hair on the neck and back, raised to show aggression or fright.
• **HARE FEET**
Relatively long and narrow feet.
• **HARLEQUIN**
Black or blue patches set against white, as seen in the Great Dane.
• **HAUNCHES**
Back of thighs, in contact with the ground when the dog is sitting.
• **HOCK**
Hindleg joint – the dog's heels.
• **JOWLS**
The fleshy part of the lips and jaws.
• **LEATHER**
Ear flap.
• **LOBULAR**
Lobe shaped.
• **LOINS**
Region from last rib to back legs.
• **MANE**
Long hair on and around the neck.
• **MASK**
Dark, masklike shading on head.
• **MERLE**
Marbled coat pattern, caused by darker patches on lighter background of same basic color.
• **MUZZLE**
Portion of head in front of eyes.
• **OCCIPUT**
Highest part on back of skull.
• **PASTERN**
Lower part of leg, between wrist and foot.
• **PLUME**
Soft hair on the tail.
• **POINT**
Immovable stance of a hunting dog, indicating location of game.
• **POINTS**
Body extremities, usually referring to the coloration of ears, face, legs, and tail.
• **ROACHED**
Convex arching of the back.
• **ROAN**
Mixture of white and another color, in even proportions.
• **ROSE-EARED**
Typically small ears, which fold down and show the inside.
• **RUFF**
Long, thick hair encircling neck.
• **SABLE**
White coat, shaded with black.
• **SABER TAIL**
Tail in the shape of a semicircle.
• **SADDLE**
Black markings in the shape and position of a saddle.
• **SOFT MOUTH**
A characteristic of hunting dogs, indicating ability to retrieve game without damaging it.
• **STAND-OFF COAT**
Long, heavy coat standing out from body, as in the Keeshond.
• **STIFLE**
Hindleg joint, the angle of which is important in breed standards.
• **STOP**
Depression between the eyes, where skull and nasal bone meet.
• **TICKING**
Coat pattern in which spots of color stand out against the basic background color.
• **TRIM**
Grooming that involves clipping or plucking.
• **WHELPING**
Giving birth to puppies.
• **WITHERS**
Highest point of the shoulders, behind the neck.

INDEX

I

J

K

L

M

N

O

P

ACKNOWLEDGMENTS

THE AUTHOR AND PUBLISHER are indebted to a number of institutions and people, without whom this book could not have been produced: Mia Sandgren, Magnus Berglin, Thomas Miller, Maria Bruga, Steve Fielder, Jovan Serafin, Luis Isaac Barata, Luis Manuel Calado Catalan, Dr. J.L. Slack, Anita Bryant, Sergio Montesinos Vernetta, Ann Houdijk, Antonio Consta, Jose Carrera, Steven Boer, Egon Erdenbrecher, Mr. & Mrs. Lawlor, Mr. K. Bent, E. Vanherle, Dr. Herbert R. Axelrod, John Miller, M. Peonchon, Patrick Schwab, Mme. Dhetz, Stella Smyth, Mandy Hearne, Heather Head. Special thanks are also due to Sabine Weiss of SDK Verlags GmbH; Vicki A. Rand of the United Kennel Club; Susanne Marlier of the Fédération Cynologigue Internationale; Susanne Lindberg of the norsk kennel klub; M. Noblet of the Société Centrale Canine; Mme Mila of the Fédération Cynologique de Yugoslavie; Mme. Durando of the Société Canine de Monaco, and Her Serene Highness, Princess Antoinette de Monaco.

Photography by Tracy Morgan, except for: p.6 (left) Bridgeman Art Library; p.7 (center & bottom) The Kennel Club; p.8 (bottom), p.13 (top & bottom), p.151 (bottom) Animal Photography; p.8 (center), p.174, p.178, p.179 Marc Henrie; p.152, p.153, p.154 (top), p.157, p.187, p.245 (bottom), p.268 Sandra Russell; p.155 (bottom), p.249 (bottom) Neil Fletcher; p.11 (right), p.12 (bottom), p.16 (top) Bruce Coleman Picture Library; p.39 (top), p.206 (right) Sally Klein; p.145 (top right & center) TFH Publications, Inc.; p.181 (top) Sunset NHPA.

The author would like to thank the many kind dog fanciers around the world who have allowed their dogs to be photographed. A particular debt is due to Tracy Morgan who, with the help of her husband, Neil, undertook the bulk of the photography, and to Andrea Fair who arranged the overseas trips. He would also like to thank Neil Fletcher, Marc and Fiona Henrie, James Harrison, Bob Gordon, and Jonathon Hilton for their input at various stages of the book. Thanks go to everyone at Dorling Kindersley, Richmond, who have contributed: in particular Jonathan Metcalf, Carole McGlynn, Constance Novis, Alison Edmonds, Mary-Clare Jerram, Gill della Casa, Spencer Holbrook, Anne Thompson, and Sam Grimmer. Last, but not least, thanks to Rita Hemsley for her typing skills, and Les Crawley and John Mandeville for their invaluable contributions.

Dorling Kindersley would like to thank: Lemon Graphics, Adam Moore, Pauline Bayne, Elaine Hewson, and Sharon Moore for design assistance; Mike Darton and Amanda Ronan for proofreading; Michael Allaby for indexing; Julia Pashley for picture research; Helen Townsend, Angeles Gavira, and Lucinda Hawksley for editorial assistance.

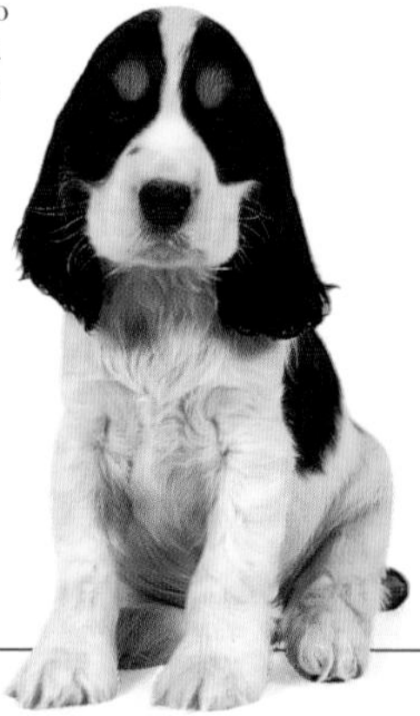

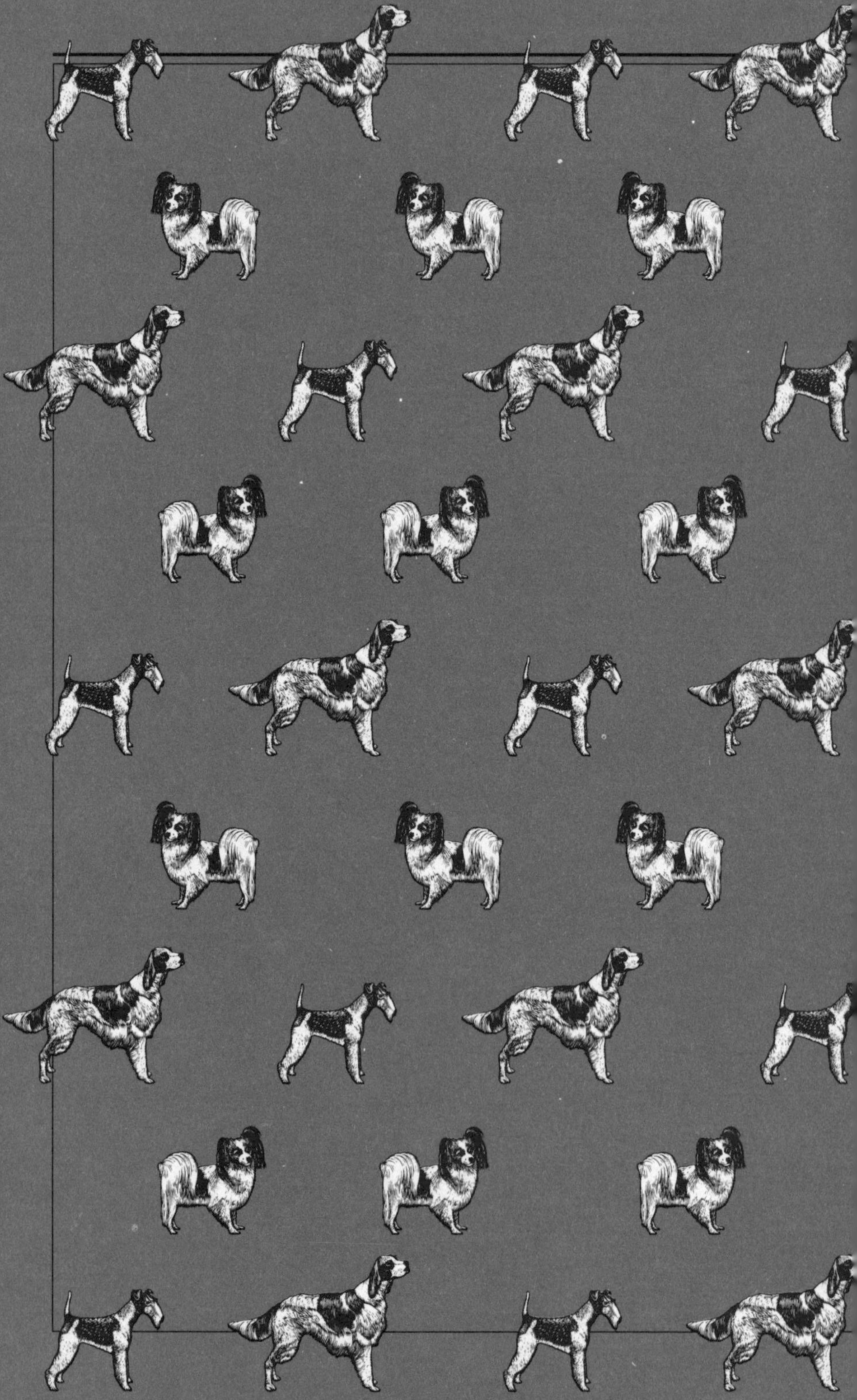